# MARGARET MITCHELL'S
## GONE WITH THE WIND

# Margaret Mitchell's
# Gone With the Wind

## A Bestseller's Odyssey
## from Atlanta to Hollywood

ELLEN F. BROWN
and JOHN WILEY, JR.

TAYLOR TRADE PUBLISHING
Lanham • New York • Boulder • Toronto • Plymouth, UK

Published by Taylor Trade Publishing
An imprint of The Rowman & Littlefield Publishing Group, Inc.
4501 Forbes Boulevard, Suite 200, Lanham, Maryland 20706
http://www.rlpgtrade.com

Estover Road, Plymouth PL6 7PY, United Kingdom
Distributed by National Book Network

British Library Cataloguing in Publication Information Available

**Library of Congress Cataloging-in-Publication Data**

Brown, Ellen Firsching, 1969–
   Margaret Mitchell's Gone with the wind : a bestseller's odyssey from Atlanta to
Hollywood / Ellen Firsching Brown and John Wiley, Jr.
      p.   cm.
   Includes bibliographical references and index.
   ISBN 978-1-58979-567-9 (cloth : alk. paper)—
   ISBN 978-1-58979-527-3 (electronic)
   1. Mitchell, Margaret, 1900–1949. Gone with the wind.   2. Best
sellers—History—20th century.   3. Publishers and publishing—History—20th
century.   4. Book industries and trade—History—20th century.   5. Mitchell,
Margaret, 1900–1949—Film and video adaptations.   I. Wiley, John, 1958–
II. Title.   III. Title: Gone with the wind.
PS3525.I972B76   2011
813'.52—dc22                                                              2010035748

∞ ™ The paper used in this publication meets the minimum requirements of
American National Standard for Information Sciences—Permanence of Paper for
Printed Library Materials, ANSI/NISO Z39.48-1992.
Printed in Canada

With love to Orran, Read, and Drew,
for their endless encouragement and patience.

EFB

~

To Mom, who first took me to see the movie *Gone With the Wind*.
To Dad, a Southern gentleman in every sense of the word.
To Linda, who bought me my first copy of
Margaret Mitchell's novel.

JW

~

*In memory of Emyl Jenkins Sexton,
who had Scarlett's zest for life and Margaret Mitchell's
love for the written word.*

# Contents

# Cast of Characters

ATLANTA

Margaret Mitchell Marsh, author
Stephens Mitchell, her brother and legal adviser
John Marsh, her husband and business manager
Margaret Baugh, her longtime secretary

NEW YORK

Lois Dwight Cole Taylor, assistant editor and friend of Margaret Mitchell
Harold Latham, vice president and editor in chief
George Brett, Jr., president
Richard Brett, treasurer
James Putnam, vice president and assistant to the publisher
Alec Blanton, sales manager
Marion Saunders, foreign rights agent
Walbridge Taft, lawyer

HOLLYWOOD

Annie Laurie Williams, movie rights agent
Kay Brown, Selznick's story editor, later agent for Mitchell Estate
David O. Selznick, movie producer

# Introduction

Anyone writing about Margaret Mitchell's *Gone With the Wind* stands on the shoulders of a vast body of work, including at least five biographies of the author, three collections of her letters, and numerous essays about the novel's place in the American literary canon. A complete bibliography of every book and article published about *Gone With the Wind* (*GWTW*)—including those on the famous 1939 movie version—would fill a large volume. So, why another?

Timed to coincide with the seventy-fifth anniversary of *Gone With the Wind*'s 1936 release, we present the first comprehensive history of how Mitchell's novel became an international publishing blockbuster. This is not a biography of the author but rather the life story of her book, from its origins in Mitchell's childhood to its status today as a controversial cultural phenomenon. We follow the novel on its journey from a small apartment in Atlanta to the Macmillan Company's Fifth Avenue headquarters in New York, and then across the country and around the world. We tell how Mitchell's book was developed, marketed, and groomed for success in a bygone era of typewriters and telegrams, as well as of the author's love-hate relationship with her publisher and agents, each of whom held divergent views on how best to manage the book and its legacy. Along the way, Mitchell changed the course of international copyright law through her struggles to maintain control over the *GWTW* literary rights. As one of the first U.S. authors since Mark Twain to cause an international sensation, she fended off unauthorized editions of her book around the globe, calling attention to the inadequacy of copyright protection for American writers.

1

And, because this is not a biography of the author, the story does not end at her death. The saga continues to the present day, exploring the tumultuous years since her passing during which Mitchell's husband, then her brother, and finally a group of Atlanta lawyers protected and capitalized on one of the world's most valuable literary properties.

Readers familiar with the history of *Gone With the Wind* will notice that the version of events we tell varies in some respects from previously published accounts. Many of the differences are attributable to our having access to information never before available to *GWTW* researchers, most importantly, a private archive of correspondence between Mitchell and Lois Cole, the associate editor at Macmillan who discovered the manuscript. These documents—including an initial assessment of the novel by Cole, the first person outside the Mitchell family to read *Gone With the Wind*—offer a new understanding of how the manuscript made its way to Macmillan and was developed there. We are grateful to Cole's children, Linda Taylor Barnes and Turney Allan Taylor, Jr., for entrusting us with this rich resource. In addition, the *GWTW* Literary Rights office recently donated a large volume of its business records to the University of Georgia. These files offer fascinating details about the novel's early history, as well as more recent developments. Also, Paul Anderson and Thomas Hal Clarke, lawyers who have worked with the literary rights for decades, agreed to be interviewed for this project. Their comments offered valuable insights into the complexities of the *GWTW* phenomenon.

Of course, there is an inherent risk in attempting to re-create history from the records of a born storyteller like Margaret Mitchell. As a friend of the author's once said, you could run into her at a department store when you both were exhausted and in foul moods and then later hear her tell the story of your meeting and barely recognize the two lighthearted and attractive people she described. Many of the other characters involved in this story also did not lack a silver tongue; the truth was often not as important as telling a good story, and if that story changed from telling to telling, so be it. Taking such embroidery into account, we have done our best not to accept anything at face value. We have been cautious in handling contradictory, incomplete, or otherwise questionable descriptions of events and noted when we were unable to meld various accounts. Throughout this process, we have come away with new interpretations of events that have become treasured parts of *GWTW* lore. We have solved mysteries, corrected misunderstandings, and hopefully offer readers the most thorough, accurate, and up-to-date exposition on the remarkable life of a remarkable book. We do not claim to have rewritten the history of *Gone With the Wind*, but we have refocused the lens.

Ellen F. Brown
Richmond, Virginia

John Wiley, Jr.
Midlothian, Virginia

# 1

## This Woman Has Something

### *1900 August 1935*

Margaret Mitchell's *Gone With the Wind* has its roots in that Sunday afternoon tradition of visits with family. As the adults whiled away hours on porches and in parlors of their Georgia homes, a young Mitchell listened to stories of the War Between the States, which had ended just thirty-five years before her birth in 1900. She later recalled being swept up and perched "on the bony knees of veterans and the fat slippery laps of great aunts," where she heard firsthand accounts of battles, disease, deprivation, and loss not "as history nor as remarkable events but just as part of their lives and not especially epic parts."[1] Mitchell also had fond memories of playing on the remains of Civil War–era earthen fortifications that still ringed her hometown of Atlanta and horseback riding with Confederate veterans who spiritedly refought the war, much to her enjoyment.[2] "I heard so much when I was little about the fighting and the hard times after the war that I firmly believed Mother and Father had been through it all. . . . In fact I was about ten years old before I learned the war hadn't ended shortly before I was born."[3]

Mitchell's mother, Maybelle, was well educated for a lady of her generation and known in Atlanta for her support of women's suffrage. She had high aspirations for her daughter. When as a young girl Mitchell announced that she did not like arithmetic and was not going to school anymore, her mother gathered her in a carriage and set out for nearby Clayton County, which still bore the scars of Union general William T. Sherman's famous March to the Sea in 1864. Across the landscape, lone chimneys rose above burned ruins—"Sherman's sentinels," as they were known in the South. Maybelle told her daughter how the people who had resided in these houses thought they lived in a secure world, but it had exploded around them, and how Mitchell's own world might explode under her some day. God help her if she did not have some weapon with which to meet the new order. Mitchell's mother was talking about the necessity of a good education and perseverance.[4] The young girl took the message to heart.

Eugene Mitchell, her father, was a lawyer. A founding member of the Atlanta Historical Society, he was known for his intelligence and punctiliousness. Under his watchful eye, good manners and taste prevailed in the Mitchell home, along with a love of reading. But appreciation for the finer elements of life did not mean the author's youth lacked childhood pleasures. She and her older brother, Stephens, freely roamed their neighborhood flying kites, playing ball, and racing ponies. Shy as a young child, Mitchell grew into a tomboy with a gift for gab. She enjoyed writing and filled copybooks with short stories—adventure tales, mostly, with lots of action.

In 1912, the family moved from the comfortable Jackson Hill neighborhood overlooking downtown Atlanta to a stately home Eugene had had built on Peachtree Street, one of the city's most prestigious thoroughfares. Mitchell attended high school at Atlanta's Washington Seminary, where she joined the Literary Club and had stories published in the school's yearbook. A description of Mitchell in her senior annual of 1918 portrays her as a vibrant young woman:

> Appearance: Swaggering
> Hobby: Aviators
> Pet Aversion: Civilians
> Favorite Expression: "Curses!"
> Highest Ambition: To send them away with a smile![5]

That spring, she found love. The United States had entered World War I the previous year, and Atlanta teemed with soldiers training at nearby Camp Gordon. Clifford Henry, a young Harvard-educated officer who grew up in New York and Connecticut high society, caught her eye, and over her father's objections, the two became engaged.

After Henry set sail for France in July, Mitchell left Atlanta to attend Smith College in Northampton, Massachusetts. She had barely settled in to college life when, in late October, Henry died of wounds received in battle. A few months later, word came from home that her mother had fallen ill with Spanish influenza, which was sweeping the globe. Mitchell immediately took a train to Atlanta but arrived too late; her brother met her at the station with the news that their mother had died. After the funeral, she finished her freshman year at Smith, then returned home to keep house for her father and brother. She never resumed her formal education.

Not one to sulk, Mitchell threw her "swaggering" self into the Atlanta social scene. She was a strikingly attractive girl with reddish brown hair and brilliant blue eyes—bluer even than Paul Newman's, according to one of her godsons.[6] Just shy of five feet tall and weighing less than a hundred pounds, she charmed people with her quick and mischievous wit. Mitchell's name frequently appeared in the society pages of the local newspapers. A March 1921 notice in the *Atlanta Constitution* described how she and a Georgia Tech student performed a risqué French apache dance at a charity ball sponsored by a group of Atlanta debutantes. According to the paper, Mitchell "offer[ed] herself and all she was on the altar of charity" with the performance.[7] Atlanta dowagers were not amused. The older women were further irritated when Mitchell and several friends insisted that the young guard, having done most of the work for the ball, should have a say in how to spend the money raised. Afterward, when the Atlanta Junior League issued its list of prospective members, Margaret Mitchell's name was not included.

The slight did not faze the spirited and restless Mitchell. In college, she had referred to herself in a letter to a friend as a "dynamo going to waste."[8] That feeling was returning. In September 1922, Mitchell married one of her many beaux, Berrien Kinnard "Red" Upshaw. The marriage was a tumultuous one; rumor had it that Upshaw was an alcoholic and physically abusive. He left town after a few months, and Mitchell turned for comfort to Upshaw's former roommate, John Marsh, who had been best man at their wedding. With his help, she managed in late 1922 to get an interview for a job as a reporter on the *Atlanta Journal Sunday Magazine*. Having no newspaper experience, she claimed to have landed the position by telling "outrageous lies about how I had worked on the *Springfield Republican* . . . and swearing I was a speed demon on a Remington [typewriter]."[9] She wrote feature articles on a wide range of topics, from profiles of local eccentrics to interviews with famous people visiting Atlanta, including silent screen idol Rudolph Valentino and millionaire murderer Harry K. Thaw. The cub reporter honed her writing skills and established herself as a popular member of the local press and literary scene.

Mitchell obtained a divorce in late 1924. On July 4, 1925, she married

Marsh, who was the opposite of Upshaw in almost every way—quiet, methodical, and settled. She was twenty-four, he was twenty-nine. They made a striking pair: her dark-haired, diminutive good looks contrasted sharply with the bespectacled and blond Marsh, who, at more than six feet tall, towered over her. A former college English instructor and newspaperman from Kentucky, Marsh had recently joined the publicity department at Georgia Power Company. The couple moved into a three-room, ground-floor apartment on Crescent Avenue that she affectionately dubbed "the Dump." Never shy about tweaking society's nose, she posted individual calling cards on their door: "John Robert Marsh" and "Margaret Mitchell." She continued to work for the *Atlanta Journal* and, in her spare time, tried her hand at fiction writing. She started with a short story about a Jazz Age youth named Pansy Hamilton but abandoned the work after about thirty pages. She next completed a draft of a Civil War–era novella called "'Ropa Carmagin" about a reclusive woman from a wealthy family that had come down in the world. Apparently not satisfied with it, she took no steps to have it published.

The early days of the Marsh marriage were lean. Ill for much of the first year, he ran up a large hospital bill. She, too, had an assortment of medical issues, and it took several years of scrimping to pay the debts they accrued as a result of their poor health. Asking her father for financial support seems to have been out of the question, and according to Marsh's sister, Frances Zane, the couple became used to living a simple life. Zane told of sending Mitchell a hand-me-down blue velvet dress that was accepted with tears of joy.[10]

In the spring of 1926, a recurring ankle injury aggravated by arthritis led Mitchell to quit her full-time job at the newspaper. On crutches much of the time, she found it too difficult to get around town pursuing interviews and story leads. Over the next several months, as she recuperated at home, she worked on occasional small pieces for the paper, including an advice column. But the "dynamo" ex-reporter soon grew impatient and bored. Her husband brought home armloads of books from the library to keep her entertained; as Stephens Mitchell once said of his sister, "books were her narcotic."[11] However, she needed something more to occupy her time and mind. She toyed with the idea of finishing her degree at Atlanta's Oglethorpe University but could not afford the tuition or expense of the new clothes she would need.[12] She returned to writing fiction. Using a portable typewriter Marsh gave her, she decided to write a novel on a topic close to her heart—the lives of Georgians in the 1860s and 1870s.

Although the book would not find a title for almost a decade, this was the genesis of what would become *Gone With the Wind*. The author set her story amidst the Civil War, but it was not about the war itself. She wanted the heat of the major battles—Manassas, Gettysburg, and Vicksburg—felt through their effects on the home front. The action would take place around Atlanta, a vital crossroads of the Confederacy that found itself in the shadow of Virginia, the major battleground state and home to the Confederate capital of Richmond. She felt that military histories and fictional accounts of the war concentrated too much on the Virginia and Mississippi River campaigns and slighted the 1864 retreat of Confederate general Joseph E. Johnston from Chattanooga to Atlanta, which, to her, had "far more drama than anything else in the whole war."[13]

The characters in Mitchell's book would be vibrant men, women, and children—free and slave—who found their world turned upside down and had to deal with hunger, disease, death, and a new world order. At the center of the story would be a spoiled Southern belle named Pansy O'Hara, who reaches adulthood in time to watch her comfortable life at her family's plantation be swept away by war and its aftermath. Pansy will fight for survival and emerge a rich woman but fail to win the affection of Ashley, the man she believes to be her true love. Through various adventures, she will fall for a rapscallion blockade runner named Rhett, who plays with her affections as expertly as she does his. The warm-hearted Melanie, Ashley's wife, serves as Pansy's foil and conscience.

With the plot sketched out in her head, Mitchell started writing the story at its conclusion, a technique she used as a reporter. Working from the end made the rest of the story flow more easily, she claimed, because she knew where it was headed. It also helped her control her characters: "I had every detail clear in my mind before I sat down to the typewriter. I believe . . . that is the best way to write a book—then your characters can't get away from you and misbehave, and do things you didn't intend them to do in the beginning."[14]

As she sat down to write the last chapter, the logical ending seemed to her an open-ended one that left it up to the reader's imagination whether Pansy and Rhett made a life together. With two such determined characters, she left it to the fates to decide what happened to them.[15] From the finale, she worked her way backward, not following any set order or formal outline. She skipped around, focusing on whatever part of the story interested her at a given moment. "Suppose I got bored with chapter five—I wanted to write about love, and here I was stuck with the Battle of Atlanta," she explained. "Why sit glaring at that paragraph when I could go on to chapter sixty and write about love! Very often, your subconscious will work out the problem you've been stuck on, and then you can come back and grab that paragraph when it least suspects it!"[16]

As she completed her chapters, she placed them in individual manila envelopes. Gradually, piles of envelopes began to clutter up the living room where she worked. They came in handy to prop up an uneven leg on a sofa and as scratch pads for grocery lists and phone messages. When the piles eventually took over their small living room, she moved some of them to the bedroom and others into a hall closet.

Mitchell descended from a family of lawyers who, she claimed, were famous for writing wills so clear and easy to read that a child could understand them. With that model as her guide, she put great effort into developing her story with a mode of writing devoid of literary flair. "I sweat blood to make my style simple and stripped bare," she said. "I'm sure if I had evidenced any style in early childhood, if would have been smacked out of me with a hair brush!"[17] She went to great pains to eliminate verbiage that did not further the plot or develop a character. She relentlessly omitted "pretty words" that did not mean anything, aiming to write so clearly and crisply "that every word could be read from a galloping horse."[18] The process proved a struggle for the loquacious Mitchell, whose natural tendency was toward detailed and colorful language. A chronic rewriter, she struggled over almost every word and sentence. "I don't have that facility for just dashing along," she said. She labored day and night, whittling pages-long passages to a few lines.[19] Even after finishing a chapter, Mitchell rarely let it be. She thought it important to let her drafts sit and reconsider them later with a fresh eye. "Put your work up for two months and then when you take it out again," she advised other writers, "the errors will fairly leap out at you till you wonder why you ever thought it was good."[20]

From the stories she had heard all her life, Mitchell knew the historical background of the region and the period she wrote about by heart. And so she did not bother with organized research. Yet, throughout the years of writing, Mitchell read about the Civil War era in old newspapers, diaries, government records, and firsthand accounts of life in antebellum Georgia. She also had access to letters between her grandparents written during the war and benefited from articles her father and brother wrote for the *Atlanta Historical Bulletin*. She would call out for special attention a piece Stephens Mitchell published in 1929 about wartime industries in Atlanta in the 1860s.[21] She rarely made notes on any of what she read, using these historical details more for inspiration rather than literal adaptation. She once said the only notes she took were when an idea came to her in the middle of the night and she did not want to get out of bed to work on the manuscript.[22]

She was not one for outlines either; much of Mitchell's work went on inside her head. One section in particular frustrated her—a scene in which Pansy flees Atlanta and returns home through the war-torn countryside, only to find her mother dead and the plantation in ruins. "I prowled around it mentally for a long time, looking at it from all angles and not getting anywhere," she said. "I could never write a line of it and never made a try at it, on paper. I didn't seem able to capture the smell of the cedars; the smell of the swamp; the barnyard odors, and pack them into those chapters."[23] But like so many writers, for whom the most unusual and unrelated stimuli—a smell, a remark, or a glimpse of scenery—can trigger a flood of thoughts and words, Mitchell had an epiphany. The words came to her at the Ritz Hotel in Atlantic City, New Jersey, where she had accompanied Marsh on a business trip:

> I was not even thinking about the story when all this came to me very simply and very clearly. It was cold, wet winter . . . and yet I could see clearly how dusty and stifling a red clay road in Georgia looks and feels in September, how the leaves on the trees are dry and there isn't any wind to move them and how utterly still the deep country woods are. And there is the queerest smell in the swampy bottom lands at twilight. And I suddenly saw how very haunted such a section would look the day after a big battle, after two armies had moved on.[24]

Now that she had the "atmosphere" she had been trying to capture for so long, the couple cut short their trip so Mitchell could return home and continue writing.

She worked on her manuscript for the next several years at an inconstant pace. She suffered several spells of poor health, including bouts of eyestrain, pleurisy, and "the jitters." Also causing her to pause was "an attack of the humbles" brought on by reading books about the Civil War such as Stephen Vincent Benét's *John Brown's Body* and Mary Johnston's *Cease Firing*. Benét, Mitchell said, had caught what she was trying to capture "so clearly, so vividly and so simply" and with such "a heart-breaking beauty" that she could not write for months. Likewise, Johnston had "done what I'd wanted to do and done it so much better that there seemed little use of me trying."[25] Toward the end of the decade, Mitchell wrote a friend that her work on the book progressed at a snail's pace.[26] She reviewed what she had written so far. Much of it seemed silly, and her expectations for ever having the story published were not high.

The novel was substantially complete in 1929. In her own words, Mitchell hit it "a few more licks in 1930 and 1931,"[27] then put it out of her mind, not having any particular impetus to add the finishing touches. After that, she "worked on the book only now and then," Marsh later recalled. "She had reached the point where most of the creative job was done and there was nothing more to do except the drudgery of turning a rough manuscript into a finished one."[28]

~

Throughout all the years of writing, Mitchell's husband was the only person with whom she discussed the novel in any detail. He reviewed drafts, made comments, and talked her through difficulties. The rest of her family and friends knew only that she was working on a book about the Civil War. She refused to disclose any details, making it clear she did not want to talk about the project. Even friendly inquiries about how her work was going were met with a bristled response. Mitchell would later explain that her stand-offishness was bred of insecurity. She was not one of those authors who felt so sure of themselves that they happily talked up their latest endeavor to anyone willing to listen.[29]

Although most of Mitchell's friends did not push her about the book, one had a special interest in the project. Lois Dwight Cole was the office manager of the Atlanta branch of the Macmillan Company, one of the largest and most esteemed publishing firms in the United States. A handsome brunette with blue eyes that crinkled when she smiled,[30] Cole first met Mitchell in 1927 through Medora Field Perkerson, a writer with whom Mitchell had worked on the *Journal*'s Sunday magazine and who had served as matron of honor at the Marsh wedding. Perkerson introduced Mitchell to Cole at a luncheon, and the two literary-minded women hit it off right away. Cole was just two years younger than Mitchell and had graduated from Smith. If not for the death of Mitchell's mother, the two would have almost certainly met years earlier at the small college. They made up for lost time and formed a lasting friendship that would change their lives and literary history.

Cole's office was near the Marsh apartment, and she often stopped by to visit Mitchell on the way home from work. Their bond was cemented when Mitchell introduced the unmarried Cole to a reporter named Allan Taylor, with whom Mitchell had worked at the newspaper. Cole and Taylor eventually wed, and Mitchell considered herself the godmother of their marriage. The couples socialized regularly. If the two men worked late, Cole and Mitchell often spent evenings together, talking and performing domestic chores like turning the collars on their husbands' shirts.[31] Their conversations gravitated toward discussions of people, poetry, history, and books. But there was one book they did not talk about—Mitchell's. Cole asked her about it several times, but the author stayed tight-lipped. On one occasion, when Cole dropped by the apartment and found her friend at the typewriter, Mitchell tossed a towel over the table to hide the manuscript.[32]

Even knowing almost nothing about the book, Cole could not help but suspect it would turn out well. Mitchell was smart, articulate, and funny, a winning combination for a novelist. She also was a natural storyteller, who told tales with such fun and skill that she could entertain an entire roomful of people.[33] If Mitchell wrote as well as she spoke, Cole thought, the book was sure to be a humdinger.[34] On various occasions, Cole let Mitchell know that Macmillan would like to see the manuscript. Mitchell shrugged off the idea, saying she would probably never finish the "damn thing."

In 1932, Marsh received a promotion at the power company, and the couple moved to a larger apartment on East Seventeenth Street. That same year, Cole accepted a job as an associate editor at Macmillan's New York office. In her new position, she reported to Harold Latham, Macmillan's editor in chief, the leading editorial force at the company and one of its vice presidents. Among Cole's host of responsibilities was vetting manuscripts for her new boss. In the back of her mind, she considered Mitchell's book as something that might interest Latham. In the fall of 1933, Cole heard a rumor that Mitchell had completed the manuscript except for the first chapter. The associate editor wrote the author a formal letter of inquiry from Macmillan. Did Mitchell want to send what she had so far to the publisher for its advisers to read and make suggestions? "I do hope you haven't made arrangements to send your manuscript to any other house, as we have always been counting on seeing it," Cole said.[35] Mitchell responded with an equally formal letter, saying that Cole had heard wrong. the book was not done. She doubted it ever would be finished but agreed that, if she managed to pull it together, she would let Macmillan see it first.

Cole tried again in 1934, this time by telegram. Mitchell still would not budge about letting Macmillan see the incomplete novel.[36] However, after several months of neglect, the author did redirect her attention to the manuscript and give it a thorough assessment with the idea of finally wrapping it up. The first three chapters failed to impress her, and she also noticed a lack of action toward the middle of the book. She decided to start there and began reworking several chapters, hoping to lift them out of their "sag."[37] Her plans were interrupted when, on November 22, she and Marsh were in an automobile accident while driving a friend home after a dinner engagement. The two men suffered neck strain, and Mitchell injured her back. For the next three months, she lay in bed, unable to work. After regaining her mobility in the spring of 1935, she remained in chronic pain. Sitting at a desk was difficult for her, so the manuscript remained on the back burner.

⌒

Although Macmillan received hundreds of manuscripts in the mail every year, Latham did not linger at his desk waiting for the next bestseller to fall in his lap. Beginning in the late 1920s, he took regular scouting trips to cities across the United States and England, looking for promising new authors. While on the road, he attended meetings, lunches, dinners, and cocktail parties with agents, publishers, and writers, hoping to ferret out hot prospects. These trips were a crapshoot at best, often full of disappointing leads and wasted time. Occasionally, though, the dice fell just right.

Such was the case in the spring of 1935 when Latham embarked on his first scouting tour of the South. Many of America's best-known writers came from that part of the country, and Macmillan wanted to publish more Southern novels of merit. En route to California, one of his regular destinations, he planned to visit Atlanta, Charleston, New Orleans, and Austin.[38] Latham came to the South with an open mind and an earnest desire to learn about the area.[39] He also came armed with some inside information that an ex-reporter in Atlanta named Margaret Mitchell Marsh might have a manuscript worth looking at. The tip had come, of course, from Cole, who recommended Latham seek out her friend.

The editor arrived in Atlanta the second week of April and sent local authors—established and aspirant—into a flutter.* The *Atlanta Journal* reported that "desks were ransacked, papers dusted" as writers scurried to

---

* Over the years, the exact circumstances of Mitchell and Latham's first meeting in April 1935 have become muddled. In an account the editor wrote in 1936, he made it sound as if he met Mitchell and obtained the manuscript on the same day. This comports with Mitchell's version of the story as well as press reports that Latham was in town for a single day—Thursday, April 11. In an article he wrote in 1939, however, Latham claimed he approached Mitchell about her novel on three occasions over a two-day period; he repeated this general version in his 1965 autobiography, *My Life in Publishing*.

pull together manuscripts for his consideration.[40] Still in pain from her injuries, Mitchell did not join in the fray. Although Cole had told her in March that Latham would be in town, she had not been well enough to finish the book in time for his visit, and she had no plans of showing it to him in its incomplete state. As a special favor to Cole, however, Mitchell agreed to meet the editor and do what she could to make his stay pleasant and productive.

On Thursday, April 11, Latham attended a luncheon at Rich's department store as a guest of the *Journal*'s Perkerson. Like Cole, the newspaperwoman knew little about Mitchell's book but suspected it would be worth the editor's time. At the luncheon, Perkerson arranged for Latham to sit with Mitchell and encouraged him to speak with her about her writing. Perkerson warned, though, that it would not be easy to wrest the manuscript from the budding novelist. Intrigued, the editor asked Mitchell whether she had a novel for him to see. She admitted to having worked on something for years, but said it was in no condition to be evaluated.[41]

The pair crossed paths again that afternoon at a tea, to which Mitchell brought along several fledgling authors eager to meet the New York editor. When Latham mentioned her manuscript again, Mitchell changed the subject and offered to take him on an outing with the group to see Atlanta's famed dogwood trees. It is hard to imagine a busy editor like Latham agreeing to spend an afternoon driving around looking at the local scenery, yet something about Mitchell interested him. She had impressed him with her intelligence, and he thought her a "nice little thing."[42] Latham accepted the invitation. During their tour, he steered the conversation to Mitchell's manuscript, and she again denied having a novel ready for him to review. At the end of the day, she told him she enjoyed their visit and promised that, if she ever finished her book, he would be the first to see it.

After the group dropped the editor off at his hotel, one of Mitchell's companions asked why she had not given Latham her manuscript. Another aspiring author in the group overheard the question and expressed shock that Mitchell had written anything that would be worth the editor's time. Mitchell later recalled the woman bragging that her own book had been refused by the best publishers, as if that was a badge of honor. Although the story has an apocryphal ring to it, the comment supposedly got Mitchell's dander up and caused her to wonder whether she ought to give Latham the manuscript so that she, too, could brag about having been rejected by the best.[43]

When Mitchell returned to her apartment, she agonized over what to do. She did not want to expose herself, her story, or the South to anyone's ridicule. At the same time, she trusted Latham, sensing he would treat her fairly. Mitchell telephoned her husband at work and told him of the editor's interest. Marsh encouraged her to let Latham see the book. What did she have to lose? Mitchell agreed.

The editor had tentative plans to return to Atlanta the following week. Mitchell could have used those few days to pull the manuscript together. Or she could have taken her time to finish the rewrites and send the manuscript to him in New York later. But impulse had taken over. It was now or never. Latham was scheduled to leave that evening by train, and Mitchell did not waste any time getting the document to him. She hurried about the apartment gathering envelopes, many from under the bed and out of a closet. None of the chapters was numbered, and there were multiple drafts of several, but she did her best to pull together enough material to present a cohesive story. She had never written an acceptable first chapter so hastily drafted a synopsis of what she had in mind for the opening pages.[44] She also grabbed her old novella, "'Ropa Carmagin," and threw that in her car with the rest of the envelopes.

"Hatless, hair flying, dust and dirt all over my face and arms and worse luck, my hastily rolled up stockings coming down about my ankles" is how Mitchell once described her appearance upon arriving at Latham's hotel.★ Bellboys followed behind, picking up envelopes she dropped as she crossed the lobby.[45] Mitchell called the editor's room and asked him to meet her downstairs. When he arrived, Latham found the author sitting on a divan next to a towering stack of envelopes. Mitchell acknowledged the shabby condition of her manuscript and told him she wanted his opinion on whether, as raw material for a book, it was worth bothering with. He agreed to look it over and, at her insistence, promised he would not share the manuscript with anyone else.[46] She told him to take it before she changed her mind.

In that pre-computer era, bulky manuscripts were standard fare. Many authors still wrote by longhand, and typewritten documents often contained hand edits. Cutting and pasting required scissors and paste. Even so, Latham was flabbergasted by the sheer mass—and mess—of what Mitchell had given him. He would later describe it as the largest manuscript he had ever seen.

---

★ It is not known in which hotel Latham stayed while in Atlanta. Mitchell biographer Anne Edwards says it was the Georgian Terrace but offers no source. Lois Cole recalled it was the Biltmore, while Margaret Baugh, a Macmillan secretary in the Atlanta office, insisted it was the Ansley.

According to Mitchell, he "kept a straight face" and arranged for a bellboy to buy a disposable "please-don't-rain suitcase" for him to carry it in.[47] He wrestled the manuscript onto the train that evening, along with a half dozen others he had picked up in Atlanta.

At some point over the next two days, Latham glanced through Mitchell's envelopes. Good editors have noses like hounds that enable them to ferret out the best manuscripts, and Latham's told him her story had promise. But, with a long trip ahead of him, he did not have time to assess the work thoroughly. That was a task best left to his associate editor, Cole, who was manning things back in New York. In today's world, Latham might have called Cole from his cell phone or dashed off an e-mail explaining the situation. In the 1930s, though, not even long-distance telephone calls were a routine tool of the business world. Operators had to place the calls, and it could take up to twenty minutes to make a connection, depending on the distance involved. The lines were unstable, often resulting in poor sound quality. And the calls were expensive, especially during business hours. Calling long distance was generally done only in the most urgent circumstances. Telegramming was another option but also could be prohibitively expensive. Latham fell back on the most popular form of business communication in those days—a letter.

On Saturday, April 13, 1935, Latham wrote Cole from Charleston, South Carolina, using a typewriter he carried with him on the trip. He gave a status report on his Atlanta visit. After praising the assistant editor for being one of the most popular people in town and for having been a "good girl" while stationed there as the Macmillan office manager, he mentioned having obtained the manuscript from Mitchell. What he had read so far was promising, but he was unable to make a complete assessment because of its disorganized state. Moreover, it was as "big as a house," and he could not carry it with him cross-country. So, although he had promised Mitchell he would not show the manuscript to anyone else, he was shipping it to Cole. He asked her to be prepared to talk with him about it when he returned to New York. Latham recognized getting Cole involved was a tricky matter given his promise to Mitchell, so he instructed Cole not to let on to her friend that she had it. He rationalized the deception, saying he knew Mitchell would be fine with Cole seeing it eventually. He promised to tell the author the truth at some point, but now was not the right time.[48]

Meanwhile, Mitchell fretted over having turned over the enormous pile of stained envelopes. With great embarrassment, she realized she had forgotten to give Latham some of the chapters and had included duplicates of others. She also worried about what would happen if the book was published. She feared a harsh critical reaction and thought she had "been several kinds of an ass" to get herself in "so vulnerable a position."[49]

Amidst her throes of regret, she received a letter from Latham on April 15. He liked what he had seen of her manuscript. He wanted to give it a careful reading and circulate it to others at Macmillan for their input. Would she mind if he kept it until June? Mitchell had a hard time accepting his praise. "I am oppressed with the knowledge of the lousiness of what I write for even though I may not write well, I do know good writing," she replied on Tuesday, April 16.[50] She offered to take back the manuscript so she could tidy things up before anyone else at Macmillan attempted to muddle through her story. Embarrassed as she was, though, if he could do something with her work in its present condition, she was fine with him keeping it.

A week after leaving Atlanta, Latham typed Cole a letter on a train from New Orleans to Austin. Having trouble hitting the keys because the train was moving so fast, he vented that he was killing himself with the travel and the constant stream of engagements. The heat also distressed him: "It is as hot as HELL." Nevertheless, he was pleased with his trip so far, especially Mitchell's manuscript. He wanted to know whether Cole agreed that "this woman has something" and asked the associate editor to send her impressions along as soon as she finished reading. Meanwhile, he wanted to play along with Mitchell carefully. Cole still should not let on that she had the manuscript. He instructed her to hold on to his letter for future reference but to make sure its contents remained secret.[51] That same day, Latham also wrote Mitchell again. He assured her that he understood about the unfinished condition of the manuscript and asked her to be patient. Her manuscript had great potential, and he intended to keep at it.[52]

After the manuscript had made its way to New York, Cole took the pile of envelopes home to sort through with her husband's assistance. Physically, it was a disaster, as Latham had warned. A few of the chapters were typed neatly on clean white paper, but the rest were on yellow pages covered in pencil notations. In many cases, there were lengthy revisions of scenes. For instance, Mitchell apparently had trouble making up her mind about the best way to kill off Pansy's second husband, Frank Kennedy. In one version, he died of pneumonia after Pansy forced him to go out in a rainstorm to evict a family. Another had him killed by federal troops in a Ku Klux Klan raid. Cole and Taylor organized the chapters and sorted through the duplicates, trying to bring some order to the chaos.

In a fifteen-page report to Latham, Cole analyzed Mitchell's work in detail.[53] She presented him an outline of what appeared to be a thirty-chapter story, with five chapters missing. Overall, it was in extremely poor condition. The time sequence was hopelessly muddled. Important scenes were missing. Yet, Cole knew right away Macmillan had a winner on its hands. According to her assessment, the atmosphere was exceptionally well done; the plot was almost "sure fire"; the dialogue was "well in character and natural." As for the characters, she thought Pansy especially good and Rhett "the strongest and most clearly drawn in the book." Cole's impressions of Ashley and Melanie were less glowing but still positive. She described him as "shadowy" and her as "almost too good" yet still believable.

Overall, Cole deemed the characters memorable. Vivid sections of the story remained in her mind long after she finished reading. She liked the ending, praising it as "severely logical in its outline as a Greek tragedy." She quibbled only slightly with Mitchell's decision to present Pansy returning to Tara, her family plantation, with a sense of hope for what tomorrow would bring. Cole thought this "implies an insouciance, a callousness, and a hope, which are all out of keeping. Pansy has lost everything she has, and even her limited intelligence must tell her that." Cole wanted the book to end on that note so there would be no doubt Pansy was doomed. Beyond that, the editor had just two concerns: Would Mitchell be able to bring the story together into an acceptable whole, and was there a market for a novel about the Civil War and Reconstruction? Those concerns aside, the manuscript was too good to pass up.

Latham wrapped up his scouting trip at the end of May and returned to Macmillan's Fifth Avenue headquarters. Busy working on the firm's fall releases, he also wanted to get things moving on Mitchell's manuscript. He decided to send it to Charles W. Everett, an English professor at Columbia University who served as a freelance reader for Macmillan. Latham had tremendous confidence in Everett's judgment and wanted a second opinion on Mitchell's manuscript with a particular focus on what she needed to do to complete it.[54]

By July 1935, Mitchell had still not heard back from Latham with his final verdict on whether her story was worth publishing. And, apparently, Cole had followed Latham's instructions about not letting the author know of her involvement. After almost three months of no news, Mitchell began to get antsy. She had been mulling over the plot since Latham left Atlanta and wanted to finish the book once and for all. But, because he had the manuscript there was not much she could do.[55] She tried working from memory and with the duplicate chapters she did have but found it impossible. On July 9, she wrote Latham explaining the situation and asking him to return the manuscript. She acknowledged this was a crazy thing for an aspiring author to do but said she could not restrain herself.

Reading perhaps a little too much between the lines, Latham worried that Mitchell wanted the pages back so she could show them to other publishers. He had no intention of letting that happen.[56] The editor replied on July 15, apologizing for the delay in getting back to her. He assured her he remained keenly interested in the book. He thought it had every chance of becoming a considerable success and hoped she would be patient a little longer.[57]

That same week, Latham received Everett's assessment of the manuscript. It was an even more glowing review than Cole's. The professor thought the book "magnificent" and "breath-taking," and praised the author's control of the plot's tempo.[58] He recommended Macmillan offer Mitchell a contract immediately and predicted the novel would likely be a bestseller.[59] Despite its rough appearance, the manuscript needed little work before it would be publishable. Everett suggested Mitchell bridge a few gaps in the plot and tone down what he saw as negativity toward Reconstruction. Like Cole, he thought the ending needed to be reworked. However, he took a different approach and recommended pulling Pansy away from the brink of certain doom by leaving open the possibility that Rhett might return someday. Finally, Everett offered a title for the as-yet-unnamed book: "Another Day."[60]

With Cole's and Everett's ringing endorsements—and having read it himself with great enthusiasm—Latham prepared to convince his boss, Macmillan president George P. Brett, Jr., to buy Mitchell's manuscript. Brett had recently taken over the reins of Macmillan from his father, George P. Brett, who still sat on the firm's board. The dynamic between the younger Brett and Latham was an interesting one. Brett had no formal education beyond high school and had joined the firm in 1919 after serving in the U.S. Army in France.[61] He and his younger brother, Richard, the company's treasurer, worked their way up the ranks under their father's tutelage. By contrast, Latham had joined the firm after graduating from Columbia University in 1909 and had climbed the ladder on his own. Although there was a mere six-year age difference between him and Brett, they might as well have been father and son. Brett played the role of young and impulsive leader to Latham's refined elder statesman.[62]

Latham approached Brett and the firm's editorial council on July 17, 1935, and suggested they offer Mitchell a publishing contract. Certain the book had great potential, the editor predicted Macmillan would make a terrible mistake not publishing it. He wanted to act quickly and stretched the truth to make that happen. Not only did he say that other publishers were after her. A family gem is on his part—but he also attempted to paint Mitchell as an established literary figure. Perhaps sensing that the council would be wary about investing in an unknown author, Latham shamelessly bolstered her resume, claiming she was an editor at the *Atlanta Journal*, had written for magazines, and was counted as a figure of importance in the Southern literary world. He predicted this book would certainly make her.[63] Mitchell would have been horrified by Latham's exaggerations. A stickler for the truth, she had no pretensions about her literary qualifications. She had worked as a reporter, not an editor. While she had plenty of friends in Georgia literary circles and remained a member of the Atlanta Women's Press Club, her name carried no more weight than that of any other ex-reporter/ aspiring novelist. But puffery aside, Latham was correct about what mattered—this book would be the making of Margaret Mitchell.

How did Latham know this? He didn't. Public taste cannot be predicted with any accuracy. Editors take risks on every title they go after. The best they can do is hope that what interests or entertains them will interest or entertain a mass audience. Having been in the publishing business for nearly twenty-five years, Latham was an experienced gambler. He thought Mitchell had written an intriguing story and was sufficiently confident of his own taste—and that of Cole and Everett—to think the average reader would agree. Brett, also a gambler, trusted Latham's judgment. He gave the editor permission to offer the Atlanta author a contract. Latham wired Mitchell that same day with the news that the Macmillan advisers shared his enthusiasm for her book and had high hopes for its success. The firm offered her a royalty deal under which she would earn a percentage of the book's profits, with a guaranteed up-front advance payment of five hundred dollars. He directed the author to wire him her approval so he could send the specific terms immediately.[64] And so began negotiations on one of the most successful contracts in publishing history.

Mitchell was stunned to receive Latham's telegram, plus an ebullient one from Cole, adding her congratulations. She replied to Cole, "Do you really mean they like it? You wouldn't fox an old friend, would you?"[65] She also wrote Latham, thanking him for the offer and his kind words, admitting that his telegram put her "in to a happiness that can best be described as a 'state'—a 'state' which necessitated a luminal tablet, a cold towel on the forehead and a nice, quiet nap."[66] Despite her excitement, Mitchell did not get carried away. She well knew that when it came to contracts, the devil was in the details, so she told Latham she could not wire back an immediate acceptance. She had a list of questions that had to be answered first. She wanted to know if there would be a specific delivery date for the revised manuscript and, if so, what would happen if she broke her neck or came down with "the Bubonic plague." Would she have access to the comments the Macmillan readers had made about the manuscript? She wanted to see their suggestions to make sure she would be willing to accept them. She hoped her comments were not overly "brusque," but she did not plan on accepting any contract, "no matter how nice," without reviewing the terms.

If Latham was amused or offended by Mitchell's forthrightness, he did not let on. He assured her there would be nothing in the contract about a delivery date; the submission date would be entirely up to her. He suggested only that he hoped she would finish in time for it to be published in 1936.[67] As for the specifics of the contract, it would be Macmillan's standard form, and he took the liberty of suggesting it contained nothing objectionable. He enclosed for her consideration the comments Everett had made on the manuscript and called her attention to his proposed title. "Another Day" worked well, Latham thought, and Macmillan was entirely content with it.★

On July 23, 1935, Latham put in a rush order for the Macmillan staff to prepare a draft contract. While Mitchell waited for the document to arrive, she wrote Cole again and expressed appreciation for her efforts in bringing the deal together. Although Mitchell did not know Cole had been the first one to read the manuscript and sing its praises, she suspected her friend had been working behind the scenes on its behalf. "I know perfectly well that Mr. Latham wouldn't have taken such a kindly attitude if it hadn't been for your nice press agenting," she wrote. "Even before he laid eyes on me, you had gotten in such good work that I had Hell to pay trying to live up to your advance notices. Any way, I do thank you from the bottom of what passes as my heart."[68]

She also wrote to Latham expressing her pleasure over Everett's comments: "I certainly did not expect so swell a report."[69] She went through the professor's suggestions one by one and agreed to take them into consid-

---

★ Latham appears never to have informed Mitchell that Cole had also read the manuscript, nor do the records suggest he sent her Cole's comments.

eration. As for two characters who seemed to spring out of nowhere in the text—Pansy's daughter Ella and a convict named Archie—Mitchell thought she had included chapters introducing them but admitted the envelopes may have been omitted in her haste to get Latham the manuscript that harried afternoon in April. She found drafts of the relevant parts amidst the envelopes still cluttering her apartment and sent them along. Lest he have any worries that she was offended by Everett's frank assessment, she encouraged Latham to always be honest with her. "I am not a sensitive plant and can take criticism," she assured him. Her skin had been toughened by her husband's review of her work: "I fear that nothing you or your advisers could say would be quite as hard boiled as what he has already said to me. So please speak your mind." As for the proposed title, she preferred "Tomorrow Is Another Day" or, perhaps, "Tote the Weary Load." Still, she had concerns about those. The first, she thought, had just been used for another novel, and the second might be "too colloquial." Could she have a "little leeway" before making a final decision?

As Latham promised, the contract contained nothing controversial. Macmillan's offer was typical of that era—10 percent royalties on the first ten thousand copies of the book sold and 15 percent for any copies sold beyond that. In the event Macmillan ever issued a low-end edition of the book, Mitchell's share of the profits would be adjusted downward. The five-hundred-dollar advance would be paid in two parts—half on signing the contract, the remainder upon delivery of the final manuscript. The document also detailed what would happen if, after Mitchell delivered the manuscript, she wanted to make corrections; if she made changes too far down the production line, she would have to pay for the alterations. Finally, Macmillan wanted the author to agree to submit her next novel to the company for its consideration.

Under Macmillan's offer, the firm would obtain the right to publish Mitchell's book in the United States, as well as in all markets worldwide. At that time, foreign rights to American novels were not seen as having significant value. Few overseas readers were interested in what writers in the United States had to say. And publishers were wary of the high cost of translating American books into foreign languages. But American publishers often acquired those rights as a matter of course on the off chance a book proved to have international appeal. Macmillan had no interest though in the dramatic and motion picture rights to Mitchell's story. Today, those subsidiary rights are integral to many book contracts, but publishers in the 1930s did not have the time or expertise to deal with movie and theatrical producers. Macmillan published books; Mitchell could do what she liked with any nonprint formats of her story.

Overall, Mitchell was pleased with the contract, so much so that she saw no need to bring in an outside adviser to assess the document. She appears to have never considered hiring a literary rights lawyer to haggle over the proposed terms or bringing in a literary agent to shop the book to other publishers with the hope of generating a bidding war. Mitchell trusted Latham and wanted the company where her friend Cole worked to have the book. She was content to review the contract with the counsel of her family. She and Marsh had experience in newspaper publishing, and her father and brother were lawyers, albeit specialists in real estate law. Mitchell felt confident the Mitchell-Marsh clan was savvy enough to review a basic contract.

On August 1, she wrote to Latham that she was "quite willing to sign up with Macmillan," subject to a few points of clarification. At the risk of being "pickayunish," she thought it important that she speak her mind before signing on the dotted line. One of her primary concerns was that she wanted input on the dust jacket design. She claimed to "have seen many books about the South which had illustrations on the jacket which were of such un-Southern appearance as to arouse mirth and indignation" and would feel better if she could see the final design before it was "closed up."[70] She also wanted to clarify her serial rights—publication of her story in installments in newspapers and magazines—and establish what would happen if Macmillan should go bankrupt. She concluded by asking if the company would keep the deal quiet until the manuscript was finished. If word got out, she would be inundated with friends wanting to know details, and she preferred to work without interruption for the time being. "I only hope you do not lose money on me!" she added. Mitchell returned the contract—unsigned—so Latham could look over the suggested changes.

The editor again accepted Mitchell's queries with aplomb, going so far as expressing pleasure at having received her "long letter." He did not want to modify the contract but offered assurances on the matters that concerned her. She could have approval rights on the book's cover, dust jacket, and even typeface. Proceeds from a serialization would be divided equally between the publisher and the author. As for the possibility of Macmillan going bankrupt, he assured her that was not likely to happen and, if it did, appropriate arrangements could be made at that time. He agreed Macmillan would not broadcast news of the book outside the company but cautioned her that he would begin talking it up to his own staff so that when release day came the salesmen would be ready to believe in her book and advance its interests.[71] Tossing on the charm, he added that he was leaving for a month's vacation and wanted to bring this matter to a happy conclusion before he left. He would not be able to enjoy his holiday otherwise, he said. Latham returned the contract to Mitchell by special delivery airmail and told her, if these assurances were not adequate, he would adjust anything that caused her concern.

Less gracious was Cole, who could not believe her friend's nerve. She, too, was getting ready for vacation and did not like the prospect of Mitchell holding things up. In Cole's mind, the author should have signed and returned the contract without hesitation. Thousands of Macmillan authors had; Cole herself had signed one for a young adult book she coauthored with her husband. Where did Mitchell get off splitting hairs? She gave her friend some hard advice in a letter airmailed to Atlanta on August 5. She assured Mitchell that Macmillan was trustworthy as well as solvent— "Gibraltar itself is no more firmly founded"—and let her friend know that Macmillan was "exercised" about the list of questions. Straddling her double role of ally and editor, Cole closed, "For heaven's sake, don't think I am trying to influence you. I am only being the most ordinary of friends."[72]

Mitchell signed the contract the following day without further ado and telegraphed her approval to New York. When returning the executed document, she apologized for having caused any trouble. She characterized Latham as being "mighty patient and long suffering" in his dealings with her: "After reading Lois' letter, I got the idea that you all might think that I suspected you and your company of bad faith or double dealing. That upset me for *that* idea hadn't occurred to me and I hasten to beg you to put such an idea out of your minds."[73]

Was she seriously worried she had offended Macmillan by asking questions about the contract? This seems unlikely. No damsel in distress, Mitchell knew she was within her rights to raise concerns before signing the document. A more likely explanation is that she wanted to avoid causing problems for Cole and getting off on the wrong foot with Latham. Regardless of her motivation though, she managed to retain the upper hand with her amiable regrets to Latham for being a bother. He rushed to apologize for the way things had been handled, claiming that her questions were legitimate and that he had not felt the least bit of impatience with her questions.[74] Mitchell had signed Macmillan's contract but now had Latham eating out of the palm of her hand. Margaret Mitchell may not have been a member of the Junior League, but she knew a thing or two about Southern charm.

# 2

A Manuscript of the Old South

*August 1935 January 1936*

O n August 7, 1935, the day after she signed the contract, Harold Latham shipped Margaret Mitchell the reorganized manuscript, which he now referred to as the "MS of the Old South." Under separate cover, he returned the novella "'Ropa Carmagin," which he deemed a splendid story but too short to be of commercial interest as a book. The editor suggested Mitchell try to place it with a magazine later.[1] For now, he wanted her to focus on the saga of Pansy and Rhett. The reality of Mitchell's new life as a professional novelist was hammered home when, on August 21, Macmillan sent the first installment of her advance—a check for $250.

With Latham and Lois Cole on vacation, Mitchell settled in to what she knew would be a formidable task: creating a book out of her loose and incomplete assemblage of chapters. She hoped to get the job done quickly. Latham had been kind to her, and she wanted to do something nice for him. Finishing the book in a hurry might show her appreciation. Almost immediately, though, Mitchell felt miserable about what lay ahead. The plot needed organizing. Gaps in the narrative had to be filled. She had to write a first chapter. She also wanted to rework the ending to address Macmillan's concern that it sounded too much like Rhett left for good. Her intention had been to leave the ending open even though she knew many readers might not find that satisfactory. As she once said, "My idea was that, through of several million chapters, the reader will have learned that both Pansy and Rhett are tough characters, both accustomed to having their own

27

way. And at the last, both are determined to have their own ways and those ways are very far apart. And the reader can either decide that she got him or she didn't."[2] Mitchell was willing to make adjustments short of giving readers "a happy ending."

In addition, the manuscript needed a title. Mitchell was not satisfied with those mentioned so far, or with several others she had come up with such as "Bugles Sang True," "None So Blind" and "Not in Our Stars."[3] The only one that struck a chord with her was "Gone With the Wind," a line she had run across in an 1891 poem by English poet Ernest Dowson, a piece with a lengthy Latin title but commonly referred to as "Cynara." She liked the sound of the phrase, and it had the added plus of appearing in her manuscript when Pansy makes her way to Tara after fleeing Atlanta: "Was Tara still standing? Or was Tara also gone with the wind which had swept through Georgia?"[4] On a list of twenty-two possible titles, she put a star beside "Gone With the Wind" and a note stating it was her favorite but that she would agree to any that Macmillan liked.[5]

She also wanted to find a new name for Pansy. It occurred to Mitchell that people in some parts of the country used the word "pansy" as slang for homosexual. In her uninhibited way, she had told Latham back in July that, in the South, "we refer to Pansies as Fairies or by another less euphemistic but far more descriptive term. However, if you think the name of Pansy should be changed please let me know and I will try to think of another name, equally inappropriate."[6] She had generated a list of possible substitutes by scanning the society pages of the *Atlanta Constitution* for the names of visiting belles, but none of those were quite right.[7] She would have to give it further thought.

Beyond these big picture issues, there were many small details that required tending. Over the years of writing, the author had not paid much attention to practical matters such as punctuation and spelling. Once the narrative was straightened out, every page would have to be thoroughly edited. The same careful scrutiny would have to be applied to the hundreds, maybe thousands, of historical references in her story, most of which she had incorporated from memory.[8] Coming from a family of history buffs, Mitchell was adamant that the book be as historically accurate as possible. She especially wanted her accounts of the war "air tight so that no grey bearded vet [can] rise up to shake his cane at me and say, 'But I know better.'"[9]

With the encouragement of her husband, who promised to take off two weeks from work to help, Mitchell mustered the energy to get started.

She began by tying up loose threads in her story line. In some cases, years had passed between the time she wrote a particular chapter and those preceding and following it. When the different parts were fitted together, it came as no surprise that there were many gaps, overlaps, and conflicts in the plot. There also were scenes that now seemed extraneous. She deleted several sections, including a chapter of more than thirty pages in which Rhett lends one of Pansy's neighbors money to buy some horses; a chapter about what happened after General William T. Sherman entered Atlanta; a lengthy discussion detailing when the slave Mammy leaves Pansy and goes back to Tara; an in-depth description of the education of young women in the Old South; and two long sections on the lives of various minor characters after the war.[10]

As fast as she completed her work of cutting and rewriting, John Marsh followed behind editing for grammar, accuracy, and uniformity. As Mitchell described his role, "He painstakingly compiled a glossary of all Negro dialect words used by my characters, and Cracker words, too. He 'styled' the manuscript for consistent spelling, capitalization and punctuation. He summarized my notes about the fighting from Dalton to Atlanta and around Atlanta, to make certain that the actions and statements of my characters conformed to the actual historical events." Marsh also created a chronology of the characters' lives to ensure there were no inconsistencies, such as having babies born at inconvenient times.[11]

Once she got started, Mitchell was relieved and surprised to find the work smooth sailing. While the original drafting had involved much drudgery, on September 3, she wrote to Latham that, "for the first time in my life, working is comparatively easy." She had a fresh sense of optimism that the book would come together in short order. "As John says there's nothing like signing a contract, having a conscience about delivering the goods and burning your britches behind you."[12] Mitchell predicted that, if all went well, the work would be done in six weeks—by mid-October.

When Latham returned from vacation in early September, he was pleased to read Mitchell's status report. Eager to get her book to market, he replied that if she managed to finish the manuscript the following month, it could be published in the spring of 1936. Yet, the editor knew that getting the book ready for production in such a short period of time would require a prodigious effort on Macmillan's part. The company already had a long list of books for spring release, and it would be no small feat to fit another one into the schedule. Macmillan's spring catalog would be issued in January, so time was short. With all this in mind, Latham made it clear that

Mitchell was under no pressure to push for a spring publication. Although Macmillan would be delighted to go to press then, she should take as much time as she needed. He did not want to hurry it: "That would be fatal, and the book is too important to do anything to jeopardize it."[13]

Latham's admonition that Mitchell take her time fell on deaf ears. The Marshes seemed to have gotten it in their heads that the book should be released in the spring, and that is what they set out to accomplish. As the editor had predicted, rushing would prove dangerous.

In their hurry to meet the self-imposed October deadline, the couple worked nonstop, seven days a week, with Marsh sometimes putting in twenty-hour days between his job at Georgia Power and his responsibilities on the manuscript.[14] And there seemed to be no end in sight, especially when it came to verifying the historical references. In describing the fall of Atlanta, for example, Mitchell needed to determine when the outer fortifications were built, what time of day the news arrived of Confederate general John B. Hood's defeat at Jonesboro, what the weather was, and what hours the retreat started and ended. There also were minor details to verify, such as when hoopskirts went out of fashion and bustles became popular, and what ladies' shoes were made of during the Union blockade.[15] With no Internet or centralized databases available, this meant hands-on research. The reference librarians at Atlanta's Carnegie Library were glad to help track down information for Mitchell, but not all the answers she needed could be found in books. The author took precious time away from rewriting to interview senior citizens who had lived through the conflict and to drive around the Georgia countryside searching for obscure information such as the correct planting time for certain types of cotton. On one occasion, she ran into an old farmer spreading manure on a garden. After answering her questions, he asked Mitchell about the life of a writer. She gave him a dreary report: "You sweated, and groaned and itched and broke out in rashes and then felt like you smelled bad." The farmer thought a minute and replied, "When you come right down to it, writing a book ain't so very different from spreading manure, is it?" She was hard-pressed to disagree.[16]

Adding to her workload, Mitchell was determined that none of her characters have the same names as anyone living in that part of Georgia during the time period covered by her story. She did not want to embarrass anyone by making it appear as though she were writing about their relatives. To that end, she spent countless hours in county courthouses around

Atlanta, combing through tax records, Confederate Army muster rolls, wills, and jury lists. In one instance, she changed the name of the Yankee overseer at a neighboring plantation a dozen times. She went to equally great lengths to place her characters' homes in imaginary locations. She put Tara, Pansy's plantation, on a long-since abandoned road she found referenced on one of General Sherman's maps. She also mixed up Atlanta geography, placing houses where they could not possibly have stood.[17]

Amidst the frenzied research and rewriting, Cole touched base with the Marshes and inadvertently added to the couple's stress. Operating on the assumption that Mitchell would have the revisions finished in time for a spring release, Macmillan was readying the novel for production. One of the first steps was creating a mock-up, or dummy, of the book and its dust jacket. Cole sent proposed language for the blurb, the descriptive text about the book and its author that would be used on the jacket and in marketing materials. A public relations professional, Marsh had his own ideas about how the blurb should read and took time away from the manuscript to rewrite the language. Mitchell worked on the wording as well. Among several issues, she specified that she wanted to use her maiden name on the jacket and press materials because that was how she had been known as a newspaper reporter.[18] Cole also had noted that the marketing department needed a publicity portrait of the author, and Mitchell dropped everything to find a photographer, buy an outfit, have her hair styled, and sit through a photo shoot. She hated the finished product, saying that the stress of reworking the manuscript was taking a toll on her appearance. She had lost weight and developed boils on her head. Her scalp, she thought, looked "as though I had just been rescued from the Indians and not a minute too soon, either."[19] She asked for more time so as to give the photographer another try.

Mid-October 1935 came and went without a sign of a finished manuscript at Macmillan. Although late in the game to have nothing in hand, not even a title, Cole did not panic. She trusted her friend had things under control. One positive sign came toward the end of the month when Mitchell proposed that Pansy's name be replaced with Scarlett. She had come across the surname Scarlett in Irish literature and already had used it as Pansy's grandmother's maiden name.[20] Cole agreed it was a good substitute. At least that matter was settled. On October 28, Cole assured the sales staffers, who were eager for work to start on the dust jacket, that sample chapters would be in New York by the middle of November.[21]

Two days later, a package arrived at Macmillan containing a draft of the first chapter. Cole was pleased to get it but wondered where the rest of the novel was. She wrote the author that same day asking her to send along copies of whatever other chapters were ready so as to give the artist who would be designing the dust jacket an idea of the story's setting and characters.[22]

If Cole assumed things were looking up, her bubble burst when the next day's mail arrived with a lengthy letter from Mitchell to Latham explaining why she had sent a single chapter. It had been the only one fit for submittal, and she was not happy even with it. Although Mitchell had been working doggedly for two months, she felt what she had so far for her opening was "amateurish, clumsy and, worst of all, self conscious." She had struggled with the beginning for years, and it did not flow any easier now. "I cannot work on anything else but keep coming back to the first chapter, pouncing on it, worrying it and then leaving it," she said. "Each time I hope that by creeping up on it I will catch it off guard and find it more pliable but I have had no luck, so far."[23] She wanted Latham to review her effort and offer an honest assessment.

Mitchell went on to say that she remained troubled by the book's title. Macmillan seemed content with "Tomorrow Is Another Day," but she had confirmed her suspicion that another novel had recently been released with that title. Moreover, Marsh, a former advertising man, had blocked out the words and ruled it too long and ungraceful. Mitchell hated to "seem a chopper and a changer" but pressed again for "Gone With the Wind." She explained to Latham, "Taken completely away from its context, it has movement, it could either refer to times that are gone like the snows of yesteryear, to the things that passed with the wind of the war or to a person who went with the wind rather than standing against it."[24] What did he think?

Next, the author expressed concern about the production details. She worried about her haggard appearance in the publicity shots, claiming she might have to be "photographed like T.E. Lawrence in a turban."[25] She was unhappy with the wording of the blurb and how it depicted her family's history in Georgia. She offered a litany of amusing but irrelevant details of Mitchell lore, including that her family did not fight in the Spanish-American War "because they thought it a piddling sort of war at best." And, as if she did not have enough on her plate, she concluded with the news that she was hot on the trail of a new author for Latham to consider publishing. She had not had time to get the particulars yet but promised to send more information when she finished her own work.

The letter offers interesting insight into Mitchell's emotional state that fall. She asked for help on the first chapter, but as later would become clear, the problems ran much deeper. The entire manuscript was in far worse condition than she let on, and there was no way it would be ready any time soon. Yet, she rambled on about an assortment of oddball matters and failed to admit she needed more time. What was going through her head? Was she in the throes of writer's block and unable to comprehend the seriousness of the situation? Was she too proud to admit that she had underestimated the job? Perhaps it was a matter of not wanting to disappoint Latham.

Regardless of the reason, Mitchell put on such a casual air that Cole saw no need for undue concern. Latham was on a business trip, so she forwarded Mitchell's letter and the chapter to him on the road. Although he found the opening pages moved a bit slowly, the rest was fine, even admirable. Latham assumed the author just needed a little encouragement to get her moving. He wrote Mitchell, telling her to forget about the first chapter and get on with finishing the manuscript. He confirmed that Scarlett was a good replacement for Pansy and agreed that "Gone With the Wind" was an intriguing title. As for her trouble with the photograph, he did not take her worries too seriously, referring to her descriptions as undeniably humorous. He concluded with a comment that was probably the last thing the overwhelmed Mitchell wanted to hear: "I may tell you in all honesty that there has rarely been a novel about the publication of which I have been so excited and to the appearance of which I have looked forward more eagerly."[26]

Assuming Latham's comments had calmed Mitchell's nerves, Cole told her friend to hurry and have the photograph retaken. She also suggested Mitchell give more thought to the name Scarlett, worrying that it sounded like a *Good Housekeeping* story and might be confused with *Sylvia Scarlett*, a recently released and widely panned motion picture starring Katharine Hepburn and Cary Grant.[27] Cole's second-guessing of Scarlett threw Mitchell into a panic. After two months of around-the-clock effort, her nerves were wearing thin. In addition to the case of boils, her eyes bothered her, as did the back injury from the 1934 car accident.[28] If Cole had a better idea for the character's name, Mitchell was glad to hear it. But Macmillan had to make up its mind. Upon receiving Latham's stamp of approval for Scarlett, Mitchell had paid a typist fifty cents an hour to convert all the Pansy references in the manuscript to the new name. The frustrated author did not relish paying to have them changed again. "Personally, we could call her 'Garbage O'Hara' for all I care," she wrote to Cole. "I just want to finish this damn thing and take my busted back and bacilli staphylococci to bed for a long period."[29] Until Macmillan decided what the name would be, Mitchell refused to go any further on the manuscript.

Regretting having opened this can of worms, Cole immediately apologized to the frazzled author and told her to get back to her writing. "For heaven's sake, don't stop work of any sort and go right along with Scarlett," the editor replied.[30]

In the midst of those discussions, Mitchell bought herself some time by sending Cole the second and fourth chapters and sections of a few others she thought might be useful to the dust jacket artist.[31] She also identified scenes that might work as a cover illustration, such as Scarlett and Mammy arriving at Atlanta's train yard; Scarlett leading a broken-down horse and cart over a hill; and Scarlett standing on a porch looking at the cavalry in the distance against a sunset. Mitchell offered suggestions for the format of the book, recommending that Macmillan use the same font as in its recently released *Time Out of Mind*. As for the binding, she opposed silver or gold lettering on a light-colored cloth, fearing the type might wear away over time and leave the exterior blank.

Latham thought little of Mitchell's ideas for the artwork, but at least they were something to work with.[32] Macmillan hired freelance artist George Carlson to design the cover. Considering Mitchell's insistence that the jacket have a Southern sensibility, he was an unusual choice. Not only was Carlson a lifelong New England resident with no connections to the South, but his mother had worked as a housekeeper for Union general Ulysses S. Grant.[33] Had Mitchell known of his background—there is no evidence she did—one wonders if she would have appreciated the irony, given her state of mind that fall.

With Macmillan satisfied for the time being, Mitchell's energies that November focused on fact-checking the many still unsettled historical details. Her father and brother reviewed parts of the manuscript and suggested several adjustments. She also brought in outside reinforcements. She admitted to Wilbur G. Kurtz, a local history expert, that "in a weak moment" she had written a Civil War novel and needed his expertise with the military descriptions in the section about General Sherman's march on Atlanta.[34] For help on the Reconstruction-era chapters, she turned to Clark Howell, editor of the *Atlanta Constitution* and author of a book on Georgia history. And, not willing to let the minutest detail go untended, she even wrote an agriculturist for assistance pinning down a saying she had heard as a child about the difference between "wheat people" and "buckwheat people"—terms used to distinguish between those who were flattened by life's storms versus those who bent with the wind and bounced back.[35]

By now, word had leaked in Atlanta that Mitchell had a book deal. Although the new author had tried to keep it quiet, she was irritated to discover Cole had mentioned the project to a friend with Atlanta connections.[36] A publishing contract was big news in Mitchell's circles, and friends began calling and dropping by to revel in her accomplishment. The author found it virtually impossible to work amidst a constant stream of interruptions. On December 3, she finally came clean with Cole that the manuscript was not even close to finished.

Three days later, Cole responded, full of remorse for having caused Mitchell any distractions. She was sympathetic about the research and encouraged Mitchell to take her time. Macmillan's sales conference was scheduled for the end of the month, which meant the editorial staff would be busy until then. Cole assured her friend it was fine to submit the manuscript the first full week of January. Mitchell should feel free to take the time she needed with a clear conscience; having a quality finished product was the most important thing. Cole encouraged the author to find a quiet place in the country to finish the book in peace. "If you will pardon my saying so, it sounds to me as though you had been working too hard and that we have been applying too much pressure."[37] Cole encouraged her to take things easy and not get so jittery.

Any relief Mitchell felt at these comforting words would be short lived. Cole, it appears, had spoken out of turn. Latham did not want to wait until after the sales conference to see the final manuscript. Twice yearly events, the sales conferences were held at the home office in New York and attended by Macmillan's sales staff from the branch offices in Atlanta, Boston, Chicago, Dallas, and San Francisco. For Mitchell's book to reach any level of success, it would have to appeal to these people, who would be responsible for generating interest in the title at bookstores and libraries. Latham knew the sales staff well; they would be no pushovers. Their livelihood depended on them offering an honest assessment of a book's chances, and he would have to make a strong case for *Gone With the Wind*'s salability. Convincing them to get behind a novel of which he had read only an incomplete rough draft was far less than ideal. Moreover, Macmillan had decided on a publication date of April 21, 1936, just four months away. Among other issues, the cover art still had not come together. As Latham had predicted, the images drawn up from Mitchell's suggestions had not proven workable, and he wanted the artist to read the text. The second week of December, Latham and James Putnam, George Brett's assistant, approached Cole and laid down the law: Mitchell had to turn over the manuscript right away.[38]

Uncomfortable being the heavy, Cole wrote to her friend on December 18: "I am sure you are working your head off, and I hate to hound you, but do shoo it along." Cole claimed she had been trying to save Mitchell from overwork and had been operating on the theory that, as long as the book was behind schedule, another week would not hurt, but Macmillan could not wait any longer. Mitchell had to send it all now. If it was not up to snuff, there would be plenty of time to make corrections later, Cole promised. She followed up with a telegram the following day instructing Mitchell to rush all available pages to New York.[39]

On the afternoon of December 19, Mitchell airmailed another portion and promised more would be on its way soon.[40] For the artist, it was too little, too late. By the time Macmillan received Mitchell's package, the decision had been made to go with a dust jacket that focused on the book's title instead of a pictorial image. This bought Mitchell some extra time. Cole returned what she had of the manuscript—except for the first chapter, which was used to create a book dummy for the sales conference—and told her to take another week. She assured the author that Macmillan was doing its best by her and urged her to send the finished book as quickly as she could.[41]

The extra time must have been appreciated, but Mitchell was not ready to dance a jig just yet. Her back pain had worsened to the point where her doctor feared surgery might be necessary; he ordered her to bed, where she worked propped up on pillows.[42] With Mitchell unable to get about, Marsh assumed a more active role in wrapping up the manuscript. He took additional vacation time and hired his secretary, Rhoda Williams, as well as Georgia Power employees Grace Threlkeld and Connie Pearson, to help with the typing after hours.[43] Also assisting was Margaret Baugh, a secretary at Macmillan's Atlanta office whom the Marshes had met through Cole.

Even with this support, the couple did not manage to complete the manuscript in that extra week. Marsh would later say that the harder he worked, the less progress he seemed to make. "And I wasn't writing a book. I was just reading it. . . . I just couldn't seem to get through with the job. I'd work myself blue in the face and then go out and take another look at the stack [of pages] and I hadn't even made a dent in it." He began to think he was slipping. "I just couldn't put the stuff on the ball like I used to could."[44] The pressure drove Mitchell into a complete state of misery. She used to think that "a lady author was a lady of leisure," but that romantic notion had evaporated.[45] She reached the point where she was scared to pick up the telephone or open the mail for fear it might be Macmillan urging her along or a friend asking for details on her progress. Matters got so out of hand, the pair felt compelled to sequester themselves, refusing visits from friends and family. Allan Taylor, Cole's husband, passed through Atlanta on a business trip during this time, and they declined to see even him.[46]

As legitimate as Mitchell's excuses were, her failure to get the manuscript to New York by the conference posed serious problems for Latham. He was worried not only about the sales staff's interest in the novel but also because Hugh Eayrs, president of the Macmillan Company of Canada, would be present at the meeting. Macmillan Canada was an independent affiliate that Latham hoped would issue its own edition of Mitchell's book. Although the retail book market in Canada at that time was small, Macmillan New York had a vested interest in having a Canadian edition published. The American company owned stock in the Toronto firm and would benefit financially if the book sold well there. But, more importantly, due to a quirk of international copyright law, having a Canadian edition issued simultaneously with the American one would offer Macmillan automatic copyright protection on Mitchell's book throughout most of Europe and in other parts of the world without the firm having to file for protection in each individual country.

Unfortunately for American authors and publishers in that era, the United States was not a member of the Berne Convention, an international treaty under which Canada, most of Europe, and some South American countries automatically granted each other's citizens copyright protection. This meant that, if Macmillan wanted to protect its publications overseas, it had to register the copyrights country by country. Without such registrations, publishers in Berne nations were free to sell their own editions of Macmillan books without asking permission or paying royalties. The only way around that quagmire was a loophole in the Berne treaty that allowed authors from nonconvention countries to obtain copyright protection in signatory countries by having their books published simultaneously in their home nation and a Berne nation, such as Canada. Macmillan was fortunate to have the Canadian affiliate to facilitate the process, often referred to as "backdoor" Berne coverage.

With the conference looming, time was of the essence for Latham. Assisting him in making the presentation about Mitchell's book would be Alec Blanton, Macmillan's sales manager. In contrast to Latham's old-school demeanor, Blanton was a charismatic businessman full of big ideas.[47] The two were a dynamic duo of the New York publishing world, credited with many of Macmillan's successes. As one industry executive put it, between Latham's sense for picking winners and Blanton's skill at selling, there was not a publishing house in the United States to compare with Macmillan.[48]

Making a successful pitch at a sales conference depends on many variables. If the staff has already read and approved a manuscript, or when the author is well known, it can be a simple process. Presenting a new writer demands more effort, especially in a case like Mitchell's where none of the sales team had yet read the manuscript. Armed with little more than a title, a plot summary, and a few chapters, Latham and Blanton had their work cut out for them. Yet, according to Eayrs, they gave a masterful performance. The two men demonstrated wild enthusiasm for Mitchell, and their excitement spread through the assembled crowd. The Macmillan sales team was thoroughly impressed and convinced that Macmillan had never experienced such a book as *Gone With the Wind*. Everyone in the room sensed that the publisher was on to something special. On the spot, Eayrs requested the right to publish a Canadian edition.[49]

Evidence of the sales team's approval can be found in Macmillan's decision to order an initial print run of ten thousand copies, a generous number given that a typical book of the era sold only five thousand copies in its lifetime. Blanton's enamored staff also decided to send five hundred autographed copies to major booksellers with hopes of grabbing their attention.[50] Equally impressive, Mitchell earned a spot on the inside front cover of Macmillan's preliminary list of upcoming spring releases. A testament to how rushed things were, the book was listed as *Come With the Wind*; a handwritten note on Mitchell's copy assured her the title would be corrected in the final catalog. Inside, the novel was given a full-page description, with a small photograph of the author and this bold declaration: "The stirring drama of the Civil War and Reconstruction is brought vividly to life in this really magnificent novel." Rhett and the newly christened Scarlett were off to a good start.

～

The beleaguered team in Atlanta worked through the holidays, most evenings past midnight.[51] While Mitchell and Marsh continued revising the narrative and smoothing out the rough edges, the secretaries returned the corrected pages. The work ground to a halt on Christmas Day, when Stephens Mitchell's father-in-law died of a heart attack at the Mitchell home on Peachtree Street. The author tended to familial responsibilities while trying to keep work moving on the manuscript. Finally, on January 7, 1936, Baugh forwarded three-quarters of the completed pages to Macmillan.[52] Upon receiving them, Cole wrote to Atlanta and pushed for an expected arrival date for the rest of the sections.[53] In response, Baugh sent another batch of pages on January 16, promising that the rest would follow as soon as possible.[54]

Two days later, George Brett happened to be in Atlanta on business. Despite *Gone With the Wind* being Macmillan's next big thing, Brett was not carried away quite yet. According to Baugh, when he dropped by the Macmillan office for a brief visit, he did not say a word about Mitchell's book and "acted like he didn't know anything about it at all."[55] He also made no effort to meet Mitchell while in town, for which he later apologized.[56] Perhaps he wanted to read the book before passing judgment. However, his trip did lead to what appears to be the first announcement of Mitchell's novel in the press—a plug that probably came from the local Macmillan office. After reporting Brett's thoughts on the current state of publishing, an article in the *Atlanta Journal* noted that his company's spring list "prominently includes *Gone With the Wind*, by Margaret Mitchell (Mrs. John Marsh), of Atlanta, about which the publishers are most enthusiastic."[57]

Although Brett had presented a disinterested front, the *Journal* was correct that Macmillan was well pleased with the results of Mitchell's labors. With time getting short, the book's release was pushed back two weeks, to May 5, just to be safe. But otherwise, all systems were go. On January 25, the publisher ran an eight-page ad in *Publishers Weekly*, the leading industry trade journal, announcing its upcoming catalog as Macmillan's "strongest" list in the company's history. Although no one at the firm had yet read the book from start to finish, *Gone With the Wind* was the first title promoted in the notice and one of only three that included a photograph of the author. The ad categorized Mitchell's work among accomplished writers H. G. Wells and Phyllis Bentley. Taken aback when she saw the announcement, Mitchell wrote Cole: "Good God, this book isn't good enough to be there. I know you know your business—but I hope you haven't made an error in judgment because of a kind and loving heart."[58]

As of January 28, Macmillan still did not have all the chapters. Cole sent a terse telegram to Atlanta that day demanding to know when Mitchell would be finished. Rhoda Williams, who handed Marsh the telegram, later recalled that he responded with a mixture of fury and exhaustion.[59] The manuscript was nowhere near ready. Several sections had not been edited, and many pages needed retyping. However, they had no choice but to send it off. Marsh wired back that the rest of the pages would be mailed the following day. Good, bad, or ugly, the final sections were in the mail on January 29, 1936.[60]

# 3

# In Cold Type

*February–March 1936*

The editorial review of a manuscript can take weeks or even months. In Margaret Mitchell's case, Macmillan did not have time to be so meticulous if it hoped to meet the early May publication date. Lois Cole knew John Marsh had editing experience from his years as a teacher and working for newspapers and trusted he would have caught any significant errors.[1] As Mitchell had sent sections of the manuscript to Macmillan over the previous weeks, sales manager Alec Blanton reviewed the copy and decided it was good enough to go directly into production without detailed editing.[2] When the final chapters arrived, they were shuttled off to join their compatriots that were already being typeset, a process by which the text was set onto printing plates that would be used to mass produce the book's pages.[3] If Marsh had let any major mistakes slip through, Cole trusted they would be caught later during review of the galleys—the draft typeset pages of the book.

Two days after Marsh mailed the final pages of the manuscript, he wrote a lengthy letter to Cole detailing the harrowing experience he and Mitchell had endured over the previous weeks and their utter lack of enthusiasm for the literary life. The opening sentence set the tone for what was to come: "My Dear Lois—I hope my telegram and the g d manuscript have reached you long ere this."[4] He then set forth a detailed list of concerns. First, he wanted to squelch any expectations Macmillan had about his wife publicizing the book's release. Though many aspiring authors dream of becoming famous and embarking on book tours, Mitchell dreaded the idea of public events where she would be expected to charm a crowd with amusing or enlightening anecdotes and then sign books with clever inscriptions. She had always felt sorry for authors put on display like that and wanted none of it. Her contract with Macmillan did not obligate her to take part in publicizing the book, and the Marshes wanted to make sure Macmillan had made no false assumptions about her role in the marketing process. After the "prolonged strain" of the previous weeks, Marsh announced to Cole that Mitchell would not be coming to New York any time soon or, perhaps, ever. If she came at all, it would be on her own terms, not Macmillan's. He explained about her aggravated back and said she hoped to have enough strength to get through reviewing the galleys. Beyond that, Mitchell would need rest.

With that clear, Marsh turned to technical matters such as the wording of the blurb and the numbering of the chapters. Near the end of the letter, he inadvertently dropped a bombshell on Cole by inquiring about the process of copyediting the manuscript. After sending the final chapters to New York, he said, Mitchell had continued to make corrections on a set of carbon copies and had identified several stylistic concerns about chapter formatting and punctuation. Overall, she was embarrassed by the poor condition of the manuscript. Mitchell assumed Macmillan would be responsible for making sure the manuscript was in good order before it went off to the printers but was willing to help if necessary.[5]

Cole panicked. Had they rushed too quickly into typesetting? If the manuscript was as bad as Marsh said, it would be complicated and expensive to make changes down the line. Though loath to slow things down, Cole contacted Everett Hale in the production department and explained the situation. Recognizing the practicalities of their predicament, she conceded that if there was no time, they would have to trust the printers to catch any major mistakes.[6] Hale called in copy editor Susan Prink and asked her to reassess the manuscript in light of Marsh's comments. At a minimum, he wanted her to do what she could about catching errors in punctuation, spelling, continuity, and tone.

With the manuscript under at least a cursory review, Cole responded to Marsh's letter. She broke the news that there was no time for formal editing but assured Marsh they were going back to reassess the pages. She encouraged him to send along corrections on the carbons and to forward guidelines on punctuation and dialect that could be used by the typesetters. As for Mitchell's refusal to participate in the book's release, Cole expressed surprise and disappointment. Enthusiastic about the project, Cole had taken for granted that Mitchell, as a first-time author, would want to enjoy the fun of her success. The editor agreed, however, not to force the issue, given Mitchell's health. Cole was astonished that the previous months had been so taxing and assured Marsh that, if Macmillan had known what Mitchell was going through, the release could easily have been put off a year. It would not have been the end of the world.[7]

With Marsh's concerns addressed, it was now Cole's turn to raise some issues on behalf of Macmillan. With all the pages of the manuscript finally together in one place, the company had come to the startling realization that the novel contained more than four hundred thousand words, which meant about one thousand pages of printed text.[8] In July 1935, when Latham had only a disjointed pile of papers to go by, he had estimated the book would be about one hundred and fifty thousand words.[9] The Macmillan editorial staff had predicted it would be closer to two hundred and fifty thousand or three hundred thousand words and, based on that estimate, had announced a retail price of $2.50.[10] The firm now realized it had grossly underestimated the size and, thus, expense of publishing *Gone With the Wind*. To earn a profit on such a lengthy book, Macmillan would have to raise the price or cut its costs. The publisher decided to do both.

Depending on how well the book sold, a suggested retail price of $2.75 or $3.00—both of which were at the top end of the market for fiction— would be needed for the firm to break even. Yet, the Macmillan sales team was worried that a high price tag would scare away readers. With the nation in the throes of the Great Depression, disposable income was scarce. Only one other publisher in recent memory was known to have asked readers to part with $3.00 for a novel—Farrar & Rinehart for *Anthony Adverse*, an epic historical saga of 1,244 pages published in 1933. Cost had not hampered that book's success; it had gone on to be a mega bestseller. Was *Gone With the Wind* good enough to carry the same price as *Anthony Adverse*? The team approached George Brett with the dilemma. According to Macmillan lore, Brett heard what the sales and marketing people had to say and then leaned back in his chair and asked if Mitchell's book could possibly be as good as everyone said. When they assured him of its merits, he told them to go with $3.00. If it was that good, people would want it, he said.[11] It was a bold decision, of which Brett was proud the rest of his life.[12]

To further protect its bottom line, Macmillan also decided that Mitchell should accept a reduced royalty. According to the contract, Macmillan owed her 10 percent of the suggested retail price on the first ten thousand copies of the book sold, and 15 percent on any copies beyond that. The firm now wanted her to accept a 10 percent royalty on all copies of the book, with no increased percentage for higher sales. Latham was in Europe, which left Cole to break the news to Mitchell. The associate editor did her best to soften the blow. Cole explained that, if Mitchell did not agree to the revised royalties, the publisher would have to cheapen the book's format by using a smaller font and scale back on advertising. On the bright side, with the book priced at $3.00, the total royalty payment on the first ten thousand copies would be $500 higher than if the book sold for $2.50 under the original royalty rate. For additional copies, Mitchell would receive less than she had been entitled to under the original agreement, but Cole predicted the loss would be minimal, given the increased sales associated with an attractive volume. Laying it on thick, Cole promised her friend that Macmillan planned a splendid-looking book to match its splendid content. Lest Mitchell have any hesitation, Cole appealed to the author's vanity, noting that they would not want *Gone With the Wind* to go out into the world looking other than its best.[13]

The Marshes were not pleased. Macmillan had known from the beginning that the finished product would be long and had never hinted this would pose a problem. Moreover, the final manuscript was shorter than the original one given to Latham. If she had known length was an issue, Mitchell felt she should have been allowed to make additional cuts. Mitchell and Marsh also worried that pricing the book at $3.00 would kill its chance of success.[14] And perhaps most irritating, Marsh suspected Macmillan forced Cole to ask for the concession, knowing it would be difficult for Mitchell to say no to her friend.[15]

Despite these reservations, Mitchell accepted the reduced royalty. The author consoled herself that the book would not sell enough copies for the royalty terms to make much difference. Although claiming Mitchell's "Scotch ancestors must be turning over in their graves," Marsh told Cole that Mitchell wanted the book to do well and hated the idea of it being published in a substandard format. However, she could not accept Macmillan's casual attitude toward copyediting. If the company failed to edit the manuscript prior to production, she thought the publisher ought to assume the cost of correcting errors. The couple also declined to send a list of stylistic rules. Mitchell did not have such a list and did not think an understandable one could be created. She would be glad to answer any questions Macmillan had and would catch what mistakes she could down the line.

With those issues settled and the manuscript in the hands of the production department, Cole turned her attention to the book's release, now three months away. Few people at Macmillan had seen the entire novel, but many, including Brett, were eager to do so.[16] Cole especially wanted the salesmen responsible for promoting *Gone With the Wind* to get a chance to read it before the release date. These "travelers," as they were called, played a key role in disseminating important industry news and gossip to remote locations around the country. Wanting to keep the troops enthused, Cole asked Mitchell to send along any extra copies of the chapters that she might have for Macmillan to pass around.

As it turns out, Cole had nothing to worry about. Excitement remained high among the Macmillan ranks. Convinced that *Gone With the Wind* was a winner, the travelers had been spreading the word since the year-end sales conference. Having only a skeletal understanding of the plot, they took the commonsense approach of focusing on the universally appealing tale of how a big-city editor discovered a spirited Southern female reporter-turned-housewife who spent a decade toiling in obscurity to write an epic American novel. (Absent from the cast of characters was Cole as the fairy godmother.) The stirring account caught on like wildfire. As a columnist in the *Atlanta Constitution* would note a year later when describing the book's fantastic success, "The story of Miss Mitchell's strike is almost as fascinating as the story she wrote between the boards."[17] Some of Macmillan's salespeople got so carried away that they dramatized the story almost beyond recognition. Marsh's sister, Frances Zane, worked in a Wilmington, Delaware, bookstore at the time and relayed to the couple the story of a Macmillan salesman who told her the manuscript had been presented to Latham in a wooden box by a Mitchell family servant. When Mitchell reported the exaggeration to a Macmillan representative in Atlanta, the man expressed regret that he had not thought of it himself.[18]

In the middle of February 1936, a letter arrived at Macmillan headquarters offering unmistakable proof that interest was building. Samuel Goldwyn, Inc., a major Hollywood production firm, wanted information on *Gone With the Wind*, the new book by "Mary Mitchell."[19] Not bad for a book by an unknown author that only a handful of people had read.

～

In Atlanta, Mitchell waited for the galleys to arrive from Macmillan and continued to fret over the manuscript. One issue in particular that caused her to worry was whether she had identified the appropriate planting season for pre–boll weevil cotton. Unable to put her mind at rest over the detail, she wrote to the agriculturist who had helped months earlier on the buckwheat question to see if he could offer any assistance. Mitchell conceded that nobody outside of Georgia would know if she got it wrong, "but I would know and would probably wake up screaming in the night about it."[20] He assured her she had the correct date.

On February 12, a mere two weeks after the final chapters had been sent to New York, the Marshes received the initial set of galleys. Printed on long sheets of paper with several pages of text per sheet, the galleys are an author's first glimpse at what the finished book will look like.[21] Seeing them tends to be a difficult experience, especially for a novice like Mitchell. Cole summed up the experience: "There is a certain amount of excitement, as well as anguish, in seeing your brain child in cold type."[22] Some authors barely recognize their own work in this new form. The words often take on a new relationship with each other, and a new rhythm may appear. Defects can pop out that had been hiding in the text, or in happy circumstances, the work appears in a new—and brighter—light.

The evening the *Gone With the Wind* galleys arrived, the Marshes stayed up most of the night reading the pages and taking notes. They thought Prink, Macmillan's copy editor, had done a "sympathetic and understanding job" in tidying up the manuscript. She had ironed out irregularities in punctuation and grammar and caught a few contradictory statements that might have been embarrassing. That said, Mitchell and Marsh had an extensive list of concerns they wanted addressed before they could finish proofreading the document. The following morning, Marsh stayed home from work and compiled nine pages of comments, which he sent to Cole that afternoon by airmail. Of chief concern were adjustments Prink had made to the dialect and punctuation, such as removing quotation marks Mitchell had put around Scarlett's thoughts. Mitchell thought the marks helped "brighten up" the page and let the reader "hear" what was going through Scarlett's mind. The author also had strong feelings about exclamation points, preferring to use them on rare occasions, and colons, which she never used. As for semicolons, she was "definitely Anti," preferring a comma, or a period and starting a new sentence. Marsh did not want the firm to think Mitchell was being picky: "I know your editor thinks by this time that Peggy is finding fault with everything. She isn't really, only with things which are important . . . to her." Until she heard back, she would delay making further corrections. Marsh closed the letter with the wish that "may we all live through this tough experience—and then have more sense than to write any more books."[23]

If the Marshes were troubled by the liberties Macmillan had taken with the manuscript, imagine their reaction when they learned, a few days later, that the galleys had gone into production without waiting for the author's comments.[24] There had been a storm on the East Coast that week, and the plane carrying Marsh's letter had been grounded. Given the time crunch, and not realizing the extent of their concerns, Macmillan had gone ahead and revised the galleys based on its own edits. By the time Cole received Marsh's letter, almost all of the type had been set.

She had no choice but to call the production department and stop the presses. She responded to Marsh by special delivery letter, apologizing and agreeing that Macmillan would cover the costs of revising the type in accordance with their concerns.[25] But Macmillan would bend only so far. In the company's defense, Cole pointed out, Marsh's earlier letter had made it sound like he wanted Macmillan to take the lead on editing. The Marshes had declined to send a style guide, and thus Prink had done what she thought appropriate. Going forward, Cole stipulated, any other changes Mitchell wanted would be charged to the author. Cole wrote again a few days later, cautioning Mitchell that, given the length of the book, she should not go overboard. The minutest edit—even adding or deleting a single comma—could throw off a printed line, and it cost nineteen cents per line change. In her experience, Cole said, authors tended to begin by making a slew of revisions and then would stop, horrified, and give up. She understood how unpleasant proofing could be and hoped it had not become "too much of a bore."[26]

One thing the Marshes were not was bored. On February 25, 1936, Mitchell wrote her mother-in-law that the couple was reviewing the galleys every day until two or three o'clock in the morning. It seemed a nightmare.[27] They were exhausted and overwhelmed, but certainly not bored—nor would they be for months, or years, to come.

∽

Before *Gone With the Wind* caught its eye, Macmillan was famously conservative in the publishing industry for its approach to book promotion. On the theory that marketing campaigns could not transform just any title into a bestseller, the publisher spent advertising dollars only on those books that had some special quality suggesting that the investment would be worthwhile. Even then, the firm proceeded with caution. Splashy campaigns with blatant ballyhoo and extravagant superlatives were not the firm's style, except in rare cases.[28]

Mitchell's manuscript did not have any obvious earmarks of being one of those exceptions. Written by an unknown author, the story was long and took place during a thorny era of American history. The characters did not fall into neat categories; whether Scarlett and Rhett were to be admired or reviled was not clear. Perhaps most troubling, the story had an unresolved ending. Still, Latham and Blanton believed the book had terrific potential and had gone to bat for it at the December sales conference. They had convinced the sales team to give it a prime spot in Macmillan's spring catalog, a remarkable feat in and of itself. But did the book deserve more?

In February 1936, as the galleys finally circulated within the firm, Latham, Blanton, and Cole must have breathed a sigh of relief. The book was as good as they had predicted—maybe better. The pages passed from person to person with growing excitement. One of the first to read *Gone With the Wind* was treasurer and business manager Richard Brett. His daughters recall their father bringing sections of the galleys with him in the evenings to read on the train ride home to Fairfield, Connecticut. He raved about it so much that they had to jockey with their mother over who got to read the pages next. The girls spent several nights stretched out on the floor or curled up on the couch poring over the long sheets of paper. On more than one occasion, Elizabeth Brett arrived late to pick up her daughters at the train station after school because she had been at home reading.[29] In Atlanta, Norman Berg, trade manager of Macmillan's southeastern office, took portions of the novel along with him on a camping trip and stayed up reading by flashlight. At three o'clock in the morning, friends recall, he dashed out of his tent, proclaiming *Gone With the Wind* "the finest book ever written."[30]

With reactions like this, Macmillan decided that Mitchell deserved some ballyhoo. Her book would be given a national marketing campaign; rumor had it that Macmillan was budgeting the most advertising dollars ever for a first-time author. Cole shared the exciting news with the Marshes in response to an inquiry from them on February 9 about how they should handle their many friends in the Southern press who were interested in running stories about the book.

A few days earlier, *Gone With the Wind* had generated its first headline in a piece by Yolande Gwin, society columnist for the *Atlanta Constitution*: "Margaret Mitchell's Novel Depicts Three Major Periods." Gwin explained that the story covered the antebellum, war, and Reconstruction eras and was scheduled for publication that spring.[31] It was a watershed moment for Mitchell. "Until I read your article about me, I didn't really feel like an author," she wrote Gwin. "I've worked so hard and been so tired and sick that the only emotion I could feel was one of numbed relief that the stuff was out of my hands and in the mail. And I wasn't thrilled or excited as I've always heard authors are. And I felt irritably that I was being cheated out of whatever fun there was in writing." But, she said, seeing her name in the headline stopped Mitchell in her tracks: "My heart began to bump and I stopped feeling numb and suddenly, I felt like an author!" She thanked Gwin for her kind words and "bringing me back to life again."[32]

Atlantans, pleased to read of Mitchell's success, inundated her with questions and congratulations. She joked of having a bad case of "author's feet," an ailment caused by being forced to stand on the sidewalk and explain to everyone who stopped her that she had written a book and that it would be out soon.[33] Realizing things were starting to heat up, the Marshes wanted Cole's guidance on how to handle the local press over the coming weeks. As Marsh explained, "The situation is that about 95 per cent of all of our friends—both Peggy's and mine—are newspaper people. They are scattered all over Georgia and they include both the high and the low, folks on the big dailies and on the little country weeklies." Marsh anticipated that once the local papers got a head of steam going about Mitchell, there would be no stopping them. The Marshes wondered how to hold off press attention until the book's actual release and also worried about how to distribute information to the local papers in an evenhanded manner.[34]

Incredulous that the couple wanted to keep Mitchell's name out of the newspapers, Cole told Marsh to let his wife discuss the book as much as she wanted. In a situation like this, Cole said, she would not "dream of shushing anyone or anything."[35] As for keeping their friends in the Southern press happy, the editor told the Marshes not to bother. Macmillan planned to focus its promotion of *Gone With the Wind* on the major urban markets. She warned Marsh that Macmillan would not bother sending review copies to many of the Georgia papers. Promotional copies, she explained, would be directed to the major national newspapers, since Macmillan aimed to cover the entire country, and even then, only to places where a review would generate a volume of sales. The Marshes' newspaper friends, Cole said, would have to understand that the purpose of reviews was, after all, to sell books.

While pleased her book merited a national campaign, Mitchell felt Macmillan was shortsighted to neglect the Southern papers. In the author's mind, the novel would have little chance of success if it were not accepted below the Mason-Dixon Line. Although today *Gone With the Wind* is considered the quintessential Southern American novel, before its release

Mitchell feared fellow Southerners would not appreciate her depiction of the Old South. She descended from Confederates and respected the memory of their suffering but was no unreconstructed rebel. Her book did not celebrate the Lost Cause or take pride in the institutions of slavery and the Ku Klux Klan.

In *Gone With the Wind*, Mitchell presented four distinct Southern viewpoints on the Civil War and the Confederacy. Scarlett, the main female character, is a self-centered belle who pines for the Confederacy when it suits her but just as readily associates with carpetbaggers. As Mitchell described her, she "does practically every thing that a lady of the old school should not do."[36] Rhett, the lead male character, is cynical about the South and scoffs at its hypocrisy. Ashley, landed gentry, slave owner, and Confederate soldier, fights for the ways of the past but crumbles when faced with adjusting to the realities of life off the plantation. Steel magnolia Melanie, who represents the Old South, dies after much suffering. Only Scarlett and Rhett, the two ill-mannered characters who refuse to cling to the past, thrive and carry on to help build the New South. Mitchell worried that influential groups such as the United Daughters of the Confederacy and the Sons of Confederate Veterans would balk at her portrayals. As she explained, "I was a little frightened because, while I had written nothing that was not true, nothing that I could not prove and much that I heard, as a child, from eyewitnesses of that era, I feared some of it might not set well upon Southerners. I suppose Southerners have been lambasted so often and so hard, in print, that they have become unduly sensitive."[37] She also wondered whether Confederate veterans and their descendants would resent that the story focused on Scarlett, a strong female character. Mitchell feared that any negative reaction in her home state would cast a pall on the book's integrity and impede its acceptance elsewhere.

As a former newspaperwoman, she felt the best way to generate enthusiasm for the book in the South would be through the Southern press. If Macmillan could not see that, it would fall upon her to advance the book among the home team. Mitchell did not debate the issue with Cole but provided her a list of key editors and publishers at Southern newspapers that she felt must receive a review copy. Of special importance to Mitchell were John Paschall, her former boss at the *Atlanta Journal*; Clark Howell of the *Atlanta Constitution* and a director of the Associated Press; and Bill Howland of the Nashville *Banner*, who, Mitchell joked, would write a glowing review "regardless of how rotten" the novel was and "cram it down" his book editor's throat.[38] She identified editors of several smaller papers as well and sent Macmillan a detailed explanation why each merited the investment of a promotional copy. Beyond that, Mitchell and Marsh would work behind the scenes to court the favor of the regional papers whose survival they thought essential. This lady author's life was sorely lacking in leisure.

~

*Gone With the Wind* was good—damn good—but it would not sell itself. Although the generous advertising budget would help, that was not enough to satisfy the ambitions of Macmillan's editorial department. To create a bestseller, a publisher needs word of mouth excitement or, in modern terms, buzz. Without it, a publisher can run full-page ads in the *New York Times* and offer free copies of a book in Times Square and find no takers.[39] While the Macmillan travelers were doing their part by spreading the word to the industry rank and file, Latham and Cole were doing yeoman's work to get the word out on a national and international scale.

On a scouting trip to England that February, Latham spent time promoting *Gone With the Wind* to British publishers, hoping to find one willing to release its own edition of the book. Having a British edition would lend Mitchell an air of import and credibility and add a few dollars to the bottom line. The editor focused on Macmillan's London affiliate, Macmillan & Company, Ltd., the former parent company of the American publishing house and its current majority stockholder. Although the two firms were independent organizations, they remained allies. The Bretts' father and grandfather had worked closely with the Macmillan family who controlled the London house, and the Brett brothers enjoyed a good working relationship with the younger generation of Macmillans. The New York office normally gave London first chance to obtain British rights on its books, and the London office returned the favor on its titles. Giving preferential treatment to an affiliated overseas publisher—known as "courtesy of the trade"—was a regular practice in those days. It was an efficient system that allowed large firms with British and American counterparts ready access to a supply of new books. At the same time, the good ol' boy aspect of the practice stifled competition among publishers, artificially dampening the market. Adversely affected were the authors, who lost the opportunity for their work to be sold to the highest overseas bidder. Although she never knew it, Mitchell would become one of many victims of this antiquated system.

During his visit, Latham spoke with both Harold and Daniel Macmillan, the two brothers who ran the London house, and described *Gone With the Wind* as a major novel worthy of special attention. Despite the editor's best efforts though, the London house could not be sold on the book sight unseen. The brothers would wait to see the galleys. Sensing the Macmillans were reluctant to back an unknown housewife-turned-author, Latham hedged his bets and touted the book to other British publishers. His main target was the Glasgow firm of William Collins and Sons, which had recently acquired other titles that Macmillan London had turned down. Latham must have done his work well because, by the end of February, several British firms, including Collins, were queuing up for a chance to bid, all waiting for the Macmillan brothers to make up their minds.

With Latham focused on England, Cole tried to catch the eye of the Book-of-the-Month Club, a major player in the American book distribution field. Founded in 1926, the club was a subscription service through which members, many of whom lived in small towns with no bookstores, could learn about and buy new books by mail at discounted prices. A panel of distinguished literary critics picked the best and most important new titles each month for the club to offer, thereby saving readers the trouble of keeping up with and sorting through the thousands of books published each year. By 1936, about two hundred thousand people had signed up for the service.[40] If the club selected *Gone With the Wind* as one of its titles, Cole knew it would mean big things for Macmillan and Mitchell. The club placed large orders for the books it offered and promoted them extensively. The organization insisted on buying books from publishers at a deep discount, but Macmillan was happy to play along.

Cole feared the length of *Gone With the Wind* might work against the book's selection but thought it worth the effort to make a pitch. At an industry luncheon on February 19, she approached two of the club's principals, Meredith Wood and Basil Davenport, and sang Mitchell's praises. Intrigued, the two men asked for galleys and promised to give the book special consideration.[41] When Cole returned to the office, she asked Brett's right-hand man, James Putnam, to send the galleys as soon as possible, along with a personal note of recommendation.[42] Putnam was a respected voice in the industry, and his personal imprimatur might help convey the seriousness of Macmillan's enthusiasm for the book. On February 26, he sent Davenport three sets of galleys and a note declaring that *Gone With the Wind* was one of the greatest novels Macmillan had ever published.[43]

In Atlanta, Mitchell and Marsh were still combing through the galleys, and it came as no surprise that Macmillan complained they were taking too long.

When the couple had not finished by March 7, the production department approached Cole en masse wanting the pages back. She, in turn, advised Mitchell that the deadline was March 15 and not a day later. Any delay would mean the release date would have to be pushed back again. Mistakes, she said, could be fixed in future printings.[44] Cole instructed the author to send sections back as she got through them and to send as many as she could at one time.[45]

Mitchell shipped the final batch of galley pages to New York by airmail on the morning of March 15.[46] Exhausted, she told her sister-in-law that she "didn't know when one day ended and another began." She could not imagine ever writing another book and being foolish enough to let herself in for such misery again.[47] And there was no time to relax quite yet. As Macmillan began processing Mitchell's edits, it identified several potential continuity problems in the story line and sent a flurry of telegrams to Atlanta—sometimes up to five a day—trying to clarify details: How old was Ella when Frank died? How long before Scarlett married Rhett? How old was Scarlett when Bonnie was born? How old was Bonnie when she died? How old was Scarlett at the end?[48]

Macmillan also kept Mitchell busy working with Cole on the advance promotional copies the sales team wanted autographed. As enthusiasm for the book grew, so did the number of signed copies Macmillan planned to distribute—from five hundred to seven hundred and fifty. The logistics of getting such a mountain of books signed were complicated, given the books were not even printed yet. Macmillan fell back on an old ploy of the publishing trade and asked the author to sign a stack of blank sheets that would be incorporated into the books as they were bound.[49] These presigned sheets would be the endpapers, the blank pages that appear before the title page in most books. To the people who received such copies, it would seem Mitchell had handled those volumes and taken the time to sign the books especially for them.

The Marshes thought the entire process absurd. Calling it a "dirty Yankee trick," Marsh wrote to his mother: "Macmillan is getting these copies autographed so they can present them to 'key people' [all] over the country with a sly smile and a wink, telling the recipient how they went to no end of trouble to get the great author to autograph the book 'just for you.' "[50] Beyond the ethical qualms, Mitchell doubted her ability to sign that many pages. Over the previous months of work, she had developed a painful growth on the middle finger of her writing hand.[51] And, as an unknown writer, she did not think her signature would add any value to the books.

But she was willing to do what her publisher asked. It was, Marsh said, the least she could do to join Macmillan's "heroic efforts to prevent the book from being a complete flop."[52]

Using a sample sheet from Cole showing her where to sign, Mitchell felt like "all kinds of a fool" writing her name over and over again. She finished in five days and joked that she had run "amuck and autographed every thing in sight, including wall paper."[53] Macmillan's Atlanta office shipped the sheets back to Cole on March 23. On most of the pages, the author simply had written "Margaret Mitchell," but she also inscribed many to specific individuals identified by Macmillan. Cole checked through the sheets and noticed two instances in which Mitchell had left off the "Mrs." in front of a recipient's name. Cole reported to Mitchell that she took matters into her own hands—literally—and added poor imitations of Mitchell's "Mrs." on the inscriptions.[54]

In mid-March, the Book-of-the-Month Club's preselection committee gave Mitchell's novel a thumbs-up and asked Macmillan to send additional galleys to the club's final review committee.[55] Latham shipped copies to, among others, committee member William Allen White, the Pulitzer Prize–winning editor of the *Emporia Gazette* in Kansas. In a telegram, Latham declared *Gone With the Wind* one of the most important novels his firm had ever published and encouraged White to advocate the book's selection.[56] The Macmillan editor followed up with an enthusiastic letter saying that Mitchell's book had taken the firm by storm and the publisher would pull out all the stops to make it an enormous success.[57]

White must have seen an earlier copy of the galleys provided to the club because he responded the next day with lavish praise that he had already finished reading *Gone With the Wind* and thought it "a whale of a book." He declared that Mitchell had the "narrator's magic," praising her skill at storytelling and "creating suspense." He assured Latham he would advance the book's cause with the caveat that the story might not appeal to the literary elite because of its setting in America, a locale unpopular with sophisticates.[58] Latham now had an outside review, and, for the most part, it was a rave.

Latham sensed Mitchell had the makings of a star. She was attractive, interesting, and witty, a powerful combination that could do wonders to advance *Gone With the Wind*. Hoping to capitalize on her charisma, he contacted the Leigh Bureau of Lectures and Entertainments, a firm that arranged speaking tours for major artists and celebrities, including First Lady Eleanor Roosevelt. Latham told W. Colston Leigh, founder of the firm, how Mitchell's manuscript was discovered and surrendered the bureau to sign her for a tour. Eight weeks in, and apparently without having read a word of the manuscript, Leigh wrote Mitchell on March 27 and offered to hire her for a brief tour in late 1936, with the possibility of a transcontinental one for the 1937–1938 season.[59] Most authors on book tour are paid nothing, their only remuneration being royalties on sales spurred by their appearances. Here, Mitchell was being offered a paid speaking tour orchestrated by one of the top players in the entertainment industry, a prize afforded only the biggest names. Latham must have assumed Mitchell would be thrilled.

Cole, however, had an inclination her friend might not react so warmly. Back in January, the Macon Writers Club in Georgia had asked Cole to recommend an author to speak at its annual breakfast meeting. She thought Mitchell the obvious choice and passed the request along to the author. Mitchell had little desire to speak in public about her book and apparently never responded. Anticipating Mitchell would also not have an interest in Leigh's proposal, Cole wrote her explaining the importance of his offer. Cole characterized Leigh as one of the most efficient and powerful players in the lecture field, and appealed to Mitchell's practical side, noting there was nobody who could make the author more money.[60]

The promise of riches did not sway Mitchell. On the heels of receiving Leigh's offer, she had an experience that convinced her she was not cut out for giving speeches. She had succumbed to pressure from friends in Macon to give a talk to the writers group when its speaker canceled at the last minute, and the event, in her estimation, had been a disaster. Rushed for time, she had hurried to buy something to wear. The stress of the previous months had caused her to lose weight, and she ended up wearing a "juvenile" outfit that she felt did not give her an "authorish" appearance. She was no happier with the quality of her remarks. As Mitchell described the scene in a letter to Cole, she had prattled on for several minutes about Latham's trip to Atlanta the previous spring and gave the audience a less-than-genteel discourse on the "horrors of galley proofs." In her frank way of speaking, she told the room of writers that she was not picky about grammar and would not be able to identify a dangling participle unless it "rose up and gave me a Bronx cheer." She also claimed that when she told the crowd she didn't think her book would sell "because the heroine was in love with another woman's husband for years and they never did anything about it," two members of the United Daughters of the Confederacy "fell on the floor." Mitchell swore to Cole she would never speak in public again, calling it a horrible experience, second only to when "I dropped my drawers in the church aisle when I was six or seven." There was no chance she would subject herself to a speaking tour.[61]

Mitchell thanked Leigh for his offer but declined. She said Latham must have been pulling Leigh's leg when suggesting her: "I have made only one speech in my life, and that was last week, and, God helping me, I never intend to make another. I am small, unimpressive, afflicted with stage fright and have a loathing for crowds of strangers." Claiming to have nothing of interest to lecture about, she said, "I'm not a speaker, I'm not yet a writer and may never be one if the critics don't like me."[62]

Mitchell's charming rejection whetted Leigh's appetite. He thought her delightful and, in her short letter, saw the spark of star quality. As he explained to Latham, "Your Margaret Mitchell Marsh must be about as nice a person as I can ever hope to meet. This is what I call a real letter from a mighty genuine person and it makes me feel that I want to manage her, if she can talk at all. There is no bluff or pretense about her—just a grand woman, and I am for her in a big way."[63] Over the following month, Leigh tried to convince Mitchell that a tour would be worthwhile. He assured her she did not have to expound on any weighty topics, suggesting she could talk about anything she liked, perhaps something as simple as "The Urge to Write." Getting down to brass tacks, he reminded her of the money at stake: "Inasmuch as you are undoubtedly besieged with requests for engagements, you might as well be paid for them, instead of doing them free."[64]

Leigh was right about one thing. Mitchell would soon be besieged by requests for public speaking engagements from all manner of people—other lecture agencies, writing groups, schools, clubs, and civic associations. He failed to appreciate, though, that she had no plans to accept any of them, including his, regardless of the money involved. After her experience in Macon, she scoffed at the idea of standing before a crowd pontificating about writing. She told Latham she "fell on the sofa and bellowed" at the idea: "I have no urge to write and never had, loathing writing above all things, except perhaps, Wagnerian opera and tap dancing."[65] Her answer was "no" and would stay "no."

Amazingly, Mitchell's position did not seem to trouble anyone at Macmillan. Perhaps they assumed she would change her mind. Or they might have been too distracted to focus on Mitchell's case of the nerves. Other pressing issues required their immediate attention.

# 4

~

# A Book with Definite Possibilities

*April–May 1936*

As spring 1936 approached, Macmillan realized it had made a mistake in not acquiring the motion picture rights to *Gone With the Wind*. That first letter of interest from Samuel Goldwyn had been followed by similar letters from other studios, as well as inquiries from a host of literary agents who handled movie rights. All were eager to learn more about Macmillan's hot new release. The level of activity signaled a potential goldmine for Margaret Mitchell but, alas, not for Macmillan. Yet, the firm saw value in Hollywood's interest. If Mitchell sold the movie rights to a major studio, Macmillan would benefit from publicity surrounding the deal.

In the midst of Mitchell reviewing the galleys and signing the endpapers, Lois Cole began nudging the author to sell her movie rights. When Cole first presented the idea, the author dismissed it as ridiculous: "I can't imagine the movies buying it anyway. I don't see how it could possibly be made into a movie unless the entire book was scrapped and Shirley Temple cast as 'Bonnie,' Mae West as 'Belle,' and Stepin Fetchit as 'Uncle Peter.'"[1] Creating a manageable screenplay out of such a long story with so many characters seemed an impossible task. She was certain no studio would make an offer once its producers read the entire book. And if someone were crazy enough to try, she was not so sure she wanted to sell. Could a movie preserve the historical authenticity of the story over which she had agonized so long? Mitchell doubted it but promised to keep an open mind. She understood the value of a movie contract and wanted her book to have the best chance of success.

Macmillan had no in-house staff with the experience to negotiate movie contracts, so it suggested Mitchell hire an agent to broker a deal. One candidate Cole had worked with in the past was Annie Laurie Williams, whom the editor described to Mitchell as a girl from Texas who had made a name for herself in the big city.[2] The agent was a former vaudeville performer and bit player in silent movies, who, when stardom did not call, worked as a features writer and movie reviewer for the *New York Morning Telegraph*. Hoping to capitalize on her show business connections, she opened a literary agency in 1929. Standing four feet ten inches tall—an inch shorter than Mitchell—with blonde hair and a penchant for elegant designer clothes, Williams was widely known for her striking looks, spunky personality, and shrewd skills. Mae West with a steel-trap mind is how one client described her.[3] Williams had already expressed an interest in *Gone With the Wind*. Being a Southerner, she told Cole, it would break her heart if she lost out on the chance to sell Mitchell's story to Hollywood.[4] Even before reading a word of the book, Williams had sung its praises to several studios and was likely responsible for them already having reached out to Macmillan.

On paper, Williams seemed like a good match for Mitchell—a petite, Southern female with plenty of gumption. Also in her favor, she worked closely with Elizabeth Otis, a friend of Cole's. Yet, Cole hesitated to recommend Williams to Mitchell. She saw Williams as pushy, and it irritated her that Williams was acting as if she already had the job.[5] Although Cole did not want to offend Otis, she presented other options for Mitchell's consideration, including Ann Watkins, a grande dame of the agency business who had been in the field since 1910, and Leland Hayward, a former movie producer known for his Hollywood connections. Cole encouraged Mitchell to pick whomever she deemed best but urged her to make a decision quickly so the galleys could be distributed to film producers as soon as possible. She also asked that Mitchell keep the publisher posted on details of the negotiations. Macmillan intended it to be a big book and wanted to make sure Mitchell earned a big price for the movie rights.[6]

Still reviewing the galleys at that point, Mitchell had little time to focus on selecting a movie agent. She contacted both Williams and Watkins, saying she would get back to them when she finished editing. "I am as nearly insane as a person can get and still remain at liberty," she explained.[7] To Cole, Mitchell expressed no preference between the two women and said she would be glad to retain Williams if it would "ease you out of any embarrassment, great or small."[8] She assured Cole there would be no hard feelings if Williams failed to sell the rights; Mitchell did not expect any offers. Again, Cole told Mitchell to pick whomever she liked best and not to worry about offending Otis. "I don't give a damn about [Williams], and I can get out of anything," the editor wrote. Cole wished that she could say for sure who the best agent would be for she thought the book had "definite movie possibilities."[9]

With each passing day, the possibilities looked rosier. The April 4, 1936, issue of *Publishers Weekly* referenced *Gone With the Wind* in its "Forecast for Buyers," a list of noteworthy upcoming titles. By the second week of April, Cole told Mitchell producers and agents were pursuing the book "with their tongues hanging out."[10] Interest reached such a fever pitch that Harold Latham began to think Macmillan should sell the rights for Mitchell itself rather than having her go through an agent. He was about to embark on another scouting trip out West and would be in Los Angeles. Maybe he could negotiate a sale to one of the studios in person. With him acting on Mitchell's behalf, Macmillan would earn the agent's commission—typically 10 percent of the selling price—and make up some of the loss of having let Mitchell keep the movie rights. On April 9, Cole reversed course and told the author that Latham might be able to handle things. "Don't do anything yet," she advised, telling the author to stall if any agents wrote to her directly.

Cole need not have worried. The agency issue was the last thing on Mitchell's mind after she finished reviewing the galleys and signing the endpapers. The author was focused on getting her health in order. She continued to suffer chronic back pain and was treating it by applying icepacks and wearing a brace; with rest, she hoped to avoid an expensive surgery her doctor had recommended. On April 11, she had the growth removed from her finger and was relieved to be on the mend three days later. As for the movie rights, she told Cole it would be "perfectly marvelous" if Latham sold the rights for her. Knowing how busy he would be on his trip, Mitchell appreciated him offering to try. "I swear you Macmillanses are the nicest people."[11]

The first printing of *Gone With the Wind* came off the presses in early April—10,245 copies, including overruns. Commensurate with Cole's promise that the book would have a quality appearance, Macmillan invested in a substantial weight paper and used a generously sized typeface. Bound in Confederate gray cloth with blue lettering, the 1,037-page book weighed nearly three pounds. Although Mitchell had thought her story would work best in two volumes, Macmillan decided on a single book because it was cheaper to produce and might appeal to a broader audience. Other economies were made as well. There was no attached ribbon bookmarker or decorated endpapers, two add-ons the company had considered but rejected because of the cost.[12]

The dust jacket focused on the book's title, presenting the words "Gone," "With," and "Wind" in tall, dark brown capital letters filling almost two-thirds of the cover. With the large words set against a yellow background, the book had the feel of a miniature billboard announcing its contents. The bold appearance led one commentator to remark that Macmillan must have wanted to make certain the words were readable from a great distance in stores and even in the arms of pedestrians walking down the street.[13] The publisher included only one pictorial element on the front, a small scene by George Carlson of a Southern belle and two gentlemen under the title. The yet-to-be-famous author's name appeared in a narrow green bar along the bottom. As a signal that Macmillan was offering readers a historical story with a modern edge, it presented all the words in a vintage-looking typeface set against a series of Art Deco–style graduated stripes.[14]

Another significant feature was the dedication page. Mitchell paid tribute to her husband, John R. Marsh, in succinct terms: "To J.R.M." The brevity of the sentiment might seem impersonal or inadequate given the amount of work he had done on the manuscript, but to those who knew the couple, it was in perfect keeping with their relationship. A family friend described the inscription years later: "If it had been as flowery as the inscription which precedes the Sonnets of Shakespeare it could no more clearly have conveyed the completeness of the bond between Margaret Munnerlyn Mitchell and John Robert Marsh."[15] Public professions of love and gratitude were not the Marsh way. As would become clear in the coming months, they were a private couple who preferred to keep personal matters between themselves. Ironically, this most personal of sentiments almost did not make it into the book. The previous fall, the dedication page had been inadvertently omitted from the book's mock-up that had been sent to Mitchell for approval. She noticed its absence but almost let it go, assuming dedication pages were not included at that stage. Only as an afterthought did the Marshes mention the omission to Cole, who acknowledged the error.[16] Cole directed the production department to correct what would have been an embarrassing oversight: "You will be sure it is not left out, won't you? There would be trouble—that is the lady's husband."[17]

Ironically, one of the most significant components of the book in years to come would be a feature that many readers ignore—the copyright page. All books published in the United States contain a statement indicating the year the volume is published and registered for copyright protection with the Library of Congress. Macmillan went further in its books and, for the sake of historical reference, identified the month of publication in addition to the year so book dealers and collectors easily could identify first editions.[18] For *Gone With the Wind*, the first printing bore the notation "Printed May, 1936," a reference to the book's scheduled release date. Including that one extra word would turn out to be a costly and potentially catastrophic mistake, though it would be several years before the full effects were realized.

On April 15, Macmillan received the news that Cole had been waiting for: the Book-of-the-Month Club wanted *Gone With the Wind* and would make the novel available to its readers that summer, although it had not yet decided which month.[19] The club offered Macmillan ten thousand dollars for the right to publish fifty thousand copies using Macmillan's printing plates, with a royalty of twenty cents per copy on club sales beyond the initial order. There was just one catch. Macmillan would have to delay publication of the book until the club could fit the novel into its calendar of releases. A standard condition of all club contracts, this provision ensured club members received the latest releases within a week of their appearance in bookstores.[20]

The prospect of delaying the book was cause for concern. Macmillan could not afford to throw away the ten thousand copies already produced bearing the May date but worried that having an inaccurate date on the copyright page might pose a problem when it came time to register the book's copyright. In addition, the firm had already spent a considerable amount of money and energy promoting the May release. Macmillan did not relish the idea of waiting indefinitely while the club made up its mind about which month to distribute the book. Despite these hurdles, the money and publicity associated with the club's offer were too good to pass up. The May release was canceled for both the American and Canadian editions of *Gone With the Wind*. As for the now incorrect copyright date in the first printing, Macmillan decided it should not matter as long as the actual book registered at the Library of Congress carried the correct date.[21] This assumption would prove to be wrong, but for the time being all seemed well. The delay even came to be viewed as a blessing in disguise because it gave Macmillan additional time to ramp up its marketing and for reviewers to read the book.[22]

Mitchell's novel was now a guaranteed bestseller. Cole reveled in the success and wrote the author saying she had better be pleased.[23] Mitchell replied, "Dearie, I was knocked flat when the news came."[24] Although the author's father expressed surprise that a "sensible" organization like the Book-of-the-Month Club would choose such a book[25] and Marsh's family thought little of the club—"a few editors sitting around a table in New York were not going to select the books we would read," his sister recalled— Mitchell could not help but be pleased.[26] She would get half of the club's ten-thousand-dollar payment and half of any future royalties if the club sold more than fifty thousand copies. This was a remarkable sum of money, given that the average per capita income for a full-time worker in 1936 was $1,235.[27] *Gone With the Wind* appeared to be signaling the end of Mitchell and Marsh's financial worries.

After the book club announcement, the publishing industry chomped at the bit to read *Gone With the Wind*. The time had come to send out advance review copies, including the ones with Mitchell's signature bound inside. Contrary to Cole's earlier statement that Macmillan would distribute copies only in the major cities, it now prepared to send books to markets large and small, North and South. Publishers rarely invested advertising dollars so broadly, but Macmillan planned to take a chance on Mitchell, whose book was proving to have a unique appeal.

For the major urban areas, Macmillan had established relationships with the important newspapers and industry players. To pique their interest, George Brett sent personal appeals along with the books, encouraging the recipients to take a careful look at Mitchell's work, which he predicted would have a significant impact on the American literary scene.[28] In the smaller markets, Macmillan relied on a new industry marketing tool to spread the word—the National Guild of Book Reviewers. The organization promoted book sales in small towns by bringing publishers and bookstores together to create word-of-mouth interest in new titles. Participating publishers selected books to be featured and sent review copies and promotional materials to participating stores. The store owners would then choose prominent persons in the area to review the books, display those reviews in their stores, and maybe pay to publish the reviews locally.[29] More than three hundred small-town bookstores were scheduled to participate in a round of reviews to begin in the summer of 1936, and Macmillan probably had little trouble getting Mitchell's book selected as one of three featured titles.[30]

As soon as the publisher began shipping promotional copies, waves of enthusiastic responses began rolling in. Although formal reviews by book critics would not appear in newspapers and magazines until the release, the trade let Macmillan know it loved Mitchell's novel. A Midwestern bookseller had not been able to put it down and convinced seventy-eight friends to order copies, sight unseen. The fifteen-year-old daughter of Macmillan's Boston manager complained the book was not long enough.[31] The head of a rental library appeared hollow-eyed and late to work on a Monday morning, saying she had started the book the previous afternoon and had been dragged away from it at 3:00 a.m. Her boss let her go home early to finish.[32] A self-proclaimed "hard-boiled" bookseller from North Carolina described Mitchell as having all the attributes of a great writer—"a grasp of material, a sense of drama, and the most perfect faculty for choosing what is necessary in the enlargement of her narrative." The woman felt Mitchell's satire was on par with Jane Austen's and predicted "immortality lies in store for our young lady."[33] A California bookseller called *Gone With the Wind* "the best novel on an American theme that has appeared in years and years" and upped his advance order from ten to one hundred copies. Another from Tennessee enthused, "Isn't it gorgeous? Was such a book ever written before? Not in America, I daresay."[34]

This reaction was music to Macmillan's ears yet also cause for concern. The company wanted booksellers to be excited about the book but not go overboard in a way that could jeopardize the release. Specifically, Macmillan did not want any copies of the book to fall into the hands of the general public before the publication date. Review copies had to be distributed early, of course, but if copies of a new title reached the public prior to registration, the copyright could be jeopardized. In particular, if a book was released in the United States prior to distribution in Canada, even on a small scale, the publisher might not be able to invoke "backdoor" Berne coverage.

Most publishers, Macmillan included, followed a strict rule that, other than review copies, new books were not to be circulated before publication, even to family and friends of the author or of book retailers. Everyone in the industry knew there would be hell to pay if a copyright was jeopardized by early distribution. If a bookstore released a title early, the seller would be blacklisted from receiving new releases in the future. Mitchell's book would test the limits of this honor system, even within Macmillan itself. The temptation to share the book proved irresistible to Cole, whose enthusiasm got the better of her that April when she sent a copy of *Gone With the Wind* to National Broadcasting Corporation executive Lewis Titterton, a mutual friend of the Taylors and Marshes. Titterton's wife, Nancy, had been recently murdered and Cole thought the book might help take his mind off matters. In a letter that would make any lawyer defending Macmillan's copyright cringe, Cole admitted to Mitchell that doing so was in violation of company rules.[35]

It appears Macmillan's Atlanta office may have broken the rule as well. On April 27, Mitchell signed and dated several books to be sent as review copies to Southern newspapers. In the process, she seems to have gotten her hands on at least two copies of the book. A first printing of *Gone With the Wind* inscribed by her to Margaret Baugh "with thanks for her patience with a new author" contains in Mitchell's handwriting the date May 1, 1936.[36]★ And the author had at least one other early copy, as indicated in a letter to Cole on May 5 in which Mitchell describes reviewing the first printing for errors. It was slow going, she told Cole. "I can't even endure to look at the book because I nearly throw up at the sight of it. One shouldn't feel that way about one's first and only child and I hope I'll recover but the sight of it reminds me of the nightmare of getting it ready." She forced herself to go through it again and identified several typographical errors that she sent on to Macmillan for correction in future printings.[37]

Later that month, at Mitchell's request, Cole again broke the rule against early distribution and sent the author six copies of *Gone With the Wind* to share with family. In her transmittal letter, Cole acknowledged that having these extra copies floating around before publication day could "very seriously jeopardize" the copyright but said the company was willing to make an exception with the understanding that Mitchell did not distribute them beyond members of her immediate family.[38]

The book club decision brought a sense of urgency to the movie rights issue. If Mitchell was going to hire an agent, now was the time. Although she had expressed an interest in Latham selling the rights for her in California, no formal arrangement had been made designating Macmillan her representative. Outside agents continued to plead their cases as well. One tried

---

★ Beneath the date, Mitchell also wrote "Number 16." Was the author creating her own series of signed and numbered books? Did the number have personal significance for the author and Baugh? To date, the numbered book is the only known copy of its kind.

to harangue Cole into arranging an introduction to Mitchell, admitting that "agents are something like vultures, I suppose, and one is considered a poor business person unless one does most anything to get good material."[39]

Williams also remained hopeful. She had a business trip to the South coming up and wanted to stop in Atlanta to talk things over with the author. Still hoping Macmillan could get its cut by acting as Mitchell's agent, this is the last thing Cole wanted, so she wrote Mitchell on April 21 telling her that, if she met with Williams, not to believe a word the agent said. Cole told the author that Williams was acting as if Mitchell had already hired her; Cole had had to correct the agent twice on the matter.[40]

On April 25, Williams telephoned Mitchell, hoping to set up a meeting. The agent caught the author at the end of a bad day when she was on her way out the door and in no mood to talk about the nagging question of the movie rights. Things went from bad to worse when Williams suggested that she had begun talking to studios on Mitchell's behalf. As the author later admitted to Cole, "I blew up" and told the agent that no such authority had been granted. It was "just the last straw of a day full of straws," she said of her bad manners.[41] The only inroad Williams made with the author was that Mitchell agreed to let the agent have a copy of the galleys.[42]

Thrilled to hear Mitchell had set the agent straight, Cole assured the author she had done the right thing. Williams, the editor said, had "a vicious tongue and isn't the sort of person a publisher can row with."[43] For reasons not specified in the Macmillan files, Latham apparently did not pursue the movie rights issue while on the West Coast and was already on his way back from California. However, the firm had no qualms about handling the job from New York and wanted to obtain Mitchell's official designation as her agent. Latham arranged to visit the author in Atlanta on April 29 to discuss, among other things, Macmillan's role in helping her sell the movie rights.[44]

Latham used his time in Atlanta wisely. He reassured Mitchell that the release would go well and tried to smooth over the rough edges that had cropped up in her relationship with Macmillan over the previous year on issues such as the copyediting and the reduction in royalties. He promised great things were in store for her and predicted that within six months she would have half the population of North America at her doorstep.[45] Mitchell told Cole afterward that it was lucky he did not visit more often because "my head swelled enormously under his words and I spread my tail feathers like a peacock."[46]

The editor and author also discussed the languishing issue of the role Mitchell would play in promoting *Gone With the Wind*. As a personal favor to Norman Berg of Macmillan's Atlanta office, Mitchell had promised to attend a celebration, either a tea or a cocktail party, to be hosted by the local office during release week.[47] She also agreed to sign additional promotional copies for Berg to distribute among regional booksellers and had spent a day at his desk while Baugh wheeled in wooden crates full of books and placed them before her one at a time. She had even allowed herself to be talked into attending book signings at local department stores. Although she disliked the idea of appearing in front of a crowd, Mitchell felt she could not say no to Berg without appearing peculiar and ungracious.[48] She also wanted to show her appreciation to the local stores that had expressed an interest in her.

The question remained though as to when Mitchell would make an appearance in New York City. In January, she had warned Macmillan that she was too worn out to make such a trip, but Latham hoped that given the delay in publication she would be rested enough by release day to travel. He presented this idea at their Atlanta meeting, but Mitchell declined. She claimed she was too busy and that she dreaded the idea of going to New York during the dog days of summer. And, if she did make the trip, she did not want to sign books there, saying she would rather never sell a copy than have to go through such an ordeal.[49] Although he was not willing to let her off the hook, Latham did not push the issue that day. Perhaps he did not want to rock the boat given the other important matter on his agenda—the movie rights.

Latham made the case that Mitchell should let Macmillan act as her movie agent, hinting that the company was starting a new department to handle such matters.[50] Although Mitchell had no particular desire to sell the rights at that time, she agreed to let Macmillan represent her. She trusted the company's reputation for fair dealing and assumed that such a large and experienced firm would have a staff of lawyers, as well as copyright and contract experts, who could guide her through the process.[51]

On May 6, 1936, Cole broke the news to Williams and the other agents that they were out of the running because Mitchell wanted Macmillan to handle the movie sale. Proclaiming to be disappointed at the author's decision, Cole wrote that there was nothing she could do to change Mitchell's mind. Knowing Williams expected to receive a copy of the book, the editor claimed there were none available to send. Moreover, given Mitchell's decision, Cole felt the agent did not need to see it.[52]

If what Cole had been saying about Williams was true, she should have known the Texan would not ride quietly into the sunset. By now, the agent had been promoting Mitchell's book to movie producers for several months and would not tolerate Macmillan swooping in and taking credit—and the commission—for a film deal. Williams wrote Cole on May 11 thanking the editor for her "fine letter" and her help: "I do appreciate all your effort in my behalf and am only sorry that things have gone the way they have."[53] She then went behind Cole's back to make sure Macmillan knew it could not steamroll her. Williams called Everett Hale, whom she had heard through the grapevine was working with Latham on the movie rights. In fact, the day she called, May 18, Hale was shipping copies of Mitchell's book to almost a dozen movie studios. Williams told him that Macmillan could talk to the studios if it wanted, but it could not cut her out of the action. If the firm secured a contract with one of the producers Williams had been courting, she promised to stake a claim to the commission.

Hale reported the threat to Latham but recommended throwing caution to the wind and ignoring the agent.[54] Rumor had it that Darryl F. Zanuck, head of Twentieth Century-Fox, had received an advance report on the book through someone who had a bootlegged galley and was anxious to acquire the rights before other studios had a chance to bid.[55] Although Hale did not think they should jump at any offers yet, it was time to take action: "The plum is ready to be picked, the melon to be sliced, whenever we decide to let it fall in our (collective) lap." Regardless of whether Williams raised a fuss, Hale wanted Macmillan to "take the gravy" for itself.[56]

Not one for making rash decisions, Latham arranged to meet with Williams the next day. She made a persuasive argument that, regardless of her commission, Macmillan would be foolish to cut her loose. Sending out books to studio story editors was the least of the work involved.[57] She had years of experience in the motion picture industry and knew how to approach the studios, how to answer their questions, and how and when to apply pressure. She claimed to have already elicited offers of up to twenty-five thousand dollars for Mitchell's movie rights and was sure she could get more, maybe as much as sixty thousand dollars.[58]

Latham saw no way out. He and Hale knew nothing of playing hardball with Hollywood types, and *Gone With the Wind* was too valuable a commodity for them to cut their teeth on. Williams had to be brought in. But he was not willing to give up Macmillan's stake, nor did he want to admit to Mitchell that he was not quite as qualified as he had led her to believe. With Brett's approval, the editor struck a pact with Williams under which she and Macmillan would represent Mitchell jointly and divide evenly the standard 10 percent commission.[59] Mitchell was to be told nothing about their arrangement. All negotiations with the author regarding the movie contract would be conducted by Macmillan as if it were her sole agent.[60]

∼

Macmillan's confidential arrangement with Williams was not the publisher's only deception in the spring of 1936. At the same time the company worked through the movie issues, it continued to market the British rights to *Gone With the Wind*. As Latham had suspected, Macmillan London had only a lukewarm interest in Mitchell. Rather than buying the rights to produce a distinct British version of her book, the firm had offered on April 2 to purchase sheets of the American edition that it could bind and distribute in England.[61] This would allow the London house to negotiate a flat rate price with its American affiliate and avoid paying a royalty to the author. This was another standard courtesy of the trade practice between associated publishers. Here, too, Mitchell had something to lose and not just the additional advance money. Having a book deemed worthy of a completely distinct foreign edition offered greater bragging rights and publicity value than having the American pages bound overseas. Also, authors generally earn more from a distinct foreign edition because publishers tend to be more diligent about selling their own volumes than they are for ones cobbled together from another firm's pages.

Latham understood these limitations and did not embrace London's proposal. On Friday, April 3, he wired the Macmillan brothers that two other British publishers were interested in Mitchell, both of whom were willing to manufacture the book in the United Kingdom. He wanted to delay accepting London's proposal until he knew how attractive the other offers would be.[62] The Macmillan brothers did not like the hint of competition and sent another telegram Monday morning, requesting Latham's assurance that he would not sell the book to any other British publisher without giving them a chance to counteroffer. They also asked what royalty payment would be required if they agreed to manufacture their own edition.[63] When Brett's assistant, James Putnam, replied the same day that London would have a chance to bid against the other interested parties, Macmillan London changed course. It wired again on Tuesday, claiming it was entitled to buy one thousand copies of the American edition and expected Macmillan to set the price. Macmillan London instructed its New

York counterpart to not make arrangements with any other publisher until London had the opportunity to consider the matter further.[64]

Latham had terrific hopes for Mitchell's book in England and saw no reason to shuffle it off to the Macmillan brothers for a quick sale. He threw courtesy of the trade to the winds and continued to suss out other interested British publishers. On April 6, he sent an unbound copy of *Gone With the Wind* to the Scottish publisher William Collins and Sons with the bold declaration that Macmillan had unbounded confidence in Mitchell and believed her book had a potential for large-scale sales over many years.[65] Latham then demonstrated a willingness to go to bat for Mitchell even if it meant going against Macmillan London. Fudging the truth, he advised William A. Collins that the London house had already made a "substantial offer" and that he was only giving Collins a chance at the book because the author had requested he do so. Latham asked Collins to read it and cable back a decision right away. In a not-so-subtle hint that Latham was bending the rules, the editor told Collins to keep the matter confidential.

When the Book-of-the-Month Club announced its selection of *Gone With the Wind* a few days later, the news spread to England, and letters of interest arrived from other British publishing concerns.[66] A bidding war was in the making, but what should be done about the Macmillan brothers, who seemed to think *Gone With the Wind* would be handed to them on a silver platter? By this time, Latham had left on his scouting trip out West, so George Brett stepped in to resolve matters. He telegraphed London, insisting that, if the Macmillans wanted to sell Mitchell's novel in England, they would have to issue a separate British edition. He asked the brothers to make an offer immediately so he could obtain approval from Mitchell, whom Brett blamed for the present situation.[67] In another example of truth stretching, Brett claimed she objected to exportation of the sheets because the book was sure to sell more than one hundred thousand copies due to the Book-of-the-Month Club selection. Sensing it had overplayed its hand, London changed its tune again and expressed a willingness to publish a British edition and pay Mitchell royalties. Although it made no mention of an advance, London expected it would obtain the rights, no further questions asked.[68]

Macmillan was still not ready to hand Mitchell over so easily. After receiving London's offer, Putnam wired Collins on April 22, instructing him to send an offer without delay if he was interested in bidding.[69] Collins replied the next day expressing tremendous enthusiasm for Mitchell's book and offering a 150-pound advance or whatever amount Macmillan thought reasonable.[70] In a follow-up letter, he assured Putnam that his firm would get behind Mitchell's book and go all out to make it a big success.[71] By offering a blank check, Collins had every reason to be optimistic that he would win the rights.

It was to Collins's disadvantage—and, ultimately, Mitchell's as well—that Brett had stepped in to handle matters in Latham's absence. Like Latham, Brett was not willing to give away *Gone With the Wind* to the London affiliate. However, his loyalties were different. He had a personal relationship with the Macmillan brothers but had never met Mitchell. Although he wanted a fair price for her book, he could not afford to breach his association with the Macmillan family to get it. He cabled Harold Macmillan on April 23, explaining about the Collins bid and suggesting that London raise its offer to a two-hundred-pound advance and bump up its proposed royalties to equal what Macmillan expected from Collins. In a follow-up letter that same day, Brett justified his demand with a fantastic story about how several American publishers had been after Mitchell and how Latham fought to bring her to Macmillan. There had been a question in the author's mind, he said, as to whether she would let Macmillan have the world rights because she was afraid the firm would not make any great effort outside the United States. According to Brett, she gave up the foreign rights only after Latham persuaded her that Macmillan would aggressively promote the book in the world market. Mitchell wanted a distinct British edition and had been promised one, Brett claimed. That said, he professed embarrassment about how matters had been handled on the British edition and assured London that Latham had offered the book to Collins only on the possibility that London would not be interested in a first novel by a young Southern woman.[72]

Harold Macmillan had no choice but to up the ante. He accepted Brett's terms by wire on April 24, agreeing to pay Mitchell the suggested advance and royalties subject to a minor qualification on the Colonial sales, which covered Australia, India, New Zealand, and South Africa.[73] Brett wrote to Latham the same day, explaining where matters stood and admitted he may have gone somewhat "wide of the truth" in his letter to Harold Macmillan.[74] The publisher also wrote Mitchell a brief letter in which he mentioned in passing the matter of the British edition. Notably, he failed to say he had reached terms with Macmillan London, that an open offer remained on the table from Collins, or that multiple other publishers were interested. In fact, he made it sound like Macmillan London was on the fence, and he was doing his level best to negotiate favorable terms: "Alas, now it appears that it will be next week before we have any definite word." He felt sure matters would work out for a British edition and that she might even earn an advance of up to two hundred pounds.[75]

On April 27, without waiting for a reply from Mitchell, Brett wired London that it had won the rights to publish *Gone With the Wind* in Britain. He followed up the next day with a letter stating that Mitchell had agreed to the proposed contract and that the matter was therefore settled. On April 30, Mitchell wrote, asking for more information about the British rights, such as how much two hundred pounds was worth in American dollars. Brett responded on May 2, estimating the advance would be eight hundred to one thousand dollars, twice what she had received in her American contract. Implying there had been a subsequent communication from London, he informed her that the deal had been finalized.

Mitchell was not the only one being kept in the dark. No one at Macmillan had bothered to break the news to Collins that he had lost out. On April 30, thinking he had won the rights to *Gone With the Wind*, the Scottish publisher wired Macmillan expressing his continued enthusiasm and asking for specifics about the U.S. publication date.[76] When he did not receive a response, he sensed trouble. On May 4, he wired Latham, noting that he and his wife had finished reading the book and thought it a guaranteed success. Wondering if his offer was too low, he stated that he would pay whatever Macmillan suggested.[77]

Latham had some explaining to do. On May 5, just back from his visit with Mitchell in Atlanta, he wrote to Collins and Harold Macmillan, both of whom had reason to be unhappy with him. His letters offer a stark portrait of the dog-eat-dog, every-man-for-himself publishing industry. To Harold Macmillan, Latham apologized for any awkwardness in the handling of the British rights to *Gone With the Wind* and expressed hope the London house was not irritated over how things had transpired. He had not intended to create a bidding war, he said, and had promised Collins the chance to publish the book only if London declined. The Scottish publisher could not make a case that he had been used unfairly, Latham assured Macmillan. Also, the editor did not want Macmillan to think he had played one publisher against the other; he acknowledged that Macmillan London could have any of the New York firm's books it wanted.[78]

To Collins, Latham reported that Macmillan London refused to let Mitchell's book go and had made a splendid offer that was entirely acceptable to the author. The London house had always been in the running, Latham said, and that point had been made clear to Collins when they had spoken in February and again when Latham sent him the proofs. The editor tried to soften the blow by adding that he would have liked Collins to have the book because Latham had a "personal enthusiasm" for Mitchell and enjoyed working with Collins.[79] Making slight acknowledgment of possible error, he conceded this was the first time in his experience that such a conflict had developed.

Latham either had a bad memory or, having been out of town, perhaps did not have a full understanding of what happened. In both letters, he overlooked the correspondence of April 6 and April 22 soliciting bids from Collins with no mention of Macmillan London being in the picture. If what Latham said was true—that Collins would not have a chance to acquire the book unless London bowed out—then Collins would have reasonably assumed London was not interested. Latham also failed to address the fact that Brett offered the terms to London before giving Collins a chance to make a final offer.

Collins did not take the brush-off well. He could not understand how Latham let the book go to Macmillan London. In his recollection of their meeting in February, Latham had said that *Gone With the Wind* was not being handled the regular way and that Collins was being given preference over the London house. Irritated at the time wasted—he had spent two weeks reading the galleys—as well as the expense of the various cables he had sent, Collins declared he would never do business with Latham again.[80] He liked Mitchell's book better than any other he had seen since entering the publishing business and was crushed at losing the opportunity to be part of its success.[81]

Latham regretted the way things had played out and sympathized with Collins's disappointment. He assured the publisher that he deplored any break in their friendly relations and agreed that it probably had been a mistake to circulate the book to him while the London office was still considering it. That said, he maintained Collins had misunderstood the circumstances.[82] As for Collins's assertion that he no longer wished to do business with Macmillan, Latham called that unwarranted and trivial.[83]

While Collins stewed, Latham wrote to Mitchell confirming the British deal had been wrapped up. Unaware Brett had halted a potential bidding war, she was pleased with the results. She thanked Latham for his role in obtaining what she called an "unbelievable advance royalty."[84] To his credit, Latham showed some evidence of chagrin over the situation. He downplayed the advance by explaining that British firms tended to pay higher sums than American houses. He also informed her that, although publishers and authors typically split the proceeds of foreign sales, Macmillan would be more generous in her case and take only 10 percent, the same amount an agent would have charged.[85] Presumably having no idea of the source of Macmillan's generosity, Mitchell wrote to Latham expressing her appreciation, noting that she would "feel even happier about it if I knew that *you* were getting the ten percent!"[86]

Although both Macmillan firms and the author considered the matter resolved, Collins held out hope. He went to London and asked Harold Macmillan to waive the rights to publish *Gone With the Wind*. He also approached Macmillan New York again and upped the ante to a five-hundred-pound advance.[87] Neither effort got him anywhere. Having accepted Brett's and Latham's version of events, Harold Macmillan refused to give Collins the rights, declaring him to be "rather an excited young man who may well be allowed to cool off a little."[88] Macmillan New York appears to have ignored the increased advance offer.

Latham still had Collins on his mind though and wrote a memo to Brett explaining what had happened.[89] He maintained he had been clear with Collins but admitted perhaps he had let the Scottish publisher believe that Macmillan London was certain to turn the book down. Either way, Latham's enthusiasm had gotten away from him, and he had created a mess. Going forward, he claimed, he would never again be tempted to offer a book to a British publisher until the situation with the London house had been definitely settled. Latham admitted Collins would have been a better choice for Mitchell's book: he was more enthusiastic about it and, thus, would likely promote it more aggressively. Yet, Latham maintained he had not played unfairly with either Macmillan or Collins. Missing from the memo is whether Latham felt he had played unfairly with Mitchell, the obvious victim of this trade courtesy debacle. Her book was being handled by a publisher that Latham acknowledged was not the best choice, and she was missing out on an advance more than double what she had agreed to accept. Macmillan had waived part of its royalty, but was that enough to make up the difference?

# 5

~

# Fanning the Flame

*May–June 1936*

Magazine publisher B. C. Forbes once said that a shady business never yields a sunny life. Such did not appear to be the case for Macmillan in the spring of 1936. *Gone With the Wind*'s streak of good luck continued when, on May 15, the Book-of-the-Month Club selected the novel as its main offering for July. This meant the book could be released on June 30, a mere six weeks away.[1] Macmillan ran a full-page notice in *Publishers Weekly* announcing the good news.[2]

With the publication date set, Harold Latham prepared to get things going in Hollywood. He wrote Margaret Mitchell on May 21 to formalize their agency relationship. He promised her that, before any final deal was made, Macmillan would provide her with all the facts and would be glad to express its opinion if she desired. In exchange, the company would earn a 10 percent commission on the amount Mitchell received for the movie rights. True to his secret pact with Annie Laurie Williams, Latham never mentioned that the Texan would handle the sale and receive half the commission.[3]

Mitchell accepted the terms. On May 25, she wrote Latham that she trusted him to handle the matter and was relieved to have it in his hands instead of an agent's. She did not mean to disparage the agents who had expressed an interest, but she did not know them "and I do know you." She had just one lingering concern—what Hollywood might do to her story. She felt she ought to have some say in the final screenplay to make sure the inevitable cuts and adjustments were not too drastic. She would not insist on a strict presentation of her text, she assured him, but wanted to make sure the producers did not do something outrageous like have "Scarlett seduce General Sherman."[4]

The editor replied on May 27, promising he would, to the best of his ability, see that the contract gave Mitchell some degree of protection on the screenplay. He also renewed his efforts to get her to come to New York to promote the book's release. Accepting that she could not be pressured, he proposed a compromise. If she did not like the summer heat, would she come in the fall instead? Early July was not an ideal time to host a big event anyway, he explained, because a lot of the Macmillan staff would be on vacation, himself included, for the Fourth of July—the weekend after publication day. In the fall, the weather would be more pleasant and the city back in full swing. He concluded his note with the announcement that Macmillan again was adjusting her royalties—this time upward: "I hope you will take this as one more evidence of our desire to deal fairly, even generously, with you and to have you a happy and contented author."[5]

The following day, Lois Cole officially notified Mitchell that Macmillan wanted to go back to the idea of bumping up her royalty to 15 percent if the book sold particularly well. This time, though, she would have to top sales of twenty-five thousand copies to earn the bonus as opposed to the ten thousand specified in the original contract. Cole explained that the book club order gave the firm an additional margin of safety under which it could afford to do the novel justice in terms of advertising and break even at that level. The only qualifier was that Mitchell would have to accept a flat 10 percent royalty in any year in which less than five thousand hardback copies were sold. In a personal letter that same day, Cole crowed about her employer's generosity, calling the decision an amazing gesture on Macmillan's part. She said the firm wanted Mitchell to feel it was doing everything it could to see that she shared in the book's anticipated financial success.[6]

Despite Cole's statement crediting the decision to the Book-of-the-Month Club contract, the timing raises the question of whether the firm's generosity may have been otherwise motivated. Latham gave Mitchell this news in response to the author placing her trust in him on the movie deal when he knew he was deceiving her about Williams's involvement. Moreover, this is the same week Latham scrambled to make things right over the British deal. Was Macmillan tweaking the author's American royalties to adjust for some of the shenanigans that were going on behind the scenes? If so, did Cole know and had she deceived her friend, too? From the surviving documents, it appears Cole was in the dark with Mitchell. Her name is not mentioned in any of the correspondence relating to either the British rights or the secret deal with Williams. Apparently not knowing of Latham's behind-the-scenes maneuverings, Cole could not have been happier how things were shaping up. She proclaimed that everyone had been "atwit" about Mitchell's book at Macmillan's recent spring sales conference. The salesmen proclaimed that they enjoyed selling it more than any novel Macmillan had ever issued. Cole teased Mitchell that she had to drive North for a visit when she bought a Rolls Royce. "Didn't I always tell you Macmillan was the one publisher for you?"[7]

The Marshes were not so sure. Although the book was now guaranteed to sell beyond their wildest imagination, the revised terms were not as favorable to Mitchell as her original contract. This rankled John Marsh to no end. It was bad enough that the firm had modified the contract in the first place.[8] Although Mitchell and Marsh would carry a grudge over the royalty issue for years to come, the author bit her tongue and responded amiably. She wired Cole:

> HURRAH FOR MACMILLAN HURRAH FOR MACMILLAN HURRAH FOR MACMILLAN PLEASE THANK ALL CONCERNED FOR KINDNESS AND GENEROSITY IN MATTER OF ROYALTIES IF YOU ALL DONT STOP SENDING ME GOOD NEWS MY NERVOUS SYSTEM WILL BE COMPLETELY WRECKED.[9]

She also thanked Latham, claiming that the firm had been more than generous and that she had already put the matter of the reduced royalties out of her mind.[10] As for his invitation that she come to New York in the fall, she appreciated that Macmillan was investing large sums in advertising her book and regretted her lack of cooperation. She had "felt guilty of rudeness" ever since he mentioned it during their April meeting and now accepted his invitation with a gracious prevarication: "The prospect of coming in the Autumn appeals to me greatly." However, in case Latham had any ideas that she would be making speeches in New York, she made clear that would never happen. She had given a talk the week before to the Atlanta Library Club at Margaret Baugh's behest.* This speech had gone as poorly as the

---

* The night before the library talk, Mitchell apparently gave a speech to the Studio Club, a local organization composed of Atlanta-area painters, writers, musicians, and actors. As a club member, she was set to appear on a program featuring three others who had "won distinction in their several fields," according to a notice in the *Atlanta Georgian* on May 28, 1936. It is interesting to note that Mitchell frequently joked about her talks at the Macon writers and library clubs but assiduously avoided referring to the Studio Club event. Years later, Baugh said she felt the author would not have wanted her membership in the club publicized. The secretary did not speculate why.

one in Macon, according to Mitchell, and she was more convinced than ever that she did not have the knack for lecturing. She had planned on discussing the reference materials she had used in her research but got flustered and rambled on with "indelicate stories," like the one about the old farmer who compared writing to spreading manure. Recounting the look on the face of the head librarian that evening, Mitchell predicted, "I think I am perfectly safe from having to address librarians in the future." She labeled the event her "swan song as a speaker."[11]

Macmillan's good luck continued when Mitchell's book began generating buzz on the European continent. Publishers in Denmark, Germany, and Sweden expressed an interest in releasing translations. Because it was such a rare event in those days for foreign publishers to consider an American book worthy of translation, Macmillan was ill suited to manage these transactions. In addition to language barriers—English was not as widely spoken in Europe as it is today—there was the inherent difficulty of long-distance communication. Currency issues and international copyright laws added further layers of complexity. To handle the details, Latham decided to turn matters over to an outside agent who specialized in these types of deals. On May 11, he wrote to Sonia Chapter of Curtis Brown, Ltd., an esteemed British literary agency, and asked her to see what she could do about selling the foreign rights.[12] The editor did not expect any of the overseas publishers would come through with an offer, given the length of the book and its distinctly American story, but thought it worth a try.[13]

Unknown to Latham, however, another agent had already been marketing *Gone With the Wind* to European publishers. Her name was Marion Saunders. An ambitious Brit who operated a small firm from her New York City apartment, she claimed to be from an aristocratic family that had lost its fortune in World War I. Forced to support herself as a young adult, she had come to America to make a living off her European connections. Although respected in the industry, she had a reputation as something of a cutthroat. French author Simone de Beauvoir once referred to her in a letter to philosopher Jean-Paul Sartre as a "real old horror."[14] Saunders had represented other Macmillan authors in the 1930s and was anxious to stake her claim on its latest discovery. Instead of approaching Latham, though, she went straight to the horse's mouth: Margaret Mitchell. Saunders wrote to Mitchell in early May 1936, announcing, in what appears to be a bald-faced lie, that she was handling the continental European rights of *Gone With the Wind* for Macmillan. She asked to represent Mitchell for any future work, such as short stories the author might be writing.[15]

Given recent events with Williams, Mitchell had little interest in dealing with agents at the moment. She responded that she did not write short stories and, therefore, did not need an agent, nor did she have plans to write another book any time soon. "If the Lord lets me keep what little sense I now possess, I never will write anything else. If I'd had any idea of the amount of grief that *Gone With the Wind* entailed, I'd have shot myself before starting it."[16] In Mitchell's mind, this ended the matter. But she made a mistake that left the door open for Saunders to continue the conversation. Mitchell had assumed, given the spelling of the name Marion with an "o," that Saunders was male and addressed her as such. Saunders used this as an excuse to write back, clarifying that she was a "woman agent."[17] A model of civility, Mitchell could not let the error regarding Saunders's gender go unacknowledged. She replied on May 13, apologizing for the mistake and for the abruptness of her first letter.[18] Saunders had not managed to secure Mitchell as a client, but the two were now on personal correspondence terms, a status of which agents all over the country would have been envious.

The following day, Mitchell mentioned to Cole the communication from Saunders and asked what continental rights were: "Does she mean translations? God forbid. How can dialect be translated?" In any event, Saunders made a favorable impression on Mitchell. "She didn't jump down my throat, try to high pressure me or lay it on so thick that I got sick at my stomach," the author reported to Cole.[19] In what must have seemed like déjà vu, Cole responded on May 18 that Saunders was another overeager agent claiming to represent *Gone With the Wind* without having bothered to obtain the authority. Saunders was not handling the continental rights, Cole explained; another agency had been hired.[20] While Cole's letter expressed no opinion about Saunders, someone scribbled a note across the top of a file copy of Latham's May 11 letter to Chapter saying, "Make sure Miss Saunders doesn't get it."[21]

Unaware or unconcerned about Macmillan's feelings on the matter, Saunders continued to pursue Mitchell. She wrote the author again on May 22, describing her work generating interest in overseas publishers. She hinted that she had sent galleys to France and Holland, which seems an unlikely assertion, given that she would have had little opportunity to obtain proofs of the book.[22] Saunders also explained to Mitchell that the foreign rights often did not amount to much money by American standards but that she welcomed the chance to work on other deals for Mitchell such as any future books she might write.

A few days later, Saunders finally got around to discussing matters with Macmillan. She contacted Latham, informing him of her advance promotional efforts. The conversation was reminiscent of the one he had had the week before in which Williams demanded credit for her advance efforts with the movie studios. Saunders must have made a persuasive case. The following day, Latham wrote to Chapter and told her to stop working on *Gone With the Wind* because, unknown to him, another agent had already secured the rights.[23] An unsigned, handwritten note across a copy of this letter in the Macmillan files states, "Tell Miss Saunders it's all hers."★

Saunders's powers of persuasion must have been strong indeed. Not only had she convinced Latham to let her handle the foreign rights, but she also managed to ingratiate herself with Mitchell. Despite Cole's warning that Saunders had lied to her, Mitchell remained on friendly terms with the eager agent. On May 27, Mitchell thanked Saunders for her interest in *Gone With the Wind*. Although she did not agree to hire the woman as her personal agent, she offered an encouraging note: "I don't believe I could be lucky enough to be translated—but I sincerely wish you luck in the matter." She then threw in some uncharacteristic gushing: "At the risk of sounding overwhelmingly girlish, I'll say that you sound like the nicest agent of them all and, God knows, I've heard from plenty!"[24] It was a solid month's work for Saunders. She had wrestled the translation rights from the Curtis Brown agency—meaning she would receive a 20 percent commission on all the overseas royalties—and made a dazzling impression on Mitchell. Though she had not snagged Mitchell as a client, she had a foot firmly planted in the author's door. In the years to come, Saunders would push that door wide open, establishing herself as one of the leading characters in the *Gone With the Wind* saga.

More important to Mitchell than flashy advertisements, book clubs, agents, and foreign publishers was the Southern press's warm reception of *Gone*

---

★ The handwriting on this note and on the May 11 letter to Chapter do not appear to match.

*With the Wind*. As soon as the review copies began to circulate, regional newspapers embraced the book, and the author did what she could to spur their affection. She sent thank you letters to the reporters who wrote about her and made herself available to answer their questions. One of the first inquiries was from the *Chattanooga Times* in late April. When asked for information about her life, Mitchell played coy. She claimed to have no idea what the press would find interesting about little ol' her, then rambled on cheerfully for a handful of pages describing in colorful detail her family history and how the book came to be written. When a reporter she knew at the Associated Press wrote an article about her, she showered him with appreciation, proclaiming that his story was the first thing her family had been impressed by since she signed her contract: "Short of shooting John or winning the Nobel Prize I never expected to get on the A.P. . . . I am sure that when my publishers see it they will look at me with great respect and with awe, thinking me a far more important personage than they had here-to-fore imagined! And, being only human, I will endeavor not to undeceive them."[25]

With the help of a clipping service Marsh had retained, Mitchell tracked the news coverage in meticulous detail. By mid-May, more than two hundred articles about her had appeared in newspapers in Georgia and neighboring states.[26] The three Atlanta newspapers led the way, especially her former employer, the *Atlanta Journal*, which, in Marsh's words, "beat the drum for Peggy and the book like nobody's business."[27]

By the beginning of June, bookstores were inundating Macmillan with advance orders for *Gone With the Wind*. The publisher ordered a second printing of twenty-five thousand copies.[28] These books would look almost identical to the first, with a few noteworthy exceptions. Macmillan modified the dust jacket to reflect the growing certainty that *Gone With the Wind* would be its star book of the season. For the first printing, the back of the jacket had identified seventeen Macmillan "Spring Novels," with *Gone With the Wind* tenth on the list. On the back of the new jacket, Mitchell's novel now led a list of thirteen "New Macmillan Books." And, as would become important later, the revised copyright page showed the new publication date of June 1936. Although Macmillan considered leaving well enough alone and indicating only the year of publication, the company again included the month as a means of distinguishing this second print run for the sake of book collectors, who would want to know the difference between this printing and the original one.[29] This, too, would cause trouble later.

On June 6, *Publishers Weekly* ran a detailed story about Macmillan's advertising and promotion strategy for *Gone With the Wind*. The article announced to the book trade that the publisher had a major success on its hands and described how Macmillan was aligned firmly behind Mitchell's novel. An unnamed company official was quoted as predicting that advance orders would be one of the largest in years and that the book would prove to be a real "wow." It is hard to imagine any booksellers reading the story who would not want to hitch their wagon to Mitchell's rising star. Indeed, some retailers were so enthusiastic about the book's prospects that they developed their own promotions to generate interest. An Ohio bookseller sent his patrons a letter soliciting prepublication orders, staking his reputation on the appeal of *Gone With the Wind*. Acknowledging that "efforts to pre-select books to suit other literary tastes are, we believe, in general practice as fruitless as they are thankless," the store owner nonetheless recommended Mitchell's book as a novel that would give them "more solid entertainment" and would stay longer in their memory than any book in years.[30]

When the second printing came from the bindery in the middle of June, Macmillan began shipping crates of *Gone With the Wind* to wholesalers and distributors. At George Brett's direction, books from the first two printings were commingled so that copies of the May printing, which might have collectible value some day, would be spread throughout the trade, rather than concentrated in shipments to a few lucky stores.[31] Macmillan also sent booksellers colorful, eye-catching placards, posters, and postcards to use in displays.

In late June, with advance orders continuing to roll in, the company ordered a third printing of fifteen thousand copies.[32] Including the fifty thousand for the Book-of-the-Month Club, this meant one hundred thousand copies would be in print before publication. The firm also geared up to start advertising the novel to book buyers through a carefully orchestrated campaign that would begin release week in the large urban markets and then, if all went well, expand into the regional markets. Macmillan reserved advertising space in major newspapers and magazines for the important cities on both coasts, with special attention paid to the South. The publisher announced it planned to cover "Dixie like the dew," borrowing the tagline of the *Atlanta Journal*. A variety of advertisements was designed to appeal to a range of readers. Some commended Mitchell's literary skill and included praise from respected authors such as Ellen Glasgow. Others focused on the upcoming holiday and encouraged readers to take Macmillan's new novel away with them on the Fourth of July as insurance against rainy weather.

Macmillan Canada likewise prepared for the big day. It had purchased one thousand sets of printed sheets of the book and one thousand dust jackets from New York. These materials had been shipped to Canada, where the pages were bound in a light gray cloth with blue lettering, trying to match the American edition as closely as possible. The Canadian firm implemented its own marketing campaign, which included newspaper and magazine advertisements, as well as an encouraging letter from Hugh Eayrs to 250 booksellers, libraries, and universities. He confessed that he had not been as moved by a romantic story "in donkey's years" as he was by Mitchell's novel.[33]

Now the official—albeit secret—movie rights agent, Williams, finally merited an advance copy of *Gone With the Wind*. Her enthusiasm soared after reading the book for herself. She thought it one of the grandest motion picture sagas ever written and loved that it was a "natural co-starring story" with roles for four leading actors.[34] Inspired by the possibilities, she raised her estimate of what the rights were worth to one hundred thousand dollars, more than double what a novice author had ever received.

Although Latham had assured Mitchell he would look out for her interests in dealing with Hollywood, Williams was working alone. After formalizing the agency relationship with the author, Latham left on an extended vacation, with plans to be out of town for the rest of the summer. Williams was also working in the dark: Latham apparently had not bothered to tell her about Mitchell's desire for script review. As an unknown first-time author, there was almost no chance Mitchell would be granted such input. Latham, having little or no experience negotiating movie deals, perhaps did not know enough to advise her of this. Or perhaps he did know and simply hoped Mitchell would not cause a fuss when the time came. In either case, Latham's negligence likely changed the course of cinematic history. Had the author been told the truth up front, she might well have refused to shop the movie rights to Hollywood at that time.

Even without knowing Mitchell wanted to review the script, Williams encountered difficulties bringing offers to the table. For starters, although it was standard practice for deals to be reached based on plot summaries of books, Williams felt strongly that the key decision makers in this case needed to read the book in its entirety. She wanted the studio executives and the potential stars to experience firsthand the novel's power and had her hands full convincing them to read such a long book.[35] She also faced the unassailable fact that Mitchell's complex novel would be expensive to produce, a serious problem considering that the film industry was still reeling from the Great Depression. The financial risks were exacerbated because the Civil War, as a topic, was considered bad box office. Fresh on the minds of industry players was Paramount's *So Red the Rose*, a Civil War saga based on a bestselling novel; the film had bombed the year before.[36]

Williams gradually came to accept that she had overestimated the value of Mitchell's rights. Paramount had removed itself from consideration, and Fox had offered only twenty-five thousand dollars. Metro-Goldwyn-Mayer remained in the running, and there had been warm interest from independent producer David O. Selznick, as well as Warner Brothers and RKO.[37] However, none of them had talked about an offer anywhere near one hundred thousand dollars. Williams began to suspect that fifty thousand was the best they could hope to earn. Selznick and the others were balking even at that price, but she held out hope that the studios would come around when good reviews started appearing in newspapers during release week.[38]

With such a drastic price reduction from her last estimate, Williams needed to know whether fifty thousand dollars was acceptable to Mitchell. The agent had earlier alerted the vacationing Latham to "please stand by," and she now needed him to step forward.[39] If an offer came through, Williams wanted to say yes right away and not risk an interested studio reconsidering while she tracked down the editor for Mitchell's consent. Williams called Latham's home multiple times the first week of June and left messages. When he failed to respond, she wrote a letter urging him to contact her immediately. Still getting no reply, she sent him a telegram on June 12. She must have been frustrated knowing she had to share half her commission with Macmillan, yet Latham could not be bothered with the details.

The telegram managed to get his attention, although only marginally. Not interested in interrupting his vacation to deal with the movie rights, Latham decided to come clean with Mitchell on his arrangement with Williams. He wired Mitchell on June 14 about the agent's involvement and followed up three days later with a letter explaining that he had decided to bring in the agent because of her experience approaching movie studios. He assured Mitchell that Macmillan's arrangement with Williams did not have any effect on the author's agency relationship with the firm. He promised to present the final contract to her and that Macmillan would pay Williams's fee out of its commission.[40] Latham expected Williams to receive an offer soon and termed fifty thousand dollars a fair price. He asked the author to wire Cole if she would accept that amount.[41]

Mitchell was shocked. She had trusted Latham, and he had betrayed her. She intended to give him a piece of her mind but did not have time with all the activity swirling around her.[42] Mitchell held her tongue and replied to Cole that she would accept fifty thousand dollars provided she was satisfied with the terms of the contract.[43] Although she did not say so to Cole, in the author's mind, Macmillan remained her agent regardless of what Latham and Williams had agreed to. She had not hired Williams and planned on having no interaction with her.

When Cole gave the go-ahead, Williams set about convincing RKO to come through with an offer. Its leading female star, Katharine Hepburn, wanted to play the role of Scarlett, and Williams sensed the studio president was ready to make a move. To her frustration, he insisted on running the project by producer Pandro Berman, who vetoed it on the grounds that Hepburn would not be sympathetic enough in the part. Williams reported the disappointing news to Cole, predicting that Hepburn was "not going to like it one little bit."[44] The agent remained optimistic though that another studio would make an offer soon. The Macmillan salespeople had been touting the firm's high expectations for the movie deal, and newspapers were speculating wildly about the money the studios were willing to throw at Mitchell. Surely, something would shake loose soon.

Still interested was Selznick, a thirty-four-year-old producer whose family had roots in the earliest days of Hollywood history. Although Selznick had built his reputation making films based on classics such as *A Tale of Two Cities*, *Anna Karenina*, *David Copperfield*, and *Little Lord Fauntleroy*, his East Coast story editor, Kay Brown, thought Mitchell's book was splendid and wanted her boss to take a chance on the unknown author. A savvy Hollywood insider—described by Selznick biographer David Thomson as "small, feisty and snub-nosed pretty"[45]—Brown had a strong intuition about Mitchell's book and had been urging her boss since May not to let another studio snatch it up. Because she and Selznick worked on opposite coasts, they communicated regularly by teletype, a typewriter-like machine that allowed private parties to send written messages without going through a telegram service. Many of the printouts from their communications survive and offer a behind-the-scenes glimpse of how important Brown thought Mitchell's book was. In one, Brown told Selznick of a meeting with Williams and her impression that the agent would be satisfied with a fifty-thousand-dollar offer. Brown thought that absurdly low, predicting the book could sell for up to one hundred thousand dollars in the hands of a more skilled agent. Brown characterized Williams as a nice person but inexperienced in negotiating a deal like this.[46]

After reading Brown's synopsis of Mitchell's novel, Selznick agreed the story had potential. But, he refused to pay even fifty thousand dollars for a book by an unproven author. He also had concerns about being able to afford the big-name stars who would be needed to bring the story to life.[47] Brown gave Williams the bad news but continued to plead Mitchell's case with her boss. Urging him to take a gamble on the Atlantan, Brown encouraged him to read the book, or at least part of it, for himself. Mitchell's story, Brown said, carried an emotional wallop akin to having your heart ripped out of your chest.[48] Somewhere along the way, her impassioned pleas must have resonated with Selznick. By June, Brown was scrambling behind the scenes to pull an offer together. Could Selznick's small, independent studio come up with the money to buy the rights and produce a movie worthy of Mitchell's epic novel?

While Macmillan and Williams oversaw developments in New York and Hollywood, Mitchell kept the home fires burning. Consistent with her goal of courting Southern acceptance, she participated in several events that thrust her and *Gone With the Wind* into the local spotlight. At the Georgia Press Association's annual meeting in mid-June, she saw a particularly valuable opportunity to promote her book. She was recognized at the convention for her forthcoming achievement and put her time there to good use connecting with members of the press. According to Marsh, she was the "belle of the ball" and "the center of attention at every gathering." Newspapers throughout the South ran stories about her appearance, many including her photograph. "If I was publicity man for Macmillan, I would expect a raise in salary for getting an advance write-up of the book and picture of the author [in so many papers]," Marsh told his mother. "But no publicity man could or did get it done." Mitchell deserved all the credit, he said. The members of the press embraced her because they liked her.[49]

Mitchell also worked with Norman Berg to schedule a series of autograph sessions for release week. Their efforts focused on three Atlanta venues: Rich's, the city's hometown department store; Davison-Paxon, the local division of Macy's; and the lending library at Sears, Roebuck. Mitchell was not eager to appear before crowds but wanted to support the local retailers who had gone out on a limb and placed large advance orders for *Gone With the Wind*. At a June 20 dinner party at the home of the book buyer at Davison-Paxon, Luise Sims, Mitchell teased her hostess that she would lose her job for having ordered seven hundred and fifty copies.[50] But the author was willing to go only so far to help Sims and the other booksellers. She let it be known that she would not give any speeches at the events and that these were one-shot deals that had to be scheduled during release week. The only public speaking Mitchell agreed to was a radio interview by her friend Medora Field Perkerson.

As the big day approached, Mitchell stayed busy, answering questions from reporters and responding to a steady stream of letters, much of it fan mail from bookstore employees and reviewers who had read advance copies. To Mitchell, it all seemed like a dream. She could not believe that the "old dog eared and dirty bunch of copy paper" that took up so much space in their small apartment and seemed to get worse with each writing was causing such a stir.[51] "Every step along the way of this book has been so unexpected and exciting and everyone has been so kind that I feel like the old woman in the nursery rhyme who screamed, 'Lawk a mercy on me! This is none of I,'" she wrote of the experience. "I invited my husband to pinch me so often that he now refuses, saying the black and blue spots on a new author do not look well and may, justifiably, lead to talk."[52] Marsh wrote his mother on June 26 that they were getting a "tremendous kick" out of the excitement. The book's reception had exceeded their "fondest expectations" and surpassed "anything we might have dreamed of in the wildest of dreams."[53]

But Mitchell did not place too much stock in all the enthusiasm. Having been a reporter covering the celebrity beat, she saw all the fuss as a passing craze that would fizzle in a month or two, which was something she looked forward to.[54] Being from a reserved, Southern family, she had no affinity for a life in the spotlight. Those close to her helped keep the author's feet firmly planted on terra firma. She once told an interviewer that if her beloved housekeeper, Bessie Jordan, had sensed she was putting on airs, "she'd walk out that front door, crushed and broken, like Napoleon retreating from Moscow."[55] Mitchell's father also kept her grounded by commenting he would not have bothered to read the book had it not been written by his daughter.[56]

The author did not even get carried away by the promise of big money heading her way. Although she would be earning far more from the book than she ever thought possible, the Marshes decided not to make any major changes in their lifestyle. They did not want to move, nor did they let the constantly ringing telephone cow them into changing or unlisting their phone number. The book was being published under her maiden name, so they figured they were relatively safe because the directory listing appeared under the name John R. Marsh. According to her brother, Mitchell's approach was entirely reasonable and consistent with her common sense. "What better could she have done than to stay and be what she was—a person who had hit the jackpot and was enjoying it in a quiet way?"[57]

Whether Mitchell would be a celebrity, however, was not up to her. The public's whim and fancy would make that determination, and from the way things were shaping up, it appeared she would be cast into that realm regardless of her desires. It was a startling realization to Mitchell that she and her husband could not simply shut their door and be left alone. And, more distressing was that some people might take offense at their attempt to do so. She described their predicament to a friend in the press:

> Being in the public eye is something neither of us care about but what good does it do to say it? No one believes a word of it or if they do believe it they get indignant. I have been caught between two equally distasteful positions, that of the girlishly shy creature who keeps protesting her lack of desire for the limelight but who only wants to be urged. . . . And that of a graceless, ungracious, blunt spoken ingrate who refuses to let people do her honor.[58]

It was an uncomfortable situation for a woman who had been reared to believe it was unseemly to draw attention to yourself and better to commit murder than be rude.

But the author was no pushover. Mitchell had already demonstrated a willingness to set limits, and as the release neared, her resolve showed no signs of weakening. The Sears lending library learned this lesson when its overeager manager, Ruth Hinman Carter, almost caused Mitchell to back out of its book signing. On June 20, Carter sent the author a copy of the "Sears Library News" bulletin promoting the event and told her to be ready to give a few remarks, suggesting that one more talk should not be any bother. Mitchell, whose every spare moment was dedicated to preparing remarks for the radio interview with Perkerson, had no time to come up with something for Sears. She called Carter immediately to explain the situation. Unable to reach her, she sent a letter making it clear that she would not make a speech. "I am frantic now thinking you misunderstood me for

I know I said at least four times I couldn't make a talk. . . . If making a talk is the price of the tea, I'll just have to stay away."[59]

Not even Cole could cajole Mitchell into embracing her newfound fame. When the editors of a trade publication, *The Retail Bookseller*, asked the author to write a short feature article for an upcoming issue, Cole thought it a good opportunity and something Mitchell should do to promote *Gone With the Wind*. She told her friend to accept the invitation. Cole acknowledged that Mitchell did not like publicity but encouraged the author to be reasonable about it and "damn glad" that people were interested in her and the book. It was a tribute to Mitchell's work, and Cole wanted her to be gracious.[60] Mitchell appears to have ignored the plea.

Cole hit another roadblock when she asked Mitchell for permission to copy the letter about the horrors of the Macon speech. Latham had read the letter aloud at the spring sales conference to great effect. The staff thought her comments hilarious and wanted copies. Mitchell went ballistic at the thought of her personal correspondence being shared with strangers. She threatened never to write Cole or Latham another letter if they ever did such a thing again. Chalking it up to a case of beginner's nerves, Cole decided not to push the issue for the time being. She promised the salesmen to ask Mitchell again when things settled down for the new author.[61]

Mitchell had serious doubts she would get used to being an author anytime soon. A friend warned her, "I know you are plum wo' out being famous—but hold your horses!—think what's coming! You have to pay the price of fame!"[62] Part of that price was the incessant worry of whether all the fuss would be merited. Word on the street had it that Mitchell's book was being compared favorably to Leo Tolstoy's *War and Peace* and William Makepeace Thackeray's *Vanity Fair*. Mitchell knew many of these stories emanated from Macmillan's sales team and was astounded by the word-of-mouth advertising "those fine, bare faced liars" had generated. She had no idea how she could live up to the expectations.[63] As Marsh wrote on June 25, "Waiting for the book's birthday has been quite a strain on both of us. It will be out next Tuesday and then we will know the worst."[64]

A moment of calm before the storm came for Mitchell on Sunday, June 28, when the Atlanta Historical Society hosted an afternoon reception in honor of the author and *Gone With the Wind*. She was proud to see "every pioneer family in town" represented, though she joked afterward that "they all looked a trifle alike!" The recognition of friends and acquaintances meant more to the new author than any of the accolades or hysteria surrounding her.[65] She had written a book about the hometown she loved and was being celebrated in that community. That was what mattered most to her.

In less than a year, Mitchell had gone from unemployed reporter and housewife to the proud parent of an imminent bestseller. Her reference that spring to the book as her first and only child was an apt one. Since the contract's signing, she had spent approximately forty weeks bringing the manuscript to full term. Like any first-time mother, the thirty-five-year-old author was nervous. And, as with parenthood, no matter how stressful the pregnancy, the biggest adjustments were yet to come.

# 6

# The Making of a Colossal Upper-case Success

## June–July 1936

The final step in securing *Gone With the Wind*'s future was protection of the copyright. In the days leading up to the book's release, Macmillan sent two copies of the June printing to the Library of Congress in Washington, D.C., along with an affidavit affirming that the novel had been produced in the United States. With that procedural technicality taken care of, *Gone With the Wind* was protected in the United States and officially released to the American public on June 30, 1936. In order to invoke "backdoor" Berne coverage, Macmillan Canada likewise released its edition that same day. When the book hit the market as scheduled in both countries, Macmillan believed its copyright was secure in most of the Western world.

Lois Cole wired Margaret Mitchell on release day, congratulating the author and reporting the remarkable news that shipments to stores had exceeded fifty thousand copies.[1] The editor was thrilled with the book's success and proud of her own role in making it happen. Mitchell certainly recognized Cole's contributions, as indicated by her inscription in the Taylor family's copy of *Gone With the Wind*: "To Lois Cole, who fought by my side with great gallantry in the engagements of Dalton, Resaca, Peachtree Creek and the siege of Atlanta and who managed to get me to press on time."★

---

★ To Cole's husband, Mitchell's former deskmate at the *Atlanta Journal*, the author added, "To Allan Taylor, who fought by my side in the major engagements of the younger generation."

June 30 was also the day major reviews began to appear in the press. Edwin Granberry of the *New York Sun* ranked Mitchell with Leo Tolstoy, Thomas Hardy, and Charles Dickens. Herschel Brickell in the *New York Post* raved about Mitchell's skill and promised her book would be a subject of discussion for months to come. But the day was not without its disappointments. *New York Times* columnist Ralph Thompson gave Mitchell a barely passing grade. He acknowledged her extensive research and lively writing but described the plot as unconvincing and somewhat ridiculous. He characterized her work as undisciplined and suggested the book would have been better if it was five hundred pages shorter.[2] The review struck fear in the heart of Annie Laurie Williams, who had been promising her Hollywood contacts that the critics would erase any doubts the studios had about Mitchell's book. The agent began receiving consoling phone calls from her studio friends, who worried she had gone too far out on a limb for *Gone With the Wind*.[3] Cole eagerly tracked the press coverage, a process she likened to watching election returns.[4]

Things in Atlanta were not quite as rosy as Macmillan would have liked either. Although Mitchell had agreed to signings at three Atlanta department stores, only two had taken her up on the offer. A disagreement had arisen between Rich's and Davison-Paxon over where Mitchell should appear first, and, when Macmillan gave Davison-Paxon the first slot, Rich's canceled its event. Secretly relieved to have one less appearance to worry about, Mitchell reported for duty on the afternoon of June 30 to Davison-Paxon's Peachtree Street store for an autograph party in its sixth-floor tea room. *GWTW* lore holds that the event was a madhouse with eager fans falling upon Mitchell in a frenzy,[5] but the evidence does not support this oft-told tale. Frank O'Gara, the store's merchandise manager, recalled that a generous crowd turned out and purchased about 250 books but made no mention of frantic fans.[6] Luise Sims termed the event "poorly attended" and noted that, had Mitchell appeared a month later, the store would have been "swamped."[7] And no articles about the event ran in the press at a time when the local newspapers were covering Mitchell extensively. The second signing in the Sears lending library the following day also failed to garner any news coverage.

One negative review and two tame book signings did not dampen Macmillan's enthusiasm for *Gone With the Wind*. Richard Brett, Macmillan's business manager, demonstrated the utmost faith in Mitchell when, the day after the release, he ordered a second set of printing plates for the book so the firm could keep up with demand.[8] That same day, his father, the senior George Brett, sent Mitchell a check for five thousand dollars in his capacity as chairman of the Macmillan board.[9] Although she was not entitled to any royalty payments until that fall, he wanted to pay her early given how far sales had exceeded the firm's expectations. Macmillan also carried through with its record-breaking advertising campaign. Throughout the holiday weekend, the major papers proclaimed Macmillan's joy over *Gone With the Wind*. Mitchell could not believe her eyes. "My God, woman!" she wrote to Cole. "How much advertising *are* you putting behind me? I quail every time I see another one! And are they grand."[10]

The publisher's faith turned out to be well placed. Although Thompson was not the only critic to find fault with Mitchell—the *Nation* said she wrote "with the bias of passionate regionalism," resulting in a work of "shallow effect," and the *New Republic* deemed her book "competent but neither very good nor very sound"[11]—the vast majority of reviewers that weighed in were impressed. The *Los Angeles Times* called the novel "the most satisfactory, the most convincing, the most powerful presentation of what took place during reconstruction that has ever been written."[12] The *New Yorker* deemed it a "masterpiece of pure escapism" and judged Mitchell "a staggeringly gifted storyteller, empowered . . . with some secretion in the blood for effortlessly inventing and prolonging excitement."[13] On July 5, the *New York Times Book Review* devoted the entire front page to Mitchell's novel. Its editor, J. Donald Adams, disagreed with his colleague Thompson and declared that, for "sheer readability," nothing in American fiction surpassed Mitchell's book.[14] The *New York Herald Tribune* book section also featured a front-page review, this one by esteemed historian Henry Steele Commager. Calling *Gone With the Wind* "a dramatic recreation of life itself," Commager said the story was told "with such sincerity and passion, illuminated by such understanding, woven of the stuff of history and of disciplined imagination."[15]

Readers loved *Gone With the Wind*, too, and flooded Macmillan with letters. A fan from Virginia wrote that Mitchell's book "really and truly *is* the best novel ever written by any Southerner—and I wonder if it is not the best novel written by any American."[16] Another from Massachusetts said her enthusiasm had to be communicated to someone, "else it will surely blow something up."[17] Many reported being unable to put the book down and of ignoring everything else in their lives to keep up with Scarlett and Rhett's story. The company received several letters from book collectors asking guidance on how to identify a first edition, the first time it had seen such a reaction to a new title.[18]

Industry insiders congratulated Macmillan on a job well done. Robert Garland, the drama critic for the *New York World-Telegram*, wrote, "Gentlemen: May I, for no reason other than my enthusiasm, tell you that if *Gone With the Wind* isn't the great American novel, there is yet to be one? Thank you for publishing it."[19] A movie studio executive sent a congratulatory note referring to the hoopla surrounding Mitchell's book as a "colossal upper-case" success.[20] Indeed it was. On July 4, Macmillan announced that demand for copies of the book was so incessant that it might be out of stock for a few days. The publisher promised to make every effort to keep bookstores supplied.[21]

Although the book signings seem to have been relatively sedate, the same could not be said for the rest of Mitchell's life during release week. Suddenly, she was one of the most famous people in America. Although the book had been published under her maiden name, well-wishers had no trouble tracking her down at the Marsh apartment to offer their congratulations. Speaking invitations streamed in from schools, community groups, and literary organizations. Fans and autograph seekers stopped her on the street, and some bold ones showed up at her apartment door. She claimed to have lost ten pounds from leaping whenever the phone rang and scurrying like a rabbit to avoid being waylaid by fans.[22]

Beyond being enamored with the book, people were fascinated by the possibility of the story being made into a movie. Rumors circulated that Mitchell had sold the rights for various amounts up to five million dollars. "People are driving me crazy, folks on the relief rolls asking for a hundred because I won't miss it out of my millions etc.," she reported to Cole. "Friends wondering why in Hell I persist in driving a 1929 model car and wearing four year old cotton dresses and fifty cent stockings and calling me an old Hetty Green to my face." Speculation also ran wild about who would play the characters on the big screen; Clark Gable supposedly called Mitchell from Hollywood saying he would cut his throat if she did not let him play Rhett. Assuming that Williams had spread the stories to run up the price on the movie rights, Mitchell asked Cole to find out "what the Hell" the agent was up to, because the "damn movie rumors" were driving her nuts.[23] Trying to assuage Mitchell's frazzled nerves, Cole blamed the furor on the enthusiastic Macmillan salesmen who were promoting the book by talking up the movie angle. Cole asked Alec Blanton to rein in his sales staff, but there was little he could do to calm things down.[24] It seemed the nation had a raging case of Scarlett fever.

By Thursday, July 2, the author had had enough. "I just came to the end of everything yesterday and blew up with loud explosions and went to bed and have the tired shakes so bad this a.m. that I can hardly hit the keys," she wrote to Cole. Mitchell planned to leave town to get away from all the attention: "Everyone has been wonderful, so wonderful that I'm nearly dead."[25] Promising Cole there would be no more appearances by Margaret Mitchell, the author, "unless they come after me with a rope,"[26] she finished up her obligations by meeting with three reporters from the Associated Press and giving the radio interview to Medora Field Perkerson. Mitchell then jumped in her car and fled Atlanta alone, leaving John Marsh to keep an eye on things at home.

The author ended up at a hotel in Gainesville, Georgia, north of Atlanta, where she stayed for a few days to catch her breath. She had brought her typewriter along and used the quiet time to write thank-you letters to reviewers all across the country who had commented on her book. Full of wit, her missives to the national press established the author as an articulate and endearing character. To Adams of the *New York Times*, she wrote:

> I am Margaret Mitchell, author of *Gone With the Wind* and I am yet so new an author that I do not know whether it is good form for an author to write a critic and say "thank you"! For all I know of literary etiquette an author should keep haughtily silent, thus intimating that marvelous reviews were only what she expected. Or only address a critic to ask why in Hell the review wasn't better and point out sad lacks in the critic's critical abilities.[27]

In many of these letters, she cast herself as something of an ingenue who never intended to have her book published. Perhaps it was a defensive device in case the book faltered. A skeptic might surmise she was pulling out the Southern belle version of playing dumb. Regardless of her motive, she charmed many of the reviewers and, in several cases, developed long-lasting friendships with them. She forged especially meaningful associations with Brickell of the *New York Post* and Granberry of the *Sun*. Their bond was so immediate that, after her getaway, Mitchell accepted Brickell's invitation to attend a literary retreat later that month in Blowing Rock, North Carolina, with him and Granberry. The two men became staunch Mitchell advocates and would write favorably about her throughout her life. Referring to the role they played in developing her reputation, she once told George Brett, Jr., "Yes, it does seem that I get a million dollars worth of free publicity."[28]

While she courted the national critics, her husband looked after their friends at the Southern newspapers. They had treated Mitchell respectfully over the previous weeks, and he wanted to keep on their good side. He sent multiple letters to New York making sure Macmillan did right by the local press. He insisted that the Atlanta papers receive all relevant news releases and that the *Atlanta Journal*, Mitchell's former paper, be given the opportunity to break the story of any movie deal.[29] He also wanted the publisher to include in its advertisements quotes from all three Atlanta newspapers, especially the influential morning *Constitution*, as well as some of the smaller newspapers in other Southern states. This would give Northern reviewers a broad perspective on the South's acceptance of the book.[30] That he might come off as pushy appears never to have crossed Marsh's mind. He knew how to play the publicity game on his home court and felt well qualified to school Macmillan on the applicable rules. James Putnam responded amiably but without apology for any slight to the local papers. The firm had tried to use a line or two from the *Constitution*'s review, he said, but, alas, after going through it with great care, had found nothing worth quoting.[31]

~

By the second week of July, *Gone With the Wind* topped the bestseller lists in major publications such as the *New York Times*, the *New York Herald Tribune*, and *Publishers Weekly*. And orders continued to arrive, even from bookstores in little Southern towns where Macmillan did not typically sell any books. Although some of the orders were small—as few as two copies—this delighted the author to no end. As Marsh wrote his mother, these sales pleased "Peggy far more than the news you may have seen in the New York papers that the book had gone to the top of the best-seller list in eight out of ten cities the first week it went on sale."[32]

News of Mitchell's success spread overseas, and publishers from around the world expressed an interest in translating the book. By the middle of July, Marion Saunders had feelers out in Czechoslovakia, Denmark, France, Germany, Hungary, Italy, Norway, and Sweden.[33] With this level of interest brewing, it occurred to Putnam to make sure everything was in order regarding protection of the copyright in Europe. On July 13, he telegrammed Hugh Eayrs at Macmillan Canada to confirm that *Gone With the Wind* had been published and copyrighted there on June 30, the same day as in the United States.[34] Eayrs's assistant, Ellen Elliott, informed Putnam that her boss was out of town but confirmed the novel had been published in Canada on June 30. However, she noted, the copyright had not yet been registered at the Copyright and Patent Office in Ottawa.[35] Though not a mandatory requirement, American publishers frequently used the registration to document compliance with the Berne Convention's simultaneous publication provision. Elliott promised to take care of it right away. She submitted the necessary paperwork to the Canadian government on July 16.

Did Macmillan Canada's failure to register the copyright simultaneously with publication jeopardize the "backdoor" Berne filing? If so, publishers in Europe were free to print their own editions of *Gone With the Wind* without seeking permission from Macmillan or paying royalties. In the face of what must have been a disconcerting situation, Putnam played it cool. He thanked Elliott and told her not to worry. Though admitting the Berne issue was complicated, he assured her they would be all right.[36] There is no hint in the Macmillan records that Putnam broadcast the potential problem around the firm or brought it to the attention of Saunders or the Marshes.

As Williams had hoped, the successful book release—once past the Thompson review hiccup—energized the movie negotiations. On Tuesday, July 7, Williams told Kay Brown that another studio was on the verge of making an offer for an unspecified amount above fifty thousand dollars. Brown wired David O. Selznick at home that morning and asked for permission to bid fifty-five thousand dollars.[37] After several frantic cross-country messages, Selznick authorized Brown to offer Williams fifty thousand. Brown conveyed the offer that day, and the agent accepted on the spot. Williams called Cole at home at ten o'clock that evening to report the news. Although the offer was half of what Williams's gut told her the rights were worth, she assured Cole they could do no better. The agent dismissed the rumors swirling in the press about the fantastic sums producers were willing to pay and convinced Cole none of the other companies would go any higher. Williams declared it the highest price ever paid for the movie rights to a first novel.[38]

Cole shared the details with the Marshes by letter the following morning, assuring them it was a fair deal. With summer vacations approaching, Macmillan and Selznick hoped to have matters finalized by the middle of the following week, so she promised a draft contract would be on its way in a matter of days.[39] Marsh responded on July 13 warning Cole that the document would not be hurried back to New York "five minutes" after its arrival in Atlanta. "The Mitchell family just doesn't work that way, as you all may have discovered last summer," he wrote, referring to the book contract negotiations. "With their legal training and legal habits, they wouldn't sign *any* contract without careful consideration and due deliberation."[40]

The Marshes and Stephens Mitchell planned to review the document thoroughly. In the midst of all the excitement that summer, the author had asked her brother to serve as her legal counsel on any issues that arose out of *Gone With the Wind*. That he had no experience with international publishing or movie contracts did not trouble her. In that day, few lawyers, especially in the South, handled such transactions. Stephens had more important credentials—he was smart, and he was family. Margaret trusted her brother implicitly and promised him 10 percent of her earnings in exchange for him serving as her permanent legal adviser.[41]

In Marsh's July 13 letter, he also put Cole on notice that Macmillan needed to do a better job of shielding Mitchell from the media attention surrounding the movie negotiations. The author did not want the sales price for the rights made public, and Marsh warned Cole that Macmillan should not leak it for publicity purposes. He explained:

> The excitement stirred up by the book's success has already just about driven her crazy and she knows the excitement would be intensified many times if the figure involved is published. The over-active interest of her friends and total strangers is bad enough as it is, but publication of the figure would attract to her a new horde of curiosity-seekers, salesmen of all kinds, beggars for money, etc., that would make her life miserable. She doesn't want to become the object of the same type of curiosity as is centered on the winners of the British lotteries and the Dionne quintuplets. Some people might like that sort of public prominence but she heartily despises it.[42]

Mitchell was capable of writing again and willing for Macmillan to profit from it, but that would never happen unless the publisher gave her time to get her strength back from the strain she had been under the previous year. "She isn't ungrateful to you for all that you've done and she isn't unappreciative of the money that's rolling in," he wrote. "But money isn't as important as health, and no amount of money could compensate her if her too sudden success should wreck her health."[43]

∽

Meanwhile, Williams was busy behind the scenes tying up loose ends. One issue pressing on her mind was tracking down the copies of *Gone With the Wind* that had been sent to the various studios in May. She wrote to several of her contacts, asking them to return the books. The records do not make clear what she intended to do with them, but it may have been that she understood the value of those copies, which were all first printings. At least two of the companies complied. Richard Halliday, a producer at Paramount to whom Macmillan had sent two copies, sent back one and expressed appreciation to Williams for letting him keep the other. William W. Hawkins, Jr., at Samuel Goldwyn, returned his with good wishes. Hawkins regretted that he would not be the one to produce the film but was eager to see a quality production come from it. He hoped the book sold millions of copies and that Selznick's picture would be the "finest ever made."[44]

On July 14, Williams arrived at Macmillan headquarters with Selznick's draft of the movie contract. Cole sent it to Marsh right away, promising him Macmillan would do what it could to keep the press at bay. Macmillan wanted Mitchell to write more books for the firm, Cole said, and was concerned about the author's health.[45] As for the contract, Cole encouraged Marsh to take his time reviewing the document but cautioned him not to go overboard in suggesting changes. The contract was apparently a standard form used by all of the major producers, and Selznick would not be amendable to making major revisions.

When Marsh received the document the following day, he telephoned Cole to complain that the draft did not give Mitchell the one thing she had insisted upon: script review. Cole checked with Williams to see what could be done in that regard and came back with bad news. There was no chance the studio would allow Mitchell to pass judgment on the movie. As Cole explained to Marsh, authors do not generally have an instinct for what should go in a film scenario any more than a motion picture producer would know what should go in a novel. But, Cole assured him, Mitchell should not worry about the script. The studio people loved the book and wanted to follow it as closely as they could.[46] Considering that issue resolved, Cole went on vacation, leaving Putnam to await the signed document in the mail.

On July 23, with no contract in hand, Putnam wired Atlanta, asking if the Marshes had identified any further difficulties with the document. They had. In an eleven-page, single-spaced typed letter to Cole and Putnam, Marsh detailed a litany of problems that had to be resolved before Mitchell would consider signing the contract. Anticipating that his comments might raise a few hackles, Marsh began by stating that Mitchell did not doubt Selznick's good intentions. "This statement is made," he explained to Cole, "because of the fact that you yourself were somewhat disturbed over some of the changes [Mitchell] requested in the Macmillan contract [the previous summer], although these changes seemed entirely proper to us and Macmillan later agreed they were proper."[47]

The most significant point of contention, beyond script review, related to copyright issues. The draft contract contained basic factual errors including a statement that Mitchell was the copyright holder instead of Macmillan. The agreement also held Mitchell liable for any infringement claims made against Selznick, such as if someone claimed that a character in the film was based on a real person. The document imposed liability even if a problem arose through no fault of Mitchell's and, making matters worse, gave the author no right to intervene in any ensuing lawsuits. Thus, Marsh posited, if a person in New Zealand made a fraudulent claim of copyright infringement against Selznick, and the producer decided to settle for one million dollars, Mitchell would be on the hook for the judgment, regardless of whether the case had merit. He also worried that Mitchell would be liable for possible actions Selznick took to create an infringement. She stood behind *Gone With the Wind* but did not have any notion of "signing her life away by agreeing to a lot of unreasonable and unfair commitments and liabilities that ought not be asked of her." In addition, Marsh expressed concern over a provision giving Selznick rights to something called "commercial tie-ups." Unclear what this meant, Marsh wanted to ensure his wife retained the rights to her characters and that Selznick would not use her name to market any *GWTW*-themed products. "She would not like to discover herself endorsing 'Wade Hampton Hamilton Bran Flakes' or 'Scarlett O'Hara-Hamilton-Kennedy-Butler Toilet Water,'" he wrote. Marsh closed the exhaustively detailed letter, "And I hope the job of getting the contract revised and signed won't be as laborious as the job of getting this very long letter written."[48]

Given the time crunch, Marsh and Putnam tried to resolve the issues by telephone but were unable to make much progress. They considered using telegrams, but Marsh feared the wire operators were responsible for feeding rumors to the press. The only other option was to negotiate in person. Marsh was busy with work at the power company, and so it fell to Mitchell and her brother to make a trip to New York.

The Big Apple was the last place on earth Mitchell wanted to be that July. Exhausted from the excitement still swirling around *Gone With the*

*Wind*, she abhorred the prospect of a long train ride in the summer heat and lamented not having time to buy any decent clothes to wear. Nonetheless, she resolved to go and straighten out what she deemed "the stupidest contract" she had ever seen, a document "no rational person could sign, regardless of the amount of money involved."[49] She would lose her mind, she swore, "if this thing isn't settled soon."[50] On July 28, the siblings boarded a train for New York.

The following morning, the two reported to Selznick's Park Avenue offices, where they were met by Cole and Richard Brett. Also present was J. Swords, an attorney from Cadwalader, Wickersham & Taft, a firm that often advised the publisher on copyright matters. Noticeably absent was Harold Latham, who remained on vacation and had expressed no interest in the movie contract after having disclosed Williams's involvement. Williams was there, but Mitchell refused to acknowledge the Texan as her agent. In Mitchell's mind, Brett and Swords represented her, and Williams was there solely on behalf of Macmillan. That said, there was no hostility between the women. They chatted about their Southern heritage and discovered that Williams's husband's grandfather had served in the same Confederate Army company with Mitchell's grandfather.[51]

On the other side of the table were Brown and Selznick's attorneys John F. Wharton and M. D. Mermin. Neither of the Mitchell siblings was a shrinking violet, yet they could not help but be intimidated going up against this crowd. In the author's words, they were "as ignorant as a babe unborn" about the issues before them.[52] Wharton, one of the top theatrical lawyers in the country, posed particular concern.[53] As Stephens Mitchell described the scene decades later, "All of a sudden there I was—wham! I had never done a movie contract before."[54] Despite their nerves, the Mitchells found all of the "Selznickers," as they dubbed them, pleasant, especially Brown.[55] Years later, Stephens Mitchell admitted to Brown that he and his sister had been impressed the moment they met her: "Margaret and I had not been in New York fifteen minutes in July 1936 before we both whispered to each other that you were the smartest person around . . . so we decided to get you on our side when we could."[56] They struck up a friendship with Brown, even sharing cocktails with her during the trip.

The convivial atmosphere did not signal smooth sailing though. Using Marsh's lengthy letter as his guide, Stephens Mitchell went over their concerns point by point. As Cole had warned, Selznick wanted to stick with the standard contract. The request for script review was a nonstarter, and the studio dismissed complaints about the copyright problems as hypertechnical. The Mitchells turned for guidance to Brett and Swords but found little support. Macmillan seemed to agree with the studio that the contract was fine.[57] By the end of the day, the only issue the Mitchells obtained any satisfaction on was the tie-ups. The studio representatives clarified that the term referred to dolls, toys, and other such articles based on the characters in the movie. Stephens Mitchell took this to mean that his sister retained the rights to her characters as used in the book and let the issue drop.[58]

The author and her brother were exhausted, their resolve weakening. They had traveled all this way to negotiate terms and were being stonewalled, not only by the studio but also by Macmillan, Mitchell's agent. That evening, they rehashed the day's events at supper with Cole and Allan Taylor. Weighing heaviest on Stephens Mitchell's mind was whether they should hold out for more money. Not having any official advisory role, Cole spoke frankly as a friend of the family. She did not think Selznick would raise his offer but proposed an idea for getting him to sweeten the pot. Pointing out that the studio had included the theatrical and radio rights to *Gone With the Wind* among those Mitchell was transferring to Selznick, Cole suggested that the author carve them out from this deal. Cole predicted these rights might prove valuable in the future and suggested that, if Selznick wanted them later, he could pay for them separately.[59]

Stephens Mitchell took seriously the responsibility of protecting his sister's interests and wanted to judge for himself what the movie rights were worth. The following morning, he called on several movie production offices to get a sense of what other deals might be out there. He quickly realized he was in over his head. None of the people he visited knew who he was, and he had difficulty getting their attention. He did not elicit any offers more than fifty thousand dollars. One company said it was absurd to think the rights were worth that much and offered him thirty-five thousand.[60]

Unsure how to proceed, the Mitchells telephoned home for guidance. Marsh, with the benefit of physical distance, saw things in clear terms: if his wife was not happy with the deal, they should come home. But it was not so simple for the siblings, being in the thick of the discussions. They worried that rejecting the contract would make Macmillan look bad and hurt sales of the book. Also, fifty thousand dollars was a lot of money, more than they ever dreamed possible.[61] Stephens Mitchell later described their mind-set: "The panic was on and had hardly let up."[62]

The two returned to the negotiating table and, as Cole had suggested, asked to keep the dramatic and radio rights. When Selznick's representatives countered that she could keep the stage rights, the Atlantans agreed to close the deal despite the problems with the document. The author knew that, if she left New York without signing, the move rights would be a constant source of irritation in the future. She also accepted that the studio did not want her involved with the movie's production and grudgingly had come to see this as a positive: it would be one less problem for her to handle. According to her brother, "She did not want the worries which Hollywood could bring to her. So she would not bother them, and they should not bother her. They had the movie rights; she had the $50,000 less commissions; and we were all happy."[63] Putting a bright spin on the situation, Marsh wrote that day to Brickell and Granberry: "Peggy went to New York . . . to take the Selznick scalp and has taken it."[64]

# 7

## That Book About the Wind

### *August–October 1936*

Consistent with Margaret Mitchell's wishes, Macmillan refused to release the sales price for the movie rights. But it did proclaim with obvious pride that Mitchell had earned the highest amount paid for a book by a first-time author. In the wake of the movie deal announcement, *Gone With the Wind* became the most talked-about subject in America. According to journalist Frank Luther Mott, the interest reached such a level that anyone who admitted to not having read the book was left out of conversations, missed the point of jokes, and was treated as "an illiterate outsider." In self-defense, the uninitiated hurried to the nearest bookstore.[1]

Demand for the book grew frenzied. People clamored for copies of *Gone With the Wind*, although in some cases they struggled to remember its exact title. Bookstore clerks received requests for "Wind in the Night," "One Windy Night," "The Wind Blows," or "that book about the wind."[2] The early concerns about the three-dollar price were for naught. People who could not afford the book either swamped libraries, where waiting lists stretched for weeks, or pooled their money to buy copies to share. Mitchell's novel also became the fashionable gift du jour. A woman about to embark on a trip to Europe received nine copies before she set sail on an ocean liner.[3] And she was not the only one enjoying her trip with Scarlett and Rhett as company. Macmillan estimated that, on a single day in July, close to one thousand copies had been purchased by or for passengers on transatlantic ships departing from New York.[4]

Macmillan Canada, likewise, experienced unparalleled demand for

*Gone With the Wind.* The company quickly sold out its first order of a thousand copies and rushed to import more sheets. Given that the average book in Canada sold 250 to 350 copies in that era, it was a remarkable achievement. After producing more than seventeen thousand copies of its own edition that summer and fall, Macmillan Canada gave up and began importing copies of the American edition.[5]

Macmillan felt certain publishing sales records were being broken. Popular wisdom held that the bestselling novel in the United States up to that point was *Anthony Adverse,* by Hervey Allen. Its publisher had received advance orders of fifteen thousand copies and sold up to two thousand copies a day for a total of 235,000 in six months.[6] *Gone With the Wind* already had more than two hundred thousand copies in print four weeks after its release, and there were no signs of the pace slowing. Macmillan publicly claimed victory, implicitly challenging other publishers to come forth and identify a book that had sold more quickly in the United States. None raised its hand.

Being in uncharted territory, there were no rules for Macmillan to follow on how to manage or sustain this level of intensity. The sales team had to think on its feet and figure things out as it went along. The first order of business was making sure Macmillan had enough books to satisfy the demand. Even though it churned out copies around the clock, the firm could not keep up with the orders. Not willing to risk any going unfulfilled, the firm contracted with an additional printer and bindery to handle the overload.[7]

Some publishers might have worried that *Gone With the Wind* was close to reaching its saturation point, but Macmillan continued to market the book with verve.[8] One stunt of which Alec Blanton's sales team would be proud for years to come was hiring an airplane on Labor Day weekend to fly over beaches from New Jersey to Connecticut, pulling a trailer of sixteen-foot-high kites urging sunbathers to read *Gone With the Wind.* As the publisher turned out each new printing, it issued press releases and print ads announcing the latest astounding figures. The firm also updated the front of the book's dust jacket by adding the *New York Times* quote about the book's readability and a tally line along the bottom—such as "Eight Printings . . . 201,000 Copies"—to track the ever-increasing totals.* On

---

* Macmillan did not, however, disclose the number of copies sold to anyone except the author. Sales figures are typically tabulated once a year, when returns are accounted for and it is time to pay royalties. On occasion, the press failed to understand the distinction and oversensationalized the figures by reporting the number of copies printed as the number sold. However, with demand outpacing production, the distinction proved a

the back of the jacket, Macmillan replaced the list of its other spring novels with enthusiastic reviews for *Gone With the Wind*.

To reach rural consumers not exposed to the major urban newspapers, Macmillan began advertising in popular weekly magazines such as *Time* and a monthly journal issued by the Elks Club, a fraternal organization with chapters all over the country.[9] Not only would subscribers see the ads, but so would people flipping through these publications in libraries, waiting rooms, beauty parlors, and barber shops. Macmillan also expanded its reach into the regional newspapers in cities such as Baltimore, Cleveland, Dallas, Detroit, Pittsburgh, and Richmond. The publisher urged local booksellers to keep the book in stock and feature it prominently in window and counter displays. Macmillan promised strong sales would be rewarded with additional advertising dollars; no outlet was too small to benefit from "the golden windfall" of *Gone With the Wind*.[10]

Booksellers in Southern cities needed little encouragement. They jumped on the Mitchell bandwagon, creating eye-catching window displays featuring Confederate flags and memorabilia. They developed promotional gimmicks to bring book buyers into the stores. In Texas, for example, retailers vied for customers by offering live *Gone With the Wind* reviews. Sanger Brothers Department Store in Dallas sponsored a presentation by a recent attendee of Columbia University. A rival store, Titche-Goettinger Company, set a record for local literary events when a woman named Evelyn Oppenheimer spoke about her impressions of *Gone With the Wind* to a standing-room-only crowd. More than two thousand people filled the aisles, stage, and doorways of the store's auditorium. Hundreds more were turned away. The program proved so popular that the store scheduled four encore performances.[11]

Northern stores reportedly did not get quite so carried away. One Macmillan representative in the Northeast suggested to Lois Cole that she "get a corner on Stars and Bars bunting" to send around to retailers to perk

---

minor one. As with many sales figures from yesteryear, a note of caution is warranted. Even documents and letters in the publisher's files cannot always be taken at face value. From the beginning, sometimes the running totals figures added to the dust jackets and the printing history inside the books did not match each other and often did not match Macmillan's official records or its print ads. But it is understandable how the ever-changing figures sometimes got ahead of the typesetters and Blanton's advertising staff. Sales departments at Macmillan's main office in New York and at the branch offices across the country took orders over the telephone, as well as juggled requests from sales reps in the field and from individual bookstores, all using pen and paper, not computers and spreadsheets.

things up. But even without the frippery, Northern stores had little difficulty finding buyers. Macmillan's reputation and the enthusiastic press reviews were enough to sway even skeptical Yankees. A bookseller in Lancaster, Pennsylvania, reported that a customer browsing a *Gone With the Wind* display commented that she did not know anything about the author, but "Maximillian's" always published good books.[12] When Cole heard the tale, she pondered, "Do you think the lady in Lancaster was confusing our august house with the late demented emperor?"[13]

Sales of Mitchell's book were so remarkable in all sections of the country that John Marsh wondered if *Gone With the Wind* might "prove to be the new industry that will help to pull the nation out of the depression."[14] He was not far off, at least regarding the publishing world. The stock market crash of 1929 had devastated the book business. The industry's saving grace had been bestsellers such as *Anthony Adverse* that helped generate traffic in struggling stores. Customers came in to buy a bestseller and often walked away with another book as well. These blockbusters are sometimes referred to as vitamins of the publishing industry. Using that analogy, *Gone With the Wind* was an extra-strength multivitamin.

Bookstores were not the only ones looking for an energy boost. One side effect of the bestseller phenomenon was that nonbook retailers, such as drugstores and department stores, often used a popular book's success to pull customers into their stores. An old industry yarn tells the story of a flapper looking to buy lipstick who walked into a bookstore and excused herself when she realized that she had made a mistake: "I'm sorry, I thought this was a drugstore, I saw books in the window."[15] In the case of *Gone With the Wind*, a variety of retailers bought vast quantities of the book hoping to lure customers. *Publishers Weekly* reported that book sales at Macy's department store in New York that summer were the highest since 1928. The book buyer at Gimbel's reported that its book business had been going up since June, July was "exceptionally good," and August was better than any year since 1928. She predicted steady book sales that fall and a merry Christmas for Gimbel's.[16]

As *Gone With the Wind*'s popularity continued to build steam that fall, department stores and drugstores began slashing the price on Mitchell's novel. They did not care if they made a profit on the book as long as they could use the title to draw customers into their establishments. In October, one of Mitchell's roommates from her Smith College days, Ginny Morris, wrote saying that Macy's was in the midst of "an exciting price war" over the book. The store kept changing the price every few hours to make sure it could advertise the best deal in New York. She reported the markdown had gone as low as eighty-nine cents, and gamblers were issuing wagers on what the price would be at any given hour as a way to relieve the monotony of wagering on "football pools and election odds."[17] Reports circulated in the press that copies were being sold for as low as sixty-nine cents in some cities.[18]

The price cutting became so aggressive that it posed a serious problem for traditional book retailers who could not afford to be so liberal with their pricing. One bookseller in North Carolina complained to *Publishers Weekly* that *Gone With the Wind* had sold well for her until a nearby drugstore priced the book at $1.98. She had fought all through the Depression to maintain high standards in her inventory, never carrying cheap books or office supplies to defray her losses. Now, she wondered, whether she should offer specials on vegetable shortening and coffee to get people in the door.[19] Mom-and-pop bookstores demanded action from Macmillan, insisting that the firm force its vendors to accept a minimum price below which the book could not be sold.

Although sympathetic to their plight, Macmillan did not have much incentive to take action. The price wars were a much-followed story in the media, all to the greater good of bringing publicity to the book. In any event, there was not much the company could do to prevent price cutting given that most states allowed the practice. Some had enacted anti-price-cutting laws in recent years, but in many instances, the statutes had been challenged on constitutional grounds. Litigation was pending, and until those cases were resolved, Macmillan's hands were tied. The company tried to assuage complaints by running an announcement in *Publishers Weekly* asserting that the situation was temporary and should not have an undue effect on traditional booksellers. Macmillan put a bright spin on things, claiming most people preferred to purchase books at full price from a reputable bookstore, where they could have the volumes wrapped and shipped as presents, a service many discount retailers did not provide.[20]

The U.S. Supreme Court finally resolved the problem in early 1937 when it upheld the anti-price-cutting laws, and several states, including New York, moved quickly to authorize manufacturers to set prices on their goods. Macmillan bowed to industry demands and established a three-dollar retail price on *Gone With the Wind*, a decision to which Macy's did not take kindly. The retail giant had more than thirty-seven thousand copies of the book in stock that had been purchased prior to Macmillan setting the price floor. The store suggested that if Macmillan did not want Macy's selling the book at a discount it should buy the books back.[21] Macmillan agreed, and the store returned almost thirty-six thousand copies. Macy's also canceled a previously placed order for an additional ten thousand copies.[22] Relations between Macmillan and Macy's suffered, but Macmillan shed no tears over the rift. Thousands of retailers snapped up the returned copies and happily sold the book at its full retail price.

One place Mitchell failed to generate much attention in the summer of 1936 was England. By the end of July, Macmillan London still had not released its edition of *Gone With the Wind*. Although the two Macmillan firms had not agreed to a specific publication date, common sense suggested that the London house would rush the book's release to take advantage of its enthusiastic reception in North America. When Mitchell began asking questions, James Putnam agreed to find out what was going on and to stir up the Brits.[23] He was surely not happy to learn that, although the British publisher already had the books printed, it planned to hold the release for another month. Also disappointing, the British house had ordered a first run of only three thousand copies and did not sound optimistic that a second run would be necessary.[24] On August 25, Putnam gave Marsh the unhappy news that the British edition would not make its debut until September 29. He tendered the weak excuse that maybe the delay gave the London house additional time to build anticipation for the book.[25] Insult was added to injury when Mitchell realized she had never received her advance from London. When she raised the issue with Macmillan New York, it must have been unsettling to learn that the check had been sent to the U.S. firm but nobody had bothered to credit the funds to her account.[26] Although a simple mix-up, it was one of many wakeup calls the Marshes received that they needed to be vigilant in protecting Mitchell's interests.

At the opposite end of the excitement spectrum from Macmillan London, David O. Selznick could barely contain himself in his eagerness to capitalize on *Gone With the Wind*. As the book catapulted into publishing history that summer, his purchase of the movie rights for fifty thousand dollars now seemed a tremendous bargain. Twentieth Century-Fox and Warner Brothers offered to buy the rights from him, but Selznick refused to sell, even at double what he paid.[27] Great things were in store for Scarlett and Rhett, and he intended to go along for the ride.

Selznick was wrapping up one film and beginning work on another, so he knew it would be months before he could turn his full attention to *Gone With the Wind*. He asked his staff to keep the fires of public interest stoked. That September, the studio arranged for a scene from the book to air on CBS Radio. Popular movie stars Robert Montgomery and Constance Bennett were hurriedly cast in the lead roles, earning them the distinction of being the first actors to bring Scarlett and Rhett to life. But they would not be afforded the honor of immortalizing the famous lovers on screen. Selznick wanted to create a sense of excitement about the film's casting and, through his publicist Russell Birdwell, planted items in the Hollywood gossip columns that the producer was looking for fresh faces for many of the roles in the film. The studio's efforts succeeded beyond Selznick's wildest imagination. The producer was flooded with mail about the project. Actors begged for the opportunity to bring Mitchell's characters to life on the big screen. Moviegoers suggested which of their favorite stars should be cast in the picture. By the end of the year, he had received seventy-five thousand letters about *Gone With the Wind*.[28]

Macmillan, of course, welcomed Selznick's efforts to draw attention to Mitchell's book. A representative of the publisher's San Francisco office told Birdwell that the producer's campaign was one of the best, if not the best, he had ever seen. Delighted with the compliment, Birdwell suggested that the two firms should put their heads together and develop ideas that would prove mutually beneficial. He promised that Macmillan could count on Selznick to fully "exploit" *Gone With the Wind*.[29]

Exploitation is a word to which Mitchell could relate. With Selznick and Macmillan pushing the publicity over the movie deal that August, the pressure on her grew unbearable. The phone continued to ring around the clock. People begged for her autograph wherever she went. Invitations for her to give speeches arrived on a daily basis. The press hounded her for interviews. Marsh responded to a *Time* magazine inquiry on August 3 with a telegram indicating she had had enough: "MRS MARSH SICK IN BED AS RESULT OF STRAIN OF BECOMING FAMOUS TOO SUD-DENLY."[30] Mitchell was suffering from a severe case of eyestrain and, under doctor's orders, needed to rest in a dark room with a bandage over her eyes.

Heeding Marsh's earlier warning about what would happen if Macmillan did not shield Mitchell from the glare of the spotlight, Cole and Putnam did what they could to divert attention from the weary author. When fans sent books to Macmillan asking for the author's signature, they refused to forward them. Putnam declined to turn over Mitchell's contact information to the many people asking for it, including the prestigious Bread Loaf Writers' Conference.[31] Cole discouraged anyone who wanted to offer Mitchell writing assignments, even their mutual alma mater, Smith College, which hoped the author would write a short piece for its alumnae magazine. Cole also refused to write the piece herself, knowing Mitchell did not want any more publicity and would not appreciate her capitalizing on their relationship. Putnam wrote Marsh on August 11, proclaiming to understand the author's reluctance to join the media hype: "I personally cannot but feel that if she had been the sort of person who could she might never have written the book she did—so let those who can, satisfy the curiosity of the mob, and let her rest on her laurels, or better yet behind them for they are certainly piled up high enough to serve as an excellent screen."[32] He hoped that her eyes improved rapidly and assured Marsh that his wife's reluctance to be in the public arena was of no importance.

With such a gentle hand, Cole and Putnam might have eventually drawn Mitchell out of her shell. While she was not ever likely to embrace the spotlight, they harbored hope of her returning to New York that fall for some sort of publicity event. It would look odd if she did not make any appearance, and they were doing their best to keep Mitchell happy so she would be willing when the time came. The ultimate test of Macmillan's patience with its new star author was yet to come though. There were still issues to deal with on the movie contract, and it is here Mitchell would learn how far her publisher was willing to go—or not go—on her behalf.

After signing the movie contract, Mitchell returned to Atlanta confident she had done the right thing. The bloom quickly faded from the rose though when rumors spread that Selznick had been willing to pay more than $100,000 and that other studios had offered Selznick $150,000 for the rights.[33] Mitchell bristled at stories that she had been swindled by the slick movie company.[34] Her discontent grew when the Mitchell-Marsh family reviewed the contract again and realized there were many "pits and deadfalls" in the document that could come back to haunt the author, in addition to those they had identified in July.[35] Marsh asked several pointed questions that his brother-in-law could not answer. "When Margaret sat down with us and talked, it was apparent that we had not known what was happening, and that the contract was an onerous one," Stephens Mitchell said years later.[36]

One clause that stood out was a provision they dubbed the "God Almighty clause," which required Margaret Mitchell to protect *Gone With the Wind's* copyright even in foreign countries. The Marshes understood why Selznick included the provision—it offered him comfort that foreign movie producers would not be able to release their own cinematic versions of Mitchell's story to compete with his. But, the Atlantans thought, it was absurd to expect the author, who knew nothing about international copyright law, to take on responsibility for fighting foreign movie producers. In any event, Macmillan owned the copyright both in the United States and abroad and, therefore, ought to be the one protecting those interests. Stephens Mitchell accepted responsibility for having let Richard Brett and J. Swords gloss over the copyright problems and placed the blame on himself for his sister ending up in such a mess.

Not willing to admit Selznick got the best of her, Margaret Mitchell refused to ask the producer for concessions. The Mitchell family honored its contracts. But she did have a bone to pick with Macmillan for letting her sign the burdensome document. The publisher had talked her into selling the rights, so she expected the firm to step in and fix the situation by assuming responsibility for protecting its own copyright. Not only was this fair, it made practical sense as well. Macmillan was far better qualified than she to track copyright renewal deadlines and the intricacies of international copyright law.[37] Marsh wrote to Putnam the first week of August, presenting the situation to him. Hoping to keep Mitchell happy, the amiable Putnam felt sure the technical points could be adjusted satisfactorily. Macmillan would be glad to do anything it could to relieve worry on Mitchell's part. He noted, however, that the matter would have to be resolved by George Brett, Jr., who was on vacation.[38]

The situation simmered on the back burner for several weeks until Brett returned to the office. But even then, the publisher did not focus on Mitchell's complaints about the Selznick contract. His father had taken ill and died suddenly on September 19. Distracted, Brett did not take the time to investigate what had transpired on the movie deal before formulating a response to Marsh's demand. Based on what Brett knew of the negotiations, which apparently was not much, he saw no reason for Macmillan to get involved. If the author did not like the movie deal, she should blame her agent, Annie Laurie Williams, or her lawyer, Stephens Mitchell. Brett acknowledged that Macmillan had originally agreed to act as broker in the negotiations but took the position that the publisher absolved itself of responsibility when Williams was substituted for Macmillan in that capacity.

Moreover, because Mitchell brought her own lawyer to New York, Brett asserted that the Macmillan lawyer participated in the negotiations only on behalf of the publishing company.[39] In other words, tough luck.

On September 21, the day of the senior Brett's funeral, Stephens Mitchell, in his role as the author's legal counsel, responded to the publisher. The lawyer blasted back at the junior Brett's characterization of events. Apparently not aware there had been a death in the Brett family, the lawyer pulled no punches. In an eight-page missive, he set forth in excruciating detail how the movie contract came to be signed under the auspices of Macmillan acting as the author's agent. When he and his sister arrived in New York, they were met by Macmillan representatives, all arrangements were made by Macmillan, and they were accompanied by Macmillan personnel every step of the way. During the negotiations, neither Richard Brett nor the Macmillan lawyer denied being her agent, though that term had been used throughout the meetings. As for Williams, the Mitchells never had any business discussions with her or otherwise dealt with her as an agent. Giving George Brett the benefit of the doubt, Stephens Mitchell assumed the publisher had not been aware of these facts when he wrote his initial response. With the correct information now before him, the author's brother demanded that Brett reconsider his position. Anything less than a retraction would have serious repercussions: "Mrs. Marsh's present and future dealings with your company on other matters will unavoidably be affected by her ability to feel the same confidence in The Macmillan Company in the future that she has felt in the past."[40]

Upon receipt of this written assault, Brett delved deeper into the matter and realized he had misstated the essential facts. He called Stephens Mitchell to apologize and extended an olive branch by inviting him to New York at Macmillan's expense to talk through the movie contract. They were on the verge of reconciling when the author's brother pushed his luck. He wrote Brett that he would be pleased to come to New York with the understanding that Macmillan would pay his travel expenses, as well as the billable hours he had spent drafting the September 21 letter and the time he would spend away from the office for their meeting.[41]

To those familiar with the Mitchell-Marsh family, this response was nothing unusual. Stephens Mitchell had a good sense of humor, as one of his law partners recalled years later, unless "he suspected someone was trying to take advantage of him. . . . [Then] he could be as rough as a cob."[42] The Mitchells took pride in being meticulous in their affairs and keeping a careful eye on every penny. If they were owed money, they expected to be paid.

If they owed a debt, they paid it when due. Brett would come to learn that this scrupulousness was part of the family's unique charm. However, he did not see it that way at the time. He was incensed by the lawyer's gall and wrote back, telling him once again, in effect, to get lost.

Oblivious to how their fastidiousness came across to others, the Atlantans were at a loss to understand Brett's reaction. The publisher seemed "highly incensed about something," Margaret Mitchell acknowledged, but she could not figure out what.[43] If Brett did not want her brother to come to New York, why had he asked him to? If he objected to the attorney's fees, why had he said all expenses would be paid?

With Harold Latham still on vacation, Cole was stuck squarely in the middle. Her husband, Allan Taylor, wrote to Mitchell on October 3, explaining that Cole came home from work "pretty much cut up" over the discord between her boss and friend. Out of concern for Cole's nerves, Taylor tried to act as an intermediary by assuring the author that she was misjudging Brett. Taylor described the publisher as a fair-minded person, "a nice chap and a gentleman, with many qualities that a southerner in particular would appreciate." If Mitchell assumed that he was some "slick Yankee trying to do anybody in," she was off base. "Like a lot of other people he is pleasant to deal with when he figures he is being met halfway, but like most of the rest of us, he may be inclined to get his back up when he thinks he is being pushed around. He is not a lawyer, remember. . . . He is a nice fellow, with normal human reactions." Taylor hoped that with this perspective, Mitchell might be willing to make peace with Brett.[44]

Mitchell respected Taylor's opinions but was not ready to mend fences. She had been frustrated with Macmillan on several occasions over the previous year but had kept things on a professional level. As long as they were working toward a common goal—the success of *Gone With the Wind*—she could overlook many things. Here, for the first time, Mitchell took Macmillan's position personally. Her trust was damaged. Apparently unwilling to discuss matters with Brett any further, she looked to Latham to make things right.

After all, the editor was arguably at fault for the entire situation. He was the one who convinced her to sell the movie rights and to let Macmillan represent her, then dropped out of sight on an extended vacation, from which he had yet to return. If Latham had been in New York throughout the summer, they would likely not have reached such a perilous point. The editor could have made sure Mitchell's concerns about script review were vetted earlier in the negotiations. He could have counseled Mitchell during the New York meeting more sensitively than had Richard Brett and the Macmillan lawyer. And, after the fact, he almost certainly would have handled matters more gently than did George Brett.

Yet, she did not browbeat Latham into fixing the mess he had helped create. In her dealings with him, she always used her best manners. On September 23, 1936, she wrote the editor, begging his pardon for bothering him, but stating there was a serious matter he needed to know about. She described how Brett had denied that Macmillan was her agent and how "upsetting and distressing" this had been. She reminded Latham, "as you know, I was besieged with requests from people wanting to be my agent, Miss Williams among others. I refused them all and would never have had any agent had you not offered the service of Macmillan."[45] She did not criticize Latham for his lack of attentiveness on such a crucial matter or ask him for any form of assistance. She closed by stating that she just thought he should know.

She followed up with another, much chattier, letter two days later. She asked the editor for his advice about the serial rights to her book and inquired about his vacation. She continued for two pages in a friendly tone with no mention of the movie contract. Only in the closing paragraph did she broach the subject of her discontent. It must be one of the most artful rebukes ever written:

> The end of your vacation is drawing near, I suppose and how sorry you must be! But what a grand long one it was! I envy you your vacation. I only hope that some time, some day I'll be well enough to take one and that the pressure of work will let up on John so that he can get away, too. His work has been doubled because of my eye trouble for he has had to do so much of my work. He's fagged and so am I.[46]

Then, in a postscript, she mentioned the elephant in the room: "As you can see, I am still writing to you frankly and freely about things on my mind, in spite of my disagreement with The Macmillan Company. . . . I certainly hope that difficulty can be cleared up promptly, for I want to regain the feeling of confidence in The Macmillan Company which I have had all along until that trouble arose."[47]

On October 6, the day Latham returned to the office after his four-month absence, he read Mitchell's letters and also got an earful from his co-workers about what had gone on in his absence. Eager to quell the unrest, he wrote Mitchell that same day stating how relieved he was, given all that had happened, that she had written him in such candid terms. He assured the author that everyone at Macmillan remained enthusiastic about her work and he was at her service for any advice and assistance she might need. That said, Latham did not accept responsibility for what had happened, nor did he agree with Mitchell's description of herself as the innocent victim. In the first place, Macmillan did not appreciate her unleashing her lawyer brother on the company. Never in his twenty-five years in the publishing business, he said, had the firm been required to deal with an author's lawyer. He professed to have difficulty expressing the hurt feelings that his associates felt over the matter. Latham also let her know that she had nothing to complain about as far as Macmillan's efforts on her behalf: "If I can say so without appearing to brag, I think that we have done a job of publishing for you which could not have been done by any publisher in America." He related how that very afternoon a man who had been in publishing for forty years stopped him on the street and congratulated him, saying that Macmillan's work on *Gone With the Wind* was the best promotion job he had seen in his entire career.[48]

Latham then considered the issue at hand—whether his absence over the previous months was at the root of Mitchell's complaints with the movie contract. He concluded probably not. Holding the party line, he claimed that Macmillan had been her agent only in obtaining the offer but that she had been represented in the sale negotiations by her own lawyer, as if the mere act of bringing her brother to the meeting had terminated the agency relationship with Macmillan. Regardless of whether Latham could have prevented the problem or whose fault it was, he wanted the damage repaired. Matters were now in the hands of the lawyers, so he worried about the propriety of writing to her in such a personal and frank manner but felt it was necessary if they were to resume the cordial relationship they had enjoyed over the previous year. He and everyone at Macmillan wanted the "misunderstandings" cleared up.[49]

What were Latham's feelings about the discord between Mitchell and Macmillan? On the face of it, he seemed to want to make amends despite Brett's position. Though some sources have cast Latham in the role of Mitchell's white knight, he was a Macmillan employee, and that is where his primary loyalties lay. In fact, Latham ran his letter by Brett before sending it to Mitchell. Brett, in turn, had the company's legal counsel review the reply.[50] While that does not negate the sincerity of the sentiments expressed, it does highlight Latham's conflicted position and belies his claim that the letter was personal.

Although never admitting error, Macmillan was willing to make one concession—Mitchell could take back the foreign rights to her novel. If she accepted them, she would be entitled to keep all the royalties on any translations, thus making her obligation to protect the foreign copyrights under the "God Almighty clause" in the Selznick contract less unfair.[51] In discussing the transfer with the Marshes, Brett downplayed the gesture, saying that foreign rights were often not worth the nuisance they caused.[52] He also structured the return of rights to protect Macmillan's interests. Mitchell could have them provided she ensured all foreign translations would (1) contain the Macmillan copyright notice, and (2) never be distributed within the United States.

The Marshes took the gesture—whatever lay behind it—at face value. The couple had no clear idea of what to do with the foreign rights or whether they would prove profitable but thanked Macmillan for its "generous attitude" and accepted Brett's conditions. What the Marshes did not realize is that, as a practical matter, these were terms with which Mitchell could never guarantee compliance. She had no control over what publishers did or did not include in their books and she certainly had no way of preventing foreign books from being distributed in the United States. Further evidence of their naïveté was revealed when she signed the papers accepting the rights. The transfer instrument contained a standard legalese provision stating that the agreement was reached "in consideration of the sum of one dollar to each in hand paid." When Marsh sent Cole the signed agreement, he enclosed a check for one dollar.[53] Latham returned the check to him, explaining that the reference to exchanging dollars was a formality and did not require the transfer of any money. He pointed out that, if Macmillan accepted the check, it would have to send him its own check for one dollar.[54]

In accepting the return of the foreign rights from Macmillan, Mitchell resigned herself to being bound by the Selznick contract for better or worse. She could have fought harder for Macmillan to shoulder some of the obligations under the "God Almighty clause" but took no steps to escalate the antagonism brewing between her and the publisher. She did not have the energy for it, nor did she want to risk her complaints turning into a public controversy. However, this did not mean Macmillan and Selznick were off the hook for what she considered a bum deal.

# 8

~

# The Reluctant Celebrity

## Fall 1936

During the contract negotiations in July, the Selznick team asserted that Margaret Mitchell had no role to play in the life of *Gone With the Wind* as a motion picture. Almost as soon as she signed the contract, though, the studio realized the value the author could add to the movie's chances of success. The public had embraced this fresh, new literary star, and it would be an obvious mistake to distance the movie from Mitchell. Moreover, the studio needed her help. David O. Selznick wanted to preserve the historical authenticity of the book and had come to understand that the production could benefit from the author's guidance on everything from sets to costumes. Her assistance was also needed with the screenplay. The task of converting her massive book into a manageable script had been assigned to Sidney Howard, a Pulitzer Prize–winning dramatist and two-time Oscar nominee. As soon as he began writing, Howard agonized over where to make cuts. He desperately wanted Mitchell to guide him through the process.[1]

In the fall of 1936, Selznick offered to fly Mitchell to California to serve as a consultant on the movie. Given her request for script approval, he likely assumed the author would be thrilled. As would become a recurring pattern in his dealings with Mitchell though, Selznick's good intentions backfired. Instead of being appreciative, the author was appalled at his nerve in asking. After having been denied the contractual right of script approval, she had no intention of dropping everything and flitting off to California. Adding to her irritation were the continuing rumors that Selznick had taken

119

advantage of her in the movie deal. Since July, it had become clear she had sold for too little money and without an adequate understanding of the obligations the contract imposed on her. For the rest of her life she claimed to have no regrets about signing with Selznick, but Mitchell would have been superhuman not to have wondered how things might have differed if she had waited another month or two to sell the rights.

In this situation, it might seem odd that Mitchell did not use Selznick's predicament as an opportunity to right the wrongs she felt the contract had caused. She might have insisted on straightening out the "God Almighty clause," for example. She could have almost certainly extracted a handsome bonus from the studio. But that was not the Mitchell way. Her family signed contracts and stuck to them, and they expected others to do the same. So the author politely declined Selznick's offer. A stickler for good manners, she never rehashed any of her cause for discontent. She never even said "I told you so." She simply begged off, claiming her readers would get upset if she had anything to do with altering the story as originally written. She would not lift a finger to assist him in making his movie a success and certainly was not going to let him use her name to bring attention to the production. Mitchell expected that to be the end of it.

Had she been more direct with Selznick and expressed her dissatisfaction with the movie contract, the producer may have respected her wishes. For all his power and wealth, he was an affable fellow. And, as later events would make clear, he greatly admired Mitchell's work and wanted her to be happy. However, he failed to pick up on any resentment on her part and seemed unable to fathom that she did not want to weigh in on details of the production. To Mitchell's great annoyance, he ignored her protestations about not wanting to get involved, and the studio bombarded her with questions. But she remained firm and refused to offer any assistance. It was frustrating for both of them. She could not comprehend why he continued to bother her, and he could not understand why she was being so uncooperative. They would spend years figuring out how to come to terms with each other.

Macmillan, too, would have cause to regret not being more sensitive to Mitchell's displeasure with the movie deal. The Marshes felt that Macmillan had "put a blindfold over Peggy's eyes and tied her hands behind her back and delivered her over to Selznick."[2] John Marsh labeled the contract "bad and unfair" and said his wife never would have signed it except for Harold Latham's assurances that the firm would look after her. Marsh had warned

Lois Cole that Macmillan would pay a price if it did not handle Mitchell gently during these difficult days, and Marsh was nothing if not true to his word.

Before the book's release, the author had put Macmillan on notice that she was opposed to joining any dog-and-pony show the publisher had in mind for promoting her novel. She never wanted to be a celebrity and did not want to join her book in the spotlight. She had cooperated with Norman Berg during release week, but the question lurked as to what would happen next. Would she, as Macmillan hoped, come around and embrace her role as a bestselling author? After the debacle over the movie contract, Mitchell had little trouble saying no. Not being under contractual obligation to shill for Macmillan, she felt no desire to do so out of the goodness of her heart.

As the fall of 1936 approached, Mitchell let the company know that she would not insert herself into the public arena to help sell books. Although she had led Latham to believe she would come to New York for a promotional trip when the weather cooled, the plan never got off the ground. Throughout September and October, Mitchell maintained that her eyes were still in poor condition. She refused to attend any events, near or far, that involved a crowd. Rich's department store, which realized it had missed an opportunity by refusing to hold an autograph session during release week, offered to host a Margaret Mitchell Day including a special tea and reception in her honor. Mitchell declined without apology.[3]

Macmillan would have liked its star author to make an appearance that fall at the first *New York Times* Book Fair, a major industry event where the company could have trotted her out in all her glory. Knowing that would never happen, the publisher proposed instead to display a few *Gone With the Wind* manuscript pages in the Macmillan booth.[4] When Latham asked Mitchell to send pages for them to use, she claimed the final manuscript had never been returned to her. Panic ensued until Macmillan located the original document in a company vault. At that point, the author was so irritated that she did not want to approve the display, which she had not thought much of to begin with. Mitchell believed authors should be judged solely on their published books, not their drafts, notes, and other working papers. But she did not bother arguing and agreed to the proposal. Macmillan pulled out three pages and shipped the rest of the manuscript to Atlanta, insuring it for one thousand dollars.[5]

The book fair exhibit attracted a great deal of attention but gave Mitchell further cause for anger when Macmillan misplaced two of the pages. The publisher arranged to have the sheets displayed in a glass case each day and taken home at night for safekeeping by a Macmillan employee.[6] One morning, the staffer responsible for the pages inadvertently left two of them sitting on the display table, atop an open copy of the *Cambridge University Press Bulletin*. A visitor to the booth innocently picked up the bulletin—and the manuscript pages—and walked away. When the employee realized they were missing and how it had happened, she searched the crowd frantically, carrying with her another copy of the Cambridge booklet. She approached people she saw carrying the *Bulletin* and offered to swap copies, claiming the ones handed out earlier were damaged. "It took fifty-one tries and a lot of tact to retrieve the missing Mitchelliana," *Publishers Weekly* reported.[7]

When the author heard what happened, she vowed never again to let a single page of the manuscript leave her possession, threatening to burn the entire thing. She considered the document a personal and intimate record of her thought process and could not believe that Macmillan had been so careless. For the rest of her life she balked at sharing the manuscript with the public and declined repeated requests from institutions and collectors wanting to acquire the document, often claiming she had already destroyed portions of it.[8]

Keeping Mitchell's name in the press was good business for Macmillan, but the increasingly irritated author refused to cooperate in that regard as well. Reporters hounded her for interviews and photographs, many of the inquiries focusing on her personal life. Seeing no reason to have her private business on display for public consumption or to have her face appear in newspapers several times a week, she declined countless requests for interviews. She even turned down an invitation by the National Press Club to honor her at a luncheon or reception. The group had welcomed only one other woman in such a manner—Amelia Earhart upon her return from her first transatlantic flight—but Mitchell was not interested.[9] If she did interact with the press, it had to be for a specific reason, such as correcting rumors about her life. Even then she proceeded cautiously and made sure not to reveal too much. She famously refused to disclose her age, saying that all the public needed to know was that she was old enough to have written *Gone With the Wind*. In one case, she agreed to talk to an Atlanta friend writing an article for a Junior League magazine but insisted on approving the piece before publication. "I hope you'll understand when I ask you to omit mention of the cigarette in paragraph one," Mitchell wrote after reviewing a draft. Her father did not know she smoked, and she did not want him learning of her bad habit in the press. "Yes, I know that sounds foolish and Victorian but it's true! I wouldn't want him to be hurt about it."[10]

Macmillan was further dismayed when Mitchell declined offers from the *Saturday Review of Literature, Cosmopolitan, Redbook,* and *Ladies Home Journal,* among others, for her to write essays, articles, or short stories. To the publisher, these offers were a marketing godsend; Mitchell would be getting paid to give *Gone With the Wind* publicity. She said no to them all, appalled at the money being thrown at her to do nothing but slap her name on meaningless tripe. Some in the literary community judged her a fool for not cashing in, but Mitchell did not let any of this affect her. If she were going to put her name in print, it would be on something she was proud of, not a piece thrown together for promotional purposes.

Much to Macmillan's chagrin, Mitchell also refused to write a sequel to *Gone With the Wind.* The public was enthralled by the book's open ending and wanted to know if Scarlett and Rhett reunited. Finding it hard to believe there was no neat conclusion, people speculated that Mitchell was working on some form of continuation of the story. Rumor had it that she had written a final chapter readers could purchase from Macmillan for a dollar.[11] Others envisioned that she was writing a second book that told the rest of the story. A bookseller in North Carolina reported taking at least two hundred advance orders for the supposed sequel.[12] There was obviously a ready market for a continuation, but Mitchell would not fill that demand. She liked her story the way she had written it and did not relish being "assaulted on all sides by readers who wished the book to end in a clinch."[13] To a reader in Dallas who agreed Mitchell should leave the ending a mystery, the author expressed her gratitude: "So many people have said indignantly that I should have had a happy ending, so I am very glad you wrote that you appreciated the fact that I did not have 'Scarlett and Rhett holding hands across Melly's death bed.'"[14]

But many readers refused to accept that they would not be hearing more about Scarlett and Rhett. In November, a Missouri woman wrote the author, declaring Mitchell owed the public an answer to whether Rhett came back. The woman suggested, "How about a new book, 'Returned With the Tide,' in view of the fact that Rhett said he might go to England or some other port? I believe Scarlet [sic] has had enough hard knocks to make her see life in a different manner. . . . Please do not make her too good, but just soften her up a little so she will not appear as hard as nails on the surface."[15] A fan in North Carolina used rhyme to plead her case. She sent

Mitchell a poem about the novel, with a final stanza: "Your style I considered most pleasing / You are wonderfully clever I'd say / So please! Will you write us a sequel / To *Gone With the Wind* some other day."[16] No matter how demanding or witty the entreaty, the author could not be swayed.

It might appear Mitchell was cutting off her nose to spite her face by turning down so many lucrative opportunities. Regardless of how disappointed she was with Macmillan, her refusal to participate in the company's publicity efforts affected her bottom line as well as the publisher's. Yet, earning more money was the last thing on Mitchell's mind in the fall of 1936. Records indicate she took in more than $225,000 that year in *Gone With the Wind*–related income. This was a tremendous sum to the Marshes, who were used to living off John's power company salary. Mitchell once claimed that, when the big money began rolling in, her savings account contained only $2.75. She joked about walking into the bank with Selznick's massive check and startling the teller who had been handling her account for years. Going forward, she took care to break the news gently to the clerk when other large checks arrived.[17]

Though the Marshes welcomed their new financial security, there is a saying that the only thing wealth does for some people is make them worry about losing it. That would certainly prove true in Mitchell's case. It was the era of President Franklin Roosevelt's New Deal, a social reform program designed to bring the nation out of the Depression through massive federal spending. To pay for these initiatives, the government enacted enormous tax increases, setting the highest tax bracket at 79 percent. Mitchell fell among the higher tiers, which resulted in her having to turn over a substantial portion of her new income to the federal government. The Marshes struggled to figure out what, if anything, could be done to shelter some of the money and considered it one of the most stressful problems they faced that year.[18] Initially, they hoped to place Mitchell in a lower tax bracket by spreading the royalties out over the number of years she had spent working on the manuscript. They were dismayed to learn, however, that federal tax law did not allow authors to apportion royalties that way. The author's only hope of reducing her tax liability was to slow down the income stream. If her earnings dropped, her income tax rate would decrease, and she might be able to enjoy the fruits of her labors.[19] Until that happened, Mitchell had no incentive to take on additional paid work. As her own Scarlett O'Hara mused, "Death and taxes and childbirth! There's never any convenient time for any of them!"[20]

Macmillan did what it could to work around its reluctant author. Throughout the fall of 1936, it blamed Mitchell's absence on her ailing eyes and continued to market *Gone With the Wind* without her. To keep the momentum going, it updated the advertising campaign on a regular basis by adding timely new pitches to catch the public's attention. During the presidential election campaign, the firm proclaimed the novel "elected by acclamation." At Thanksgiving, Macmillan suggested the book would make an ideal "bread and butter" hostess gift. If there were any lingering concerns about the hefty three-dollar price, the publisher released ads declaring *Gone With the Wind* a great buy, worth five regular novels.

To fill some of the informational void caused by Mitchell's public reticence, the publisher created a booklet about her for reporters and fans who deluged the firm with questions.[21] *Margaret Mitchell and Her Novel* contained facts and figures about sales, an essay from Latham on how he secured the manuscript, reprints of several reviews, and a brief biographical essay about the author. The booklet also included a section in which Mitchell answered some of the most common inquiries people had about *Gone With the Wind*, including how to determine a first edition (it had to say May on the copyright page), where was the real Tara (there wasn't one), and, of course, did Scarlett get Rhett back (Mitchell claimed to have no idea).

It must have been to Macmillan's surprise—and relief—that the author's absence did not negatively affect the public's interest in her book. The publisher went back to press seven times in October and another four in November, increasing the individual press runs from twenty-five thousand copies to fifty thousand. If anything, Mitchell's refusal to make a spectacle of herself seemed to fuel curiosity about *Gone With the Wind*. The world was intrigued by the attractive and mysterious Southern author. As Berg remarked with amazement in November, "If all the articles on Margaret Mitchell's *Gone With the Wind*, and how it came to be written and published, were collected they would make a volume many times the size of the novel itself."[22]

Not so clear though is whether the "I-want-to-be-left-alone" routine worked to Mitchell's advantage. When the author declined to participate in Macmillan's promotional campaign, she spared herself some of the vagaries of celebrity authorship. She did not have to go on a lecture tour. She did not have to waste time writing fluff magazine pieces. However, that did not mean she was nestled away in her apartment safe from prying eyes. Months after the book's release, Mitchell remained besieged by fans and curiosity seekers. At all hours of the day and night, people called to speak to her or arrived at the apartment hoping to catch a glimpse of her. A woman from Philadelphia showed up one afternoon with a photographer and insisted that Mitchell pose with her shaking hands.[23] As the author described the situation to her brother, she felt like Stone Mountain, a popular Georgia tourist destination. Not being a celebrity gawker herself, none of the attention made sense to Mitchell. To James Putnam, she wrote, "Having so little curiosity about people, celebrities or otherwise, I will never understand strangers who ring the door bell and ask Bessie for 'just a peek' at me. I feel that this puts me in the class with an educated pig, a flea circus or a two-headed baby in a jar of alcohol."[24]

She was also buried in an avalanche of mail. On slow days, Mitchell received at least fifty letters, but the daily total was frequently triple or quadruple that. At times, there were six hundred letters in a single day. The mailman appeared before dawn some mornings, laden with special deliveries, telegrams, and letters that had accumulated the previous night. The volume of paper was so staggering within the confines of their apartment that the Marshes rented an efficiency unit in the building next door to use as an office and storage area.

Mitchell could not get over the many types of people who reached out to her. She received letters from all segments of society, rich and poor, young and old, and male and female, from doctors, judges, and teachers to elevator operators, garage mechanics, and clerks in what she called "Helpsy-Selfy" stores.[25] She was honored to hear from respected writers such as historian Douglas Southall Freeman and novelist Ellen Glasgow, as well as from fans in Canada, England, Germany, and Italy.[26] To her surprise, even children were enjoying the book; she claimed her mother would never have let her read such a story as a girl. But the author took comfort in the fact that the "sex angle" went over the heads of most children. She once described an eleven-year-old girl who had given a book report on *Gone With the Wind*, referring to madam Belle Watling's house as "the swankiest night club in Atlanta, run by a lady named Miss Watling who, I think, was sorta like a blues singer."[27]

The variety of topics about which people wrote was equally diverse. In addition to hundreds of letters about a sequel and casting for the movie, she received traditional fan letters containing testimonials of how the book had captured the public's attention. In September, a woman related her experience reading *Gone With the Wind* while on a Caribbean cruise. She was so wrapped up in the story she could not be bothered to sunbathe, play shuffleboard or ping-pong, or swim. When the novel got "too gripping," she took breaks walking around the ship's deck to calm herself. And the woman was not the only one onboard so enamored. She noticed a young couple on the sundeck, in their bathing suits, lying on their stomachs with a copy of Mitchell's book between them: "There in the glaring, broiling sun they can't leave the story long enough to save their eyesight," she wrote to the author. "They grunt at each other when ready for the pages to be turned."[28]

Other letters were of a practical nature, such as those from sharp-eyed readers who had noticed typographical or continuity problems in the book. One corrected her spelling of Cecilia, the famous ball in Charleston, South Carolina. At least two suggested she had erred by not giving Belle Watling a pet parrot. Many were curious about the pronunciation of Tara, Melanie, Scarlett, and even "wind" as used in the title. How had Mitchell chosen the names of her characters? What did the expression "broad-wife" mean? Was the story drawn from real life? Where was Aunt Pittypat's house and the real Tara? Had Melanie and Rhett had "carnal relations"? ("Dear me," Mitchell remarked to Cole after several people raised that issue, "even the most chaste women must avoid the appearance of evil and Melanie should never have closed that door.")[29]

Countless correspondents were curious about Mitchell's personal life, including many who wondered if they were related to her or had known her as a child. In a surprising number of cases, fans wanted the author to know about their personal lives. Wives reported that Rhett and Scarlett's failures had opened their eyes to problems in their own marriages and had moved them to mend estrangements. Husbands wrote that Rhett's loss of Scarlett, despite his love for her, had them worried that they might lose their own wives.[30]

People also wanted things from Mitchell. There were dozens of requests each week for the author to give speeches. Aspiring writers asked for advice. Published authors hoped she would review their books or write blurbs for their dust jackets. Strangers sought financial assistance. Some of the pleas were charitable in nature, such as a man who wanted money to help his wife get treatment for tuberculosis using a "new, very expensive" drug. Others asked for money because they assumed she had enough to go around.

Life outside her apartment had its travails as well. Fans recognized Mitchell everywhere she went.[31] Walking down the street, strangers stopped her to shake her hand and often as not asked intimate questions about her personal life. As Marsh described it, the whole world was "madly trying to find out what she likes to eat, what kind of underwear she prefers, what her hobbies are and other things that are nobody's business but hers."[32] And there were constant demands for signed books. "When I make a business appointment with someone they usually turn up staggering under a dozen copies which their friends have wished upon them," she bemoaned.[33]

So how did Macmillan's reluctant celebrity handle the onslaught? Oddly enough, not very reluctantly. While she did not have any interest in being a public figure, Mitchell embraced in an exceedingly warm and open way the public who approached her. When the phone rang, she answered it. Fans bold enough to knock on her apartment door were often invited in for a cup of tea. Students who wanted to ask her questions for book reports or articles in their school papers were granted interviews. The same approach applied to the letters. Except for those from obviously disturbed or rude people,★ Mitchell determined that nearly every one that had a legible return address deserved a response, in some cases a personal, handwritten note. She would not divulge intimate details of her own life and refused to state any opinion about Selznick's movie production but provided helpful responses to the many questions that came her way.

When it came to questions about her book, she answered most inquiries in detail, no matter how silly the question seemed. "Wind," in her title, she explained patiently, rhymed with *sinned* and *grinned*. She often provided insights into the story that she never otherwise made public. For example, she revealed to a reader that Rhett Butler's middle name was King, a question enticingly left unanswered in the story.† When a reader suggested Melanie must have known about Ashley and Scarlett's feelings for each other, she disagreed, saying that, for Melanie, "being the type of woman she was, it would have been impossible for her to dissemble even had she desired to do so."[34]

If a reader tried to nab her on errors in the historical details, the author was quick to defend herself. To a man who questioned her use of the term "La Grippe" to refer to influenza, Mitchell explained that she had interviewed many people who lived through the war who confirmed the word's usage during that time.[35] When *Time* magazine ran a letter to the editor taking Mitchell to task for her description of federal soldiers looting ceme-

---

★ She kept these letters in files labeled "Gems," "Curioso," and "Of all the gall."

† In their authorized sequels, Alexandra Ripley (*Scarlett*) settled on Kinnicutt, while Donald McCaig (*Rhett Butler's People*) went with Kershaw. Mitchell biographer Anne Edwards attempted to draw a link between Rhett's initials, R.K.B., and those of Mitchell's first husband, Berrien Kinnard "Red" Upshaw.

teries in Atlanta, the author replied, citing numerous references for her version of events.[36] She just as readily conceded error when appropriate, such
as when a reader pointed out an inconsistency in the scene where Scarlett
meets Frank Kennedy in Atlanta after the war. The text had Scarlett calling
Kennedy by his first name, supposedly for the first time, although she had
called him Frank several pages earlier. Mitchell graciously thanked anyone
who pointed out a mistake and made sure Macmillan made appropriate
adjustments in future printings.[37]

One topic she would not debate with readers was which portions of
her story had been inspired by actual people, places, and events. Mitchell
insisted her novel had been made up from whole cloth, saying she did not
care for authors who dragged their own feelings and experiences into fiction
books.[38] "Ever so often I am amused, and sometimes disconcerted, when
strangers meeting me tell me exactly whom I took some character from,"
she wrote. "It does me no good to deny it for the stranger always knows
more about the matter than I do."[39] She thought people ought to be more
generous and credit authors for having "even a little creative talent."[40] To
any reader who wrote proclaiming that a particular house served as the
inspiration for Tara or that a relative had been the real Rhett Butler, she
denied all such associations. In only two instances is she known to have
admitted specific inspirations for fictional scenarios. She said she based the
slave girl Prissy on a former Mitchell family maid and that she had placed
Scarlett and Rhett's house in Atlanta "vaguely . . . on Peachtree somewhere
between Forest Avenue and Ellis Street."[41]

Despite the press having publicly discussed ad nauseam the author's
reluctance to give speeches and make public appearances, Mitchell spent
countless hours declining invitations. She thought people should have
known better than to ask but felt each one deserved a detailed, timely, and
courteous explanation.[42] Pleas for handouts were also denied, subject to
occasional exceptions where the favor sought did not seem overreaching.
To a woman who asked for a handkerchief to be auctioned off for charity,
Mitchell sent a green one with "Peggy" embroidered on it. To fellow
authors, Mitchell refused all requests that she review or blurb books but
gave generously of her advice, especially to young writers.*

On top of responding to fan mail, Mitchell also kept up a steady stream

---

* The only exception Mitchell made for a dust jacket blurb was in the spring of 1936
for the book *Empire: Georgia Today in Photographs and Paragraphs*, by her friend Emily
Woodward. Afterward, Macmillan asked Mitchell to decline blurbing books by other
publishers and promised not to ask her to promote Macmillan titles.

of correspondence with members of the press. While she did not want to give interviews, she tracked her clippings and sent letters of correction to any reporters who published incorrect information about her or the book. To those who supported her work, the author continued her practice of writing thank-you notes. When an unsigned "Gossip of the Book World" column in the *Los Angeles Times* made a passing reference to *Gone With the Wind* being worthy of both the Pulitzer and the Nobel prizes, Mitchell wrote to the newspaper's Paul Jordan-Smith, wondering if he was the author and thanking him, saying she nearly "fainted from excitement."[43] Mitchell clearly had a knack for making friends in the press, as evidenced by Jordan-Smith's response. He pleaded guilty to having placed the blurb and was "not ashamed of it." He did not see "any good reason why you should not land one or both, save that usually the Pulitzers go to dumbbells." He added:

> I suppose the reason why prize books are commonly dull is that the committees are made up of middle-aged morons. But if old Pulitzer were alive to direct the thing, you'd certainly get it under the explicit direction of his orders. As for the Nobel folk, they're more intelligent and ought to easily see yours as the best thing America or any other dang country has had in fiction for quite a spell.[44]

Mitchell also had to respond to requests for autographed copies of *Gone With the Wind*. On a daily basis, the mail contained stacks of books that fans had sent in the hope she would sign and return them. For the first several months after publication, the author obliged, inscribing the books as instructed and mailing them back, regardless of whether return postage had been included. She only said no to bulk requests from bookstores. In late October, Rich's, still regretting not hosting an event that summer, tried to guilt Mitchell into signing two hundred copies, claiming its customers were "clamoring" for her autograph.[45] Mitchell remained unswayed by the store's attempts to flatter her.[46] Macmillan, too, wanted more autographed copies but had learned to handle her with kid gloves when asking a favor. To make it as easy as possible, the company proposed sending the author endpapers to sign instead of shipping her a case of books or asking her to stop by the Atlanta office. The solicitous routine worked. Mitchell was hard-pressed to refuse, admitting, "I don't believe this small amount of work could possibly hurt me."[47] Still, Alec Blanton walked on eggshells when he sent her the package of papers, saying there were only thirty, but she should not hesitate to stop at any point if the signing became too taxing for her.[48]

That summer and fall, Mitchell devoted her life to sifting through letters, writing responses, packing signed books, and standing in line at the post office. The workload was so intense that the Marshes hired temporary stenographers to come to the apartment in shifts—one working from nine in the morning until five o'clock, while the other covered evenings from seven o'clock until midnight.[49] Mitchell's housekeeper, Bessie Jordan, also pitched in, as did Marsh, who helped on nights and weekends. Though grueling work, answering her mail was not something the author felt she could turn her back on considering the public had showered her with kindness and admiration. Assuming the interest could not last forever, she was willing to be gracious until things died down.

As months passed without Mitchell making any public appearances, the excuse that she suffered from eyestrain or postrelease exhaustion wore thin. By mid-fall, rumors began circulating in the press that there was something more sinister afoot—that she was an invalid, blind, paralyzed, or abnormally shy and could not stand talking to people. Hating rumormongering and sloppy reporting even more than the spotlight, Mitchell had no choice but to set the record straight. She enjoyed sound health, or at least relatively so, and simply did not wish to dwell in the limelight.

Recognizing this might cause her to appear ungrateful for the attention people gave her, the Marshes wanted to present her position in a sympathetic light. As a former newspaperman with years of experience in the public relations field, Marsh had definite ideas about how a problem like this should be managed. He arranged an in-depth series of six articles by the *Atlanta Constitution*'s city editor, Lamar Q. Ball, whom the Marshes knew and trusted. They fed him information designed to create an appealing persona for Mitchell, while also excusing her reluctance to appear in the public eye. As Stephens Mitchell described it, Marsh set about to portray her as "a pleasant, gracious housewife, interested in social graces, not wishing to have her name before the public, not interested in art or music or literature except as they fulfilled the necessity of social obligations, a good housekeeper, a pleasant hostess, civic-minded in a polite sense."[50]

The articles Ball wrote are almost comical in the portrait they paint of the author as a simple housewife bewildered by the attention surrounding her. When asked to reveal her next ambition, now that "success had enfolded [her] in its comforting embrace," she responded that she wanted to get her hair washed, buy a couple of dresses, and see the next Marx Brothers movie.[51] As to why she had not yet moved to the upscale Pace's Ferry area of Atlanta with a house full of servants, she responded, "Great heavens, no! Bessie is all I need. I don't know what I would do with a personal lady's maid. I'd never feel comfortable if I hadn't put on my own clothes."[52] She professed to be an avid Donald Duck fan and to enjoy relaxing at home wearing a pair of plain corduroy trousers and one of her husband's old shirts. Her book's success was "all too glamorous," she professed. "When I hear from my publishers that they have printed another edition, all I can say is 'Good Heavens.'"[53]

In Ball's final installment, Mitchell let it be known that she appreciated the public's affection but wanted to live her life in peace. She had not set out to become a public figure, like an actress or a politician. She did not like women chasing her into changing rooms in department stores while she stood there in her slip trying on a dress. "They actually did this to me," she lamented. "They questioned me like a crowd of hard-hearted district attorneys. They wanted to know the size of my intimate wearing apparel. They screamed to one another . . . 'Ain't she skinny?' while still another observed: 'I expected her to look more middle-aged around the hips.'" She concluded the anecdote with the simple statement, "I don't like to have them comment on the fact that I have no lace on my petticoat."[54] The message was clear: Margaret Mitchell was a nice lady who wanted to be left alone.

Stephens Mitchell did not think much of the prim image they were creating of his far-from-shy-and-retiring sister. However, when he expressed his reservations, the Marshes held firm. They encouraged friends and family members to refrain from talking about her in public, especially to the press, and were vocal in their displeasure when ranks were broken.[55] When college chum Ginny Morris reported she had been asked to write an "I-knew-her-when" story about the author for *Photoplay* magazine, Mitchell begged her friend to turn down the offer. "I'm tired out. I want to get out of the spotlight more earnestly than you or anybody else could possibly believe." She also reminded Morris that she was not connected with the motion picture and saw no reason for a story about her to run in a movie magazine.[56] Morris agreed not to pursue the piece, observing, "It's indeed a shame, Peggy, that you can't enjoy the terrific success of your book."[57] Cole also thought this reclusive persona was an ill-fitting one for her outgoing friend and noted that, when the Taylors spent time with Mitchell after the book's release, it would take the author time to "loosen up and be natural even with us."[58] Cole and her husband felt sorry Mitchell did not seem comfortable with her success. At times, they were bemused by her reluctance, which, to some extent, they blamed on Marsh. The Taylors were fond of him but could not help feeling that the author might have enjoyed things more if not for his decision to build a wall around her.[59]

Marsh's plan might have worked, except for one thing: Macmillan was not going to let *Gone With the Wind* follow Mitchell into obscurity. In the first week of December, the firm announced that the millionth copy would come off the presses at mid-month.[60] The novel was doing wonderful things for Macmillan's financial health. Company records indicate that the publisher earned $1.62 for each copy sold. For the New York office alone, this amounted to a gross income on this single book of almost $1.5 million by the end of 1936.[61] Generous Christmas bonuses were in store that year for the firm's rank and file, for which Mitchell would be remembered fondly in years to come.[62]

Blanton, the company's sales manager, saw the millionth copy as a perfect opportunity to reinvigorate the advertising campaign in time for the holiday shopping season. To kick things off, he arranged for American Express, then still a delivery business, to plaster its vans with *Gone With the Wind* posters touting the big news.[63] Macmillan also spent an estimated eleven thousand dollars to run a full-page, five-color advertisement for the book in the *Saturday Evening Post*. Large ads were placed in more than one hundred daily newspapers and several major magazines, including *Time* and the *New Yorker*.[64]

The world-weary author did not even try to feign indifference to news of the millionth copy. She may not have liked the way *Gone With the Wind* turned her life upside down, but even she had to admit to being impressed by this achievement. She wired Macmillan asking if she could have the landmark volume.[65] Brett agreed, and Latham developed a special hand-lettered dedication page that congratulated Mitchell on her book's success.[66] In thanking the editor for the gesture, Mitchell wrote, "Of course, there was no possible Christmas gift that could have pleased me more, but I felt rather dazed as I looked at it for I still cannot believe it is true."[67]

Although the author would have been happy to fade away on the heels of this milestone, her adoring readers refused to cooperate. In the wake of all the attention that December, and with the gift-giving season in full force, the letters continued to arrive in bulk, and demand for signed books multiplied exponentially, up to hundreds per day on occasion.[68] And the national press showed no signs of respecting Mitchell's wishes to live in peace. Perhaps most glaringly, in December, the just-launched *Life* magazine featured a four-page spread on *Gone With the Wind*, including a photograph of the author's apartment building and the helpful tip that she lived in Unit 9.

And despite Marsh's efforts to convince the world his wife was a simple homebody, the rumor mill spun out of control. The more successful the book became, the more outlandish the stories that circulated about its reclusive author. Mitchell read she had a wooden leg, owned a yacht, went on a shopping spree in New York and spent ten thousand dollars on new dresses, was seventeen years old, had leased a penthouse in New York, had bought an antebellum Georgia plantation, was set to receive a million dollars for writing a play, and had agreed to play Melanie in Selznick's movie. She could laugh at much of the gossip but found upsetting rumors that her marriage had failed or that Marsh had died. Also troubling were reports that she had not written *Gone With the Wind*. All manner of theories circulated that she could not possibly have done the job alone. Some claimed she had pepped up a novel drafted by her father or brother. Others suggested that Sinclair Lewis was the author. Speculation also ran wild that Marsh wrote substantial portions of the book, if not the entire thing. When this rumor found its way into the *Washington Post*, Mitchell sobbed with frustration. While her husband played a formative role in the development of *Gone With the Wind*, both of the Marshes and those around them knew his role had been inspirational, supportive, and editorial. She, and she alone, had written the book. Perhaps because of these suspicions, Marsh declined to sign a copy of *Gone With the Wind* when a cousin asked him for the favor that December. He explained, "I haven't done that yet in any copy of the book and I don't aim to. It's Peggy's book, and she is the one to do the autographing. She paid me the highest compliment when she put my 'JRM' on the dedication page, and that will have to do for me."[69]

Mitchell burrowed further into her self-imposed shell, terrified of saying or doing anything that could end up in the newspapers. She felt as if she could not sneeze without appearing in a gossip column and scarcely opened her mouth in public for fear her remarks would "appear immediately in a garbled form in someone's column."[70] But there was little she could do to stop the wild stories. Many of the rumors originated from a spate of Mitchell impersonators who began popping up around the country. The imposters gave interviews, signed books, and basked in the spotlight as the famed author. One appeared at an airport in Florida with two men she claimed were her managers and demanded seats on a flight to Cuba. Another had a grand time on a cruise ship. The Seaboard Air Line Railway between Florida and Virginia had a regular wannabe Mitchell who caused a stir picking up men. The Marshes were astonished at how well the impersonators succeeded in their aims. "The majority of people these days seem lacking in suspiciousness, and if some plausible stranger says that he is Oliver Cromwell or Franklin Roosevelt, people seem to fall for it," Marsh said.[71]

With every new rumor, family, friends, reporters, and random strangers contacted Mitchell wanting to know the details. Each incident caused her embarrassment and a great deal of work, as she felt obligated to write round after round of letters setting the record straight. She fretted that if a single false tale went unchecked, her reputation would be irretrievably damaged. She desperately wanted to escape the fate of other celebrities who rode the roller coaster of fame to their downfall. One example that struck fear in her heart was Richmond Pearson Hobson, a Spanish-American War hero who permitted himself to be photographed being kissed by a group of nubile young ladies and was ridiculed the rest of his life as Kissing Bug Hobson. Though she had no desire to be acclaimed, she found the idea of being reviled or laughed at unsettling. She also worried about how the constant glare of attention would affect her relationships with family and friends. She did not want to end up like the Pulitzer Prize–winning author Caroline Miller, also from Georgia, whose marriage fell apart after her sudden rise to fame. Mitchell felt she lived "in the middle of the swirl of public emotions" surrounding her book and had to "steer a careful course every day" to "escape being wrecked."[72]

# 9

~

# *Gone With the Wind*, Inc.

## December 1936–April 1937

As 1936 came to a close, Margaret Mitchell accepted that *Gone With the Wind* had changed her life. But she had no intention of letting it ruin her life. The author decided to make some changes in the way she managed the chaos around her. One option would have been to reverse course and team up with Macmillan and David O. Selznick to control the media coverage. Not only could the two companies, with their ample resources, have offered her protection, but they might have also been willing to make concessions on her royalties or on the movie contract. As attractive as that would have been, Mitchell appears never to have considered asking them for help.

Another possibility would have been to hire a manager or a press agent, or both. She could have had her pick of the top New York literary representatives and public relations firms to help navigate the celebrity maze. Yet, Mitchell termed the idea of hiring an outsider "wholly unsatisfactory and inadequate to the needs of the job." She was reluctant to rely on a stranger, especially one who was not "familiar with the peculiarities and the personalities of Georgia and the South."[1]

There was only one person Mitchell trusted to help her through this ordeal—her husband. John Marsh had already done admirable work protecting her interests with the Lamar Q. Ball articles that fall, and it was to him she turned again. She formally retained his services as her business manager, for which he would earn 10 percent of the money she made on the book.[2] She also agreed to transfer to him the foreign rights to her novel.

Although he maintained his job at Georgia Power, it became his primary mission in life to get his "dearly beloved young lady through this without breaking her health or her nerves or her spirit."[3]

Marsh's first major initiative in his quest to return a sense of normalcy to his wife's life was to have her stop signing books. Mitchell estimated with exasperation that there had been "hundreds of thousands" of requests, with no end in sight.[4] If she autographed a copy for one person, the next thing she knew she received a stack to sign from friends of that person. A man from Toledo, Ohio, sent thirty copies and asked her to write a personal message in each. And it was not just fans. Friends hounded the author for signed copies while acknowledging the burden it placed on her. As one wrote, "Like all the other 5,000 I do not want to impose on [your] good nature—but!"[5] Her family members were harassed as well. She told Lois Cole that Stephens Mitchell and his wife, Carrie Lou, led "hunted lives because perfect strangers descend upon them, leaving copies with them and instructions that they *make* me sign them."[6] Amidst the attention surrounding the millionth copy, Marsh announced his wife would no longer sign copies of *Gone With the Wind*. At first the ban was limited to strangers, but he soon expanded it to friends, family, and charities. Although Mitchell knew the stance seemed "hardboiled" and could generate bitterness among fans she agreed with Marsh it was a necessary step. She refused all requests from that point forward, subject to only a few exceptions, such as for a fan to whom she had promised a copy before the moratorium and for people especially close to her, including Cole's mother.

Macmillan did not welcome this decision. The author's willingness to handle the inscriptions by mail alleviated some of the pressure on the firm over her refusal to conduct mass signings in bookstores. Scrambling to come up with another way to appease fans, Cole suggested a rubber stamp of the author's signature be created. Mitchell declined, wanting nothing to do with fake autographs.[7] Rumors had circulated that all the existing signatures in signed copies of *Gone With the Wind* had been created with a rubber stamp. This had caused her a considerable amount of trouble:

> Second hand book shops wanted my word of honor that I had honest to God autographed the volume they were trying to sell. I've had to say so often, with what patience I could muster, that I had never used a rubber stamp or a facsimile signature and that I never would—that anyone would be perfectly safe in buying an autographed copy because, short of forgery, the signature would really be mine.[8]

Mitchell had no plans to spend the rest of her life distinguishing stamped signatures from authentic ones. She realized her concerns might sound "invalidate" but assured Cole "this last year has been so full of incredibilities that with ease, I now believe six impossible things before breakfast every morning." Mitchell also explained that she had never understood the importance of obtaining a famous person's signature. "For of what value is a signature if you do not know the person who writes it? Of what value is it even if you *do* know them and you do not love them or at least respect them highly?" Mitchell claimed she had never bothered celebrities for their signature and could not comprehend why anyone wanted hers. In fact, she regretted having signed any books for strangers.

The ban on signing failed as a quick fix. Fans continued to approach her in public; one tactless woman, book in hand, confronted Mitchell at a cousin's funeral as the author exited the church.[9] And the mailman still brought hundreds of books for her to autograph, all of which needed to be shipped back. As incongruous as it was, in many cases she sent lengthy letters explaining why she could not sign the enclosed volume. Of course, those letters ended with her much sought-after signature. Though she saved herself little time, the ban seems to have offered Mitchell a psychological victory of sorts. She could not stop people from being curious about her. She could not control what people said or wrote about her. However, by refusing to sign books, she showed she could not be pressured into participating in what she considered a meaningless ritual.

Marsh next focused on the media situation. The Ball articles had been a good first step at distancing Mitchell from the spotlight, but the couple needed a more forceful and widespread message to set the record straight on Mitchell's life and to quell the frenzy of interest in her. Her husband selected three writers to issue a new series of articles that would further shape her public image. He asked Mitchell's close friend Medora Field Perkerson to write a story for the *Atlanta Journal Sunday Magazine*—"Double Life of Margaret Mitchell"—debunking the rumors that were swirling.[10] The novelist Faith Baldwin was given the task of writing about Mitchell's home life for *Pictorial Review*, a national ladies journal. Titled "The Woman Who Wrote *Gone With the Wind*, An Exclusive and Authentic Interview," Baldwin painted a picture of the author "with the world at her feet" wanting nothing more than to "stay at home with books and peace and friends."[11]

Finally, Marsh asked the always-supportive Edwin Granberry to do an in-depth story for the popular *Collier's* magazine on Mitchell's struggle with fame. Under Marsh's close editorial guidance, Granberry told of Mitchell's childhood, how she came to write her book, and the plight she found herself in since its publication. Marsh reviewed at least two drafts of the article and offered the reporter twenty-four pages of comments, which he insisted that Granberry return. "Edwin, if *anybody* sees these notes but you, I will personally break your neck with my strong hairy hands," Marsh vowed, obviously not wanting word to get out that he had orchestrated the piece.[12] The finished product paints a distinctly sympathetic portrait. "Miss Mitchell stands at the moment in such a spotlight of public attention as no American, excepting the President, has known since Colonel Lindbergh flew the Atlantic," it says. Granberry explained how the pressure weighed on her:

> She fears that the intense glare of the spotlight beating down upon her, month after month, may eventually drive her into complete seclusion, in the hope of salvaging some remnant of her private life; she fears that she will lose touch with the world she loves because of this seclusion; she fears that people may think her hard and unappreciative and unsociable because of her enforced necessity of refusing the public demands upon her; she fears to be set apart, to lose the easy friendships she cherishes, to be put on an eminence from which she will not be permitted to descend.[13]

The author wanted her privacy and to stand before the world, for good or bad, on the book she had written, not on what she said, the way she dressed, or her likes and dislikes. Her book belonged to anyone who paid the price for it, but nothing of her life belonged to the public. Whether her wishes mattered to anyone reading the article remained to be seen, but at least the couple had made her position clear.

Of all the actions Marsh took to bring order into their lives, the one that had the most lasting impact came about on the spur of the moment. In January 1937, Margaret Baugh, the Macmillan secretary who had helped with the manuscript revisions, went to see Marsh at his Georgia Power office for career advice. She had been let go from Macmillan in December and asked if he could assist her in finding a new position. He knew of no openings at the power company but thought she might be of assistance to Mitchell, who had been unable to find reliable secretarial help. Few of the temporary workers she had hired knew anything about publishing, and some were so starstruck that Mitchell had been tempted to "slap" some sense into them when they began fawning over her.[14] Marsh asked Baugh, a no–nonsense schoolmarm-type, if she would be willing to step in and assist Mitchell in bringing the *Gone With the Wind* correspondence under control.

The Marshes had recently returned from a brief getaway to find the mail piled almost as high as the door.[15] Baugh accepted, even though Marsh warned her the job might last only a few weeks, three months at the most. Upon hearing the news that the organized and professional Baugh was stepping in to help, Mitchell told Cole she "burst into tears of joy" with relief.[16] Three months stretched into more than thirty years. Baugh, who never married, would devote the rest of her life to the Marshes. Although she and Mitchell were close in age, Baugh became the mother hen, proving herself indispensable as the author's personal assistant, secretary, bookkeeper, confidant, and protector.

Even after reaching the million-copy mark in the middle of December, *Gone With the Wind* continued to astound. Macmillan records indicate that, from December 16 through December 28, 1936, the New York office moved another 57,000 copies and, from December 29 through the first week in February, 143,000 more.[17] And Macmillan was confident *Gone With the Wind* had more to give.

In January, the firm began running advertisements in *Publishers Weekly* hyping the novel as the big book of 1936 and predicting it would be 1937's major title as well. The notices boldly called Mitchell's story part of the nation's folklore and the greatest piece of historical fiction ever written by an American. When questioned whether it was beating a dead horse, the publisher proclaimed that the time to not give up on a proven piece of merchandise was when it showed clear signs of breaking records: "The difference between a good sales record and a great one is often merely a matter of merchandising courage."[18] Macmillan went on to blanket the country with advertisements in big-city newspapers and national magazines.

Predictably, the book's amazing success caught the attention of many ambitious souls who scrambled to grab their own slice of the *Gone With the Wind* pie. Writers wanted to quote from it in their books. Orators had grand visions of live readings of Mitchell's dramatic prose. Theatrical producers were eager to present the story on stage. Songwriters hoped to set her tale to music. Manufacturers wanted Scarlett and Rhett to help sell all manner of goods, from housedresses to greeting cards. There seemed to be no end to the ways people were finagling to make a dollar off Mitchell's story.

Every request that came in the door—and there were thousands—required careful consideration. As Mitchell would later say, preventing people from exploiting her book kept her busy twenty-four hours a day. There was far more to being a bestselling author than cashing royalty checks and signing books. Authors who do not take seriously the legal and technical aspects of permissions and infringements risk giving away their hard-earned money. Not so Margaret Mitchell. Overwhelmed by the rewrite process, the movie negotiations, and the mantle of celebrity, Mitchell hit her stride managing the business of her book.

Stephens Mitchell wrote of his sister's acumen for the commercial side of her literary career:

> I have read many lives of literary people, and . . . I realize what is the differ-
> ence between Margaret and other writers. Almost all of these people had no
> sense of business. Some of them knew it and turned over their affairs to an
> agent. Some of them did not know it, and lost their money. Some of them
> did not get any money, because of lack of business ability. One of them,
> Mark Twain, after losing money, acquired a guardian and protector in the
> great millionaire, H.H. Rogers. [The] real story about Margaret is that she
> became a woman of business, a good executive, a tireless worker.[19]

The author tackled the job with the able assistance of her husband and brother, who were both earning a percentage of her profits. The trio formed a makeshift management team, a sort of *Gone With the Wind*, Inc. The author held the post of chief executive responsible for making the big picture decisions. Marsh served as the administrator charged with managing the workload and, of course, public relations. Stephens Mitchell, with the occasional help of his father, constituted the law department. Because the men had office jobs, the team met in the evenings after dinner.[20] They analyzed issues and developed strategies, often until the wee hours of the morning.[21]

Many of the inquiries the team considered came from people who wanted to quote from the book, either orally or in writing. Macmillan technically controlled the rights to use written excerpts, while Mitchell held the rights to oral performances, but she kept a careful eye on all requests that came in. By this point in her literary career, Mitchell understood that, if she wanted matters handled to her specifications, she had to take an active role. For the most part, despite a sometimes-troubled relationship, she and Macmillan worked well together on these requests. They agreed that permission to quote should be denied to any profit-making ventures. The publisher saw no reason to share the *Gone With the Wind* wealth, and, given her tax concerns, Mitchell had no need for additional income. The publisher and author agreed, however, that students, teachers, and nonprofit organizations wanting to use only small portions of the text should be able to do so and at no cost.

As the saying goes, no good deed goes unpunished. In many cases, the Mitchell team struggled to identify those causes that were truly charitable in nature. As Marsh put it, they became "thoroughly familiar with the many abuses that masquerade under the name of charity."[22] Also frustrating were the innocent-sounding proposals that raised complex legal issues. When several charitable organizations asked for permission to create Braille editions of *Gone With the Wind*, Mitchell was pleased that her book merited translation. She agreed that the editions could be produced at no cost, as long as the publishers gave proper credit to Macmillan and did not abridge the story. Macmillan used the Braille editions as yet another golden opportunity for publicity. When Helen Keller traveled to Japan in 1937, the firm issued a press release announcing that she brought for reading on the journey *Gone With the Wind* in twelve Braille volumes. All seemed well until charities asked Mitchell to go a step further and allow broadcast readings of *Gone With the Wind* to the blind on the radio or via "talking albums." She wanted to oblige but did not know if she had the authority, given the rights Selznick had acquired as part of the movie deal. She also identified a host of copyright issues associated with such a project and had no interest spending hours resolving them. Although she disliked appearing uncooperative, she declined to give permission and palmed the matter off onto Selznick. Mitchell would comment many times that people had no idea the stress, work, and expense imposed on her in the name of charity.

Then there were myriad proposals for commercial tie-ins associated with *Gone With the Wind* and its characters. The most straightforward situations were retailers who wanted to use Mitchell's book to draw attention to their own products. For instance, at the New York Motor Boat Show in February 1937, a publisher of nautical books placed *Gone With the Wind* among a display of volumes about boating. The exhibit grabbed a lot of attention as visitors puzzled over the connection. According to *Publishers Weekly*, the man in charge of the booth stayed busy explaining that "*Gone With the Wind* was not nautical, but nice."[23] In other cases, manufacturers wanted to use Mitchell's title to promote their own products. An advertising display for a water heater proclaimed "Gone with the wind are your hot water worries." Book titles are not copyrightable in the United States, and so there was nothing Mitchell could do to stop uses like these. But that is not to say that the phrase "gone with the wind" was free for the taking.

When Pepperell Manufacturing Company asked for permission to create a *Gone With the Wind* fabric printed with scenes from the story, Macmillan and Mitchell were confident they had a propriety interest in such a product. They were not clear exactly how far those rights went though and suspected Selznick might have something to say about visual depictions of the story. After much hemming and hawing, neither the author nor the publisher were opposed to the fabric, and neither wanted to expend the time and resources necessary to figure out the legal nuances. They told Pepperell, as well as several other companies with similar plans, to proceed at their own risk. That winter, Pepperell sent Mitchell several yards of the fabric as a gift. She admitted it turned out well and Macmillan, too, had reason to be pleased when Pepperell took out a full-page ad in *Life* featuring the fabric, and bookstores put the material to good use in creating window displays.

Macmillan put its foot down, however, when third parties asked to use images of the book to promote other products. The publisher owned the rights to the dust jacket design and did not want it used in advertisements for other companies. One of the rare approvals Macmillan gave in this regard went to Winter Drittel, a clothing manufacturer, which asked to reproduce the dust jacket on hang tags for a line of *Gone With the Wind* dresses. Macmillan apparently wavered in this case because the manufacturer had already created an attractive window display at Stern Brothers department store in New York that featured the book with the dresses, thereby proving itself a good advertising partner.

Mitchell also wondered who controlled the further adventures of her characters. When fans began to accept that she would not write a sequel, some took matters into their own hands and wrote continuations of the story themselves, answering the burning question of what happened to the star-crossed lovers. Under modern copyright law, it is well established that authors have the exclusive right to prepare derivative works based on the lives of their characters. In the 1930s, however, the legality of this so-called fan fiction was less certain, and Mitchell did not know what, if anything, she could do to stop these unauthorized sequels. In the spring of 1937, she read about a Louisiana woman who could not bear the unhappy conclusion of *Gone With the Wind* and had written a happy ending, which a local newspaper published. Professing ignorance of the legalities involved, Mitchell forwarded the information to Macmillan and suggested the firm decide whether to voice any complaint.[24] Macmillan did not pursue the matter and seemed fine with fans writing their own endings. For the time being, Mitchell did not question this approach.

A related question was who controlled the names of the characters. The movie contract allowed Selznick to use those names for manufactured items related to the film. Mitchell assumed she retained the rights for all other purposes. In the late fall of 1936, when manufacturers proposed using Scarlett O'Hara to promote their products, Mitchell did not bother to consult Selznick and took an open-minded approach. If someone wanted to assert that Scarlett might have liked a certain item, she had no problem with that as long as the manufacturer did not call the item a Scarlett O'Hara such-and-such or give the impression that Mitchell endorsed it.[25] On one occasion in the winter of 1937, she went a step further and allowed a charitable group to use the name Scarlett O'Hara on dolls being sold to raise money for women on welfare.

Mitchell's liberal attitude about the use of her characters came to an end that spring when Cole had lunch with Mitchell's college friend Ginny Morris. The subject of the Scarlett dolls came up, and Morris, who worked in the publicity department of United Artists Film Corporation, expressed concern about Mitchell being so generous to the charity. She wrote the author to make sure she understood the commercial value of her characters, pointing out that Walt Disney made more from merchandise royalties than he did from his movies. Morris apologized for "butting in" but recommended that Mitchell and her brother take a careful look at the commercial tie-ups before they let a fortune slip away.[26]

Heeding Morris's warning, Mitchell approached Selznick to clarify ownership of the characters' names. To her consternation, the producer claimed that he had acquired the exclusive rights to merchandise the characters. This position contradicted what Stephens Mitchell understood the studio people to have said during the 1936 contract negotiations, and there were several heated exchanges over the matter. Mitchell stood her ground that the studio owned only the rights to the character names as they appeared in the movie. If Selznick wanted all the rights to Scarlett O'Hara and Rhett Butler, he would have to pay for them. Selznick balked, and discussions stalled. Mitchell withdrew permission for the Scarlett O'Hara dolls and declined all similar proposals pending a resolution with Selznick.

In the 1930s, the stage rights to a successful novel were often more valuable than the movie rights. This was the heyday of Broadway, and theatrical producers scoured the literary world for promising new story lines to dramatize on stage. Mitchell's book had obvious potential, but the author was in no rush to cash in. She had been through enough with the movie negotiations and did not relish the idea of complicating her life with a new round of contract talks. She turned down all offers to buy the dramatic rights.

When it came to *Gone With the Wind*, though, people seemed to have a hard time taking "no" for an answer. In one instance over the winter of 1937, a Georgia theater producer refused to accept Marsh's statement that Mitchell would not sell the rights. The Federal Theatre Project, one of Franklin Roosevelt's Works Progress Administration agencies, and the Atlanta Theatre Guild had joined forces to write an outline of a four-act play of *Gone With the Wind* they hoped to present during Atlanta's Dogwood Festival that spring. Thinking he could get a favorable response if Mitchell would read his proposal, the producer harangued friends of the Marshes, Wilbur and Annie Laurie Kurtz, to open the lines of communication with the author. The appeal got the producer nowhere. After the Kurtzes made two failed attempts to set up a meeting with Mitchell, the author's nerves wore thin. "I do not know why they still persist in the face of this," she wrote to Annie Laurie Kurtz. "Should you have any communications with them on the subject, tell them that I thank them for their interest but that I do not want the book dramatized."[27]

Also on Mitchell's mind that winter and spring of 1937 were the foreign rights to her novel. Brett had warned her that the foreign editions would not be worth much money and might be difficult to manage. But that had not deterred the author from taking an active interest in her book's reception outside the United States. Hopeful that *Gone With the Wind* would do her proud internationally, she was willing to deal with the inconvenience.

Macmillan London had finally released the British edition at the end of September 1936, along with a Colonial edition for readers in Australia, India, New Zealand, and South Africa.[28] To Mitchell's pleasure, most of the reviews were as favorable as the American ones. The London *Times* commented that few books in literary history had sustained such a consistent level of competence.[29] Although some British critics complained that the book inaccurately depicted friendly relationships between whites and blacks, Mitchell scoffed at the suggestion she wrote her book to glorify the South's position on slavery.[30] "Personally I do not know where they get such an idea," she wrote Herschel Brickell, "for, as far as I can see most of the negro characters were people of worth, dignity and rectitude—certainly Mammy and Peter and even the ignorant Sam knew more of decorous behavior and honor than Scarlett did."[31] British readers did not seem overly concerned about the racial nuances, and by December, *Gone With the Wind* hit number 1 on the British bestseller list, a rare honor for an American author.[32]

The success in Britain bode well for the other overseas rights, which were being handled by Marion Saunders. After the movie negotiations and the dustup over whether Annie Laurie Williams or Macmillan had represented Mitchell, the Marshes had been wary of dealing with another agent. However, they had no idea how to manage the foreign rights and so followed the company's lead and let Saunders continue working with foreign publishers on behalf of *Gone With the Wind*.

By February 1937, Mitchell proclaimed to Brickell that "everybody except the Chinese and the Albanians" had put in a bid on *Gone With the Wind*.[33] Though the level of activity was promising, working through so many offers proved tedious. The Marshes kept running into snags, the chief one being dealing with Saunders. The agent had specific ideas about how foreign rights should work, and her methods did not always jibe with what the Marshes wanted.

Mitchell, for instance, had concerns about quality control in the translations and told Saunders not to accept any offers for abridgements. The agent thought this unwise because it limited Mitchell's chances of obtaining contracts in small countries that did not have enough money or paper to print a book as long as *Gone With the Wind*. The Marshes also instructed Saunders that all foreign publishers had to include the Macmillan copyright notice in their books and promise, in writing, not to distribute their translations in the United States. Although both of these conditions had been mandated by Macmillan, Saunders complained about the author's cautiousness. The agent warned that foreign contracts were not as tightly woven as American ones and that Mitchell risked discouraging publishers if she insisted on such provisions. After various squabbles, Saunders agreed to do things the way Mitchell wanted, but Marsh sensed trouble lay ahead with the agent.

Cole validated those suspicions when, in January 1937, she reported that Saunders wanted to cut Marsh out of the loop on the dealings with foreign publishers. Macmillan had been receiving a steady flow of letters from publishers expressing interest in translating *Gone With the Wind* and had been forwarding copies of all such inquiries to both Saunders and Marsh. Obviously not aware of Cole's friendship with the author, Saunders asked Cole to stop sending Marsh copies. She apparently preferred to process the requests on her own without his intervention. Cole alerted Marsh, though discouraged him from letting Saunders know he was on to her.[34] Marsh agreed to keep silent but set his mind to breaking in the agent to handle the *Gone With the Wind* rights with the care and thoroughness he demanded. Cole continued to send copies of the requests to Marsh, who kept a close watch on Saunders. He communicated with the agent on an almost daily basis by either letter or long-distance telephone call.[35]

Marsh's oversight did not sit well with Saunders, a go-getter out to close deals. Operating on a commission basis, her goal was to get as many translations in place as quickly as possible. Not only that, but she considered herself an independent, free-thinking woman confident in her abilities. She explained herself to Mitchell this way: "I'm a rebel at best (that's why I like your story!)—there's Highland Scottish blood in my veins, as well as Spanish blood, and a few other things—and I've roamed around this world of ours quite a bit—and have been somewhat independent ever since the age of 19 after a fortune was machine-gunned in the World War." She goaded Mitchell to be more independent of the men in her life and to take charge of her business matters: "Or do you prefer to leave all such matters to the strong men of your family? I've never had a strong man to fight my battles for me since my father died in 1922—so I've battled alone. And it has been loads of fun."[36]

The discord between Marsh and Saunders boiled over that January when several of the overseas deals were ready to be formalized. The Marshes wanted written contracts in every country that published *Gone With the Wind*, but the agent did not think that necessary. In her experience, it was fine to handle such matters by exchanging letters and cables, and she wanted leeway to "put the business through" as she saw fit.[37] She claimed to have on the table six contracts, all of which were stalled by Marsh's insistence on dotting every *i* and crossing every *t*. She threatened that, if she lost any contracts because of his delays, Marsh would owe her extra compensation for her time.[38]

Marsh responded to Saunders in his typical no-nonsense way. He apologized that she "found it difficult to deal with" them. If she could not work "with a family that believes in abiding by its contracts, even at the sacrifice of its financial benefit," he invited her to resign.[39] Saunders did not want to give up on *Gone With the Wind*, she just wanted Marsh out of the way. His inexperience and persnicketiness were interfering with the contracts. She ignored the offer to quit, proposing instead that he pay her an additional one hundred dollars for the extra work he created for her.

At this point, the Marshes were tempted to throw in the towel and forget the translations altogether. But they were not quitters, nor were they unfair. If they abandoned the rights before any deals were closed, Saunders would receive no compensation for the months of work she had done. Although it must have stuck in his craw, Marsh agreed to pay Saunders the extra money with the understanding that all the contracts with foreign publishers would be in writing and contain the restrictions the Marshes wanted included. Saunders accepted the money and Marsh's terms.

Despite her efforts to maintain a low profile, a fresh round of attention focused on Mitchell when the awards for literary merit in 1936 were announced. She came away the big winner, landing both the National Book Award and the Pulitzer Prize. Mitchell obtained a behind-the-scenes look at the inner workings of the publishing world when she received advance notice of her selection in both instances before the official announcements were made. As Mitchell once said to her mother-in-law, "Publishing circles gossip more than newspapers or ladies homes."[40]

At the end of February 1937, the American Booksellers Association presented its National Book Award, anointing *Gone With the Wind* the most distinguished novel of 1936.★ This was an industry prize selected by booksellers to honor the books they admired and enjoyed selling.[41] Although the winners were officially announced at a luncheon in New York on February 25, Mitchell had apparently heard the news weeks earlier. A cryptic message from Cole to the author dated February 5, 1937, congratulates Mitchell about an unspecified accomplishment and instructs the author not to leak any details. Only a few people at Macmillan were in the know, and if the information found its way to the press before the official announcement, Cole warned, Macmillan's name "would be mud" in the industry. Mitchell had little incentive to draw attention to herself, and there is no indication she let the cat out of the bag.

She kept another secret that spring when Julian Harris, executive editor of the *Chattanooga Times*, wrote Marsh and tipped him off that Mitchell had won the Pulitzer Prize for the most distinguished novel. The letter had been directed to Marsh's office, and he called his wife at home to give her the news. Mitchell later told Harris that Marsh had to read the letter to her

---

★ This National Book Award is not affiliated with the award of the same name sponsored since 1950 by the National Book Foundation.

three times before she could take it in.[42] On the afternoon of May 3, hours before the Pulitzer committee sent her official word, Mitchell wired George Brett to expect good news: "GO TO THE PARTY AND DON'T FORGET TO TAKE THE BRASS BAND WITH YOU."[43] She likely also shared the scoop with Harold Latham, who probably already knew, as evidenced by the fact that he had arranged to be in Atlanta the week the awards were announced.

When the official wire arrived that evening at the Marsh apartment, the author was not there to receive it. The Marshes and Latham were visiting at the Mitchell family home on Peachtree Street. An editor and photographer from the *Atlanta Constitution* tracked Mitchell down at her father's house to record her reaction to the news. She later joked to Brett that the press was "indignant because I hadn't stayed home where they could catch me with ease."[44] For the benefit of the reporters, she acted suitably surprised, never letting on that she already knew of her selection.

Despite her desire to stay out of the public eye, Mitchell gracefully accepted the attention the award brought, even agreeing to attend a party in her honor hosted by Latham and Norman Berg at the Atlanta Athletic Club the following evening. She also gave an interview on WSB Radio in Atlanta, saying that winning the award was an honor far beyond any she ever expected for her book. In describing her feelings about the award to Latham, Mitchell said she did not feel like a Pulitzer Prize winner and had a hard time believing "that I am sitting in the seats of the mighty."[45]

Although some critics, including the *Saturday Review of Literature*, questioned bestowing such an esteemed literary accolade on a work of popular fiction, the award signaled good news for the book.[46] *Publishers Weekly* reported that fourteen thousand copies of *Gone With the Wind* were sold the day after the announcement, more than three times the daily average for that year. Never shy about keeping Scarlett and Rhett the center of attention, Macmillan increased advertising in major cities and sent retailers posters announcing the award. The company also printed the news on more than thirty thousand green foil bands that were wrapped around copies of the book.[47]

To Mitchell's relief, the Pulitzer did not cause an influx of fan letters or visitors. In fact, just the opposite occurred. "We were afraid the Award would serve to stir up public interest in me personally again and were all set for another awful siege," Mitchell wrote to Marsh's family. "But, fortunately, it worked just the other way, and from the date of the announcement the mail, phone calls and tourists have fallen off sharply. Life is beginning to wear its old face again."[48] Perhaps the award distanced the author from her admirers; she was now considered a verified literary talent, not a fairytale housewife who had stumbled into incredible good fortune. Many may have felt she was no longer one of them, someone they could treat like an old friend. It is a tribute to Mitchell's good nature that it took people so long to come to that conclusion. As a college student wrote her that May, thanking her for helping with his school's *Gone With the Wind*–themed yearbook, "My highest regards to you for remaining a very real and human person while the world knelt at your feet."[49]

The only major literary prize Mitchell did not receive that year was the Nobel Prize in Literature, an international award issued by the Swedish Academy. However, she was nominated for the award in 1938 by geographer and explorer Sven Hedin, a member of the academy. She did not win and, due to the strict secrecy surrounding the Nobel process, likely never knew she had been under consideration. The Nobel Foundation restricts disclosure of information about nominations for fifty years, meaning that information about Mitchell's nomination was not publicly available until long after her death.[50]

In the spring of 1937, *American Business* magazine published an article about Mitchell's novel titled "The Making of a Best Seller." The piece went into painstaking detail about the marketing strategy behind the *Gone With the Wind* publishing phenomenon, covering sales figures, advertising plans, the money spent, and the savvy decisions by Macmillan that contributed to the book's blockbuster achievement. What the article failed to mention, even in passing, was the role Mitchell played in the success of her book.

The omission is hardly a surprise, given the perception of the author that first year as something of a recluse. Yet, it is a glaring error if due credit is to be afforded to what made *Gone With the Wind* such a triumph. Beyond having written the book, Mitchell endeared herself to fans by being approachable and accommodating. The Margaret Mitchell mystique sold books—and still does today, long after Macmillan's flashy advertisements and window displays have been forgotten. She protected her famous asset from exploitation and tried to give it the opportunity for a life overseas. By the author's own standards, which are the only ones that mattered to her, she had done her best to support her brainchild.

# 10

# Defending Scarlett's Honor

## Spring–December 1937

By the spring of 1937, *Gone With the Wind* started to cause increasingly complicated problems for its attentive mother. Margaret Mitchell would be forced to blow her cover as a reclusive Southern belle and establish herself as a steel magnolia prepared to defend her rights at any cost. Her first inkling of big trouble came from a seventy-six-year-old fellow Southern author named Susan Lawrence Davis. With Mitchell's novel still entrenched atop the nation's bestseller lists, the distinctive yellow dust jacket became increasingly famous, and that made Davis see green.

The Alabama author, who claimed to be descended from Confederate president Jefferson Davis, had published in 1924 a volume titled *Authentic History of the Ku Klux Klan, 1865–1877*. The book had not been a commercial success, but Davis hoped it would one day obtain the recognition she felt it deserved. In the years before *Gone With the Wind*'s publication, she made a name for herself as something of a literary narcissist, lodging charges of plagiarism against people who wrote about the subjects covered in her *Authentic History* without acknowledging her contribution to the field. She demanded millions of dollars in damages when Claude G. Bowers, the American ambassador to Spain, released a book titled *The Tragic Era: The Revolution after Lincoln*. She sued the *Atlanta Journal* for running a photograph of General Robert E. Lee that she had used in her book. Neither of those claims succeeded, but she did finagle a five-hundred-dollar nuisance settlement out of the *New York Times* for a story she claimed used her work as an unattributed source.[1]

When *Gone With the Wind* became the most talked-about book in America, Davis must have thought she hit the jackpot. She combed through every word of Mitchell's book, looking for similarities between the novel and her Klan history. After amassing a list of hundreds of parallels, she found a lawyer willing to file a plagiarism lawsuit against Macmillan. In a 461-page complaint, Davis sought five thousand dollars per alleged instance of infringement of her copyright. If taken to mean each copy of Mitchell's novel sold so far, this translated to 6.5 billion dollars. Among hundreds of accusations, Davis found fault with Macmillan for having bound *Gone With the Wind* in Confederate gray, the same color fabric used on her book. She also thought actionable Mitchell's references to people, places, and events mentioned in her *Authentic History*, including poet-priest Father Abram Ryan, the Freedman's Bureau, General Wade Hampton, General John B. Gordon, scalawags, carpetbaggers, and the federal commissioners who tried to see President Abraham Lincoln before Fort Sumter fell. She also pointed to similarities between Mitchell's phrasing and her own. They had both referred to the crosses of the Klan as fiery and called people from Charleston Charlestonians. Davis seemed to think she had a copyright on the history of the Confederacy.

Mitchell was flabbergasted when she read the allegations. She took pride in the research she had done to support the details in her book and had been open about her reliance on historic records, books, manuscripts, and diaries. She denied, however, that she had ever heard of either Davis or her book. Moreover, coming from a family of lawyers, she knew the fundamentals of copyright law and insisted she would have never usurped another author's work, even inadvertently. Although she dreaded the prospect of a drawn-out lawsuit, she was determined to fight Davis in court. She feared any sign of weakness would encourage copycat lawsuits and cause people to doubt her integrity.[2]

Adding insult to injury was the expense the suit would cause Mitchell. Even though Davis had not named the author as a defendant, Mitchell was on the hook for responding to the allegations. In her 1935 contract with Macmillan, she accepted responsibility for defending plagiarism claims related to *Gone With the Wind*. George Brett predicted the legal fees in this instance would be nominal and offered to share the cost. Continuing to nurse her wounds over the movie deal, she was reluctant to accept charity from him. She declined. She told Brett to bring in his own lawyers and send her the bill when the case was resolved.

Brett hired Walbridge Taft, a partner at Cadwalader, Wickersham &

Taft, to represent Macmillan's and Mitchell's interests. Taft, a nephew of former president and Supreme Court justice William Howard Taft, assessed the matter and concluded Davis had little chance of success. No author had exclusive literary rights to the people and events of the Civil War, and Davis's track record made it unlikely a judge or jury would be sympathetic to her cause. Brett promised Mitchell that the case would be resolved in their favor: "This has all the earmarks of a shake down, and if that's all it is I reckon they'll find us hard to shake!"[3]

Brett took an assertive stance against Davis and released indignant press releases promising to fight her. Although Mitchell probably did not like her name being bandied about in any discussions of plagiarism, Brett saw it all as for the greater good of publicity. The lawsuit received extensive news coverage and yielded many supportive letters from the public, including several that gave Macmillan helpful information about Davis. Reed Harris, assistant national director of the Federal Writers' Project, wrote Macmillan about the woman's unsuccessful attempts to obtain work with his agency; he labeled her one of the most annoying people on earth. She had staged a one-woman sit-down strike in the agency's office and confronted Harris after hours. He assured the publisher that, if he had not been a government employee, "I am sure that I would have dropped whatever dignity I had and socked this old lady."[4] Another letter gave rise to a light moment between Brett and Taft. A purported friend of a friend of Davis sent an ink-stained note in a scrawling handwriting, offering to broker a settlement for somewhere in the neighborhood of a billion dollars. The letter writer warned Brett that, if the publisher ignored the "kindly offer," the firm would "sup sorrow" in the end.[5] Brett forwarded the letter to Taft, noting, "Here's our chance! We can now settle for a billion dollars."[6] Taft replied, "I have your letter of June 21, but couldn't find your billion-dollar check to settle the case. However, I just advanced that amount from our funds, and at your convenience you will reimburse us!"[7]

Stephens Mitchell, who still fretted about the unfairness of his sister's income tax liabilities, managed to find a silver lining in the Davis cloud. Sales of his sister's book remained strong, and 1937 was shaping up to be another collection windfall for the Bureau of Internal Revenue, forerunner of today's Internal Revenue Service. He wondered whether the Davis suit could be used as a way to defer some of his sister's income until 1938, when sales were sure to slow and she might be in a lower tax bracket. He asked Harold Latham if Macmillan would be willing to withhold a portion of her earnings as a bond pending resolution of the litigation.[8] Latham appreciated

Mitchell's difficulty but, in a letter dated May 20, declined to help, stating that the company had to pay her in accordance with its contractually established schedule. Only if the Davis suit assumed serious proportions, he said, would Macmillan consider asking for a bond or authority to withhold royalties.[9]

The author's brother did not give up on the idea. In July, he broached the topic with Brett and traveled to New York so they could discuss it in person. Although the specifics of that trip are not documented, it is known that the attorney and his family enjoyed an outing on Brett's yacht. Sometime during the visit, Brett overruled Latham and agreed to defer $175,000 of the author's 1937 royalties in case of an adverse judgment in the Davis litigation. What ensued next is something out of a slapstick comedy.

First, someone at Macmillan, presumably Brett, handwrote a note ordering the destruction of Latham's May letter. That order was not carried out: both Latham's letter and the note remain in the files today. Then Stephens Mitchell and Brett went back and forth, drafting a letter for Brett to sign that would give the appearance that it had been Macmillan's idea to withhold the royalties. They had trouble getting their act together, and at one point, Brett instructed the Atlanta attorney to be more specific about what he wanted and offered some advice about the art of surreptitious business schemes: "Now if you will tear up this letter it won't be in your files. It is simply to say that if you will write me an informal letter and tell me just exactly what it is you do want to do we shall be very glad to co-operate in every possible way."[10] Brett, or maybe his secretary, did not follow his own advice. A copy of his note to Stephens Mitchell—along with the draft letters—were filed in the Macmillan records. By July 27, they finally worked out mutually agreeable language, and Brett sent the author's brother a demand for the bond, along with a note saying he thought this version ought to "hold up under scrutiny."[11]

They reached their deal just in time. The next day, a federal trial court in New York dismissed the Davis case. The judge found that because both authors were "Southern women steeped in Southern tradition, writing about the South" it was natural there should be some similarities in their writing, but there was not enough resemblance to be actionable. While the ruling negated the excuse for Macmillan to retain Mitchell's funds, the judge left for vacation the following day, which meant there would be a delay of several weeks before he could enter a dismissal order. Brett directed Macmillan personnel not to release any formal announcement on the decision until the judge returned.[12] Even after the judge dismissed the case that fall, the firm still held on to Mitchell's money on the theory that Davis might challenge the court's ruling. Not until March 1938, when the appeal period expired, did Macmillan pay Mitchell the overdue royalties.[13]

With the Davis case disposed of, Cadwalader, Wickersham & Taft sent the author a bill for services rendered. Based on Brett's earlier prediction about what the case would cost, Mitchell had expected to owe a few hundred dollars in legal fees. But the New York lawyers were asking for a remarkable $7,581.83. The amount surprised even Brett, who thought the bill might be $2,500 at the most. He offered to pay that amount toward the invoice.[14] Admitting Cadwalader's bill took her breath away, Mitchell again declined Brett's offer to help; she wanted to live up to her obligation to pay the cost of the suit.[15] The only relief for Mitchell was that the court had ordered Davis to pay two thousand dollars of Macmillan's legal fees. It was a Pyrrhic victory though because Davis refused to pay and died of a heart attack in a Washington, D.C., hotel before Mitchell could wrest any of the money from her. Mitchell went after the estate and was not surprised to learn Davis was insolvent.*

~

The spring of 1937 presented further difficulties when the Marshes learned that a Danish newspaper, *Politiken*, had been running a serialization of *Gone With the Wind* without having signed a contract or paying royalties. It was, in publishing terms, a literary piracy. John Marsh was also concerned that the newspaper had failed to include the Macmillan copyright notice in its installments and had not agreed in writing to refrain from distributing its publication in the United States, the two requirements Macmillan had imposed on Mitchell's acceptance of the foreign rights. To make matters worse, Marion Saunders knew what *Politiken* was doing and had done nothing to stop it.[16] When questioned, the agent explained she had been in negotiations with the publication for a royalty agreement and saw nothing wrong with the paper getting started with its serialized version while the details were being finalized. As for *Politiken*'s failure to comply with Macmillan's requirements, Saunders gave a proverbial shrug. She did not think any foreign publisher would accept such terms and thought it absurd to ask.

---

* Mitchell purchased the meager assets of Davis's estate when it was auctioned in 1940. Consisting mostly of the elderly woman's personal papers and other assorted "junk," Mitchell paid thirty dollars for the lot and considerably more than that to have the items shipped to Atlanta. Perhaps she was curious to learn more about Davis or wanted to make sure that any papers related to the lawsuit did not end up in the hands of the press or a third party.

Stephens Mitchell contacted Brett, begging forgiveness: "We are exceedingly regretful that this has happened and that we have failed unintentionally in safeguarding Macmillan's rights. . . . It is a matter of great embarrassment to us, and Mr. and Mrs. Marsh ask me to say to you that they stand ready to make whatever is the proper restitution." What did Macmillan want them to do?[17] In a magnanimous mood, Brett told him not to worry. The publisher admitted that Mitchell would never be able to prevent distribution of translations in the United States and agreed to waive the requirement on one condition: Mitchell would have to indemnify Macmillan if a foreign serial translation was ever used to create an unauthorized edition in the United States. He acknowledged this was an onerous term but noted Mitchell could afford to bear the risk if she were careful about making the newspaper publishers agree in writing that adequate copyright notices would be included in every translation. Having accepted the foreign rights, Brett thought the responsibility ought to be hers.[18]

Stephens Mitchell could not argue with Brett's logic. His sister had signed a contract with Macmillan specifying how the foreign rights would be handled and had to assume responsibility for its compliance. He thanked the publisher and assured him it would not be an issue in the future. Realizing it would be almost impossible to control foreign newspapers and magazines, the Marshes decided not to allow any other serializations overseas.[19] As for *Politiken*, Margaret Mitchell reluctantly agreed the publisher could finish running the story on the condition that it include in all future installments an appropriate statement regarding Macmillan's copyright.

Mitchell put the *Politiken* matter to rest just in time to face another problem. In June, the *New York Herald Tribune* announced that Broadway producer and lyricist Billy Rose was preparing a theatrical production of *Gone With the Wind* as part of an upcoming revue in Fort Worth, Texas. A thirty-six-year-old former nightclub owner, Rose was a small man— nicknamed the Bantam Rooster—known for big ideas. Married to Ziegfeld Follies "Funny Girl" Fanny Brice, he achieved fame co-writing musical standards such as "Me and My Shadow" and "It's Only a Paper Moon." In 1935, he staged a spectacular musical circus extravaganza, *Jumbo*, at New York's Hippodrome Theatre and, the following year, in commemoration of the one hundredth anniversary of Texas's independence from Mexico, mounted a massive revue called the *Fort Worth Frontier Centennial*. The show featured a restaging of *Jumbo* and fan dancer Sally Rand hiding her curvaceous charms behind a balloon.

His new show, *Frontier Fiesta*, also promised to be quite a spectacle. The *Herald Tribune* described the planned *Gone With the Wind* segment:

> You will see a plantation in the Old South. Ladies and gentlemen will appear at a garden party, and Harriet Hoctor, famous ballerina, will arrive in a carriage drawn by four horses. She will portray Scarlett O'Hara, characterizing the romance of the book in dance. Mr. [Everett] Marshall will portray Rhett Butler and will sing *Gone With the Wind*. . . . Pickaninnies will dance and there will be an ensemble dance. The distant booming of cannon is heard, and Marshall gallops in on a horse, to shout that the end of a civilization is at hand. As the huge stage begins to turn, the mansion bursts into flame.[20]

The Fort Worth city fathers had high hopes that Rose would recapture the previous year's success with another extravaganza.

For all his elaborate planning, Rose forgot one essential detail—to ask Mitchell for permission to dramatize her novel. The author was shocked at his gall in laying claim to her story and characters. However, she was unsure how to proceed. With all the press attention over the Davis case, Mitchell was loath to take any action that would put her name back in the spotlight. She also did not want to cause trouble for a community event, especially in Texas, where her paternal grandfather had served in the Civil War. Yet, with the guidance of her brother and father, she decided to take a stand. If she allowed Rose to walk away with the dramatic rights for free, no one else would be willing to pay for them should she ever decide to sell. The day before the scheduled opening on June 26, 1937, Stephens Mitchell wrote the Frontier Fiesta Association, the planning organization in Fort Worth, pointing out that his sister owned the dramatic rights to *Gone With the Wind* and had never granted those rights to Rose or anyone else. The Fiesta's lawyers were nonplussed. They claimed to understand the author's rights in her literary property but said Mitchell had nothing to worry about because not a word of her text would be used in Rose's production. Suggesting that she should not place too much reliance on newspaper reports, the association invited Mitchell to Texas to see the show, which opened as planned.[21]

Mitchell had no intention of traveling to Texas or of being brushed off. As soon as Rose's show opened, press reports confirmed that the producer had usurped *Gone With the Wind* for his own benefit. On July 7, the *New York Evening Post* carried a report confirming the parallels, and a four-page feature in the July 19 edition of *Life* included two photographs from the *GWTW* sequence: one of costumed belles and beaux in front of a mansion facade, which the magazine referred to as the home of Scarlett O'Hara, and the other of a group of black children, with a caption stating "From *Gone With the Wind*." Stephens Mitchell hired legal counsel in Texas to approach the Fiesta in a more direct fashion. This time, the officials denied wrongdoing on the grounds that Rose had cleared the copyright matters through his friend, David O. Selznick. When the lawyers explained that Selznick had no authority to grant such rights, the officials reversed course and agreed to cooperate with Mitchell. However, they had no money to offer her in damages. The show was running a deficit and some of the smaller entertainment features were already scheduled to be eliminated in an attempt to cut costs. The officials warned Mitchell that Rose was committed to proceeding with the *Gone With the Wind* scenes and had discussed taking that portion of the show on a road tour.[22]

Marsh hired Howard Reinheimer, a well-known literary rights lawyer in New York, to assess whether Mitchell had a viable claim for copyright infringement against Rose. Reinheimer concluded that the author did have a case and pointed out that she arguably had a legal obligation to file suit, given that she had promised Selznick she would defend the *Gone With the Wind* copyright. The lawyer advised that the next step would be asking Macmillan to join her in a legal action. Although she owned the dramatic rights to her novel, Macmillan was the copyright owner of record and, thus, an interested party. If the publisher did not join the case, Rose would likely try to bring the publisher in involuntarily. Such action might result in Mitchell's contract with Macmillan being made public, something the author did not want to happen. She also did not like giving the impression that she and her publisher were not on the same team.

Although Mitchell wanted to get matters moving against Rose, it was not an ideal time for her to be asking Macmillan any favors. As luck would have it, this was the same week the Davis hearing was being held and all the machinations on the tax issue were being resolved. Further complicating matters, Saunders advised the Marshes that questions had been raised about the legitimacy of *Gone With the Wind*'s copyright in Europe. It would be yet another reason Mitchell needed Macmillan's assistance.

The European trouble began that busy spring of 1937. Saunders had been negotiating a contract with a Dutch publisher named W. L. Brusse when rumors began to surface in the Netherlands questioning whether *Gone With the Wind*'s copyright was protected under the "backdoor" Berne provision. The difficulty centered on the fact that the first printing of the American edition showed a publication date of May 1936, a month before the Canadian edition's publication. Brusse would not finalize the deal until Saunders proved to him that the American and Canadian editions had been published simultaneously, as required by the Berne Convention.[23] At Saunders's behest, Macmillan's Everett Hale wrote to Brusse, stating that the editions in Canada and the United States were both released on June 30, 1936.[24]

Not satisfied with Hale's statement, Brusse wanted Macmillan Canada to provide further assurances. Matters began to unravel. Hugh Eayrs of Macmillan Canada checked his records and noticed there had been a two-week delay in registration of the Canadian copyright after the June 30 publication. He wrote to Hale on May 21, 1937, claiming that his office had applied for registration of the *Gone With the Wind* copyright on June 30, suggesting the delay had been the copyright office's fault.[25] Did Eayrs not know his office had failed to file the registration until July 14? In any event, it was unclear to him how he should respond to Brusse, so he asked Hale to tell him what to say.[26]

Saunders and Hale took Eayrs's story at face value, and the party line became that Macmillan Canada had applied for the copyright registration concurrently with the American and Canadian publications on June 30. Anxious to salvage the deal, Saunders asked Frederic Melcher, editor of *Publishers Weekly*, for an expert opinion on whether the requirements of the "backdoor" Berne provision had been complied with under this scenario. The editor reviewed Eayrs's version of the facts and expressed his opinion that the delayed registration was inconsequential given that, as he understood it, application had been made promptly upon publication.[27]

Melcher's assurances were not enough for Brusse. The negotiations were scuttled when, in June, another Dutch publisher, Zuid-Hollandsche Uitgevers Maatschappij, known as ZHUM, announced it was preparing to release a multivolume illustrated edition of Mitchell's book. Citing the May publication date in the first printing, ZHUM asserted that the Canadian and American editions of *Gone With the Wind* had not been published simultaneously and, thus, Mitchell's book was not protected under the Berne Convention. The company claimed it was free to publish *Gone With the Wind* without Mitchell's permission and without paying her royalties. Saunders had a major problem on her hands. If ZHUM was correct, then publishers in all Berne signatory nations would have the same right, and her hopes of earning any commissions off Mitchell's European royalties would go up in smoke. To prevent that from happening, she approached ZHUM and tried to convince the firm to sign a contract with Mitchell.

Eager to avoid trouble with Marsh, Saunders did not initially tell her clients what was going on. She discussed the situation only with Macmillan, which she considered at fault for having released the books with the May printing date and not ensuring that the Canadian publication was registered properly. In a June 29, 1937, letter, she chastised Latham for failing to oversee matters more vigilantly, given that he had known before publication that Mitchell's book would prove valuable. Saunders warned him that if ZHUM refused to sign a contract, she would look to Macmillan to make things right, including paying any necessary legal fees. In a vaguely threatening tone she wrote, "Our friends in Atlanta do not know very much about Holland, and as there is this difference in the copyright dates, I hope you will not mind my bothering you with the details."[28]

By the middle of July, Saunders had not convinced ZHUM to sign a contract. The agent came clean with the Marshes and gave them a crash course in international copyright law. Dismayed at the perilous position of the book's overseas copyright, Mitchell was offended that the American government did so little to protect her interests abroad while taxing her within an inch of her life. More troubling, she realized what a mess the Berne problem presented in terms of the movie contract's "God Almighty clause," which obligated her to protect the copyright overseas. It was further proof to the Marshes of how ill prepared they had been to negotiate the movie contract and how poorly Mitchell had been represented by Macmillan in the negotiations.

Regardless of what the Berne treaty said, Mitchell considered ZHUM a thief. But what could she to do stop it? Taking on a character like Rose in Texas was one thing, battling international copyright law in The Hague quite another. The Marshes had no connections there, did not speak the language, and knew nothing about the Dutch legal system. Yet, if they did not fight ZHUM, they could be viewed as conceding that the copyright was not protected in Europe. Mitchell understood she had an obligation to Selznick to protect the copyright and, therefore, had no choice but to jump on ZHUM "like a duck on a June bug."[29]

So, at the same time the Marshes were working on the Rose matter, they also had to deal with finding Dutch legal counsel. With Saunders's assistance, Stephens Mitchell hired a lawyer named J. M. W. Knipscheer, whom the agent said had been recommended by the Netherlands Chamber of Commerce. He had an office in New York and worked with an associate in The Hague named Dr. Pot, who could handle any court filings and proceedings overseas. As in the Rose case, the lawyers advised Mitchell to file a lawsuit and that Macmillan should join as a co-plaintiff. She summed up her affairs on July 22, 1937: "To misquote Gilbert and Sullivan, 'An author's life is not a happy one!' Life is going to be a trifle complicated for some time to come."[30] The couple surely did not relish approaching Macmillan with news of two potential lawsuits—one across the country, the other across the Atlantic. However, they had no choice.

Perhaps to soften the blow, they did not present both cases to the firm simultaneously. On August 3, a lawyer from Reinheimer's office, William Bratter, telephoned Macmillan to discuss Mitchell's concerns about the Texas show. George Brett was on vacation, so the operator transferred the call to Richard Brett. Bratter described Mitchell's determination to fight Rose and asked Macmillan to join the cause. Brett received the entreaty coolly. The *Frontier Fiesta* was getting good reviews and coverage in major publications. He did not see why Macmillan would want to spend money fighting good publicity. Only after Bratter promised that Mitchell would pay all litigation costs did Brett agree to consider it.[31]

While Richard Brett mulled over the Rose case, Stephens Mitchell broached the subject of the Dutch piracy. He wrote George Brett on August 4, asking if the firm, as copyright owner, would join in the fight against ZHUM.[32] Here, too, the matter was referred to Richard Brett, who demonstrated little inclination to volunteer Macmillan's services.[33] The younger Brett ran the issue by Taft and learned that Macmillan was not obligated to join the lawsuit. That was all Brett needed to hear. He got back to Stephens Mitchell right away, telling him that, although he would like to be of assistance, Macmillan could not get involved.[34] He excused his lack of helpfulness on the fact that the United States had not signed the Berne Convention, as if that somehow precluded the firm from taking a stand in support of the book's copyright. In a thinly veiled brush-off, the younger Brett suggested the author ask Macmillan Canada for help. Evidence of Brett's lack of sympathy for her plight can be found in a letter he wrote to Eayrs cautioning him that Mitchell might ask the Canadian firm to join the litigation. Brett advised his Canadian counterpart to assist her only if he could do so at no expense.[35]

Richard Brett had a harder time deciding how to handle the Rose litigation. He recognized the validity of the author's claim but felt that the "Mitchell Tribe," as he referred to the Atlantans, was making an unnecessary fuss.[36] He asked Taft and the Macmillan sales department for guidance. The lawyer again advised that the publisher was not required to assist the author, and Herman Beaty, manager of trade advertising, recommended

Brett not join the suit. He warned that Rose might play the victim by claiming Macmillan had made millions off the story of Scarlett and Rhett and was picking on a poor artist trying to earn a little money for a charitable event.[37] This made sense to Brett, and he called Stephens Mitchell to tell him that Macmillan did not have a dog in that fight either. The publisher would not join the suit, and Richard Brett urged the Marshes to reconsider the idea of going after Rose.[38]

As had happened the previous summer, George Brett returned from vacation to find an unhappy Margaret Mitchell. This time, he did not dismiss her concerns out of hand. He agreed with his brother that Macmillan had no stake in the Dutch case; Mitchell had accepted the foreign rights, and she had to protect them.[39] However, on the Rose matter, he reversed course and agreed to join the lawsuit. On September 2, he wrote to Marsh and apologized for the company's unhelpful attitude. Brett understood Mitchell's anxiety about Rose's show and said that, although it was not in the best interests of Macmillan's sales department, he had no qualms about coming to her aid.[40]

With Macmillan's cooperation, Mitchell's lawyers filed suit in Texas, seeking an injunction and damages. Rose reacted with characteristic swagger, claiming the case did not worry him in the least. He extended an invitation to the Marshes to experience the *Frontier Fiesta* in person, offering to fly them down at his expense. According to Mitchell, when her husband refused, Rose threw down the gauntlet. He knew the author was averse to traveling and newspaper publicity and said he would make her come to Fort Worth to testify, where she was sure to find plenty of public attention.[41] Marsh replied that they were willing to take that chance.

Mitchell never had to make the trip. On September 14, a Texas court issued a restraining order, precluding the Frontier Fiesta Association from paying Rose any income from the performances. The judge set a hearing date of September 27 on the issue of whether to halt the show. In the face of almost certain failure, Rose agreed to bring the curtain down on September 26, three weeks earlier than scheduled. With the show canceled, the only remaining issue was damages. The parties negotiated over the next several months and reached an out-of-court settlement that called for a formal apology to Mitchell and payment of three thousand dollars in damages by Rose. The agreement required an additional penalty of twenty-five thousand dollars should the defendants again use the author's title or characters without her permission.

Mitchell's decision to take action paid off. She stopped Rose and sent a clear message that *Gone With the Wind* was not fair game. The experience gave her a new appreciation for the seriousness of the task before her. Chiselers lurked around every corner, she now felt, and it was up to the Mitchell-Marsh family to protect her rights. She might be a housewife from Atlanta, but that did not make her a doormat.

Mitchell put this new resolve to the test in dealing with Saunders. Amidst all the difficulties with ZHUM and Rose that summer, it had come to light that *Politiken* continued to omit the Macmillan copyright notice in its serialization. Saunders brushed the matter aside on the grounds that copyright notices were not required in Berne nations. She also did not see how such wording would have any practical effect deterring piracies. The Marshes were appalled by her reaction and let her know it:

> If your . . . argument were carried to its logical conclusion, you would be in the position of saying that there should be no laws against murder, arson and theft, simply because murder, arson and theft do take place in this naughty world, in spite of the laws against them. Just because there is always a danger that some evil person may attempt to steal *Gone With the Wind*, is that any reason why we should abandon any efforts to prevent theft? Is it any reason why we should not take sensible precautions to safeguard the property?[42]

The Marshes once again had to ask Macmillan for guidance.

This was another issue put before George Brett when he returned from vacation. He advised the couple that they needed to demonstrate the seriousness of the matter to *Politiken* and demand that it halt publication. Failure to include Macmillan's notice, he warned, could jeopardize the copyright, which Mitchell had an obligation to defend on behalf of both Selznick and Macmillan.[43] Marsh accepted the reproach and directed Saunders to fix things. But, once again, she balked. To her, it was not an issue worthy of expending effort, no matter what the Marshes had promised Macmillan or Selznick. The author and her husband were shocked at the agent's boldness in defying their instructions. Mitchell described their dealings with Saunders to Brett:

> We have had to write interminable letters, argue over long distance and in general wear out our nervous systems, trying to get her to do the things she had promised in her contract with me to do. Never before in the history of our legal-minded family have we ever had dealings with this kind of person,

and complete bewilderment was added to our weariness. We are all accustomed to people who do not thoughtlessly sign agreements and then refuse to live up to them.[44]

After talking themselves "blue in the face" trying to get Saunders to act, Marsh had had enough. Yet, he was not anxious to fire her. They were close to finalizing contracts in several countries; bringing in a new agent would only serve to cause further delays. He swallowed his pride and asked Brett to step in and knock some sense into Saunders.[45]

Once again, Brett proved himself on Mitchell's side. He took the agent out to lunch and set her straight on the seriousness of the situation. Coming from Brett, arguably the most powerful publisher in the United States, the medicine went down easier for her. She immediately cabled *Politiken* and demanded that the newspaper add the copyright notice to its future installments.[46] Mitchell thanked Brett for taking "a hand in the matter" and putting "things to rights." She conceded that Saunders may be "right and that we are indeed ignorant, country and prone to see trouble in the future where no trouble will ever come," but she was not ashamed of their position. "All of us would rather take steps immediately to prevent any possibility of future trouble rather than have it develop."[47]

Mitchell faced further frustration when Saunders advised that ZHUM steadfastly refused to sign a contract. With the Dutch edition scheduled to be published in November 1937, Mitchell authorized Knipscheer to seek an injunction in the Netherlands preventing the book from being released. The Marshes were not happy to find themselves in court for the third time in less than a year but had full confidence that, once again, the author's rights would be recognized. Mitchell felt comfortable Knipscheer had matters under control. Upon seeing a photograph of him, she told Brett that the lawyer was so good looking that she feared "the movie people may seize him bodily." But she hoped not, "for at just this moment I need a good Dutch lawyer."[48]

All was not doom and gloom that summer and fall of 1937. By June, the book's first anniversary, an estimated 1,350,000 copies of *Gone With the Wind* had been printed.[49] To celebrate, Macmillan issued a press release stating that, over the previous year, the book had sold an average of 3,700 copies a day, including Sundays and holidays.[50] The company developed a list of statistics to give a visual picture of what these numbers meant. In one year, Macmillan had used more than eleven tons of ink and ninety square miles of paper (four times the area of Manhattan) to produce Mitchell's book. If all the copies in existence were placed atop each other, the stack would be more than thirty-five miles high. If all pages in the books printed were laid end to end, they would reach more than ninety-two thousand miles, encircling the globe three and a half times. The dust jackets alone, if spread out side by side, would cover 425 acres.[51]

These amazing figures raised the question of how much more could *Gone With the Wind* sell in its current form. Was there anyone in the United States who wanted to read the book who had not yet purchased it or borrowed a copy from a library or a friend? Some industry insiders suggested it was time for Macmillan to replace the original three-dollar edition with a cheaper one aimed at the bottom end of the book-buying market. Others thought Macmillan should sell the serial rights to a newspaper or magazine. A long list of periodicals had offered to run serializations, and their editors were waiting for Macmillan to open bidding on the rights.

Brett scoffed at the idea of giving up so soon. In September 1937, Macmillan placed a full-page notice in *Publishers Weekly* announcing there would be no cheap edition of the book that fall because there was no doubt that the original edition would continue to sell in the upcoming Christmas season.[52] After that, the movie release, then scheduled for the fall of 1938, would be sure to generate continued interest. Macmillan's fortitude would prove well founded. The book sold well throughout the remainder of 1937 and was the bestselling work of American fiction for the second year in a row.

The authorized foreign editions also fared well. By summer, Saunders had wrapped up deals in Denmark, Finland, France, Germany, Norway, Poland, and Sweden and had several others in the works.[53] Copies of the translations started to make their way to Atlanta that fall and proved a pleasant diversion for the Marshes. The couple studied each one and expressed amazement at how the book was transformed from country to country. They had great fun deciphering the different dialects and were struck by terms such as "Gawdlmighty" becoming "Ach, Gott!" in German. Although they could nitpick here and there—the typeface in one was rather small, the paper quality poor in another—the Marshes were satisfied with how the foreign editions had come together.

Most impressive were the vivid dust jacket illustrations created by several of the European publishers. Whereas the American jacket offered only a small sketch of three unidentified persons, the foreign artists presented bold depictions of specific characters. Especially striking was the Danish edition, the first to contain interior illustrations. Mitchell said she had never thought much of "Captain Butler" until she saw the depiction of him in the book from Denmark, claiming the image gave her "a girlish flutter of the heart."[54] The German Rhett also stood out. The artist had given him a fierce, almost deranged, expression, which is largely hidden by a bristling black mustache. Latham found the depiction "perfectly terrific (in the sense of terrifying)."[55] In one case, the cover art was attractive but disconcerting. The first of a two-volume Czechoslovakian edition carried an American flag on the dust jacket. Seeing the Stars and Stripes on such a thoroughly Confederate book seemed out of place to the author, and she asked Saunders to explain the situation to the publisher.[56] When the second volume arrived, she exclaimed to Latham with relief, "They gave us the Confederate flag on this one!"[57]

As word spread about the overseas editions, Mitchell once again found herself the center of attention in Atlanta. Family, friends, and fans wanted to see what the novel looked like in a foreign language. To cut down on people ringing her doorbell and asking to see the books, Mitchell agreed to let the local library put them on display.[58] She also loaned the Danish edition and its original illustrations to the Atlanta Historical Society, which arranged them in a window of the Biltmore Hotel in downtown Atlanta. Mitchell reported to Brett that there was an "unbelievable amount of interest" and that swarms of people were "hanging about" the exhibits.[59] He complimented her savvy in letting the public enjoy the books; new publicity was always good for business, he said.[60]

Also exciting were the reviews, which Saunders helped Mitchell translate. A Danish reviewer praised the book in picturesque terms noting, "It is indeed a juicy fruit that [publisher] Steen Hasselbalch has caught in his lap. Some people may think that it is too large, too long, but do not worry—the important thing is that it really is a delicious fruit, full of juice, meat and seeds."[61] A Swedish newspaper called Mitchell's novel an "outstanding literary gem."[62] In Finland, a critic noted the parallels between that nation's history and the American Civil War and said Finnish readers would be encouraged by the greatness America had achieved after the struggles it had endured in the war.[63] The author found the reviews exciting and humbling. Reports of the public response overseas were gratifying as well. The German edition sold forty thousand copies in five weeks. The Danish publisher sold its entire first printing of ten thousand copies in eleven days and hoped to sell forty thousand more.[64]

Mitchell found herself in a new realm of fame, one far broader than she had experienced in 1936. Madeleine Baxter, a friend from Smith College who had traveled in Europe, wrote the author about the popularity of the German *Gone With the Wind.* While in a Munich bookstore, Baxter mentioned to a clerk that she knew Mitchell. Baxter reported that the man grabbed her hand and exclaimed, " 'I wish to kiss the hand of the friend of this great writer.' "[65] Now an international celebrity, Mitchell received a fresh round of fan letters. Europeans were fascinated by her and demanded to know who she was and what made her tick. A Hungarian admirer lamented:

> I don't know if you like Mendelssohn, I don't know if your heart has ever been touched by a Shelly [*sic*] poem. I don't know what you think of *Midsummer Night's Dream* and if you like Benvenuto Cellini? Again I don't know how you eat your grapefruit, peeled or just cut in half? If you pour maraschino over it or if you are afraid of gaining weight? I know nothing and I'd love to know everything [about] a writer from Georgia who wrote the book about Scarlett O'Hara.[66]

As she did with letters from her American fans, Mitchell endeavored to answer each one.

Predictably, the rumor mill began churning again, and the foreign press picked up the stories that had circulated about Mitchell over the previous year and, in many cases, expanded upon them. By the time she achieved fame in South Africa, for example, she was no longer a shy recluse but now had a "deranged" mind caused by her success.[67] This time, Mitchell tried to take the attention more philosophically, managing on occasion to find the humor in some of it. She wrote to Latham about a story circulating in France that depicted the acceptance of her manuscript as if out of a romantic fantasy:

> My faithful husband and my faithful old black Bessie (This is the literal translation) cried, "Voila, a masterpiece!" My husband felt that this book was more than a symptom of the disease. (You figure that one out. I can't.) He stole it from me and went to New York. In practically no time *une auto puissante* drew up in front of a beautiful home my husband had bought for me, and a dashing gentleman said to the old and faithful and black Bessie, "Announce to madame the presence of monsieur Harold S. Latham, Vice President and Editor of the Macmillan Publishing Company." This well prepared editor also whipped a contract out of his pants pocket. I cannot get the next idiom but it appears that I went into lady-like vapours, but my hus-

band spoke to me with kindness and firmness, and, like an obedient wife, I signed a contract just prior to a long swoon.[68]

Perhaps because of the geographical distance, she was better able to see the lighter side of such stories.

Mitchell found most of her foreign publishers to be an earnest group of people and enjoyed working with them. She could not help but be impressed by the energy they put into selling her novel. She especially appreciated the efforts of Vaclav Petr, her Czechoslovakian publisher, who had a flair for advertising. As Saunders put it, he was "pleased as Punch" to have Mitchell on his list and invested generously in the book's promotion.[69] He organized a window display contest for booksellers, as well as a public exhibition of *Gone With the Wind* foreign editions. Following Macmillan's lead, he created an informational brochure about Mitchell to distribute to newspapers and fans.[70] The author also admired her German publisher, Henry Goverts, who was new to the business and eager to prove himself with *Gone With the Wind*. Optimistic about the book's chance for success, he invested some of his personal funds to promote it.[71]

Mitchell was so impressed with her overseas publishers that she supported their efforts the best she could. On several occasions, she lifted her moratorium against book signing and inscribed foreign editions for the publishers to use in their promotions. When Denmark's Hasselbalch organized a contest offering one lucky reader a trip to Georgia, Mitchell agreed to give the winner a personal tour of local Civil War sites. The recipient was a middle-aged bookkeeper named Emanuel Christensen, whom Hasselbalch referred to as having "a certain YMCAishness." Mitchell arranged for the visitor to be squired around town by historian Wilbur G. Kurtz and an elderly Danish interpreter, and she joined them in Clayton County for a tour of the area around Jonesboro. She also hosted a dinner for Christensen that included a performance of spirituals by a quartet from Bessie Jordan's church. Macmillan got in on the act and used the Dane's visit as an opportunity to draw attention to foreign interest in *Gone With the Wind*. When Christensen traveled through New York on his way home, Macmillan showed him a grand time, taking him to the Empire State Building, Radio City Music Hall, and the circus.[72]

One challenge of handling the foreign editions was juggling the needs and personalities of so many different people. On one occasion, the German publisher became upset because the Danish publisher had obtained access to photographs of Mitchell taken by the Associated Press. Although Mitchell had nothing to do with circulating the images, she took the time to smooth things over by sending the German publisher a studio pose that had not yet been used overseas.[73] There were also instances where the foreign publishers seemed to be stepping on each other's toes, such as when the Latvian edition used the same cover art as the German edition. Mitchell had no idea whether permissions had been granted but decided to keep out of it.

She was so proud of her success overseas that she shared copies of the foreign editions with people who meant a great deal to her. On a regular basis, she gave extra copies of the treasured books to her husband, George Brett, Harold Latham, Lois Cole, Norman Berg, and Margaret Daugh— many of them signed. She also donated overseas editions to the Atlanta Historical Society, Emory University, and Wesleyan College in Macon, Georgia; some of those were signed as well. Perhaps in her mind, there was a distinction between signing copies of "the book" and signing translations.

Mitchell's enjoyment of the foreign editions fell by the wayside in November when a Dutch court denied her motion for an emergency injunction against ZHUM's unauthorized edition. Pending a full trial on the merits of the case, which could take months, ZHUM was free to sell its translation of *Gone With the Wind*. Mitchell likened the news to an explosion of shrapnel.[74] Because overseas communication was so difficult in those days, the Marshes did not have a firm understanding of what had gone wrong. The best they could figure is that the Dutch court had made its decision based on a misimpression that the first American edition had been released in May 1936, rather than June. Pot, Knipscheer's associate who had appeared in court on Mitchell's behalf, failed to explain that the May date in the first printing did not reflect the actual month of publication in the United States.[75] The Marshes blamed Knipscheer for the adverse ruling, claiming he had not consulted with them in preparing his pleadings.[76]

Angry and ready to wrangle, Mitchell explored her options for challenging the decision. Not willing to risk further misunderstandings, the Marshes looked to the U.S. government to clarify matters with the Dutch court. Expecting a speedy resolution, Mitchell and her brother traveled to Washington, D.C., where they met with Georgia senator Walter F. George, who escorted them to the Department of State. They met with, among others, Wallace McClure in the Office of Treaty Affairs, an expert on international copyright law who had experience with Dutch publishers in similar cases. With McClure's support, the department wired the American ambassador in Holland asking him to confer with Pot and to approach the Dutch government about protecting her interests.[77] Although the U.S. government could not officially intervene, Mitchell appreciated McClure's support. Over the coming months—and for many years thereafter—she would rely on him for guidance in navigating the murky waters of international copyright law.

From McClure's perspective, the timing of Mitchell's problem with ZHUM was fortuitous. The Berne treaty happened to be up for ratification before the U.S. Senate that December. If America joined the convention, American publishers and authors would automatically have copyright protection in most of Europe without having to go through the hoops of the convoluted "backdoor" provision. McClure encouraged Mitchell to take a stand. As he explained to her brother, "Patriotic citizens from Mark Twain to the present day, over a period of many years, have sought to bring about this result. If your sister can achieve it, I suggest that she may be doing a service to her fellows that is at least somewhat comparable to that of producing a masterpiece like *Gone With the Wind.*"[78] Ratification would not affect Mitchell's current case against the Dutch publisher, but she agreed to help. As she saw it, joining Berne would encourage the development of American literature if writers in the United States were protected by their government and did not have to waste time, energy, and money fighting for their rights in foreign countries.

At McClure's invitation, the author made plans to appear before the Senate Committee on Foreign Relations. Although reluctant to draw attention to herself, she seemed energized by the chance to tell her story—a rare state for her in those hectic and stressful days. She wrote to Brett that she was "all a-twit" and wondered "if I am to have a secret service man for my very own. Things do get curiouser and curiouser!"[79] To Mitchell's disappointment, the ratification issue bogged down in committee, and the hearing date was postponed. She apparently did not make the trip to Washington.★ But McClure had planted a seed in the author's mind about the importance of Berne ratification, and it became a cause she supported the rest of her life. She also became more strongly convinced that she had to fight ZHUM in court, no matter the cost or inconvenience.

When Macmillan learned that Mitchell had failed to secure an injunc-

---

★ In a 1947 letter to George Brett, Mitchell referred to having appeared before a Senate subcommittee on the issue of international copyright protection. However, no details about when such a presentation occurred have been uncovered.

tion against ZHUM, George Brett began to see that his firm could no longer take a disinterested position in the case. If Mitchell was denied coverage under Derne's "backdoor" provision, it would have serious implications for all American authors and publishers. He was not willing to accept responsibility for Macmillan's missteps that had created the problem or join the case with her—as Saunders thought the firm should—but he did reach out to Mitchell and offer support. He told the author he was frightfully worried about the "low down snide piece of business" and encouraged her to fight.[80] He suggested that she hire Macmillan's lawyer, Taft, to help develop a legal strategy on appeal. He also expressed an interest in working with the Department of State and traveled to Washington to meet with McClure.

Sensing that the legal team Saunders had arranged was not up to par, the Marshes took Brett's advice and hired Taft to assess how matters were being handled by the Dutch lawyers. Taft looked into Knipscheer's qualifications and came away underwhelmed. According to a report Taft received from government sources, it appeared the Dutchman had not been admitted to the bar in the Netherlands and had been disciplined for unauthorized practice of law. Worse, rumors were circulating that he might have been involved in a blackmail incident, although he did not have a criminal record.[81] Taft fired Knipscheer and Pot and replaced them with J. A. Fruin, whom Taft's sources assured him was one of the best lawyers in the Netherlands.

The ordeal with the lawyers behind them, the Marshes hoped things would be put to rights in short order. Through Mitchell's clipping service, the couple learned that the Dutch publisher had released the first two of its planned three-volume edition of *Gone With the Wind*. By all accounts, the books were beautifully made with attractive illustrations. Although pleased with the quality, Mitchell noted with frustration that ZHUM could well afford to spend money on the edition given that the firm was not bothering to pay her royalties. In a small attempt at humor, Saunders commented that the Dutch reviews were rather "flat" and suggested that "perhaps the flatness of the country is responsible."[82] Mitchell, too, managed to make light of a serious situation. When she eventually obtained copies of the pirated book, she sent Latham a set inscribed with a line from an old poem: "In matters of commerce, the fault of the Dutch is granting too little and taking too much."[83]

# 11

# From Greenland's Icy Mountains to India's Coral Strand

## 1938

If the Marshes held a grudge against Marion Saunders for bringing J. M. W. Knipscheer into their lives, they kept it to themselves. Yet, her handling of the matter must have been on their minds when they were confronted with a new set of problems brewing with the foreign accounts. In the early days of 1938, the couple learned of two additional unauthorized translations. The first was an Italian edition, to be published by Mondadori, a firm with which Saunders was negotiating a contract. John Marsh was waiting for the deal to be formalized when he read in a press clipping that Mondadori's edition would be on the market any day. The publisher also sent Macmillan copies of its promotional materials, as if the deal was already final.[1] Marsh wrote Saunders, demanding to know why the contract had not been signed and where the royalties were. As usual, the agent acted unconcerned; she blamed the delay on difficulties exporting money from Benito Mussolini's Italy.[2] The situation worked out amicably, but it was further evidence to Marsh that the overseas contracts—and Saunders—had to be watched carefully.

When Margaret Mitchell received the Italian edition, she could not help but be charmed. She found the dust jacket "colorful and spirited" and was amused to discover that Scarlett's name had been changed to Rossella, which she guessed meant "little Rosie."[3] She reported to Harold Latham that her hairdresser, a second-generation Italian, had been thrilled with the

book when she showed it to him: "He was so enthusiastic about the translation that he cut off most of my . . . hair while describing it."[4] However,
there were problems with the quality of the volume. She noted the covers
were spotted and warped easily. The back was so cheaply put together that
she feared it would "come apart in one reading."[5] The publisher apologized
for the substandard stock, blaming it on a paper shortage. With Europe on
the brink of war, Saunders speculated that the rag material used in higher
quality paper was being used for sandbags and soldier's kits.[6]

More difficult to resolve would be an unauthorized Spanish-language
edition circulating in South America. The book had been published in
Chile, a non–Berne nation that had signed a reciprocal copyright agreement
with the United States. An American author could obtain copyright protection there by registering a work with the government in Santiago. However, neither Macmillan nor the Marshes had done so for *Gone With the
Wind*, and the book was not protected. In the fall of 1937, two savvy Chilean publishers had realized that the book was fair game and raced to release
a translation. The winner was a firm named Ercilla that pulled together a
flimsy paperback edition.[7] When Saunders learned of the unauthorized
translation, she decided to pressure the publisher into signing a contract,
just as she had tried to do with Zuid-Hollandsche Uitgevers Maatschappij
(ZHUM). Without bothering to consult Marsh, she sent Ercilla an airmail
letter threatening to go to the newspapers and cry theft if the publisher did
not sign a contract.[8]

When Marsh learned what Saunders had done, he was furious. He
worried that negotiating with the rogue publisher would open the door for
other firms to slap together cheap editions to weasel their way into obtaining the rights to *Gone With the Wind*. He told Saunders she had overstepped
her boundaries by not consulting him. Yet, for all his certainty that Saunders
had done the wrong thing, Marsh had no idea what they should do. Mitchell's contract with David O. Selznick obligated her to protect the copyright
internationally. Did this mean she had to fight every unauthorized edition
that popped up anywhere in the world? Marsh had no idea. Again in over
his head, Marsh sought advice from George Brett. It must have been a bitter
pill to swallow, knowing that if Macmillan had done its job as Mitchell's
agent on the movie contract, foreign piracies would not be her problem.
On top of that, Brett had advised the couple that foreign rights were nothing but trouble. They had ignored his warning and now were having to

defend the copyright in countries they knew nothing about. "Our greatest difficulty in this situation," he admitted to Brett, "is that we are constantly confronted with problems that are wholly new and strange to us."[9]

The situation presented a new and strange problem for Brett as well. Other American authors had been pirated, but few had bothered to put up much of a fight, given the logistics and the relatively insignificant amount of money involved. Because Mitchell was breaking new ground, Brett could not point her to other precedents as a guide. Once again, he referred the couple to Walbridge Taft.

Marsh asked the lawyer how to deal with the Chilean publisher and what, if anything, could be done to prevent similar situations in other countries. He also instructed Saunders that Taft now called the shots on the foreign editions and nothing should be done on any of the accounts until the lawyer had things under control.[10] Saunders did not welcome this additional layer of oversight. She had several deals in the works, and her income from them would now be on hold indefinitely. She also did not appreciate Marsh's complaints about her handling of the Chilean situation and vented to the author, "I felt rather like the little boy who discovered a fire, but was not exactly in favor because it was thought he might have prevented it!"[11] To make matters worse, the Marshes were relying on the advice of Macmillan, which, after all, was at fault for not having protected the copyright to begin with. Saunders believed it had been a grave misjudgment on Macmillan's part distributing the books containing the May 1936 copyright date and failing to register the copyright in non–Berne nations. Yet, she did not want to go on record and hash it out with the powerful publisher. "I do not wish to be quoted, you understand," she told Mitchell, who bore the brunt of her frustration. "We all make mistakes, agents as well as publishers!"

Marsh also reached out for guidance to the Department of State's Wallace McClure, who contacted the American Embassy in Chile on Mitchell's behalf. McClure reported back with the unfortunate news that Ercilla had acted within its rights. Because neither Macmillan nor the Marshes had filed for copyright protection in Chile, Ercilla had violated no law.[12] After reviewing their options with Taft, Marsh understood he had no choice but to fall back on Saunders's original plan of negotiating a deal with the firm. If the publisher acknowledged Macmillan's copyright, Marsh would grant Ercilla exclusive rights to distribute *Gone With the Wind* in Chile and non-exclusive rights throughout Spanish-speaking South America, Central America, and Mexico. To everyone's relief, the firm accepted. The book was selling so well Ercilla agreed to pay royalties and also issue an improved edition.[13]

On Taft's advice, Marsh signed a contract without raising various legal technicalities that remained unresolved.[14] The lawyer convinced him that their interests were better served by getting a deal done without protracted negotiations. Even so, it was quite a feat finalizing the paperwork. Mitchell reported there were sixteen copies of the contract to be signed by assorted officials, including the governor and secretary of state of Georgia, the Department of State in Washington, and a Chilean governmental minister. In those days of wax seals on official documents, she joked to Brett that "the Seal of the State of Georgia is as big as a Smithfield ham and, as the weather was warm, the seals were very mushy." She guessed the filing fees alone ate up the royalties she would earn on the edition, not to mention the legal costs.[15]

While the Marshes scrambled to figure out what to do in Chile, the Dutch case heated up. Mitchell's appeal was scheduled to be heard at the end of January 1938, and the Marshes found themselves dealing with interminable communications between New York, Washington, D.C., and The Hague.[16] Overwhelmed by "work and worry," Mitchell lost her patience: "My mind is made up that if I do win I am going to try to hang damages that will look like the national war debt on ZHUM."[17] A week before the hearing, ZHUM expressed interest in reaching a deal, but Mitchell declined to pursue a settlement. Latham thought this foolish and suspected it was J. A. Fruin who had counseled her to fight to the end.[18]

Fruin appeared in court armed with affidavits from Brett and Hugh Eayrs establishing the facts related to the publication of *Gone With the Wind* in America and Canada. At Fruin's suggestion, Latham, who was in England at the time on a scouting trip, traveled to The Hague to testify in person. With the factual record laid out in detail, Fruin convinced the court that the initial ruling had been in error. The court ordered the sale of the Dutch edition halted and all unsold copies seized pending a full trial.[19]

While this was welcome news, it did not signal the end of Mitchell's Dutch troubles. ZHUM dug in its heels and continued the fight under a new argument. The publisher now claimed that Macmillan Canada had not published the work at all but rather acted as a distributing agent for books provided by Macmillan New York. ZHUM appealed the court's ruling, and to Mitchell's amazement, the injunction was reversed. ZHUM had the

Dutch edition back on the market in a matter of weeks. Mitchell authorized Taft and Fruin to proceed with another appeal. The author knew she was spending far more on the case than the royalties were worth but vowed to see it through.

Although Macmillan would not join Mitchell in the case, Brett followed the proceedings and did what he could to help from a distance. He apparently never admitted it to Mitchell, but he gradually realized there had been irregularities in protection of the Canadian copyright, especially the two-week delay in its registration. Eayrs defended his firm's actions, stating that it had followed standard Canadian practice, but, as Brett pointed out, this was no defense if standard practice did not comport with the law. Also lurking in the background was the early release by Macmillan of copies of the book to Lewis Titterton and Mitchell. If any of these facts came before the Dutch court, the author's case might be in serious trouble. And, if Mitchell lost, the foreign copyright to Macmillan's other titles—and those of many other publishers—would be in jeopardy to the extent similar lapses had occurred with other books. Brett now viewed Mitchell's case as one of the most important in the history of copyright law.[20] He felt so strongly about it that he traveled to The Hague that spring as a witness on her behalf at another hearing. Although the court did not allow him to testify, his trip indicated how seriously he viewed the matter.

To guide the Marshes on avoiding similar problems in other countries, Taft's firm conducted an exhaustive study of copyright laws around the globe, country by country. The good news was that Taft felt they had a strong case for "backdoor" coverage under Berne, despite the irregularities that had occurred, and recommended the Marshes take no further action to preserve the copyright in Berne countries pending the outcome of the Dutch litigation. He also identified several South American countries that gave automatic protection to any book copyrighted in the United States. The bad news was that Mitchell faced a serious risk of piracy in countries that had no copyright law, including Albania, Estonia, Iceland, Iran, Latvia, Lithuania, Russia, and Saudi Arabia. Other countries, such as Bolivia, Egypt, Iraq, Liberia, Sudan, Turkey, and Venezuela, had domestic copyright laws but were not members of any major international conventions. These countries were under no obligation to allow Americans to register copyrights within their borders; further inquiries would have to be made about what could be done to protect *Gone With the Wind*. More danger lurked in countries like Chile that had reciprocal agreements with the United States, including Argentina, Austria, Cuba, Mexico, and Romania.[21] In these countries, Mitchell's book was ripe for the picking until such time as she registered the copyright in each place.

For countries that allowed foreign authors to register copyrights, the Marshes came to the distressing conclusion that they would have to hire Taft to do so in each nation. This would be an expensive and time-consuming process because the lawyers had to research each country's procedures and dispatch the necessary documents. In countries without a protective copyright law, the Marshes decided their best bet was to find legitimate publishers to issue authorized editions in the hope of discouraging pirates from entering the market. They gave Saunders the go-ahead to arrange for contracts in as many of those countries as possible, even if the terms were not attractive. Where she could not get authorized editions in place, they would wait and see what happened.

By May 1938, Brett finally acknowledged that the movie contract had put Mitchell in an impossible situation. It did not seem fair to him that she should have to spend so much time and money preventing piracies overseas because of the "God Almighty clause." He broached the issue with Selznick's lawyers, who agreed that piracies in small and remote countries would not materially affect the studio's rights. Encouraged, Brett suggested the author ask Selznick to clarify what he wanted her to do.[22] Mitchell appreciated the gesture but declined to grovel to the producer. Although the movie contract had hung over her "like the sword of Damocles" and cost her and her family "unhappiness, worry and money," she was determined to meet her obligation to protect the copyright "from Greenland's icy mountains to India's coral strand." Only then would she approach Selznick.[23]

As *Gone With the Wind* celebrated its second anniversary in June 1938, Macmillan approached production of the 1,500,000th copy of the three-dollar edition.[24] This time, though, the landmark edition would not go to Mitchell. The previous February, Selznick had called dibs on this copy, as well as the two millionth. With Brett's permission, Lois Cole agreed to the former.[25] However, she did not go to any great pains to make sure Selznick received his heart's desire. She directed the printing department to hold a copy from the press run that included the milestone number, telling them it was not necessary to pull out the exact copy the producer wanted.[26]

That summer also signaled Mitchell's first return to New York since the movie contract negotiations in 1936. The main purpose of the trip was to spend time with Cole, who had just given birth to her first child, a son named Turney Allan Taylor, Jr. The Taylors had asked Mitchell to be the boy's godmother. During her visit, she spent a night at their Greenwich Village apartment. Allan Taylor slept on the couch so Cole and Mitchell could share the bedroom and talk.[27] They caught up on personal matters, but the business of publishing also cropped up. Cole hoped her friend might write again and nudged her in that direction, suggesting Mitchell had given people so much pleasure that she practically had a duty to produce another book. The author said she probably would some day, when the fan mail fell off and the foreign editions were all published.

When Brett heard she would be in the city, he gushed at the chance to meet her in person. "Oh, do tell us more," he pleaded, wanting to know her itinerary. He lived in Connecticut and hoped she would consider visiting him there, as well as at the New York office. He offered to host a picnic on his yacht for Mitchell and her friends and to take her to a Broadway show. Mitchell declined the boat ride, claiming she was prone to seasickness and did not think she would make a pleasant guest for Mrs. Brett if she "turned green and prayed fervently for quick death." However, she did agree to visit the Macmillan offices and go to the theater.[28]

Macmillan rolled out the red carpet for its star author. George Brett, Harold Latham, Alec Blanton, and James Putnam escorted her through the building, showing her off and introducing her to many of the people who had been working so hard on behalf of *Gone With the Wind*. The author James Michener, then a junior editor, recalled years later his secretary calling out excitedly as Mitchell approached his office. He watched from his door "as the solemn procession, much like the marching priests in *Aida*, moved past." The executives, all wearing grave countenances, surrounded the diminutive author while she nodded greetings to everyone they passed. Later that day, after Michener had occasion to shake hands with her, he could not get over how petite she was. A joke circulated around the Macmillan office that, when Mitchell went to formal dinners, she carried a copy of *Bartlett's Quotations* to put on the floor to use as a footstool.[29]

And, a sure sign that her ill feelings toward Macmillan had been soothed, the author participated in a press conference arranged by the publisher. At long last, Brett was able to introduce her formally to the press. She charmed the journalists with stories of how busy she had been over the previous two years fighting piracies and fending off starlets vying for a role in Selznick's film. She tried to dispel some of the old rumors that continued to circulate, especially that she had been working on a sequel.[30]

When she returned to Atlanta, Mitchell thanked Brett for allowing her to interrupt the company's busy schedule: "My appreciation of what The Macmillan Company has done for me increases with time rather than diminishes. That was why I wanted to meet the staff—from the telephone operators who have handled my frenzied long distance calls to the boys on the bottom floor who sent the books on their way."[31] In this letter, Mitchell addresses the publisher by his first name, something she appears to have never done before. Whereas she and Latham had been writing each other informally since 1935, Brett and Mitchell had started off on the wrong foot and had been on reserved terms ever since. After meeting Brett in person, he became "My dear George" to her, and she "Peggy" to him. Although Marsh still licked his wounds over the movie deal and would for years to come, Mitchell appeared to have moved on.

With so many copies of *Gone With the Wind* in circulation, Brett at long last considered the possibility that the three-dollar edition had run its course. In August, publishing magnate William Randolph Hearst offered to buy the serial rights for ten thousand dollars and made a compelling argument Macmillan should sell before the movie release.[32] Unsure, Brett turned for advice to Waldo McClure of the McClure Newspaper Syndicate. His friend advised Brett not to sell, predicting it would be the death knell of the book to run the entire story in newspaper installments. Brett also sought input from Mitchell, who was entitled to 50 percent of the proceeds of any serialization. She admitted to having little understanding of these types of deals but did have two concerns. First, she was in no particular hurry to sell because a lump sum payment would have increased her taxable income. Second, if now was the time to sell the rights, she wanted to be sure her former employer, the *Atlanta Journal*, would have a chance to bid.[33]

Brett rejected Hearst's offer but had come to accept that it was time to dip his toe into the low end of the market. That fall, Macmillan announced to the trade plans to issue a hardcover "cheap edition" of *Gone With the Wind* in time for the 1938 holiday season. Priced at $1.49, it would look like the original book but use a lower quality paper and binding. At Blanton's suggestion, it would be marketed as a Christmas present for those who shopped chain drugstores and cigar stores.[34] To create a sense of urgency, the new edition was made available to retailers for two weeks only, from November 1 through November 14.[35] Brett had high hopes that this special offer would do well. He wrote Marsh that Macmillan felt sure it had at least

$250,000 "in the bag," maybe even $350,000. "If we do it will be most satisfactory and, in that case, would produce—oh well just chicken feed to the Marshes! but a neat little $17,500.00." He did not want to commit any chickens before they were hatched but predicted the company might sell as many as five hundred thousand copies.[36] Marsh responded succinctly: "I won't make any comment on your reports of sales of the new edition except to say that I continue to be amazed."[37]

As Brett predicted, the cheap edition was a success. Stores promoted it enthusiastically, some paying out of their own pockets for newspaper advertising. The Emporium department store in San Francisco devoted a store-front window to the new edition, featuring a Scarlett mannequin with a skirt made of the book's dust jackets. *Publishers Weekly* reported Macmillan sold 250,000 copies in the first nine days of the promotion, with reorders pouring in at a phenomenal rate.[38] By the time the deadline expired, Macmillan had received orders for a remarkable 338,000 copies.[39]

Two years after the movie contract had been signed, Selznick had not shot one foot of film for *Gone With the Wind*. As Mitchell had warned, difficulties abounded in bringing her epic story to the big screen. The script proved a major complication and ultimately involved more than a dozen writers, including F. Scott Fitzgerald. Also slowing things down was the casting. Clark Gable, the reigning he-man of Hollywood, seemed the obvious choice for Rhett Butler, but Selznick did not have the authority to cast him. Gable was under exclusive contract to Metro-Goldwyn-Mayer (MGM), Hollywood's largest and most powerful studio that just happened to be run by Selznick's father-in-law, Louis B. Mayer. MGM's legendary boss was not about to loan his biggest star to another studio without exacting a hefty price. Family ties went only so far in Screenland. Selznick could have Gable only if the producer agreed to give MGM half the film's profits. In addition, MGM's parent company, Loew's, Inc., wanted to distribute the movie and take its own cut of the grosses. With the public overwhelmingly in favor of Gable, Selznick felt he had no choice but to accept the terms.*

Selznick International had a distribution contract with United Artists that ran through the end of 1938, which meant that for Loew's to be involved in *Gone With the Wind* the movie could not be released until the

---

* Although the Marshes refused to publicly express any opinion on casting, Gable was not their first choice. "In our opinion, his he-man stuff is synthetic," Marsh wrote his sister on August 1, 1936. "He just doesn't ring the bell."

following year. The delay worked to Selznick's advantage as he needed all the time he could get to find the perfect Scarlett to go with his perfect Rhett. Russell Birdwell, Selznick's public relations director, had launched a nationwide search for Scarlett that, much to Mitchell's frustration, had been dragging on since late 1936. Established screen sirens and would-be stars overwhelmed the studio with pleas to play the famous vixen, and many approached Mitchell as well. Despite denying that she had any responsibility for the film or its casting, people still believed the author was their inside ticket to Hollywood. She received countless letters about it; people stopped her on the street; and the telephone rang with fans anxious for the latest scoop.

The studio consumed her time as well. Although she had made clear after the movie contract was signed that she would not offer Selznick any assistance with the film's production, his staff continued to hound her with questions and pleas for help. She lost her patience and finally told them that if they did not leave her alone she would sue them for breach of contract.[40] As the months dragged into years, the author grew increasingly bothered at the annoyances associated with the movie. She complained to Kay Brown in 1938: "Selznick International Pictures may think *GWTW* is a headache to them, but, dearie, the film has been a Grade A headache to me!"[41]

With the film still in the preproduction stage, Selznick's attention wandered to future projects he might pursue with Mitchell. The producer sent a memorandum to Brown asking her to approach the author about writing a sequel to *Gone With the Wind* for the movies. If she did not want to write the story herself, he was open to the idea of the studio taking on the job and maybe releasing a series of sequels, along the lines of *The Thin Man* movies.[42] Selznick felt sure Mitchell would agree to one of these options once she understood how much money was at stake. Brown predicted Mitchell would say no and was proven right.

Mitchell had no interest in discussing a sequel to her book. She still did not want to write one herself and did not want a third party doing it for her, whether it be Selznick or one of her many fans who seemed to think they were up to the task. When readers began writing continuations of her story the previous year, Mitchell had been unsure of the legalities involved and left it up to Macmillan to decide what to do. As time wore on and Mitchell gained her bearings in the world of copyright law, she became angry at the number of people who felt no compunction about using her characters for their own purposes. One instance that especially irritated her was an elderly Christian woman who wrote a religious sequel to *Gone With the Wind* aimed at saving souls.[43] That Selznick was offering Mitchell money for the authority to prepare a continuation was a good sign that she did have some control of the sequel rights, but the author did not know whether she had the power to prevent the woman from publishing her religious tome. In the fall of 1938, Mitchell asked Cole for Macmillan's thoughts on the matter. Cole did not know, nor apparently did anyone else at Macmillan. It was not likely an issue many—if any—of its authors had faced. The publisher turned for guidance to C. L. Bouvé, the register of copyrights at the Library of Congress. Although not allowed to give legal advice to private parties, Bouvé offered his personal opinion that, because Mitchell's characters were an idea they were not protected by copyright. Therefore, Mitchell probably had no right to stop third parties from writing sequels, and the best she could do was to sue for damages if one negatively reflected upon her reputation as an author.[44]

Ultimately, Mitchell dropped the matter of the religious sequel because the woman agreed not to publish her story. Yet, the Marshes disagreed with Bouvé's interpretation of the legal rights at stake. In their minds, all unauthorized sequels were an unfair appropriation of Mitchell's skill, which inherently caused her damage, regardless of the quality of the writing or whether Mitchell could prove damages.[45] They considered it theft, plain and simple. Though no expert on copyright, Stephens Mitchell took matters into his own hands and conducted an extensive survey of the law. He unearthed a decision by a New York court that supported the idea that authors control their characters. Although not binding legal precedent outside of New York, the Mitchell team felt confident with the decision in its back pocket should anyone try to publish a sequel without the author's permission.

In the fall of 1938, the Marshes saw a glimmer of light at the end of the international rights tunnel—and it was not another oncoming train. Taft finished registering the copyrights, and Mitchell felt she had done all she could to meet her obligations to Selznick regarding protection of the copyright. With Brett's and Taft's guidance, Mitchell approached Selznick and asked for assurances that she had fulfilled her duty under the "God Almighty clause." In December, Selznick agreed Mitchell was off the hook as long as she continued to fight the Dutch piracy.

Another positive development occurred when relations with Saunders improved. For Mitchell, their association began to take on a friendly aspect when the two women finally met in person that spring. They had been communicating by letter, telegram, and telephone for the previous two years—a situation not ideally suited for building relationships. In June, Saunders visited Atlanta while on a business trip. Their conversation apparently branched beyond business into girl talk, and their correspondence afterward was chummy and good-natured.

Saunders and Marsh took longer to forge a bond. They had met on business matters during the agent's visit to Atlanta, and Saunders made a stab at sending him some friendly letters after her trip. Marsh remained distant, insisting on calling her Miss Saunders though she freely used his first name. Later that summer, they had some further disagreements over the handling of the foreign accounts, and Marsh let Saunders know he viewed her as "highly emotional" and prone to "temperamental outburst," which he found ironic given it was usually agents who complained about dealing with high-strung artists.[46] Sensing she may have finally pushed him too far, Saunders retreated. She did not exactly beg his forgiveness but apologized for her attitude and agreed to do better going forward. "To sum up: I have decided to cooperate with and represent your interests on a more liberal and tolerant basis than before, and I trust that this will be acceptable to everyone concerned, and that our relations may, through the difficulties we have weathered together, become even more close and happy than they would have been without them."[47] Her one request of him was that he stop addressing her as Miss Saunders. Marsh agreed to give her another chance and began calling the agent by her first name.[48]

The situation improved further when, later that year, Saunders took an extended tour of Europe. She corresponded with the Marshes throughout her trip, giving every impression that she was working diligently to advance *Gone With the Wind* in overseas markets. She met with several of Mitchell's publishers and sent back informative and entertaining anecdotes. After visiting the Polish firm operated by a man named Wydawnictwo J. Przeworski, Saunders regaled the Marshes with the story of an elderly white-haired woman "crouching like a bird behind the counter" who bowed deferentially to every visitor who came through the door. A few days later, while detained in Kraców by a snowstorm, Saunders struck up a conversation with a bookseller who informed her that the old woman was Przeworski's mother and the one who ran the business. According to the bookseller, the son never introduced his mother despite her being the brains behind the firm. Saunders also reported that she had discovered one of the largest publishing houses in Latvia was preparing an unauthorized edition of *Gone With the Wind.* She jumped on the problem and convinced the publisher to sign a contract, impressing Marsh with her quick work.[49]

With the foreign rights moving along smoothly—except for the pending Dutch case—the Marshes looked forward to life returning to a slower pace. *Gone With the Wind* had finally dropped off the American bestseller lists that year, an event that caused celebration in the Marsh household. "That was a happy sign that the turn had come," Marsh told his family. "We hope nothing will happen to prevent public interest from subsiding further and further."[50] As Mitchell described it, a lull had come that allowed her to attend to matters that had been neglected "while the *Wind* was blowing a gale."[51] She wanted to get her personal affairs in order, which included making arrangements for what would happen to the *Gone With the Wind* rights when she died. She had her brother draw up a will that bequeathed her literary property to Marsh and devoted several paragraphs to her feelings about privacy. It was her desire that her personal life remain personal, even after she was gone, and that her standing before the public rest upon her published work. She was not interested in the affairs of other people and did not think they should be interested in hers. She specified that she did not want a biography written and asked that her papers, including letters, manuscripts, and corrected proof sheets of her novel, not be "sold, given away, published or otherwise exposed to public view."[52] In case people remained curious about her life in the future, she wrote a brief biographical sketch for her executors to use as they saw fit. She also expressed opposition to any sort of memorial being created in her honor, something fans already were proposing. She saw no need for such a tribute.[53]

On December 10, 1938, Selznick finally began filming *Gone With the Wind*. He started with the now famous scene of the retreating Confederate soldiers in Atlanta setting fire to their supply warehouses. Scarlett had yet to be cast, but fans were thrilled the movie was underway at last.

Mitchell, too, was relieved things were moving along but dreaded the inevitable surge in public attention the movie's production was bound to bring. She had maintained her public hands-off policy over the past two years and intended to continue with that approach. However, she did not turn her back on the project entirely. She had recommended the studio hire as advisers two fellow Georgians—historian Wilbur G. Kurtz and newspaperwoman Susan Myrick. Kurtz, who had reviewed parts of Mitchell's manuscript in the fall of 1935, became a technical adviser on everything from period architecture to sign lettering. Myrick offered guidance on Southern speech, manners, and customs. Having her friends in Hollywood deflected the studio's constant questions and also provided Mitchell the latest scoop from behind the scenes.

The author knew things were certain to get stirred up again when Selznick released his movie—now scheduled for the fall of 1939—but until then she looked forward to the year ending on a quiet note. She remained one of the most famous people in the country—according to a Gallup poll, an estimated fourteen million people in the United States had read *Gone With the Wind*[54]—but the author was heartened that people no longer considered her a curiosity. The press seemed to have lost some of its fervor for tracking her every movement, and she found it easier to let her guard down among friends. After a round of Christmas social calls, she wrote to Latham, "Thank heaven, the 'new' must be off of me, for no one asked for autographs or stole my handkerchief or tried to pull off buttons for a souvenir."[55] To author Clifford Dowdey, Mitchell reported with pleasure that she was treated as no more special than "a successful lady embalmer or life insurance salesman."[56] She could not ask for anything more.

# 12

# Me and My Poor Scarlett

## 1939

The year 1939 marked a major turning point in the life of *Gone With the Wind*. After two and a half years of suspense, on January 13, David O. Selznick announced that a little-known British actress named Vivien Leigh would be his Scarlett O'Hara. At last, the movie production went into high gear, forcing the author to steel herself. In late January, Margaret Mitchell wrote to Kay Brown about how much the Marshes dreaded the months until the movie was finished, noting that hundreds of people already had asked them about getting seats to the premiere. "With interest already so high, this coming year may be even harder on us than 1936 was."[1]

Also on Mitchell's mind were the day-to-day issues of managing what was becoming an international publishing empire. The Marshes were nothing if not meticulous and kept a close eye on the financial side of the foreign accounts. They puzzled over the royalty statements that were written in a variety of different languages and used unfamiliar accounting practices. Figuring out exchange rates and tax liabilities for income earned in foreign countries proved challenging as well. That February, when Mitchell received a notification about overdue taxes in England, the couple had no idea whether they owed the money. John Marsh asked George Brett what to do, but the publisher was also at a loss and told them to ignore it: "Tear His Majesty's income tax blank up and throw it in the waste basket, or to be a little more cagey about it put it in the file and forget it."[2]

One of Marsh's chief worries that winter was France, where no edition had appeared, despite the rights having been purchased by the venerable French publishing house Hachette in 1937. The delay stemmed from Hachette's insistence on printing lengthy extracts of *Gone With the Wind* in high-end literary magazines as part of its marketing plan. Marsh had no objection to that approach, but he had to get Macmillan's approval because most of the leading French magazines were circulated in the United States. After much back and forth over a period of several months, Brett refused to grant permission. American magazines had not been given permission to excerpt the book, and he did not see why French magazines should be treated differently. When Marsh declined Hachette's request, the French publisher lost interest in *Gone With the Wind* and, in May 1938, sold its rights to the rival firm of Gaston Gallimard. Although Gallimard claimed to be enthusiastic about the project, he, too, appeared in no rush to get the book produced, leaving the Marshes to cool their heels for months.

Gallimard's edition finally arrived in Atlanta in March 1939. Although relieved to see it, the Marshes were disappointed with the finished product. By this time, France was on the brink of war with Germany, and Gallimard did not have the luxury of producing a high-quality edition. Printed on flimsy paper, Mitchell deemed it a "poorly turned out affair."[3] She took comfort in the knowledge that great care had been taken with the text. The translator, Pierre-François Caillé, had struck up a correspondence with Mitchell over the previous years. He assured her that his interpretation was as close to the original as possible while giving a colloquial French rendition. She was amused to read Gerald O'Hara exclaiming "oo, la la!" and Aunt Pittypat's swoon bottle rendered as "la bouteille aux vapeurs." Also consoling, the book received a warm reception. In March, a correspondent for the *New Yorker* reported that France had recovered from a flu epidemic only to find itself in the early stages of a *Gone With the Wind* attack. Though the translation ran eight hundred pages, one critic regretted it did not run another thousand.[4]

Unauthorized editions continued to be a problem, especially in China and Japan, where Walbridge Taft had been unable to register the copyright. China was not a signatory of any reciprocal agreement with the United States and thus under no obligation to respect the *Gone With the Wind* copyright. Japan and the United States had a copyright agreement, but it offered Mitchell no protection. Early in the century, to encourage the spread of Western ideas in Japan, the United States had given free rein to Japanese publishers interested in distributing the work of American authors; the publishers did not have to obtain permission or pay royalties. This approach was not considered unduly damaging to American authors because so few American books appealed to Japanese readers. That her work was being used for a good cause provided Mitchell little comfort. A legally pirated edition was no more welcome to her than an illegal one. And the theory that she was not losing any money did not ring true when reports surfaced that several hundred thousand unauthorized copies of *Gone With the Wind* had been sold in Japan. Mitchell thought this unfair, not only to her, but also to Marion Saunders, who earned no commission on those books.[5]

What bothered Mitchell the most though was that such publishers demonstrated little remorse over profiting from her labors. A Japanese translator sent her a silk kimono and a three-foot-tall geisha doll in a red lacquer case. He asked Mitchell to pose for a publicity photograph wearing the kimono and standing next to the doll. She was appalled: "It has never occurred to them that this request was insult added to injury—after swiping my book and paying me no money, they want me to assist in the sale! I did not answer the letter."[6] She suggested to Wallace McClure that "a nation with so much gall certainly should go far."[7] Beyond the fairness issue, the author also was bothered by the poor quality of the editions circulating in Asia, noting that one of the Chinese editions was printed on newsprint and the pages bound so tightly it was difficult to open.[8] She was glad to have a copy of it though when McClure sent her one, saying it rounded out her collection of foreign editions and would be all she ever got out of China.[9]

The political unrest in Europe resulting from Adolph Hitler's rise to power posed additional complications for the Marshes. As the Führer expanded his reach across the continent, it became difficult to communicate or do business in many countries. Exporting money to the United States was nightmarishly complicated, and the flow of foreign royalties became irregular at best. Initially, Marsh took an unsympathetic approach to the problem and expected the foreign publishers to keep trying to get Mitchell's money through. The couple paid their bills on time and expected others to do the same. Marsh made it clear that, if Mitchell wrote another book, she would not do business with any firm that had been lax about paying royalties on *Gone With the Wind*.[10] Not until war broke out in September did he come to understand the devastation Hitler wrought on the lives of Europeans. When the Germans invaded Poland, Saunders warned that the situation looked grim for Przeworski, who was Jewish. "We must obviously forget about your Polish edition," she wrote. "It is all too, too sad and I wonder if your Polish publisher and his eighty-year-old mother are still alive."[11]

~

In Hollywood, filming on *Gone With the Wind* continued, and for a while it seemed as if industry naysayers, who had dubbed the production "Selznick's folly," might be right. In mid-February, Selznick fired director George Cukor; the producer was not pleased with the daily rushes. He got permission from his father-in-law to pull director Victor Fleming off Metro-Goldwyn-Mayer's (MGM) *The Wizard of Oz* to take the helm, but Fleming demanded a new script, so Selznick hired Ben Hecht for a rewrite. The original cinematographer was replaced when the producer felt the footage was too dark, and the actor playing overseer Jonas Wilkerson died, forcing a quick recast. Every development was covered by newspapers and movie magazines. Mitchell continued to keep her public distance, but, in private, her friend, Susan Myrick, who served as an adviser on the film, kept her posted on all the latest gossip.

Despite the delays, excitement was brewing for the movie's release. Plans began for a gala premiere in Atlanta, hopefully some time that fall. Brett offered to throw a grand party for Mitchell during the festivities, but she declined, having already accepted an invitation to an event hosted by the Atlanta Women's Press Club. The author felt one major to-do in her honor was enough. Brett mentioned the possibility of Macmillan and Selznick joining forces with the press club but Mitchell did not want to slight the organization or its president, her close friend Medora Field Perkerson. The author was a charter member of the club and felt a special bond with its members who had been so supportive of her novel. The publisher graciously accepted her position and demonstrated no ill will toward Mitchell for once again denying his company the opportunity to celebrate its association with her.

In March, Mitchell heard from her college roommate Ginny Morris. *Photoplay* magazine had renewed its interest in Morris writing about Mitchell. Now that the movie was underway, Morris assumed the author would have no objection to an "innocuous reminiscence" of their college days, "a harmless little piece."[12] Mitchell exploded over the news, which she likened to a "bombshell." She fired back, quoting extensively from their 1937 correspondence in which Morris had agreed not to write about Mitchell. "Whether the article is 'innocuous' or not, its publication will mean the end of any friendship between you and me," Mitchell announced.[13]

The author also contacted *Photoplay* and asked the magazine to kill the article. The executive editor did not want to lose the story so he forwarded a copy of the piece to Mitchell, asking her to rewrite it to her satisfaction. In a twelve-page, single-spaced, typed response, the author presented her case that publishing the story would be embarrassing to both her and the magazine. She set forth her desire to avoid the public spotlight and detailed the difference, in her mind, between answering reporters' questions about a newsworthy event in her life—winning the Pulitzer Prize, for instance— and articles that "pry into my private affairs." She outlined the many factual errors in the draft article, from the misspelling of her name as "March" to the claim that Mitchell's father, Eugene, was like Gerald O'Hara. She also downplayed her friendship with Morris, calling it a "hit of schoolgirl acquaintance twenty years ago." Mitchell then came to her most important point: Morris's claim that the author "was closer to being Scarlett than anyone who ever lived" was potentially libelous. "How could anyone who read my book make such a statement without intending it as an insult?" her creator fumed. Scarlett was not an admirable person:

> About the only good qualities Scarlett had were courage and a refusal to admit defeat. But on the other side she was selfish, vain, almost illiterate, a bungler in her dealings with other people, a person with shoddy tastes and a fondness for cheap companions. She neglected her children and she was the ruination of every man who loved her. She stopped at nothing in her grasping determination to make money, including cheating, swindling, and cruel abuse of the helpless convicts she hired. She committed murder, she stole her sister's sweetheart with a lie, and she offered her body for sale at a price.[14]

The editor begrudgingly dropped the story but could not resist asking Mitchell to consider writing a piece for the magazine about the difference between publicity for a movie star and for a private individual. She declined, and Mitchell and Morris apparently never spoke again.

A more pleasant encounter with friends from her Smith College days occurred that June, when Mitchell and Lois Cole traveled to Northampton, Massachusetts, where the author received an honorary master of arts degree from her alma mater. While in the Northeast, Mitchell also conducted some business in New York. She called on Saunders at her apartment and, by all accounts, had a pleasant visit. Mitchell was surprised to discover that the agent lived and worked in an elegant art deco building in Gramercy Park. "Your apartment was the nicest and most interesting one I saw on my trip," she gushed to Saunders upon her return to Atlanta. "I did not believe New Yorkers were lucky enough to have such large living quarters, and trees too."[15]

The following month, Marsh and Stephens Mitchell traveled to New York to meet with Selznick representatives on the unresolved issue of the commercial tie-ups associated with *Gone With the Wind.* Selznick had almost finished filming, and the release was still scheduled for that fall. Before the movie promotion started, the Marshes wanted to settle once and for all who owned the rights to the characters and related products. After several days of meetings, a deal was reached establishing that such products would be managed by Loew's, which was coordinating publicity for the film pursuant to Selznick's deal with MGM.[16] The author would receive one thousand dollars, plus a sliding scale of royalties on the net profits from the sale of all *GWTW* merchandise. Mitchell also obtained assurances that her name would not be used in the advertising or exploitation of any product licensed by the movie people and that she retained control of her characters and their names, including the rights to use them in any new stories. She expressed tremendous relief at resolving this "disorder" that had been worrying her since the book's publication.[17]

Macmillan, too, had plans to join forces with Selznick. Over the previous three years, the publisher and the studio had mulled over various ideas for commemorating the movie in print. They had considered issuing a bound version of the film's script but, in August 1939, settled on a paperback edition of Mitchell's original text to be illustrated with color photographs of scenes from the film. At Brett's suggestion, the images would progress throughout the story, letting Mitchell's tale unfold from beginning to end.[18]

With the movie release a few months away, time was of the essence to get the book into production. As soon as the decision was made, sales manager Alec Blanton flew to California to review movie footage and select images of the characters in action. He wrote to New York raving about the quality of Selznick's production. Eager to get the ball rolling, he asked Selznick for sample images to take back to Brett for approval. The producer was reluctant to let any of the film out of his control for fear it would be leaked to the press. The most he would agree to share were negatives of two still images of characters in costume and a few discarded screen prints. The studio impressed upon Blanton that the images were priceless and had to be handled with extreme care.[19]

In a marked departure from Brett's policy of pricing *Gone With the Wind* aggressively, he decided on a rock-bottom retail price of sixty-nine cents for the motion picture edition. At that rate, he predicted, the firm could safely order a first printing of 350,000 copies. He did not expect to make much money on the book but hoped to get it into untapped markets. Selling that many more copies of a three-year-old title, he told Mitchell, would bring "a certain kudos . . . to the fair name of Macmillan."[20] She wished the firm luck: "I do not know to whom [Blanton] is going to sell these copies but I believe he will do it."[21]

Although a deal had not yet been finalized with Selznick, Blanton had been testing the market for weeks, and retailers already were lining up. Sears, Roebuck agreed to purchase fifteen thousand copies, with the option to purchase an additional ten thousand. The store also promised to promote the movie edition in its famous Christmas catalog.[22] With enthusiasm building, Macmillan released details of the motion picture edition to *Publishers Weekly*. On August 12, 1939, the magazine ran an article describing Macmillan's "bold move" of releasing a new edition of Mitchell's book after having already sold 1,445,000 copies of the $3.00 edition and 338,000 of the $1.49 format. The article described the new format to the "excited" trade and announced the book would be on sale in November, just before the movie opened. Macmillan promised a "high-geared" promotional campaign that would run nationwide in coordination with the film's release. The publisher assured bookstores that promotional posters and further details would be provided soon.[23]

Amidst all this activity, the question arose as to whether Macmillan should try to capitalize on the unused serial rights. Perhaps a serialization would serve as good advertising for the movie edition.[24] And, with all the excitement building about the film, interest in *Gone With the Wind* appeared to be at an all-time high. Nobody could say for sure whether that interest would remain after the movie's release. Although these were valid reasons to proceed, the idea never got off the ground. Trouble arose with the motion picture edition, and Macmillan had to focus its efforts there.

The more enthused Brett became about the movie edition, the more Selznick seemed to have second thoughts. As they haggled over the details of their joint venture, Selznick raised troubling questions about how the book should be distributed. Macmillan planned on a nationwide release in bookstores timed to coincide with the movie premiere in Atlanta. Selznick was not so sure this would work. After the premiere, the movie would open in stages from city to city, and Selznick did not want the book available in places where the movie had not yet been shown. He felt that the more the studio held back on what Scarlett and Rhett looked like, the more eager people would be to see the movie. He proposed that Macmillan wait until the following spring to release the book. Selznick also questioned why third-party retail outlets had to be involved in distribution. Why not sell the movie books in the theaters? He had millions invested in the film and had no desire to share the wealth with Sears or other retailers.[25] Macmillan balked at both proposals and, by the end of August, the publisher and the studio were in a deadlock. Brett canceled all the orders the firm had received for the edition.[26]

Financially and emotionally invested in the motion picture edition, Brett viewed this as a major catastrophe. Macmillan had spent several thousand dollars on design and print work for the new edition, and the advertising campaign was already in development. Frantic for a backup plan, Brett grasped for ways to create a special edition of *Gone With the Wind* that would not involve images from the film. He considered using generic photographs of the Civil War era. Mitchell proposed using illustrations from the Danish edition. Norman Berg suggested they could add a photograph of Mitchell and a history of the book. None of these ideas appealed to Brett, so he begged Selznick to reconsider. There was a flurry of long-distance phone calls, as well as a series of meetings in New York between Macmillan representatives and Selznick's agents. The most Brett could get out of the producer was permission to use a handful of promotional stills of the actors in costume, as opposed to actual scenes from the film.[27] Publication would be allowed, at the earliest, two months after the movie's release.

On September 14, with the clock ticking, the publisher proposed the new format to Mitchell. Now, not expecting to make any profit on the book, Brett asked her to waive her royalty if Macmillan did not sell at least 250,000 copies. If, by luck, the firm managed to top that, he offered a meager sliding scale of royalties. Mitchell wired back the next day that she would play along with Brett if she received a share of the profits should the book sell better than expected: "IF I GET NOTHING IF YOU LOSE I SHOULD GET PART OF THE PROFITS IF YOU WIN."[28] Brett understood Mitchell's point but would not adjust the proposal. He wrote back explaining that the firm was putting up the cash to produce the book and, therefore, had more to lose than she. For that reason, Macmillan should reap the benefit if the book succeeded. Furthermore, after setting out detailed cost assumptions and calculations, Brett explained that Mitchell would be earning more per copy than Macmillan.[29] If she did not agree to his terms, the motion picture edition would be scratched.

Realizing a battle of letters would get them nowhere, Marsh and Brett hashed matters out over the telephone on September 22, 1939. The Marshes understood Brett's financial justifications but pointed out that Mitchell, too, was taking a risk in authorizing the motion picture edition. If Macmillan did not release that edition, there would certainly be a surge in demand for the three-dollar edition which would earn her full royalties. She was willing to gamble that the cheap movie edition would sell enough copies to be worth it in the long run but thought she should be rewarded for the chance she was taking.[30] In the end, Mitchell accepted that she would have to waive her royalties if Macmillan sold less than 250,000 copies, and the publisher agreed to an improved schedule of adjusted royalties if the book sold more.[31]

With that settled, Brett flew to Los Angeles to finalize a deal with Selznick. He returned a few days later disheartened. The producer would not release the images until February 1940. Although Brett held out hope Selznick might change his mind, the publisher was not optimistic. He wrote to Mitchell on October 6 seething with frustration. If he had been an older man, he said, the negotiations might have given him "high blood pressure and a stroke."[32] Brett described the experience as the most exasperating of his publishing career.[33]

By this time, it appeared the Atlanta movie premiere would be delayed to December, although no date had been specified. It was to be a star-studded media event, and Brett desperately wanted a new book to sell during the celebration and in the weeks afterward as the movie made its way through America's major cities. He toyed with the idea of reprinting the cheap edition, but that would mean going back on the representation that the $1.49 price tag was a limited-time offer. He mulled over the problem with Luise Sims, the book buyer at Atlanta's Davison-Paxon department store, where Mitchell's first autograph session had been held on publication day. The two agreed there had to be some type of special edition to mark the movie's release and that they could not depend on Selznick coming around at the last minute. They decided on two special editions: a new two-dollar hardcover version for general release across the country and a deluxe two-volume set, limited to one thousand copies, to be sold exclusively at Davison-Paxon.[34]

Brett pitched the plan to Mitchell by letter on October 23, 1939. Admitting the two-dollar edition was not a slam dunk, he suggested that she accept half her normal royalty. With the confidence of a man accustomed to getting his way, he enclosed an extra copy of the letter so she could sign it to show her acceptance. Mitchell did not fall for the glib routine. She could not comprehend why Brett thought she ought to bear the cost of the proposed edition. But, her reply started with some light banter away from the heart of the matter. The author understood Brett's frustration with Selznick and suggested the publisher might now appreciate the aggravation she had endured in dealing with the movie people: "Perhaps now you may believe some of the stories I told you about them, whereas at the time you probably had the inner thought, 'Yes, this Margaret Mitchell of ours has a wonderful imagination, but just a bit too melodramatic.' "[35] She then encouraged Brett to remain optimistic—Selznick would surely recognize that the publicity benefits of the motion picture edition were too attractive to pass up.

With the pleasantries aside, Mitchell turned to the reduced royalty. After all that had gone on between them, she could not believe he had the nerve to ask such a thing. "If you want to deviate from the contract, and if you ask me to make concessions in order to help you in a gamble, then I should not be the only one to make concessions," she wrote. "You should make concessions, too, and you should *offer* to make them. It is not right for you to put me in the embarrassing position of having to ask for them each time." When she sold *Gone With the Wind* to Macmillan, the company accepted the risk of publishing her story. When Macmillan sold far more copies than predicted, its risk had paid off, but Mitchell had not come back asking for more money. "I made a contract and I stuck to it. I do not mean either that I resented the profit you made. You paid me what you had agreed to pay, and I did not expect or want anything more."[36] But if Macmillan wanted her to share the risk now, then she should be entitled to a portion of the earnings if the new edition succeeded.

Brett seemed genuinely taken aback by Mitchell's stance. He felt she had misunderstood him and blamed the disconnect on how difficult it was to do business by letter. "Conversation so quickly removes misunderstanding, doubt, confusion, where correspondence, it seems to me, sometimes serves only to make the subject more complicated."[37] That said, the numbers did not lie, and regardless of what had happened with the 1935 contract, this edition would not happen without a concession on her part. He felt that each version of the book that Macmillan released had to stand on its own, no matter how much money the author had made for the firm over the past three years. They were so far apart that he suggested scrapping the entire idea. The premiere was scheduled to take place in just a few weeks, and Brett barely had enough time to pull the new edition together anyway.

Mitchell was determined to get the publisher to concede the point of fairness. If he refused to acknowledge it, she threatened, it would impair both their business and personal relationships: "Briefly and bluntly, your proposition is the sort that a grown person might offer to a child, according to my way of looking at it."[38] Yet, once Mitchell had her say, she acknowledged there was nothing she could do if he refused to change his offer. Tongues would wag if Macmillan failed to issue a special edition tied to the movie, and she did not want to be involved in any such drama. She was too tired to get entangled in "any embarrassing situations which I can avoid" so, if he insisted, she would accept the proposed royalty reduction.

Exhausted as well, Brett wavered, albeit slightly. He insisted on the reduced royalty but agreed that if the two-dollar edition sold more than fifty thousand copies, they could renegotiate. Not wanting to stir up another letter-writing campaign, he did not even bother responding to the fairness argument.[39] A few weeks later, when the final figures came in, the two-dollar edition cost less to produce than anticipated, and he offered Mitchell an improved royalty schedule. He was "mighty happy" things had worked out so well.[40]

In the end, the fracas over the two-dollar edition turned out to be for naught. Brett had never given up on an illustrated edition coming out in December, and Selznick finally agreed Macmillan could release one in Atlanta for the premiere. After that, Macmillan could sell the movie edition on a staggered basis in each city as the film opened across the nation until February 15, 1940, at which point Macmillan could release the book nationwide. In exchange, Brett agreed that Selznick could use the image of the original book's dust jacket in promoting the movie, that Macmillan would include a list of cast and crew members in the motion picture edition, and that Loew's could have one hundred free copies and buy additional ones at the trade rate. Russell Birdwell, Selznick's publicist, also proposed Brett dedicate the motion picture edition to Selznick, but that idea went nowhere fast.[41] Brett hated not releasing the book to the entire national market at one time given the extra expense of a staggered release. And there was the matter of policing such a convoluted system. If bookstores in Atlanta and New York were selling the edition, Macmillan could not prevent shops in other cities from buying books and offering them in their own towns in advance of the movie's release dates. He agreed to play along though and hoped Selznick would change his mind.[42]

Concerned at one time that he would have no special edition of *Gone With the Wind* to mark the occasion, Brett found himself with three ready to hit the market. Though not an ideal situation, the publisher was relieved to have it all taken care of. Now he could look forward to the premiere, which Loew's had announced for December 15, and to which Macmillan planned to send a delegation.

~

As Macmillan geared up for the big event, Mitchell hunkered down. With three new editions of her book scheduled for release and a gala movie premiere set to descend upon Atlanta, the author knew another whirlwind was coming. This time around, she intended to be well braced when the storm struck. That fall, the Marshes made a concession to the changes *Gone With the Wind* had wrought in their lives and moved to the elegant Della Manta apartments on Atlanta's Piedmont Avenue. Overlooking the woods of a park across the street, the larger home would be a more secure place to ride out the coming excitement than their tourist attraction of an apartment off Peachtree Street. More importantly, the new space had an extra room they could use as a home office. Although Mitchell maintained her office in the building next to their former apartment for the time being, the additional space at home made the day-to-day job of managing her workload far more convenient.[43] The move would have been a good time to have their address and telephone number unlisted in the local directory, but they would go only so far to sequester themselves. Their listing remained publicly available under the name of John R. Marsh.

Mitchell's chief line of defense against the movie mania was sticking with her decision to have little to do with its production and promotion. This was not always an easy course of action, though, as she had a natural interest in the film and wanted it to do her story justice. One of the greatest tests of her resolve came in August 1939, when Selznick invited her to attend the first preview of the film. The lengthy footage needed drastic cutting, and he thought Mitchell might like to see the movie before the editors got their hands on it.[44] Selznick offered to hold the preview in the Midwest so she would not have to travel all the way to California. Brown suggested flying Mitchell to New York, where the viewing could be held in secret at the Long Island mansion of Selznick's business partner, John Hay "Jock" Whitney.[45] Mitchell was as eager as anyone else to see the movie and knew Selznick was offering her an amazing opportunity. As she related to Brown, "I've heard scores of people say that they would give anything to see everything Mr. Selznick had shot, even if they had to sit hours and bring their lunches in shoe boxes. . . . We are a virile race."[46] Nonetheless, she declined, not wanting to go back on her word that she would have nothing to do with the movie making. Mitchell would wait to see the finished film in Atlanta with everyone else.

Of course, there was only so much the author could do to prevent people from trying to draw her into the fray. As the premiere buzz built, opportunists began to circle. In early October, Mitchell attended a release party for *Chins Up!*, a book written by Atlanta journalist Mildred Seydell, who had reviewed *Gone With the Wind* in the summer of 1936. Mitchell had written Seydell a thank-you letter for the notice and was distressed to discover that the journalist had quoted from that letter in the preface to *Chins Up!*[47] When Mitchell expressed her displeasure at her name being used to promote the book, Seydell said she assumed Mitchell would be pleased to be referenced.[48] Unmoved, Mitchell explained that Seydell had no right to use the letter without permission. Seydell apologized and agreed to have the quotation removed from future printings. A few days later, Seydell attended a breakfast with Selznick International and MGM officials who were in town promoting the premiere. Marsh was also there and made no mention of the unauthorized quotation. The journalist thought things had blown over and told her publisher it did not necessarily have to change the preface in the next printing. She thought Mitchell should be delighted to be mentioned in her book and that the Hollywood people would welcome the plug for *Gone With the Wind*.[49] As a fellow Southerner, Seydell ought to have known better than to assume Marsh's pleasant demeanor meant all was forgiven. Unbeknownst to Seydell, Mitchell had contacted the publisher of *Chins Up!* and threatened legal action if the quote was not removed. The editor agreed to Mitchell's demand and warned Seydell "it probably will be some time before you and she will be buttering each other's muffins."[50]

Indeed, Mitchell was in no mood to butter anyone's muffins. Atlanta was in a frenzy of preparations, and despite her best efforts, the author was drawn into the whirl as friends, relatives, acquaintances, and fans begged her for tickets to opening night. The premiere would be at Loew's Grand Theatre, a venue affiliated with the film's distributor. The auditorium seated only about 2,100 people, which meant tickets were at a premium. "There was a widespread belief that I had a million tickets to the premiere in my pocketbook and for a 'pretty, please' I would gladly yield up fifty or sixty to anyone who wanted them," the author said. "People fought and trampled little children and connived and broke the ties of lifelong friendships and bribed and brought political influence to get tickets."[51]

Also, dozens of private parties were planned for release week, and it seemed as if Mitchell had been invited to every one. She kept her vow to attend only one major event—the press club party—and declined all but a few invitations to smaller gatherings hosted by close friends or associates. As for public appearances, Mitchell would only attend the premiere. She did not want to give the impression that she disapproved of the movie but was not going to upend her entire life or make a public spectacle of herself for its sake. In an effort to distance herself gracefully, she issued a statement to the Atlanta newspapers on December 2, 1939, expressing her gratitude for the city's efforts but explaining that, due to a recent bout with influenza, her participation in the public festivities would be limited to her appearance at the main event.

In the weeks leading up to the opening, Harold Latham proposed creating a commemorative copy of *Gone With the Wind* to present to Mitchell in celebration of the movie's release. His original idea had been to insert a memorandum from Macmillan acknowledging the book's remarkable success. The editor wanted to compliment the author while also indicating that Macmillan had done its part, too.[52] Latham finally settled on a letter, which was typeset and tipped into a first edition of *Gone With the Wind*. It recounts Mitchell's reluctant submission of the manuscript, the company's marketing efforts, and the book's overwhelming public reception. The salute concludes with the prediction that, for the novel, "the end is not yet, and will not be during our lifetime." The letter was signed by Latham, Cole, James Putnam, Blanton, Brett, and other Macmillan personnel.[53] The week before the big day, Brett assured Mitchell that the Macmillan team looked forward to seeing her and was "getting out the white ties and what nots" for the big event in Atlanta.[54]

The triple edition release would be a formidable test of *Gone With the Wind*'s staying power. Could the printed word compete with moving pictures? The first book to market was the Davison-Paxon limited edition released in Atlanta on December 1, 1939. Priced at a steep $7.50, the two volumes were housed in a slipcase. The first volume included a dedication page commemorating the movie premiere, and each copy was hand numbered. But slipcases and commemorations failed to capture the public's interest. Although today it is one of the rarest and most valuable editions of *Gone With the Wind*, the set did not sell well, and many copies gathered dust on Davison-Paxon's shelves for months to come.* Next was Macmillan's two-dollar hardback edition. Thirteen thousand copies were released on

---

* Although the book was couched as an exclusive Davison-Paxon edition, *Publishers Weekly* reported that Sims allowed a few other area retailers to acquire copies at a 20 percent discount.

December 7 to a national audience. The book was the same format as the three–dollar edition but with a fresh coat of paint—a scarlet red binding and the original dust jacket design printed with red highlights. Brett thought it a handsome book but did not invest in an advertising campaign given its status as a mere backup to the splashy motion picture edition. No second printing was ordered.

Macmillan saved the best for last. The illustrated movie edition had been rushed into production and made it onto the shelves of Atlanta stores just in time for premiere week. The publisher got behind it with full force, ordering an initial printing of 350,000 copies. It placed large ads in the *GWTW*-themed special editions put out by Atlanta's three newspapers, with similar fanfare planned in papers across the country. Loew's also touted the special offering with a full-page notice in the elaborate pressbook it sent to theater owners to show them the promotional material available for the movie. The motion picture edition, with a bright yellow cover featuring a color still of Scarlett and Rhett, took Atlanta by storm. With tickets to the movie a limited commodity, fans went for the next best thing.

Macmillan was not alone in its efforts to profit from the release. Thanks to Loew's, department and drugstore shelves and windows were full of tie-in novelty items. A woman lucky enough to have scored tickets to the movie could slide on her new Scarlett O'Hara slip and dab on some Flirt perfume and powder from containers shaped like Scarlett. She could wrap a scarf featuring scenes from the film on her hair and tuck into the pocket of her *Gone With the Wind* coat a Scarlett and Rhett hankie. Her husband could coordinate with a Rhett Butler bow tie and keychain. At home with the babysitter, the children could color in their *GWTW* coloring book or play with *GWTW* paper dolls. Traditionally, such widespread marketing had focused on children's movies like *Snow White and the Seven Dwarfs* and *The Wizard of Oz*, but *Gone With the Wind* was the first straight feature film merchandised to such an extent.[55]

Atlanta rolled out the red carpet for the big event. Never before had the city hosted such a star-studded occasion. Local officials worked closely with Loew's representatives and Brown to schedule a series of public events, including a parade of stars for the many cast members who were flying in for the celebration. Only two of the film's leading actors were not making the trip to Atlanta. Leslie Howard, who played Ashley Wilkes, had returned to his native England after it declared war on Germany.

Hattie McDaniel, the African American actress who portrayed Mammy, was confronted with the ugly reality that Atlanta's theaters and hotels were segregated in 1939.★ Demonstrating remarkable grace, McDaniel wrote to Mitchell the Monday before the premiere to thank the author for creating the "outstanding personage" of Mammy and to share that her grandmother, a slave, had told of events in her life similar to those described in *Gone With the Wind*. McDaniel never mentioned the uncomfortable reason for her absence, saying only that she hoped to visit Atlanta soon.[56] Mitchell replied right away, relating that she had heard about McDaniel's "splendid" performance and was looking forward to seeing her on the screen. The author added, "Should you be in Atlanta at any time, please telephone me. I would like to see you and talk to you."[57]

On the evening of Wednesday, December 13, Mitchell hosted a gathering at her new apartment for some of the movie people who had arrived that afternoon. Although Mitchell had complained many times about the impositions the movie had caused her, she would have been hard-pressed to maintain ill feelings against Selznick, who seemed to want so desperately to please her. Wearing his heart on his sleeve, the producer had sent her a telegram the week before admitting how nervous he was about her seeing the finished product and asking her to be open-minded.[58] Mitchell would let bygones be bygones, at least temporarily. According to the *Atlanta Georgian*, the author served as a gracious hostess to Selznick, Leigh, and Olivia de Havilland. (Clark Gable and his wife, actress Carole Lombard, did not arrive in Atlanta until the following day.) The newspaper described the get-together as a low-key event at which "the diminutive author . . . sat on the floor and talked animatedly with her guests." The account also reported that "in accordance with the true rules of hospitality," Mitchell offered her guests a drink, but they "refused so much as a Southern Comfort" because they needed "no other stimulus than their hostess' conversation."[59] The guests did not arrive until 10:30 p.m. and stayed until well after midnight. The next day, Leigh sent the author a note saying it had been a joy to meet her and that she hoped they had not kept her up too late.[60]

On Thursday, Richard Brett and his wife, Latham, Cole and Allan Taylor, and Blanton and his wife arrived in Atlanta on a chartered train car. (Due to a last-minute problem at the office, George Brett and his wife flew

---

★ McDaniel would have been allowed to appear on the stage of Loew's Grand Theatre as a performer but could not sit in the audience or use the restrooms. Mitchell's longtime housekeeper, Bessie Jordan, was unable to see the film until it opened at a "colored" theater in Atlanta in late April 1940.

down later that day.) The entire contingent was put up at the Georgian Terrace Hotel, where the movie stars were also staying. As guests of the city, the Macmillan team was chauffeured around town with an official escort—two police cars rolling alongside each vehicle. Cole later said of the experience, "It was just lovely. I had always wanted to ride with a police escort, and here I was."[61] Even the staid Latham was caught up in the hoopla. He told the *Atlanta Journal* that he planned on going to everything, seeing everything, and thoroughly enjoying his time in the city.[62]

The group's first stop was at Mitchell's apartment for tea.[63] Later that afternoon, the firm hosted a cocktail party in the suite of hotel rooms reserved for the Brett brothers. That evening, they attended a charity costume ball sponsored by the Atlanta Junior League. The Macmillan team sat in box seats near Gable and his wife. For years afterward, Richard Brett's wife, Elizabeth, regaled family and friends with a tale of how the King of Hollywood stepped on her foot that night, causing an ingrown toenail.[64]

On Friday, Rich's department store hosted a luncheon in its tea room to honor the Macmillan executives. At long last, the store that had declined to hold a signing for Mitchell in June 1936 and had been finagling to make up for the gaffe ever since, managed to get the author to attend an event in celebration of *Gone With the Wind*. The party got off to an inauspicious start when someone pulled out Mitchell's chair for her as she was sitting down. She missed the seat and hit the floor, injuring her weak back and forcing her to endure the rest of the events with her back wrapped in a bandage.[65]

Later that afternoon, the Marshes slipped across the street from their apartment to the exclusive Piedmont Driving Club, where the Atlanta Women's Press Club hosted a cocktail party for the visiting celebrities. The Macmillan team was invited as well. At the request of Brown's husband, Cole chatted with a lonesome-looking young Brit who told her his girlfriend was an actress. After about fifteen minutes of conversation, the dashing man shook Cole's hand and graciously excused her as she was being pulled away by some old friends. The editor later realized, much to her chagrin, that she had abandoned the actor Laurence Olivier, Leigh's future husband.[66] Mitchell, meanwhile, was escorted into a side room to have a private conversation with Gable. According to Cole, Mitchell had no idea what to say to him and, in her frank way, asked, "What in the hell are we supposed to talk about?" The world's biggest movie star gamely replied, "I don't know, if you don't." Charmed by the author's forthrightness, he later declared Mitchell the most "fascinating" woman he had ever met.[67] Caught up in the excitement of the day, the author agreed to sign a copy of *Gone With the Wind*—albeit a partial one. Members of the press club had obtained a salesman's copy of the motion picture edition that consisted of a few sample text pages and photographs but mainly blank sheets. They asked those in attendance to sign the book as a thank-you gift for club president, Medora Field Perkerson. The pages were filled with dozens of signatures, including those of Gable, Leigh, de Havilland, Brown, Latham, Cole, Berg, Marsh—and "Margaret Mitchell Marsh."[68] It is the only known copy of the motion picture edition signed by the author.

The premiere that night would be a watershed moment in the history of *Gone With the Wind*. After all the stress and disagreements over the previous years, the key people who had played a role in the book's young but remarkable life were coming together to celebrate. Mitchell and Marsh rode to Loew's Grand Theatre with Selznick and his wife. The streets were thronged with fans hoping to catch a glimpse of the arriving celebrities. Cole described the scene: "There were floodlights all over the front of the building, mobs in the street and on the sidewalk, police roping off the hoi polloi, red carpets laid down to the cars as they came up to discharge, red carpets inside the theater."[69] As Mitchell made her way inside, she stopped and gave brief comments that were broadcast on the radio and to the crowd: "This is a very happy and exciting day for me, and at this time, I want to thank everybody in Atlanta for being so nice to me and my poor Scarlett. Thank you."

Once in the theater, the Marshes were seated between Gable and Whitney. When the lights dimmed and the curtains parted, the audience was breathless with anticipation.[70] The author must have been on the edge of her seat, wondering what Hollywood had done with her story. She knew the book would not translate easily to the screen, and her concern went beyond its sheer length; she also felt the story line was too complicated. As she had told her friend Myrick, "It had taken me ten years to weave it as tight as a silk pocket handkerchief. If one thread were broken or pulled an ugly ravel would show clear through to the other side of the material."[71]

Selznick had faced just such problems. Creating a workable screenplay had taken more than two years, and as Mitchell predicted, drastic cuts had been necessary, including many of her characters. Among those biting the cinematic dust were Scarlett's children from her first two marriages, leaving only doomed Bonnie, her daughter with Rhett. Also cut were several colorful supporting characters, including Will Benteen; Dilcey, Prissy's mother; and Archie the convict. On Selznick's theory that it was better to cut entire sequences than to make minor deletions within them, numerous scenes from the book also fell by the wayside.[72] A few notable ones included Rhett getting Scarlett's father drunk and Scarlett reading Ashley's letters to Melanie. Changes were made within scenes if they moved the story along. For example, in the book, Scarlett's radish-induced vow to never go hungry again takes place in the ruined gardens at Twelve Oaks the day after she returns from Atlanta; in the movie, she makes her promise at Tara shortly after arriving home.

For the most part, the narrative and feel of the print and film versions are remarkably similar given the amount of material Selznick had to digest. However, in several important aspects, the movie offers a different experience than what Mitchell had given her readers. Perhaps most notably, while Leigh is widely remembered as one of the most beautiful actresses in Hollywood history, Mitchell's Scarlett was decidedly not a beauty, an important nuance that affected one's understanding of the story. Selznick's treatment also misses the parallels between Scarlett and Atlanta and much of the historical detail on the daily lives of Civil War–era Georgians, both essential themes in Mitchell's version. The treatment of racial issues is noteworthy as well. Anyone who judges Mitchell's feelings about slavery based on Selznick's depiction will miss the mark.

Despite the many changes, Mitchell was pleased with the movie. She thought that Selznick and his crew, as exasperating as they had been at times, did a remarkable job of bringing her book to life. Marsh, too, liked the film and was especially relieved that Gable gave a fine performance. Mitchell's husband later described the experience of sitting next to the actor during the screening: "He was so anxious for the thing to be a success, and we couldn't keep our minds on the picture for wanting to tell him, 'There, there, Captain Butler.' "[73]

After the film ended, the mayor asked Gable and Lombard to escort the author to the stage. Mitchell apologized for her nervousness and thanked the audience for its support: "You know, everybody thinks it's just when you're dead broke and you're out of luck that you need friends, but really, when you have an incredible success as I've had, that's really when you need friends. And, thank Heaven, I've had 'em. And I've appreciated everything the Atlanta people and Atlanta's papers have done for me to be kind to me and my poor Scarlett." She went on to praise the film's emotional wallop, noting that she had "a dripping wet handkerchief," and closed by paying tribute to Selznick and his "absolutely perfect cast."[74] The audience rose in a long ovation. Latham later wrote to Mitchell that her remarks were pitch-perfect for the occasion and brought a lump to "the throat of this hardened old sinner."[75]

After the premiere, the Macmillan group—still in evening dress—caught a train to New York.[76] Mitchell and Marsh attended postcelebration festivities at the Piedmont Driving Club along with many of the Hollywood contingent. At 5:00 a.m. on Saturday, Mitchell sent a telegram to McDaniel:

> THE PREMIERE AUDIENCE LOVED YOU AND SO DID I. THE MAYOR OF ATLANTA CALLED FOR A HAND FOR OUR HATTIE MCDANIEL AND I WISH YOU COULD HAVE HEARD THE CHEERS. CONGRATULATIONS.[77]

# 13

# Toting the Weary Load

## December 1939–1942

E ven after all the celebrities left town that weekend, the excitement was not quite over for the Marshes. The Monday after the premiere, as they prepared to leave on a much-needed vacation, a fire broke out in their apartment building. John Marsh rushed to protect the *Gone With the Wind* business papers, which were the first things he carried out of the building with the help of Margaret Baugh and Bessie Jordan. The blaze was extinguished just before reaching their unit, getting close enough to blister the paint on the baseboards. The couple lost some of their personal effects that had been stored in the basement of the building, but the *GWTW* documents were safe. "If I had lost the four-year record of my work as Peggy's business manager, it would have been catastrophic," Marsh said.[1]

Four days after the Atlanta premiere, *Gone With the Wind* opened in New York at two Broadway theaters, with gala festivities broadcast live on a newfangled product called television. Reviews of the film were glowing, and David O. Selznick returned home in triumph for a star-studded Los Angeles premiere on December 28, 1939, just under the wire for consideration for that year's Academy Awards. In January 1940, the film began opening in major cities nationwide, and *Gone With the Wind* became the first movie ever to gross one million dollars in a single week. Unfortunately for Margaret Mitchell, she did not earn a penny of this money. As was standard at the time, she had sold the movie rights to Selznick for a flat fee and, therefore, was not entitled to a percentage of the box-office proceeds. But that is not to say she did not profit from the movie's success. In the week after the film opened in Atlanta, sales of licensed *GWTW* products totaled $636,250. And the earnings climbed as the film's release expanded.[2] Thanks to her agreement with Loew's, Mitchell earned a small percentage of every dollar made on the merchandising.

The motion picture edition was also a hit, and as George Brett predicted, it proved impossible to keep the cat in the bag. Word about the edition's popularity spread, and booksellers across the United States wanted copies to sell right away, expressing little concern for Selznick's desire that the volume not be sold across the country in advance of the movie. When Macmillan refused to fill the orders, many bookstores purchased copies from retailers and distributors in cities where the movie was already playing. A Chicago wholesaler reported to Macmillan that the book was on sale throughout the Midwest although the movie had not yet reached there.

Brett approached Selznick and pleaded for an immediate nationwide distribution of the edition. Selznick was amenable but at a price. Under the terms of the original deal, he had let Macmillan use the movie stills without extracting a royalty; Selznick now wanted a five-cents-per-copy share of the profits.[3] Brett thought this ridiculous. As he fumed to Marsh, Selznick seemed to be forgetting that Mitchell and Macmillan were the ones who made the movie possible in the first place.[4] The staggered release had caused so much trouble and expense that Brett refused to give a cent to Selznick.[5] Faced with Brett's recalcitrance, the producer dropped the royalty demand and offered a compromise. He recognized that the motion picture edition offered valuable advertising for the film and proposed allowing Macmillan to distribute the books two weeks before the movie's release in each city. Brett reluctantly accepted.

With the expanded distribution, the first printing sold out quickly, and the publisher ordered a second run of 350,000. This printing, perhaps reflecting reader concerns that the 391-page book had been shortened, added a line to the cover proclaiming, "Complete and Unabridged." That run sold out as well, and in February, Macmillan optimistically went back to press with a third printing of 350,000 copies. The book climbed to the top of *Publishers Weekly*'s reprint bestseller list, where it stayed for several months.[6]

In March, Brett boasted to Mitchell of having supplied the public with more than seven hundred thousand additional copies of her remarkable novel: "What a history it is writing in the annals of American publishing!"[7] Lois Cole concurred that history was in the making. Macmillan had a document retention policy that called for the editorial department's records to be destroyed after seven years, and Cole wondered if an exception should be made in the case of *Gone With the Wind*. She suggested to Latham that Macmillan's correspondence relating to Mitchell's book be segregated so there was no risk of it being discarded. She predicted that, in the coming decades, the letters would prove interesting and valuable and that "perhaps, our descendants might be much annoyed at our departed spirits for having destroyed [them]."[8] Latham apparently agreed. The files were retained and later were donated to the New York Public Library, where most remain to this day.

When the Marshes returned from their postpremiere vacation, they found more than a thousand pieces of fan mail had arrived in their two-week absence.[9] Mitchell, with Baugh's help, worked through the pile one by one. To some correspondents seeking a memento of the premiere, they sent pieces of fabric trimmed from the hem of a velvet coat Mitchell had worn that special evening.[10] An elderly woman in Georgia who had the foresight to ask for a souvenir before the premiere received special attention. She had sent a piece of green taffeta for Mitchell to carry in her purse that night. Mitchell obliged and asked Baugh to return the fabric as requested, along with a camellia from the corsage the author wore to the premiere.[11]

Mitchell's ban on book signing remained in place. The author declined all requests to sign copies of the motion picture edition, even saying no when Kay Brown wrote asking for one on Selznick's behalf.[12] The author struggled with denying people such a simple favor when they seemed so interested in her work and, in some cases, offered small concessions. When Vivien Leigh asked Mitchell to sign a copy of the commemorative Davison-Paxon edition the author had sent to the actress's Atlanta hotel room as a gift, Mitchell instead sent Leigh a small sheet of paper on which she had written a few lines of a poem and her signature. Presumably, the author intended "Scarlett" to paste the memento inside her copy of the book.[13]

In the early days of 1940, the Marshes managed to keep a low profile. In mid-January, Mitchell had abdominal surgery that she had been putting off, and then Marsh, who was battling a persistent fever, found himself in the hospital as well. But, by the end of February, Mitchell was propelled back into the spotlight. At the Academy Awards ceremony on the 29th, *Gone With the Wind* won eight of the thirteen awards for which it had been nominated, including the Best Actress Oscar for Leigh, the Best Supporting

Actress award for Hattie McDaniel—the first Academy Award ever won by an African American—and the Best Picture Oscar for Selznick. Two days later, the producer wired Mitchell that he wanted her to have his gold statuette and planned to send it to her as soon as he could have it engraved with an appropriate inscription. She appreciated the gesture but knew allowing him to give her such a gift would cause a stir in the press and forever link her name with Selznick's honor. "You are amazingly generous in offering to send me the trophy but I could not think of accepting it," Mitchell responded. "The award was not for novel-writing but for movie making so the trophy's proper place is with you."[14]★

Mitchell's efforts to distance herself from the Oscar were foiled when word leaked about Selznick's offer, and the story circulated like wildfire. The truth got lost along the way, and the press reported that Selznick wanted to give her the trophy and a cash bonus—or, as famed radio commentator and gossip columnist Walter Winchell called it, "a bunch of lettuce." When rumors circulated that Selznick had sent her fifty thousand dollars, Mitchell was incensed. She found herself inundated with letters from people congratulating her on the windfall and offering suggestions for how to use the money. She worried that the Bureau of Internal Revenue would believe the story and start asking questions about her tax returns.

Matters escalated when another false story sprang up purporting that, back in 1936, Mitchell had received a higher offer for the movie rights from another producer but had rejected it, preferring to have Selznick tell her story. Now she was concerned Selznick might think she started the rumor and was "encouraging the newspaper furor" in an effort to guilt him into paying her a bonus. This struck a nerve with the Marshes, who were still sensitive about the movie deal and the speculation that she had been foolish to sell so early and for so little. Although they maintained they were happy with the selling price and had been lucky to get it, the Marshes must have had twinges of regret now that the movie was raking in millions and she was not entitled to any of the profits. Mitchell never let on that she was anything less than pleased with the deal, and the idea Selznick might suspect her of hinting around for more money mortified her.

Mitchell denied the rumors and insisted she had nothing to do with starting them. When the producer failed to issue similar denials, the Marshes

---

★ Selznick's Best Picture Oscar for *Gone With the Wind* was sold in 1999 at Sotheby's auction house in New York for a record $1.54 million; the buyer was entertainer Michael Jackson.

wondered if the studio had been orchestrating the press coverage all along as a publicity stunt. The couple was not pleased and sent Selznick a telegram letting him know it. The producer went through the roof at the accusation. He responded with a strongly worded five-page telegram denying that he had started the rumors and detailing the extraordinary efforts he had gone to over the previous years to protect Mitchell's privacy; he suggested she develop a thicker skin. Chastened, Marsh replied with an eight-page letter, ensuring Selznick they were not challenging him personally but rather the studio's publicity team. As often seemed to be the case, Marsh's bark was worse than his bite. He ended the letter assuring Selznick that they still held him in high esteem and hoped they could rebuild the "mutual understanding between us."[15] The relationship was back on an even keel—for now.

As had happened with the book's original release, the movie's success brought out opportunists looking to capitalize on Scarlett and Rhett's popularity. A handful of speculators found an easy target in the bargain-priced motion picture edition. They bought bulk quantities of the paperbacks and made a quick profit by rebinding them in hardback and reselling them at a marked-up price. The books had all the appearances of a legitimate edition—the clever culprits even cut the images from the discarded paper covers and glued them onto the new cloth-covered boards. The only sign that something was amiss was that Macmillan's name did not appear on the cover of the volumes.

When word got out about the ploy, Macmillan looked imprudent for having priced its book so low. The publisher also faced a problem with Selznick. The producer had granted Macmillan the exclusive right to distribute the movie images in the motion picture edition. The unnamed third parties had no legal authority to distribute those photographs. The publisher failed to pinpoint any law prohibiting the rebinding but took an aggressive stance and began sending threatening telegrams to anyone it thought might be involved. On February 24, 1940, Macmillan took out a full-page advertisement in *Publishers Weekly* putting the trade on notice that, while individuals were free to rebind their personal copies, the company felt mass rebindings for resale were a violation of its rights. The publisher announced it would do everything within its power to prevent further tampering with the motion picture edition.[16] The hardball routine worked. Three weeks later, a small article in the trade journal reported that the responsible parties had

accepted Macmillan's claims and had withdrawn the unauthorized rebindings from the market.[17]

Although Macmillan never publicly revealed who the guilty parties
were, its files indicate that one was its price-war nemesis, Macy's. When
Macmillan raised a stink, the store insisted on its right to rebind the text but
agreed to remove the movie photos. The store replaced the cover image of
Vivien Leigh and Clark Gable with an illustrated map showing the route
Scarlett took to Tara after she fled Atlanta. Presumably embarrassed over the
situation, Macmillan did not advise Mitchell of what had transpired. She
found out by accident months later when she ran across a copy of the
Macy's edition. She was not enamored of the book's production quality and
noticed it had two typographical errors on the map: General Stephen D.
Lee was referred to as "Lea," and Rough and Ready, a small community in
Clayton County, was listed as "Rough and Readys."[18] Assuming Macmillan
had authorized the new edition, Mitchell asked Latham to make sure the
mistakes were corrected in future printings. Only then did he come forward
and explain what had happened.[19]

Macmillan faced further difficulties with the motion picture edition
that summer when Loew's announced that it planned to withdraw the film
from the market for several months and rerelease it in early 1941. In six
months, more than twenty-eight million people—one out of every five
Americans—had seen the movie, breaking box-office records that would
stand for decades. By pulling the movie from theaters, the distributor hoped
to let the excitement settle and build fresh demand the following year. This
was disastrous news for Macmillan, which had more than three hundred
thousand unsold copies of the motion picture edition on its hands. As the
film's first run began to wind down, so did sales of the movie edition. In
June, less than seventy-five copies of the volume were sold. Left holding
almost the entire third printing, this represented a loss to Macmillan of close
to sixty thousand dollars. Brett admitted to Mitchell it had been a terrible
error in judgment to order the final run, noting that trying to predict reader
demand was always a gamble.[20]

When faced with large quantities of leftover books, publishers often
sell them at a cut rate, a process called remaindering. Brett faced an agonizing decision. Should he cut the firm's losses and dump the books now or
hold them until the film's rerelease? After riding so high on the glory of
*Gone With the Wind*, it would be embarrassing to have the motion picture
edition hawked at bargain-basement prices. He decided on remaindering
but with a twist. Rather than having the now famous paperback edition

stacked on shelves as evidence of his failure, Brett approved selling the books at a discount to a retailer who would reissue them in a new, hardcover binding when the movie began its second run.

Brett had to go hat in hand to Selznick, admit defeat, and ask for his permission to authorize the sale. Selznick was not happy about letting yet another third party take advantage of the movie images, nor was he interested in doing Brett any favors. Nevertheless, out of respect for Mitchell, he agreed. Brett also had to ask the author to accept yet another reduction in royalties. To make the deal worth Macmillan's while, she would have to take a payment of only a penny per book. Accepting Macmillan's judgment that it was time to cut bait, Mitchell agreed. With everyone on board, Macmillan sold the inventory to discount publisher Grosset & Dunlap for ten cents a copy.

As part of the deal with Grosset, Macmillan had to agree that it would not issue another cheap edition of *Gone With the Wind* for the next two years. This left Macmillan with only the standard three-dollar edition on the market, a book that appeared to have run its course for the time being. Hoping to recoup some of the company's losses, Brett gave the green light to sell the book's serial rights. Here was a way to eke out another few dollars to help balance the books in 1940. The firm's serial department combed through its records and sent an invitation to bid to all of the newspapers and syndicates that had ever expressed an interest in those rights. But it quickly became apparent that the publisher had made a mistake in waiting so long. Most of the companies did not bother to respond, and of the few that did, most said they were no longer interested now that the movie had come and gone. Only King Features Syndicate made an offer, and it was for just one thousand dollars, with a fifty-fifty split of the proceeds.

Reluctant to go that low, Macmillan wrote to several additional newspapers. When only one expressed mild interest, Brett decided to take the bird in the hand and go with King Features. Macmillan presented the offer to Mitchell, and she agreed. Alas, the publisher had more humiliation in store. King Features backed out when it realized Macmillan expected the syndicate to run an unabridged version of the story. King claimed there were few people in the United States interested in reading a full-length version of *Gone With the Wind* who had not already done so. Brett had to go back to Mitchell and tell her the deal was off. The best they could hope for was trying to sell the story to individual newspapers, for one hundred or two hundred dollars each. She gave her assent to this as well, but apparently there were no takers. To this day, no serial version of Mitchell's book has appeared in the United States.

Mitchell did not share Macmillan's dismay at *Gone With the Wind*'s seemingly dwindling fortunes. She had waited a long time for the hoopla to die down and had high hopes her life would return to a saner pace once the movie had run its course. But, once again, she underestimated Scarlett and Rhett. While *Gone With the Wind* may not have been selling many books, it had become such a part of American culture and consciousness that, four years after the book's release, rarely a week went by without some new problem arising out of unauthorized use of the author's work or some new scheme from somebody wanting to profit from it.

That summer, producer Mike Todd—a future Mr. Elizabeth Taylor—created a musical called *Gay New Orleans* for the New York World's Fair. The production included characters named Scarlett O'Hara, Rhett Butler, Belle Watling, and Mammy. The lyrics to one of the songs included the phrase "Gone with the wind are the cares I bore, gone with the wind to return no more." It was Billy Rose all over again. This time, Mitchell wasted no time debating what to do. As soon as she learned of Todd's plans, she brought in the able services of Howard Reinheimer, her attorney in the Rose case. The New York lawyer convinced the producer of the error of his ways and elicited an apology. Shortly thereafter, Mitchell prepared for battle again when word circulated that a stripper in New York named Renee Villon was performing a dance routine called "Gone With the Wind" in which an electric fan blew off her clothes. Although Villon folded up her tent before lawyers got involved, the press had a good time at Mitchell's expense. Even the loyal *Atlanta Constitution* got in on the act, noting it would take a "very large, forceful fan" to blow off the "multitudinous petticoats and pantalets of Scarlett O'Hara's day."[21]

The sequel issue also reared its head again. With Gable and Leigh now emblazoned in people's minds as Rhett and Scarlett, fans felt the story called, nay screamed, for further development. Rumors ran rampant that Mitchell had changed her mind and was working on a continuation. Friends teased the author about a report that she was writing a sequel called "Back With the Breeze," "a highly moral tract in which everyone, including Belle Watling, undergoes a change of heart and character and reeks with sanctimonious dullness." Mitchell quipped, "I am happy to announce that I have written no such book and still happier that such a book lies outside my feeble capabilities."[22] Despite her immediate and repeated denials, the rumor continued to spread and stirred up a fresh round of correspondence from readers. A pair of thirteen-year old girls from Vicksburg, Mississippi, were so enthralled with the idea of a follow-up that they sent the author two detailed plot lines they thought would work for a new book. In one, Scarlett develops amnesia; in the other, Rhett is similarly stricken. The teens told Mitchell she was free to use either plot, subject to acknowledgment and compensation. Mitchell politely thanked the girls for their letter, complimented them on their writing skills, and informed them that she had no plans to write a sequel.[23]

Mitchell was further irritated when Hollywood fan magazine *Screen Guide* ran a contest for its readers to see who could write the most interesting continuation of Scarlett and Rhett's love story. A sailor on the U.S.S. *Portland*, Arnold Manning, won the top prize of ten dollars. The magazine published an illustrated version of Manning's story in its September 1940 issue: Scarlett had Rhett kidnapped and brought to their home, where they shared a night of passion. Furious at her treachery, Rhett stormed out of the house and headed to his boat in Charleston. Scarlett stowed away and presented herself to him as a changed woman—"proud, yet mutely appealing, promising surrender." They reunited and returned to Tara. The editors of *Screen Guide* took the liberty of announcing that Manning's conclusion was thoroughly consistent with Mitchell's characters; if she had chosen to end her story more definitely, the magazine said, the final chapters might well have looked like his.

In the four years she had been dealing with fan fiction, Mitchell had become increasingly less tolerant. She accepted that fans might write sequels for their own amusement but did not think it fair for them or publishers to profit from their efforts. If someone wanted to publish a Civil War–era story set in Georgia, that was fine, but let them spend their own time developing characters, settings, and scenes. Moreover, the quality of sequels such as Manning's left much to be desired. She feared having outlandish ones in print would harm her book's reputation, in which she had a vested financial interest. Stephens Mitchell wrote a stern letter of complaint to *Screen Guide*, charging it with unauthorized use of Mitchell's "title, characters, plot, color and atmosphere."[24] Although it was by no means clear under copyright law at that time that Mitchell controlled those characters exclusively, the magazine did not put up a fight. In its December issue, the publication ran a full-page apology, declaring that Mitchell owned the exclusive right to "sequelize" her story. She won that battle, but the war continued, especially overseas, where plenty of people had their own ideas of what happened to her famous couple. Although her legal footing was even less clear abroad than in the United States, Mitchell maintained she owned the rights to her characters the world over as a matter of common sense and decency. If she heard of anyone trying to publish a sequel, she fought it as a matter of principle.

Fans were not the only ones interested in sequels. With the movie an unparalleled success, Selznick renewed his push for Mitchell to sell him the sequel rights. He envisioned Selznick International Pictures producing a follow-up or perhaps selling the rights to another producer in a package deal with the services of Leigh, who was under contract to Selznick. He wrote to Brown and Jock Whitney, encouraging them to get moving on a sequel, which he predicted would be worth a fortune greater than what they could earn on all the other pictures they had in mind combined. When the studio approached Mitchell, she turned it down without hesitation. On her behalf, Marsh explained that resolution of *Gone With the Wind*'s open ending would undermine her original story's integrity. Moreover, she did not have the time to write a sequel herself, nor would she allow a third party to create one for her. Mitchell's refusal did not end matters though.[25] Selznick was determined to obtain the rights and would, despite her repeated denials, revisit the issue with the author on many occasions over the coming years.

With no sequel in the works, Selznick turned his attention to other ideas for bringing Scarlett and Rhett to the public. That fall, he announced plans to mount a radio production of *Gone With the Wind*. He had acquired those rights as part of the movie deal, so Mitchell's permission was not required. Even so, he managed to cause the author no end of trouble when advance publicity for the show claimed that Mitchell had agreed to participate in the program to "give everything a proper Tara flavor." She had never been invited to join the program and would have said no in any case. To her great annoyance, Mitchell began receiving letters, telegrams, and telephone calls from people wanting her to help them land a role in the production. Radio producers from other programs contacted her complaining that she was participating in this program after having declined their offers.

Although the author did not blame Selznick for the false report of her involvement, she held him accountable for letting it happen on his watch and demanded that he set matters straight. She wrote him a seven-page letter declaring, "I think you *owe* me prompt and effective action in this situation. I have *earned* the right to ask it of you." She had, after all, "written the book which gave you the opportunity to score your greatest success, artistically and financially."[26] According to notations in Mitchell's file, she never mailed the diatribe; Stephens Mitchell sent a more measured statement instead. Fortunately for Selznick, the matter blew over when plans for the radio production fizzled due to problems with the sponsor.

Despite the dustup, he remained confident in Mitchell's goodwill and asked Brown to approach the author about letting him acquire the stage rights to *Gone With the Wind*. Selznick knew the movie would be a tough act to follow but wanted to try. He had visions of an elaborate, five-hour theatrical production with a dinner intermission. Brown approached the author saying that, this time around, Selznick would be willing to give Mitchell script approval.[27] Mitchell was open to selling the rights, but chances of a deal coming together fell through when the author and Hollywood became embroiled in yet another publicity conflict, this one related to the movie's second release.

Hoping to re-create the magic of the original unveiling, Loew's scheduled a "second premiere" at the Grand Theatre in Atlanta for December 12, 1940. The distributor promoted the event as a benefit for the Atlanta branch of the British War Relief fund. From the beginning, the well-intentioned plan seemed cursed. Loew's publicity department announced that, as an added attraction, Leigh and McDaniel would reenact the movie's famous corset-lacing scene onstage before the film was shown. The re-creation would feature a replica of the movie set, along with lights, cameras, and other equipment to capture the feel of a Hollywood sound stage. However, the promoters forgot to ask for permission from Mitchell, who retained the dramatic rights to her story. When news of the plans broke in the local papers, Mitchell was tempted to "sue the hell out of them." After numerous letters, telegrams, and phone calls between Atlanta, New York, and Hollywood, the author reluctantly agreed to allow the reenactment but only out of esteem for Brown and the charity and on the condition that the scene be copyrighted in her name. After weeks of nailing down the details, McDaniel announced she had a scheduling conflict and was unable to attend. The scene was canceled.

In the end, Mitchell was not prepared to let the studio people walk away scot-free after having wasted so much of her energy on the project. She wrote to Selznick and Nicholas Schenck, president of Loew's, detailing the "great deal of work, worry, trouble, annoyance and expense" she had been forced to undergo. She demanded five thousand dollars as compensation for her time and trouble.[28] It is a testament to Mitchell's growing reputation for tenacity that they agreed to make the payment with little fuss.

However, when the check arrived, Mitchell was unhappy to see that Selznick had paid the bill rather than Loew's. Stephens Mitchell threatened to return the payment; the Marshes considered Selznick an "innocent partner" in the affair and suggested Loew's should be held solely accountable. Selznick's attorney assured them it was simply a bookkeeping issue and that Loew's, through its subsidiary Metro-Goldwyn-Mayer (MGM), would bear its fair share. Appeased, Stephens Mitchell accepted the check, noting, "With the whole world at war, we would be happy to have peace at home."[29]

Even with the stage scene shelved, MGM and Loew's remained optimistic the so-called "re-premiere" would be a success. They scrambled to find a substitute attraction and arranged for Leigh to bring with her fellow Brits Laurence Olivier, whom she had married in August, and director Alfred Hitchcock. MGM also invited the Duke of Windsor and his American wife, Wallis Simpson. But plenty of hitches lay in store. King George VI declined on behalf of his older brother, causing the *Atlanta Constitution* to lament, "Gone Are the Wind-sors for *Gone With Wind* Revival."[30] The movie people suffered further embarrassment when, at a luncheon before the movie showing, the press discovered that the small American and British flags on each table were labeled "Made in Japan." Given the tenuous state of American-Japanese relations at the time, it was just one more joke in a comedy of errors. As the final act, the plane carrying Leigh, Olivier, and Hitchcock encountered bad weather, and the trio did not arrive in Atlanta until the day after the rescreening. Mitchell was forced to pinch-hit at several events.

Although not nearly the grand event Loew's originally envisioned, the gala served the purpose of again drawing attention to the movie *Gone With the Wind* as it was released for a second run in theaters across the country. The film drew large crowds, which meant good news for Grosset & Dunlap's revamped motion picture edition. The publisher sold the book, now encased in a hardcover and dust jacket, for fifty cents. The volume proved so popular it made the *Publishers Weekly* reprint bestseller list. As if any doubt remained about whether Mitchell's novel had found a distinct place in American culture, the Associated Press ran a story about a mother in Little Rock, Arkansas, who gave birth that December to triplets whom she named Gone, With, and Wind.[31]

~

Amidst all the travails on the home front, an increasingly weary Mitchell also faced difficulty managing the *GWTW* literary rights abroad. In April

1940, Mitchell was in the midst of a royalty dispute with her Danish publisher when the Nazis invaded Denmark. All communication was cut off. In May, Mitchell's Dutch lawyer, J. A. Fruin, was preparing the piracy case for trial when Germany invaded the Netherlands. The Luftwaffe destroyed the commercial district of Rotterdam, including the building that housed Fruin's firm. Showing a true fighting spirit, he managed to get word to the author in June that the courts were operating, and he would do his best to move the case along.[32] Many months passed before she heard from him again.

Then there was Poland, which had been torn asunder by Germany and the Soviet Union the previous fall. The Marshes had heard nothing from the publisher Wydawnictwo J. Przeworski and assumed he had been killed. Marion Saunders contacted an "Aryan" publishing firm she knew of, Gebethner & Wolff, to see if it would take over Przeworski's stock. As she explained to Marsh, "No money can come out of Poland, but this house is extremely reliable and I would rather see them sell the books than have the copies thrown into a dung-heap."[33] Gebethner & Wolff accepted the stock and promised the rights would revert to Przeworski if he resurfaced.

Even in nonoccupied countries, communication was problematic. Letters sent overseas were censored and often detained. International mail was typically transported by sea, an uncertain method at best given Nazi U-boat patrols in the North Atlantic. In the fall of 1940, the Marshes got wind of an Arabic piracy about to be released in Cairo. Saunders sent a letter to the American Embassy there but warned the Marshes she had no idea how long it would take to reach Egypt. It was "in the lap of the gods," she said.[34] They heard back from the American vice consul a year later that the publisher was willing to sign a contract and pay royalties. However, by that point, hostilities had escalated in North Africa, and Marsh had no way to close the deal. When, in May 1941, Mitchell received a copy of the Bulgarian edition, it scarcely seemed possible to her that a book could make it safely around the world in the middle of a war and find a quiet resting place on her shelf. She valued it greatly even though she could not read a word of the text.

The stress took a toll on Mitchell and her husband, and the couple came to regret having accepted the foreign rights from Macmillan. As Marsh described his feelings to Brett, "Briefly and poignantly, our dominant idea about the foreign rights in general is that they are a pain in the neck." The Marshes had been forced to spend a tremendous amount of money protecting those rights and, now, because of the war, the translations were bringing in little income. "We have done a good job with the foreign rights—in every respect but making money. . . . For whatever it is worth, we have the satisfaction of a job well done, but that is all."[35]

Mitchell discussed the situation with Cole, who told her about another author struggling to get royalties out of Europe. The writer, whose name Cole did not disclose, had appealed directly to Adolph Hitler for assistance.[36] Three weeks after sending the German dictator an airmail letter, the money had been wired to the woman's bank account in U.S. dollars. She accepted the payment and donated 10 percent of the funds to British War Relief. Cole wondered if Mitchell should pursue a similar route. The author's name might have carried some weight with the Führer—rumor had it that the Nazis approved of *Gone With the Wind* because it was critical of the "Yankee" government in Washington. Principles mattered to Mitchell more than money; she refused to consider asking Hitler for a favor. Mitchell told Cole she had abandoned hope of ever recouping the lost income.*

Even in the far corners of the globe where business continued relatively unaffected, successes were few and far between for Mitchell those days. In late 1940, when a South African publisher expressed interest in translating *Gone With the Wind* into Afrikaans, the couple was enthusiastic. Negotiations stalled though when the publisher indicated he wanted to have the story rewritten with a South African setting, transferring the city scenes from Atlanta to Cape Town or Johannesburg. Marsh thought the idea "highly offensive" given that the flavor of the book was "so directly a part of the original setting as Peggy created it." Saunders tried to convince the publisher to leave the geography intact, but he refused, and a contract never materialized.[37] In South America, Marsh panicked upon hearing that the assets of the Chilean publisher Ercilla were being liquidated. The firm owed Mitchell more than $3,500. Having no experience with Chilean bankruptcy law, he was at a loss as to how to protect their rights. Upon realizing Macmillan was also a creditor, he turned to Brett for guidance. The publisher managed to calm Marsh by explaining that Ercilla was reorganizing because of a "screwy" Chilean labor law, which provided that corporations had to increase employee salaries by a certain percent every year.[38] Apparently, to get around the requirement, companies routinely went out of business

---

* It may have come as some consolation to Mitchell that Hitler faced his own difficulties with World War II currency restrictions. When Boston publisher Houghton Mifflin released an English translation of Hitler's memoir, *Mein Kampf*, the book was a bestseller, earning Hitler royalties of more than twenty thousand dollars. Those funds were impounded by the U.S. Alien Property Custodian.

every few years and then started from scratch. The Marshes were relieved but described the experience as "something out of *Alice in Wonderland*."[39]

The Atlantans also continued to struggle with unauthorized translations. Fighting the pirates was draining, but Marsh did not feel they could let the thefts go unattended even when the law was not on their side. For instance, Cuba required foreign copyrights be registered in Havana within one year of original publication. *Gone With the Wind* had not been registered within that time frame, so a Cuban newspaper took advantage of the situation and ran a serialized version of Mitchell's story. When Saunders learned about it, she demanded payment of a royalty and publication of the Macmillan copyright notice in future installments. The newspaper replied in what Mitchell described as a "saucy" manner. "In fact, they practically told me to go to hell and that they would not pay me or acknowledge my rights," she informed the Department of State's Wallace McClure.[40] The Cuban publisher insisted he had the authority to publish the serial without permission and stated that if the author wanted Macmillan's copyright notice printed, she should pay the newspaper to run an advertisement for the New York publisher.

Marsh appreciated that a lawsuit would be futile but stood his ground, hoping to convince the paper to at least include the copyright notice. To everyone's surprise, the publisher eventually made an about-face and agreed to pay one hundred dollars in royalties. Mitchell's camp speculated that the hostilities in Europe had the publisher concerned about relations with the United States. In a comical coda, the newspaper sent the one-hundred-dollar check to Macmillan, instead of to the Marshes. To keep things simple, Marsh asked Richard Brett to accept the check and credit the proceeds to Mitchell's account. The younger Brett, a by-the-book numbers man, refused and told Marsh that the proper procedure was to ask the Cuban publisher for a new check. Marsh prevailed upon George Brett to cash the check, explaining that when you have "dealings with pirates and when they finally capitulate and pay money over to you it is not very wise to send the money back to them just because of a technicality."[41]

The difficulties with the foreign publishers reached a crisis point in December 1941 when the Japanese attacked Pearl Harbor and the United States declared war on Japan, Germany, and Italy. Virtually all overseas communication was cut off. Royalty payments became so few and far between that the couple was stunned when any came through. One from the Norwegian publisher took more than a year to reach Atlanta. The Marshes were not sure how the firm got the money out of Europe, but they appreciated the company's diligence and deemed its managers honest and reliable. They were also impressed by the Finnish publishing house, a business operated by a father and his four sons. During the war, the sons fought against the Russians while the patriarch ran the firm alone and somehow managed to send royalties throughout the conflict.[42]

The delinquent royalties caused Mitchell no substantial hardship, but she felt sorry for Saunders, who relied on commissions off those royalties for her livelihood. On two occasions, the author voluntarily sent the agent five-hundred-dollar advances to tide her over until money could start getting through to the United States again.[43] Mitchell told her that, if the funds never came in from the foreign publishers, Saunders did not have to repay her: "I appreciate all that you have done and I want you to have this money, so I hope you will accept."[44] Mitchell also knew Saunders still had family in England and regularly expressed concern about how they were faring. The two women drew closer, sharing a mutual disgust over Hitler's atrocities. Even Marsh apparently felt sympathy for Saunders, as evidenced by his response to an inquiry from government officials investigating foreign nationals working in the United States. The Federal Bureau of Investigation (FBI) contacted Marsh to find out whether he had any suspicions or concerns about Saunders. Marsh rose to the agent's defense and asserted there was no reason to doubt her loyalties. She had been open about her hatred of the Nazis, and Marsh told the FBI she was, in his experience, distinctly pro-American.[45]

Although Mitchell knew little of what was happening with her book in Europe, the novel continued to live a full life during the conflict. After America entered the war, Hitler banned *Gone With the Wind* in Germany and all occupied countries. The Nazis apparently realized the book was not anti-American but rather encouraged survival amidst war and occupation—a theme on which the Third Reich was not particularly keen. Mitchell took great pride in Hitler's disdain though was horrified to hear rumors that people had been shot for possessing a copy of her book.

Despite the ban, *Gone With the Wind* remained popular in Europe and continued to sell well, even in occupied countries where black-market copies went for as much as sixty dollars. Scarlett's determination served as a valued source of comfort to people suffering the horrors of war. An English actress living amidst the bombing of London wrote to thank Mitchell for helping "at least one citizen of London in the 'front line' to 'tote the weary load.'"[46] Mitchell's book struck a nerve in the Pacific theater as well. After the war, an American woman visited the Philippines to research a book on her uncle, General Jonathan Wainwright, the senior field commander of American and Filipino forces under General Douglas MacArthur. While there she met with a Filipino captain who had been through the Battle of Corregidor and the Bataan campaign. The soldier told the woman he had endured the bitter last days of the Japanese invasion by reading *Gone With the Wind* by campfire. He concealed the book and carried it with him throughout the Death March until, starving, he sold it through the prison gates for a handful of turnips.[47] Mitchell's story even provided inspiration and comfort in Nazi concentration camps. Julie Salamon, a former movie critic and columnist for the *Wall Street Journal*, wrote in her 1996 memoir, *The Net of Dreams*, about the strength her Jewish mother drew from *Gone With the Wind* during her imprisonment at Auschwitz. One of her mother's most vivid recollections from the concentration camp was when her bunk-mates recounted from memory stories from books they had read, their favorite being *Gone With the Wind*. Salamon's mother identified with Scarlett, a girl who had lost everything and triumphed.

On the home front, as America's war effort shifted into high gear, Mitchell's fans had more serious things to worry about than Scarlett and Rhett, and this meant a welcome decline in attention directed at the author. She had not exactly fallen into obscurity, though. Atlanta was filled with transient soldiers, and she remained a popular tourist attraction. On one occasion a female Marine lieutenant from New York called the Marsh home early on a Sunday morning asking for help finding living quarters. The woman had no connection to the couple; Mitchell's was the only Atlanta name she knew. She tracked down the author's phone number and put herself in the couple's hands. The Marshes were a little startled at the woman's "Yankee directness," yet made a few phone calls and found her a place to stay.[48]

According to Stephens Mitchell, the war brought out the best in his sister. Although she had refused to promote herself for the sake of the book, if the name Margaret Mitchell could help American soldiers, she gladly stepped forward. She volunteered for the Red Cross and raised money selling war bonds. She christened a light cruiser, the U.S.S. *Atlanta*, and its replacement after the first was sunk in the Battle of Guadalcanal. She agreed to write an article for the Treasury Department on the importance of buying bonds. In December 1941, she reported to Latham that she had even plucked up the courage to give a series of speeches to Atlanta schools, in "an effort to get lunch and movie money from the pockets of the little ones." Proud of making it through the ordeal "without screaming or fainting or having the children burst into uproarious laughter," the author noted the irony that "the Lord always makes people do the things they least like to do."[49]

Selznick, too, supported the war effort—he was active in Hollywood fundraising efforts—yet still seemed fixated on recapturing the glory of his greatest triumph. By late 1941, he finally accepted that Mitchell would never write a sequel and that she could not be persuaded to sell him the rights by promises of great wealth. So he changed tactics and asked Brown to gauge Mitchell's interest in granting him the rights to create a film sequel in exchange for a one-hundred-thousand-dollar donation to a charity of her choice or endowment of a Margaret Mitchell Foundation. He promised her name could be left off the film project entirely and suggested the payment would be free from income tax.[50]

Again, Mitchell declined—but this time went beyond her usual pleas of being too busy to deal with such a project. Though the author had claimed for years that she had never given any thought to Scarlett and Rhett's future, she confided to Brown that she had, and her answer to the burning question of what happened next is why she could not write a sequel: a happy ending was out of the question. Mitchell explained that when Rhett left Scarlett he was forty-five years old, a relatively advanced age for a man of that generation. His final words about not caring what Scarlett did or where she went indicated that Rhett had finally lost interest in her and would never return. Therefore, Mitchell could not write or authorize a sequel in which the two would reunite—the result she thought the public wanted.[51] As a Mitchell family friend recalled the author saying, the most optimistic thought she had for her characters is that Rhett might have taken Scarlett "back into his bed, but not his heart."[52] A sequel was out of the question.

The ever-resourceful Selznick was not prepared to throw in the towel. He had Leigh under contract and wanted another starring role for her. If Mitchell had nothing left to tell of Scarlett's fortunes, would the author consider exploring the life of Scarlett's daughter—a role that Leigh could slip into effortlessly? Yes, little Bonnie had died, but surely other children were possible. With Rhett out of the picture, Mitchell could bring other men into Scarlett's life. The producer suggested an opening scene that introduced a fourth husband.[53] He thought Mitchell should be able to churn out a novelette or short story along those lines in a few weeks. Again, Mitchell declined.

Meanwhile, Macmillan continued to sell its three-dollar edition of *Gone With the Wind*, biding its time until it could issue a new cheap edition in 1942 upon expiration of the two-year moratorium it had agreed to as part of the Grosset & Dunlap movie edition remainder deal. The full priced book continued to sell, but Macmillan was ready for the next big thing and wondered if Mitchell might be ready to write a new novel. In 1941, a member of the shipping department came up with the idea of having readers petition Mitchell to write a sequel or another book; Macmillan could distribute postcards for fans to use in submitting their pleas. Richard Brett loved the idea and proposed to Latham in August that the company create a little publicity excitement by wrapping the cards up and shipping them to Mitchell in some "ritzy" manner.[54] He was so enthusiastic that he wanted to offer a reward to the man who came up with the plan. Latham turned his nose up at the proposal and told the younger Brett to forget about it. The editor called the idea unprofessional, undignified, and not something Mitchell would like.[55] The scheme went no further. Macmillan would have to stick with the story Mitchell had already written and wait until the following spring to reignite interest in it with a new low-priced edition.

While Mitchell would not have appreciated a publicity stunt to goad her into writing a new book, she apparently was not averse to getting back to work. At the end of 1941, Marsh and Selznick were exchanging letters on the producer's continued interest in acquiring the rights to a theatrical production of *Gone With the Wind*. A stumbling block in Selznick's path was the author's concern that the producer would stage another talent search. This would, Marsh said, further postpone "the time when she can begin writing again, as she ardently wishes to do."[56]

On April 29, 1942, with the two-year moratorium almost up, sales manager Alec Blanton dropped Latham a note suggesting they start making plans for another cheap edition of Mitchell's novel. He felt sure the book would sell at least fifty thousand copies, maybe a hundred thousand. A first printing of twenty-five thousand would be perfectly safe, he assured the editor.[57] Mitchell admitted to feeling uneasy about Blanton's optimistic sales figures but gave her blessing. As she told Latham, "Your sales department has r'ared back and passed so many miracles since 1936 that I do not worry as much as formerly."[58]

Macmillan released the new edition that summer. In keeping with the times, the back of the dust jacket contained ads urging readers to buy U.S.

war bonds. The book sold well—about 120,000 copies over the next three years—but not enough to propel Mitchell back into the spotlight. On August 17, 1942, Mitchell reported to Latham that the summer had been blissfully peaceful. People were not plotting "idiocies" and expecting her "to join with them in carrying out these idiocies, there are no school children who wish to interview me for their papers, ladies clubs are mercifully quiescent, and life takes on an enjoyable dullness."[59]

As Mitchell basked in the quietude, Selznick and Whitney were getting ready to enter her life again. This time, though, she would have little cause for complaint. The two men were in the process of dissolving their partnership when, on August 22, without any forewarning or fanfare, they sent Mitchell a check for fifty thousand dollars as a token of their appreciation for her part in making the movie *Gone With the Wind* so successful.[60] They assured her the payment would remain confidential and offered her best wishes for her continued success and happiness. Mitchell wrote them a gracious thank-you letter, acknowledging that the movie had caused "periods of strain and weariness and years of disruption of life and routine," but such things were, she now understood, "unavoidable in any great undertaking, be it a great motion picture or the prosecution of war."[61] A further pleasant aspect of the transaction was that a 1939 adjustment to the U.S. tax code meant that she, not Uncle Sam, enjoyed the benefits of this windfall. The new law permitted averaging of income over a five-year period for lump sums derived from personal services. This provision did not help Mitchell on her publishing royalties because they were not considered payment for personal services, but the bonus from Selznick and Whitney did fall under the new approach.★

The dissolution of Selznick International Pictures signaled two important changes for the future of *Gone With the Wind*. On the advice of tax attorneys, Selznick sold his interest in the film to Whitney and his sister, Joan Whitney Payson. The siblings subsequently sold their shares to MGM, as did other smaller stockholders, resulting in MGM obtaining control of the movie.† The producer also severed ties with Brown that year. After receiving the credit for bringing Selznick and Mitchell together, Brown became one of the producer's most trusted advisers, earning a reputation as a top-notch talent scout. In an interview she gave late in life, Brown claimed

---

★ Congress revised the law again in 1952, allowing authors to average book royalties.
† Selznick's brother, Myron, owned a small percentage of the film, which he held on to. Years later, part of that share passed to David O. Selznick's two sons, Jeffrey and Daniel, upon the death of Myron's daughter.

Selznick fired her in 1942 because she had been receiving too much of the credit for his successes. She recalled receiving a phone call from one of Selznick's executives telling her she was being let go and asking her to circulate the story that she was quitting to take care of her children. She refused, stating that she would protest if Selznick made any such claim. She resigned without offering any public explanation and went to work as an agent for Leland Hayward.[62] Although she no longer had any official responsibilities for *Gone With the Wind*, she remained in contact with the Marshes, with whom she had developed a collegial working relationship.

Another interruption of Mitchell's idyll came that October when cartoonist Al Capp, creator of the popular syndicated comic strip *Li'l Abner*, published a three-week slapstick spoof of *Gone With the Wind* called *Gone Wif the Wind*. He depicted Abner as Wreck Butler, Daisy Mae as Scallop O'Hara, and Hannibal Hoops as Ashcan Wilkes. The parody appeared in more than six hundred newspapers across the United States. Although some writers might have considered it an honor to be lampooned by the respected humorist, Mitchell did not. On his wife's behalf, Marsh demanded that Capp apologize and cancel any further segments of the strip. The cartoonist apparently did not take kindly to the protective husband's demands. In a speech to the National Cartoonists Society, he later described a telephone conversation he had with Marsh in which the author's husband nagged at him until Capp snapped and ended the discussion with a two-word "Anglo-Saxon phrase" that he found handy for "getting rid of pests" and "beginning lawsuits."[63]

Undeterred, Marsh contacted Capp's publisher, United Features, and threatened to sue for one dollar for every copy of every paper in which the spoof had appeared. This amounted to about seventy-five million dollars, a figure that immediately caught the attention of syndicate executives, who flew a representative to Atlanta to apologize in person. The firm agreed to cancel any future installments in the series and run a public apology in Capp's strip. Pleased with their quick reaction, Mitchell decided to forgo seeking monetary damages. With one arm twisted behind his back, Capp devoted two panels of his Sunday strip to a public mea culpa. In the first, Mammy Yokum declared that "Mistah Capp" owed Mitchell an apology for hurting the author's "feelin's." The second offered a formal apology in which United Features and Capp acknowledged that he had inappropriately made use of Mitchell's characters.

The year 1942 ended with a bang when Selznick, who so recently had redeemed himself in Mitchell's eyes, demonstrated that he was not quite through with her yet—or his idea for bringing Scarlett back to life. On December 3, he dropped the author a line saying he had figured out the topic for her next book, as if she were wracking her brain looking for possibilities. He had been thinking about it for a while and could not resist presenting his idea. She would be doing a service to the nation, he said, by writing a modern novel featuring the life of contemporary Southern women. He thought Mitchell the only person qualified to take on the task and had figured out a surefire method to make the book a smashing success. Warning her to hold her breath, the producer announced that the main character, and a guaranteed crowd pleaser, would be—Scarlett O'Hara's granddaughter.[64] Would the plotting of idiocies never end?

1. *In an era when children were seen and not heard, young Margaret Mitchell grew up listening to relatives tell stories of the War Between the States, which had ended just thirty-five years before she was born. Courtesy Hargrett Rare Book and Manuscript Library, University of Georgia Libraries, Athens, Ga.*

2. In a portrait made for her debut into Atlanta society, Mitchell reveals some of the charm that would attract people the rest of her life. Courtesy the Atlanta-Fulton Public Library System, Atlanta.

3. A French apache dance Mitchell performed with A. Sigmund Weil, a student from Georgia Tech, scandalized Atlanta society—much like Scarlett did by dancing with Rhett at the Atlanta Bazaar. Courtesy of Atlanta-Fulton Public Library System, Atlanta.

4. John Marsh, Mitchell's second husband, served in the U.S. Army during World War I. With experience teaching English composition, working as a newspaper copy editor, and in public relations, he proved an invaluable helpmeet to his novelist wife. Courtesy Hargrett Rare Book and Manuscript Library, University of Georgia Libraries, Athens, Ga.

5. As a young woman, Mitchell was known for her fearless nature. Courtesy Hargrett Rare Book and Manuscript Library, University of Georgia Libraries, Athens, Ga.

6. Although Macmillan editor Harold Latham received credit for discovering Mitchell's novel, his role was not as significant as often has been reported. Courtesy Atlanta-Fulton Public Library System, Atlanta.

7. *Lois Dwight Cole Taylor met Mitchell in the late 1920s, and the two literary-minded women remained lifelong friends. Although Cole received little of the credit, she was responsible for bringing* Gone With the Wind *to Macmillan. Courtesy Linda Taylor Barnes.*

8. *Cole's husband, Allan Taylor, was a friend of Mitchell's from her days as a reporter. He assisted Cole in organizing the original manuscript and later served as intermediary when Mitchell had a falling out with publisher George Brett, Jr. Courtesy Linda Taylor Barnes.*

9. Macmillan president George Brett, Jr., locked horns with his star author on several occasions but ultimately became one of her greatest admirers. Courtesy Ann Zagari.

10. Richard Brett, younger brother of George Brett, Jr., was enthusiastic about Gone With the Wind yet never seemed comfortable dealing with "the Mitchell tribe," as he referred to the author and her family. Courtesy Clare Brett Smith.

11. Mitchell credited Norman Berg, trade manager of Macmillan's Atlanta office, as being her official hand-holder during the arduous process of revising the manuscript and galleys. He was one of the first people to read the completed manuscript and told friends it was the finest book ever written. *Courtesy Karen Berg Kushner.*

*12. Mitchell poses in front of the typewriter on which she wrote* Gone With the Wind. *Courtesy Hargrett Rare Book and Manuscript Library, University of Georgia Libraries, Athens, Ga.*

*13. Annie Laurie Williams, the agent who brokered the sale of the* Gone With the Wind *movie rights to David O. Selznick, was described by one of her clients as Mae West with a steel-trap mind. Courtesy Rare Book and Manuscript Library, Columbia University, New York.*

14. *Marion Saunders,
the agent who handled
the foreign rights to*
Gone With the Wind, *provided invaluable
assistance but proved
difficult to deal with.
Courtesy Svenska
Dagbladet.*

15. *Kay Brown, the East Coast story editor for Selznick International Pictures, fought
hard to convince producer David O. Selznick, left, to buy the motion picture rights to*
Gone With the Wind. *Shown with them are John Hay "Jock" Whitney, Selznick
International chairman of the board, center, and John F. Wharton, one of the lawyers
who negotiated the GWTW movie contract on Selznick's behalf. Courtesy Kate Barrett.*

16. *The author faithfully answered most of her fan mail, which at times numbered hundreds of letters a day. Courtesy Hargrett Rare Book and Manuscript Library, University of Georgia Libraries, Athens, Ga.*

17. *In the months after* Gone With the Wind *was published, the title and its characters entered the public consciousness and became popular marketing tools. An advertising company created book-shaped paperweights that promised to keep papers from going with the wind. Photo by Doug Buerlein. Courtesy John Wiley, Jr., Collection.*

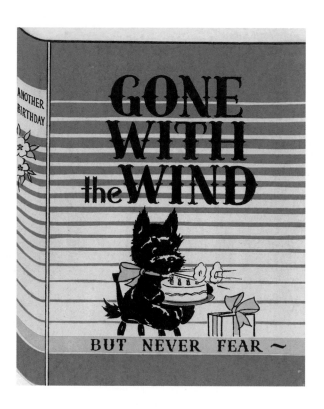

18. *Greeting card manufacturers capitalized on Mitchell's popularity by incorporating her book's title and dust jacket design into their products. Courtesy John Wiley, Jr., Collection.*

19. *The Pepperell Manufacturing Company created fabric featuring six scenes from the book.*
*Photo by Doug Buerlein. Courtesy John Wiley, Jr., Collection.*

20. An appliance company promised homeowners their worries would be "gone with the wind" if they purchased its water heater. Courtesy Hargrett Rare Book and Manuscript Library, University of Georgia Libraries, Athens, Ga.

Billy Rose PRESENTS

Frontier Fiesta

FORT WORTH 1937

25¢

21. *When showman Billy Rose included material from* Gone With the Wind *in his* Frontier Fiesta *revue in 1937, Mitchell sued him for violating her dramatic rights. Courtesy John Wiley, Jr., Collection.*

22. One of the songs in the Billy Rose show was titled "Gone With the Dawn," but the singer changed the lyrics to "gone with the wind" during the performance. Courtesy John Wiley, Jr., Collection.

23. Wallace McClure of the Department of State offered valuable assistance to the Marshes during their struggles with unauthorized overseas publishers. Courtesy Wallace B. McClure.

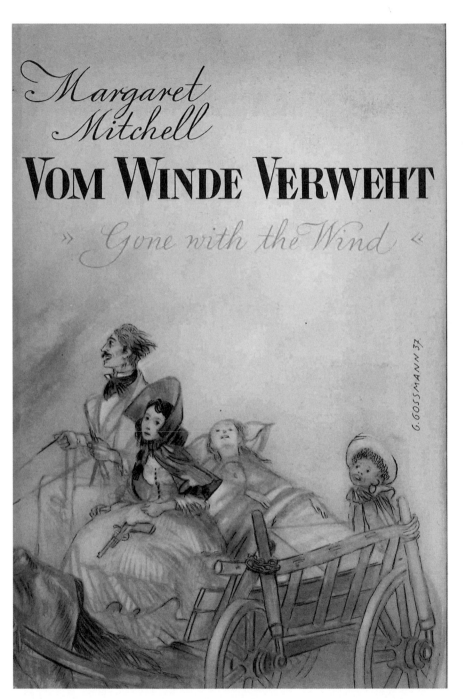

24. When friends teased Mitchell that the image of Scarlett on the dust jacket of the German edition resembled her, the author admitted there was a "maddening resemblance as far as the vacant and nearsighted look" but demurred, "I was never that sweet and pretty looking." *Courtesy John Wiley, Jr., Collection.*

25. Marion Saunders found the cover artwork on this Hungarian edition comical, terming it "sort of a la mode de Budapest." Courtesy John Wiley, Jr., Collection.

26. *Mitchell was amused when she found out her protagonist was renamed Rossella in the Italian edition of her novel. Courtesy Arnoldo Mondadori Editore.*

27. *Using posters and contests to stir up interest, the Danish publisher of* Gone With the Wind *sold its entire first printing of ten thousand copies in less than two weeks. Courtesy John Wiley, Jr., Collection.*

28. *A Czechoslovakian bookstore promoted Mitchell's novel with an eye-catching window display. Courtesy John Wiley, Jr., Collection.*

29. *On the train to Atlanta in December 1939 for the premiere of* Gone With the Wind, *Harold Latham, left, chatted with fellow Macmillan executives Richard Brett, center, and Alec Blanton. Courtesy Clare Brett Smith.*

30. Clark Gable and his wife, actress Carole Lombard, were the center of attention at a
Gone With the Wind *ball sponsored by the Atlanta Junior League the night before the*
*premiere. Courtesy Herb Bridges Collection.*

31. British actress
Vivien Leigh won
rave reviews—and an
Academy Award—
for her portrayal
of Scarlett O'Hara.
Courtesy Herb
Bridges Collection.

*32. On premiere night, Mitchell thanked the people of Atlanta for their support of "me and my poor Scarlett." Selznick is at far right. Courtesy Atlanta-Fulton Public Library System, Atlanta.*

33. *Mitchell received this doll, which she nicknamed "Madam O So Solly," from one of the unauthorized Japanese publishers that was not obligated to pay her royalties. After Pearl Harbor, she donated the doll to an American Red Cross auction to benefit U.S. serviceman fighting overseas. "Royalties of that kind are the finest I could ask," she said. Courtesy Atlanta-Fulton Public Library System, Atlanta.*

34. *During World War II and afterward, Mitchell, often aided by her housekeeper, Bessie Jordan, packed boxes of supplies for overseas publishers and readers. Courtesy Hargrett Rare Book and Manuscript Library, University of Georgia Libraries, Athens, Ga.*

35. *In the summer of 1949— thirteen years after her book was published—Mitchell looked forward to a quieter life. Courtesy Hargrett Rare Book and Manuscript Library, University of Georgia Libraries, Athens, Ga.*

LA **DOMENICA** DEL **CORRIERE**

Supplemento settimanale illustrato del nuovo CORRIERE DELLA SERA - Abbonamenti: Italia, anno L. 1165, sem. L. 625 - Estero, anno L. 1765, sem. L. 935

Anno 61   N. 35                    L. 25

*La tragica fine di una famosa scrittrice. Margaret Mitchell, autrice del celebre romanzo americano "Via col vento" investita e uccisa da un'automobile in una strada di Atlanta. Aveva 46 anni.*

(Disegno di W. Molino)

36. *Mitchell's death made news around the world in August 1949. Italian newspaper* La Domenica del Corriere *devoted a cover to the deadly accident on Peachtree Street. Courtesy John Wiley, Jr., Collection.*

37. *After his wife's death, Marsh spent the few remaining years of his life managing her literary rights. Courtesy Hargrett Rare Book and Manuscript Library, University of Georgia Libraries, Athens, Ga.*

40. *In 1972, a musical version of* Gone With the Wind *opened in London, where it played for almost a year. Courtesy John Wiley, Jr., Collection.*

41. *Stage versions of* Gone With the Wind *have been performed many times in Japan by the all-female Takarazuka Revue. Courtesy John Wiley, Jr., Collection.*

42. *An Ethiopian edition of* Gone With the Wind *was published in the 1980s by a former political prisoner who translated the novel on the backs of foil linings from cigarette packets. Courtesy Herb Bridges Collection and Road to Tara Museum.*

43. *In the late 1970s,* Gone With the Wind *was translated for the first time into Burmese by Mya Than Tint, a well-known writer and translator from Myanmar. He was awarded the Myanmar National Literature Award for the translation. Courtesy John Wiley, Jr., Collection.*

44. A seven-volume comic-strip edition of *Gone With the Wind* was published in Japan in the 1970s. The covers of these two volumes depict Scarlett and Rhett. Photo by Tasha Tolliver. Courtesy John Wiley, Jr., Collection.

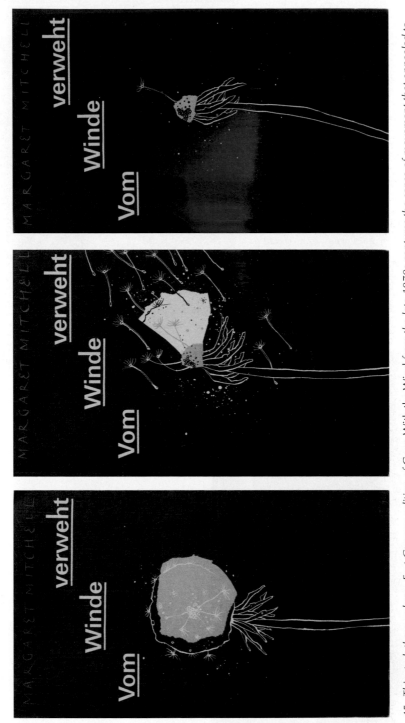

45. *This stark three-volume East German edition of* Gone With the Wind *from the late 1970s captures the sense of movement that appealed to Mitchell when she selected the title for her novel. Photos by Tasha Tolliver. Courtesy John Wiley, Jr., Collection.*

**RÜZGÂR GİBİ OCCTİ**

M. FGARET MITCHELL

46. *A pirated Turkish edition in 1976 featured a very modern-looking Scarlett and Rhett. Photo by Tasha Tolliver. Courtesy John Wiley, Jr., Collection.*

**Margaret Mitchell**

**CUON THEO CHIEU GIO**

1

47. *The cover art on this Vietnamese edition of* Gone With the Wind *released in the early 1990s featured a curious collage of images. Photo by Tasha Tolliver. Courtesy John Wiley, Jr., Collection.*

48. *Paul Anderson is one of three original trustees Stephens Mitchell authorized to manage the literary rights of* Gone With the Wind. *Courtesy Paul Anderson.*

49. *Thomas Hal Clarke, also an original trustee, met Stephens Mitchell through the Atlanta Historical Society. Courtesy Thomas Hal Clarke.*

*50. Alexandra Ripley wrote* Scarlett, *the first authorized sequel to* Gone With the Wind. *The book was a huge bestseller in 1991. Photo by Osmund Geier.*

51. *After the success of* Scarlett, *numerous unauthorized sequels appeared in Russia, such as this one, titled* Son of Rhett Butler. *Photo by Tasha Tolliver. Courtesy John Wiley, Jr., Collection.*

52. Alice Randall's "rejoinder" to Gone With the Wind— The Wind Done Gone, *told from the viewpoint of a slave— was the subject of a lawsuit by the Stephens Mitchell Trusts. Photo by Eric England. Courtesy of Houghton Mifflin Harcourt.*

53. *Author Donald McCaig, who had never read* Gone With the Wind *before being hired to write* Rhett Butler's People, *termed Mitchell's Scarlett O'Hara the "finest woman character in American literature."*

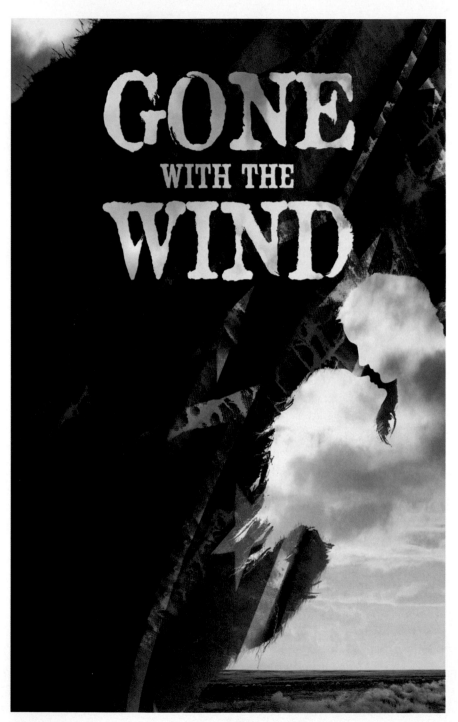

54. *In 2008, Sir Trevor Nunn directed a musical version of* Gone With the Wind *in London, but the critically savaged production closed after only seventy-nine performances. Courtesy John Wiley, Jr., Collection.*

# 14

# Reconstruction

## 1943–Summer 1947

Although war still raged around the world, the new year began quietly for Margaret Mitchell and *Gone With the Wind*. Over the holidays, she and John Marsh had enjoyed a trip to New York, which included time with the Taylors. The couples spent a memorable evening at the famous Gay Nineties nightclub. "It isn't often that people have new experiences at our time in life and John and I enjoyed it enormously," she wrote Lois Cole. "Afterwards we thought up a score of old songs we wished had been sung."[1]

The only significant business pending was David O. Selznick's continuing interest in acquiring stage rights to her novel. The matter had been in a holding pattern during the liquidation of Selznick International Pictures, but in February, the producer finally made a formal bid on the rights to mount a stage production of *Gone With the Wind*. He offered an advance of $2,500 against a percentage of the show's gross receipts. Mitchell declined, saying she wanted a guaranteed upfront payment, plus royalties, and would be "a dope" to accept anything less. The author told Selznick to adjust his terms accordingly; she was not willing to go through another one of his "foofarahs" until he came back to the table prepared to meet her requirements. He failed to come up with an acceptable proposal, and the matter languished.

Overseas, matters remained largely at a standstill, but Marsh continued to keep meticulous records of the accounts. The federal government required American citizens to document their foreign income, and in the course of preparing such a report in the spring of 1943, Marsh noticed irregularities in the few royalty statements Marion Saunders had sent. There were discrepancies in some of the figures and also informational gaps. While he understood why countries such as Poland and France could not get money through, it troubled him to have heard nothing from Sweden, a neutral country where *Gone With the Wind* supposedly continued to sell well. He wondered about the publisher in Cairo and why they had not heard from him now that the Germans were being driven from North Africa. Saunders also had failed to update the Marshes on unauthorized theatrical productions in Ireland and Spain that she had promised to look in to.

Marsh let matters slide for several months, realizing conditions in Europe were difficult and not wanting to appear a nag. However, by summer, he felt he had been patient long enough. The Allies were making progress, and he wanted to be ready to hit the ground running when Europe reopened for business. Unable to resolve the discrepancies on his own, he asked Peat, Marwick & Mitchell, an accounting firm that helped with their taxes, to review the documents.* When the accountants confirmed that the numbers did not add up, Marsh wrote Saunders on August 6, 1943, that he had concerns about the foreign income reports and was sending an accountant to New York to review her records. He also mentioned that, while the accountant was there, it made sense to audit all the *GWTW* files. On August 10, he followed up with a longer letter detailing a list of assorted "unfinished business" he wanted Saunders to address. Marsh ended the letter on a friendly note, saying he did not expect the impossible from her. He knew she could do nothing about the nations under German control, but he did want to put things in order as much as possible. He also left the door open for the chance the errors were his own: "If I have misrepresented any of the above situations, because of letters misplaced in my files or carelessness in my record-keeping, I want to apologize in advance." He sent along best regards for Saunders and "her kinfolks in England" and acknowledged "we all have much to be thankful for these days in the complete reversal of the war picture from what it was not many months ago."[2]

Saunders responded right away, acknowledging there were unresolved issues and that she had been meaning to sort things through with him. She placed much of the blame on Hitler and identified all the *GWTW* publishers who were Jewish, suggesting it might be impossible to ever figure out what happened in those cases. She promised to cooperate with the accountant but could not do so until September because she was having trouble

---

* The Mitchell in the firm's name was no relation to the author.

finding competent secretarial support amidst the wartime labor shortage. Her secretary had died in March, and the files had been in disarray ever since.³ Marsh replied on August 31 that he was glad she would cooperate and advised her that the accountant would be in touch soon.

The next document in the Mitchell files is a frantic letter from Saunders to Marsh dated September 20, by which point the accountant had paid her a visit. She cryptically told Marsh that information he would receive from the accountant was being sent at her suggestion. "I want you to know this," Saunders wrote. She also announced that she would be traveling to Atlanta with the accountant and wanted to meet with Marsh confidentially.⁴ Something was amiss.

What Saunders wanted to talk to Marsh about was a shortfall in Mitchell's royalty account of close to thirty thousand dollars. The accountant had not pinned down an exact number but had seen enough to know that Saunders had been stealing from Mitchell for years. The agent did not deny the findings and was distraught at having been exposed. Over the following days, she wrote several letters to Marsh, baring her soul. As would become a pattern in the coming months, she recognized she had committed a crime but could not bring herself to accept full responsibility for her actions. Desperate for forgiveness, she told Marsh that their meeting would not be easy for her. She grieved, recalling how kind he and Mitchell had been to her. Conceding she should have come clean long before, she did not know how she could face him: "It is made ever so much harder by reason of my feelings and admiration for you all—which may sound futile at this time. I have been too proud and optimistic."⁵ She assured Marsh that she could be trusted to continue working for them and pleaded for the opportunity to do so. She wanted a chance to restore their relationship: "To say that I am terribly, terribly upset, is to put it mildly. I have been through h_____ in the past few weeks."⁶

On October 7, she met with Marsh and Stephens Mitchell at Peat, Marwick & Mitchell's Atlanta office. Margaret Mitchell was not present; she knew what the accountants had discovered, but Marsh saw no reason for his wife to face her betrayer. At the meeting, Saunders acknowledged that since 1938 she had failed to pay Mitchell more than twenty-eight thousand dollars in royalties.⁷ The agent said she could not repay the debt because her work had dried up during the war, and her expenses had exceeded her income for some time. Although she could not specify precisely where Mitchell's money had gone, she assured them she was not doing business with the Nazis or any enemies of the United States. She wanted to repay

Mitchell and proposed that they retain her services on a reduced-fee basis so she could earn back the missing money and save them the trouble of hiring a new agent.[8]

Marsh considered her proposal but decided to part ways. The next day, Saunders and Mitchell executed a document terminating their agency relationship. Saunders agreed to pay back the missing royalties as soon as possible and to (1) promptly notify all of Mitchell's foreign publishers that she no longer represented the author; (2) provide Marsh a detailed list of contact information for all the foreign contracts; and (3) cooperate in the resolution of the ongoing audit. In exchange, Mitchell agreed to waive interest on the missing royalties and credit toward Saunders's debt any commissions owed on the foreign accounts.[9]

Firing Saunders had been an easy decision. More difficult would be whether to pursue criminal charges. The Marshes had little sympathy for the agent but were averse to embroiling themselves in a messy judicial proceeding. Admitting they had been swindled would be embarrassing. As Margaret Baugh recalled, the Marshes did not want to "look like suckers and yokels to have been so taken in by [Saunders]."[10] A trial would be time consuming and stressful. Mitchell's back was bothering her that summer, and her father was ill. After much soul searching, they decided not to report the embezzlement to the police.[11] However, they were not willing to let Saunders off the hook entirely. Given the FBI's inquiry the previous year, Marsh worried that the agent might have used the embezzled money for subversive purposes. Just in case, they reported Saunders to the FBI. Marsh and Stephens Mitchell met with agents at the Atlanta field office at least twice. Marsh explained that, although he had assumed Saunders "anti-Axis," he now worried that she had duped them. The FBI agreed to look into it but apparently found no cause to suspect Saunders of treason. The bureau kept the matter confidential, and the story appears never to have made the newspapers.[12]

The next question for the Marshes was how to oversee the foreign accounts without Saunders. The idea of bringing in a new agent held little appeal. It would be burdensome finding someone they trusted and would draw attention to the break in their relations with Saunders. Handling the foreign accounts themselves would be difficult, especially given the confused state of world affairs, but it was an option they were considering. While they developed a game plan for the future, Saunders tried to convince them that she deserved another chance. Throughout the fall, she peppered the Marshes with letters in which she struggled to come to grips with what she had done. The correspondence is striking, both for its pathos and its remarkable lack of self-awareness. One moment she was despondent with remorse; the next, she cockily warned they could not function without her

Saunders admitted she had done a "horrible thing," and that no "apology or reparation" would ever be good enough. Her actions showed "a corruption and a deadness of conscience" that made her "absolutely ill." She acknowledged this was small punishment compared to the "awful worry and sickness" Mitchell must have been suffering at having her trust betrayed.[13] She wrote Marsh that her legs were shaky as she walked the streets of New York, tormented by what she had done and the kindness with which they had treated her. Desperate for forgiveness, Saunders tried to explain away her behavior. Harking back to earlier comments about how she liked working on her own, the agent now held that independent streak responsible for her predicament. She had been alone too much since moving to the United States and wished she'd had someone like Marsh or Stephens Mitchell to advise her. She also tried to cast blame on the "impressions and influences" of her early years. Claiming to have been brought up in "luxury in Berlin and Paris," she suffered from a lack of discipline. For good measure, she also threw in that she had a thyroid deficiency and problems training secretaries.[14]

She must have believed these excuses justified her actions because she had the nerve to ask the Marshes to reconsider her termination, assuring them that she had their best interests at heart. It was unheard of, Saunders claimed, for an American author to deal directly with foreign publishers. Moreover, if word got out about the embezzlement, it would look bad for Mitchell and cause unwanted attention. And, Saunders fretted, if it became public that she had been fired, it would ruin her business and she would never be able to repay the debt. She desperately wanted to know if Marsh had told Macmillan what happened. She claimed to have "very happy relations" with Harold Latham and Cole and continued to send them manuscripts on behalf of other authors. Saunders felt uncomfortable engaging in pleasantries with the editors not knowing what they knew.[15] Would Marsh be willing to downplay the theft and not go into details about why the agent no longer worked for Mitchell?

Marsh would have none of it. Her letters showed "a fine attitude" and it was "human to indulge in self-justification" but enough was enough. If the contract with Mitchell had been burdensome to Saunders, she should have quit. He blamed matters on the agent's "unbusinesslike methods" and failure to follow "elementary principles of business and law." Whereas a "proper agent relieves her client of burdens and worries," he felt Saunders created them and put "hard labor" on the Marshes by forcing them to argue with her about matters "which should have required no argument at all."[16] At the end of October, the accountants finished the audit and declared the final amount due, including the one thousand dollars Mitchell had advanced the agent, was $30,088.22.[17] Marsh instructed Saunders to get busy notifying the publishers and agents that she no longer represented Mitchell.

As for Macmillan, Marsh had not yet told George Brett, Latham, or Cole about the embezzlement. He expected Saunders to do so and was not cowed by her threats about bad publicity. "We are free at any time to tell the whole story or any part of it," he wrote. "You will be making a serious error of judgment if you assume that we have changed our position just because we have said nothing yet."[18] Marsh would not be a partner to any deception. He recommended Saunders tell Latham and everyone else the full truth and be done with it.[19] If the agent even hinted that any fault for the situation rested with Mitchell, he said, the Marshes would not hesitate to file a lawsuit for libel or slander. They did not want to hear any more excuses. "The disruption of my life and the gray hairs I have gained these past seven years were largely because of the foreign business, and the hard job of holding you in line," he wrote, "and no amount of money in the world could compensate me for it."[20] He reminded Saunders that her career had benefited from her association with Mitchell and that she was fortunate they did not charge her interest on the missing funds or ask her to pay the cost of the audit.

After several weeks of back and forth, Saunders called the apartment in Atlanta at nine o'clock on the evening of December 1, 1943, and frantically tried to convince Marsh to keep his mouth shut. Did he want her to go out of business? If word got out about what she had done, she threatened, she would never be able to pay back the money she owed. She was most anxious to avoid telling Latham; even if the editor promised to keep it secret, she felt sure he would broadcast the news to others. According to Marsh's notes of the phone conversation, he explained to Saunders that he would not deceive other people, even if it did slow down her repayment. He summarized the discussion this way: "Throughout the conversation she displayed the same mental dishonesty, inability to grasp simple principles of right and wrong and twisted thinking which she displayed in our Atlanta discussions and which got her into trouble in the first place."[21] After half an hour of her ranting, he hung up on her.

The following day, the agent wrote to Marsh full of remorse. She apologized for having called so late but explained that she would have been unable to sleep without talking to him. She had no business making excuses and acknowledged that it had been tactless of her to suggest otherwise. It would not happen again, she promised.[22] Accepting Saunders at her word, Marsh was glad they had reached an understanding. He assured her that if the Marshes disclosed details of what happened, it would not be with pleasure but because the "only way we know how to do business is to plow a straight furrow."[23]

On December 8, 1943, Saunders broke the news to Macmillan that she no longer represented Mitchell.[24] Although the agent volunteered no details about what caused the split, the firm heard the full story from Marsh. Brett was sympathetic with what the Marshes had endured but disagreed with their decision not to report Saunders to the police. He thought they should haul her into court and obtain an order directing her to turn over the records and money immediately. He also wanted Mitchell to inform *Publishers Weekly* and the Authors League. He thought Saunders ought to be put out of the literary agency business; it was unfair to other authors not to reveal what happened. If Mitchell was not comfortable doing so, Macmillan would be glad to step forward once she provided the firm with the necessary evidence to defend itself from a libel suit.[25]

Marsh did not take kindly to the unsolicited advice. He blasted back, explaining that they had decided against legal action "not out of kindness to Miss Saunders but because it would have hurt the innocent party, Peggy, more than the guilty one." While they considered themselves to have a good sense of their public duties, the Marsh family had no regrets about not going public. As for other possible victims, Marsh doubted Saunders could afford to remain in business much longer. In any event, he felt Macmillan was in no position to be critical of them. After all, Marsh charged, Saunders would have never come into their lives except for Macmillan: "You gave her to us along with the foreign publication rights and, from that day on, she was a constant source of trouble and expense to us until we terminated her contract, and since then, too, for she left a terrible tangle and mess for us to clear up."[26]

Taken aback by the vitriol of Marsh's response, Brett forwarded the correspondence to Latham for his reaction. Latham, too, failed to see any reason for Marsh's ire.[27] Nonetheless, Brett took the high ground. He gave up on the idea of the Marshes exposing Saunders and went about privately advising Macmillan's authors to cut ties with the agent. The publisher apologized to Marsh for any discomfort his letter had caused, saying he had not meant to give the impression he was criticizing the couple.[28] Brett did dispute though that Macmillan had saddled the Marshes with Saunders. Back in 1936, Macmillan had no reason not to trust her, he explained, and it was logical that she had been allowed to continue working on *Gone With the Wind* after the foreign rights were transferred to Mitchell. Chastened, Marsh accepted the apology. "A situation of this kind is always difficult to handle, and practically any method of dealing with it might fall short of the best way," he wrote.[29]

By the spring of 1944, Marsh began to wonder if Brett had been right about how to handle Saunders. Not yet having hired a replacement agent, the Marshes found themselves in the uncomfortable position of continuing to rely on her for advice. They had been working the foreign accounts with her for more than seven years by this point but still faced a steep learning curve on almost every facet of their overseas dealings. Saunders proved irresistibly helpful, and knew it. In the months since she had been let go, the agent had been tutoring Marsh on the accounts, giving him an exhaustive report about each of the publishers, going into great detail about their likes, dislikes, marital statuses, incomes, and attitudes toward *Gone With the Wind*. She described how one was loyal because he had bought a car with the money he earned from Mitchell's book. Another, she said, was reliable but had a quick temper. She also knew which ones were Jewish or had Jewish spouses, an important consideration in trying to sort through why some publishers may have been unable to pay royalties in recent years. The Marshes further took advantage of her connections in the publishing world and savoir faire about how to operate on an international level. She alerted them to potential piracies in Canada and Iceland and helped them sort through what to do in each case.

Their failure to make a clean break with Saunders put the Marshes in a difficult position. Knowing that they needed her, Saunders again became less contrite and more demanding. She lashed out at Marsh for daring ask about her plans for repaying the debt. She criticized him for not being more sympathetic to her plight. She also started making noises that she wanted credit against her debt for the information she had been providing them since her termination. By the summer of 1944, Saunders had cast herself in the role of the victim struggling against mean ol' John Marsh.

Marsh went through several rounds with her, and it took him until July 1944, almost a full year after discovering her wrongdoing, to put matters to rest. He acknowledged she been helpful over the preceding months but explained that he had accepted her assistance with a clean conscience on the assumption that she wanted to be of service. "If I were living in a friend's house in a relationship of trust and confidence and, accidentally or intentionally, burned the house down, I would want to help rebuild it," he wrote. "If I did not have the money to pay for the damage, I would want to help in any other way I could, even if I could do nothing more than push a wheelbarrow." Sermon delivered, he offered to credit Saunders whatever amount she believed proper for providing them helpful information.[30] With that behind them, he wanted to cut ties. It would be a gradual process, but by fall, Saunders accepted the reality of her position and started making payments on her debt.

With Saunders out of the picture and the Marshes responsible for handling the foreign rights themselves, a new phase began in *Gone With the Wind*'s international history. The couple revisited the idea of bringing in another agent and contacted Hervey Allen, author of *Anthony Adverse*, for his advice.[31] They made inquiries to some of the leading agencies in New York and got as far as reviewing a draft contract from Leland Hayward, for whom Kay Brown now worked. Ultimately, they decided to continue handling the accounts themselves, with the assistance of the accountants at Peat, Marwick & Mitchell, which had a network of international affiliates.[32] The author's father had died that summer after a lengthy illness, and his passing meant that Mitchell, who had been his primary caregiver for the last years of his life, would have more time to focus on her business affairs.

At first, they were mostly in a holding pattern waiting for the war to end. Mitchell did what she could to introduce herself to the publishers and subagents around the world with whom Saunders had been working. Knowing it was unusual for them to be dealing directly with an author, she did her best to forge positive relationships. As she wrote to Jenny Bradley, the subagent in France who had worked with Saunders on the Gallimard account, "At present we are little more than names to each other, but I promise that I will contribute whatever I can toward the advancement of our mutual understanding. I want your dealings with me to be both profitable and pleasant to you, and I will help in any way I can toward that end." Mitchell needed to keep a careful eye on what was happening in the publishing world overseas and let the local agents know that she counted on them to be her eyes and ears. She encouraged Bradley to make suggestions and offer advice: "I am far away from France; I know little of French methods of doing business; I know nothing of the personality and character of my publisher."[33]

In late 1944, Mitchell began seeing signs of life on the foreign accounts when a handful of publishers expressed interest in publishing new translations of *Gone With the Wind*. Suspicious of anyone managing to do business in those difficult days, she proceeded cautiously. A Swedish publisher asked permission to run a serialized English version of the book and offered to guide Mitchell through the foreign currency licensing process. According to the publisher's representative, Mitchell could avoid some of the complications if she took an oath that she was not doing business with any enemy or anyone in enemy-occupied territories. Knowing nothing about the publisher, Mitchell could not truthfully make such a statement so decided to wait until after the war to pursue the opportunity. She preferred to lose money rather than discover later that she had been "doing business with a Nazi even three times removed."[34] She also turned down an offer from a publisher in Argentina, feeling that the country's pro-German leanings made it an unattractive place to do business.[35] One of the few new contracts she pursued during that period was with Mordecai Newman, a publisher in Palestine. Marsh considered the Hebrew translation a highlight of their collection.

Germany's surrender in May 1945 brought an immediate resurgence of activity on Mitchell's accounts around the world. Most of the publishers acknowledged their back royalties and indicated they were anxious to continue publishing *Gone With the Wind*. Steen Hasselbalch, her Danish publisher, reported he had been in hiding for much of the war but his firm had sold more than seventy-five thousand copies of Mitchell's book through 1944 and expected to reach one hundred thousand by the end of 1945. He assured the author that he had placed her royalties in a bank waiting the day when they could be transferred legally to the United States.[36] The Bulgarian publisher had likewise survived the war and was enthusiastic to get back to work. In a note that reflects the types of logistical difficulties that existed after the war, he reported that, during the bombardment of Sofia, he had lost his copy of their contract and needed Mitchell to send him another one.

These were happy days indeed. Mitchell jumped into action, thrilled to do anything within her power to help her publishers get back on their feet. She sent care packages to them, her translators, and the local subagents representing her book. If they wrote asking for specific items, such as medicine or clothing, she complied enthusiastically. To Bradley, she sent underwear, soles for shoes, coffee, rice, tea, mending thread, a toothbrush, and a sweater. She even suggested that the agent trace her shoes on a piece of paper so Mitchell could get her a new pair in the right size. Macmillan, too, was in a celebratory mood. In December 1945, a few months shy of the book's ten-year anniversary, the publisher issued a press release proclaiming, that 3,500,000 copies of *Gone With the Wind* had been printed in the English language. The book continued to breeze right along.[37]

As was often the case in Mitchell's post-*Wind* life, positive developments were followed by trouble. The Marshes looked forward to relaxing over the 1945 Christmas holidays at Sea Island, Georgia. Shortly after checking in to their room on Christmas Eve, Marsh suffered a massive heart attack. He survived but was forced to take an extended leave of absence from work—both from Georgia Power and as his wife's business manager. He would remain at home for the next two years, mostly bedridden. This left Mitchell in charge of all her business affairs, including the foreign accounts. She rolled up her sleeves and got to work with the able assistance of Stephens Mitchell, Baugh, and the accountants at Peat, Marwick & Mitchell.[38] For the next several years, Margaret Mitchell would walk a tightrope trying to balance her time between caring for her husband and overseeing the affairs of *Gone With the Wind*.

It was a time of transition at Macmillan as well. Cole left the firm to try her hand at being a literary agent. The new profession did not suit her, so she eventually returned to publishing but at a different firm, Whittlesey House. She and Mitchell remained close and communicated regularly about the book and personal issues, including Cole's son and daughter Linda, who had been born in 1943. Richard Brett, who had butted heads with his brother George about the goals of the business, also left the company. During the war, the younger Brett had volunteered for the army air force; after his discharge, he became the business manager of the New York Public Library. And, to the great sadness of Mitchell and Macmillan, advertising manager Alec Blanton, who played such an important role in marketing *Gone With the Wind* and ensuring its success, died in July 1946. As George Brett relayed the events to Mitchell, Blanton had been at the office one evening in good spirits, joking with everyone, and looking forward to an important meeting scheduled for the following morning. Word came to the office the next day that Blanton had committed suicide. "It is just one of those damned things," Brett said, shaken by the loss.[39] Blanton's absence was felt all the more keenly because Latham was ill and away from the office for extended periods during the mid-1940s.

~

Mitchell confronted myriad difficulties reestablishing business operations after the war. Perhaps most daunting was the language barrier. Whereas Saunders had been fluent in several languages and had a city full of interpreters at her disposal in New York, Mitchell spoke only a smattering of French and had to hobble along with the assistance of her husband's limited knowledge of German and her brother's familiarity with Portuguese, Spanish, French, and Latin.[40] When a publisher from Ukraine asked for rights to release a translation, Mitchell had to ask a friend what language Ukrainians spoke. She guessed it might be Ukrainian but, given her experiences so far, thought "that would be far, far too easy."[41] (The answer was Russian.) When she needed assistance translating documents, she turned for help to the international community in Atlanta, such as it was in those days. Bankers, businessmen, returning soldiers, missionaries, refugees, and war brides came to her rescue and helped her muddle through.

As for the publishers who survived the war and remained in business, Mitchell worked closely with her accountants to assess what money was due. She reviewed all the royalty statements to make sure every penny was accounted for and was not shy about standing up for what she thought was rightfully hers. She pointed out shortfalls and demanded all accounts be brought up to date as quickly as possible. But her scrupulousness was not born of greed; she just as readily corrected errors that would inure to a publisher's favor. What mattered to her was accuracy.

In countries where the publisher had died or gone out of business, she tried to make arrangements with new firms. She never heard from Wydawnictwo J. Przeworski, her original Polish publisher, and assumed he had perished. The replacement publisher Saunders found had not fared well either: his stock had been destroyed by German bombing, along with records of any sales. After the war, Mitchell contracted with a third Polish publisher to get the book back in print.[42] The situation proved most complicated in countries where it was less obvious what had happened to the people involved, such as was the case in Germany. Right after the war ended, she had received a letter from Henry Goverts saying that he had fled to Liechtenstein, where his British mother lived. He acknowledged owing Mitchell back royalties and promised he would soon begin selling her book again. But then his correspondence abruptly ceased. Had he died? Had he lost interest in publishing? Had he been a Nazi after all? She might have been able to invalidate the contract given his failure to keep the book in print, but she was not eager to do so. Goverts had been fair in his dealings with her, so she decided to give him time to get his affairs in order, even if doing so meant losing out on potential sales.[43]

A similar problem loomed in France. Mitchell had not heard from Gaston Gallimard since 1940 and was troubled by rumors he had cooperated with the Nazis and gone into hiding after the liberation of Paris. If he had been a collaborator, did that void their contract? Was she free to negotiate a new contract with a different firm? Stories circulated in France that another publisher was close to releasing an edition of *Gone With the Wind*, and Mitchell fretted that the French government had confiscated the rights to her book from Gallimard and given them away. She also wanted to know where her overdue royalties were. Mitchell contacted Wallace McClure and Bradley to see if they could offer any insight. They both assured her that Gallimard had been absolved of any wrongdoing and remained in business. In fact, it was he who was planning to issue the rumored new edition of *Gone With the Wind* and would be doing so with a splash. To make up for the substandard edition released in 1939, Gallimard's new book would be a deluxe, two-volume hardcover set illustrated by Andre Dignimont, whom Bradley described as the best-known French illustrator of the day. Mitchell also learned that a considerable sum of her back royalties had been confiscated by the Germans and that Gallimard was working on getting the money to her. When the funds arrived in 1946, Mitchell expressed to Bradley "the greatest admiration and appreciation for the way [Gallimard] handled my royalty money during the war and the occupation and the honesty of his desire to get what was mine into my hands."[44] She apologized to Gallimard for having raised the issue of whether he had been a German collaborator. She hoped he held no anger or resentment against her and said she was sure he, as a good Frenchman, understood her reluctance to do business with a purported Nazi sympathizer.[45]

Not all of Mitchell's publishing relationships withstood the war so well. Such was the case with Alice Meden, her Swedish publisher. When the Swedish edition debuted in the fall of 1937, Mitchell had been pleased to read that the publisher had invested in an extensive advertising campaign and that the book had been received enthusiastically. Over the next several years, the author heard that the book sold well. Yet, the royalties Meden paid were paltry, and Mitchell heard almost nothing from the woman for lengthy periods of time. Although some of that could be attributed to the war and the problem with Saunders, the numbers still did not add up. Sweden was neutral during the hostilities, and its communications with the United States had been fairly open. And, even after the war ended, Mitchell heard nothing. She directed an accounting firm in England—whom she fondly referred to as "Britain's bulldog breed"—to track down Meden. When confronted, the publisher played dumb, claiming she had sold just a few copies of the book in 1944 and none in 1945. Mitchell was skeptical considering the Danish publisher had fared well during those years, as had the one in neighboring Norway, who had sold almost seventeen thousand books during the German occupation. "It seems very strange to me that in two small countries under oppressive occupation by the enemy, impoverished by systematic looting, such astounding sales can be reported, while next door in neutral Sweden, which has grown wealthy by wartime trade, the report is that no sales were made this year," she wrote.[46] The accountants performed a full audit of Meden's records and determined that the firm had been withholding royalties. Meden showed no remorse: Mitchell had made enough money, so what was the harm? Outraged, Mitchell considered filing criminal charges, but the accountants advised her against taking on the stress and expense of such a proceeding. Instead, they negotiated a settlement and an agreement severing the relationship.[47]

Another headache arose for Mitchell when an American army officer in Germany asked for permission to use excerpts from the English-language version of *Gone With the Wind* in an anthology to be distributed to Germans studying English. This was not something she was eager to do. At that time, Goverts's whereabouts were still unknown, and it was not clear to Mitchell who owned the rights to produce English-language editions outside the United States. The rights arguably belonged to her because she had not specifically granted them to anyone else, but she figured Goverts, Macmillan London, and Macmillan New York might claim an interest. She predicted the contract would be "the damnedest thing to write I can possibly imagine."[48] She considered saying no, but Brett cautioned that doing so might look unpatriotic.[49] With his encouragement, she put on a brave face: "Margaret Baugh and I have charged boldly at hurdles and hedges and have cooked up something like a dozen foreign contracts each one different. So I suppose we can cook up this one."[50]

As she predicted, the project proved to be a disaster. The American official who had goaded her into agreeing to the book was transferred stateside, leaving Mitchell to deal with the German professor whose idea it had been. As it turned out, what he actually had in mind was an abridged and reorganized edition of *Gone With the Wind*. He also wanted Mitchell to waive her royalty and spared no effort in plucking at her heartstrings. He wrote to her in November 1946:

After my house being plundered and my wife finding a painful death as one of the last victims of the European havoc, it is bitter to see one's own and only child feel always hungry. With health and strength almost failing, it seems often desperate — unpractical as I am — to stand through a time when inconsiderate self preservation prevails and morals are turned upside down. The hopelessness of the situation as well as physical exhaustion threaten to stifle initiative and idealism altogether.[51]

Mitchell sympathized with the man's plight but would not give him the rights to *Gone With the Wind* for free. If she did so in this case, she would be expected to do the same in other countries. She dreaded breaking the news to the professor. As she explained to Brett, "So much of my work these days is done with the pitiful starving of Europe that I cannot take on another one; nor can I say no to another one, as I am carrying more than I really am able to carry." She was working past midnight every night on the foreign accounts and doing her best to care for her still-ailing husband. Asserting that the revised proposal created copyright implications for Macmillan's interest, she asked Brett to handle it in her stead. "George, I just can't wrestle with this, and I can't wrestle with the problem of writing a long explanatory letter to this German."[52] Brett graciously agreed to make her excuses. The following spring, Mitchell was relieved to learn that Goverts was back in business.[53]

The author also had to figure out how her contracts were affected by changes to geopolitical boundaries after the war. For example, according to the terms of its 1935 contract with Mitchell, Macmillan had the exclusive right to publish and distribute *Gone With the Wind* in the United States and in U.S. territories such as the Philippines. Macmillan did not allow any foreign translations to be distributed within its markets, and, thus, the only version of *Gone With the Wind* available in the Philippines was the American one, despite the fact that several other languages were spoken there. When the Philippines obtained its independence after the war, Mitchell assumed Macmillan no longer had exclusive rights in the island nation and that she would be free to promote foreign language editions there. As a matter of courtesy, she confirmed her understanding with Brett. He agreed and appreciated her forthrightness: "Know the reason why I am so partial to Margaret Mitchell as an author? Because she is always so frank and helpful and always confers before doing things."[54] He declared it a delight to do business with her.

Without Saunders and her network of overseas connections, the author did the best she could to keep her ear to the ground for word of new unauthorized editions. Her clipping service proved useful in this regard, as did the Department of State and Peat, Marwick & Mitchell. Metro-Goldwyn-Mayer (MGM), which had extensive overseas operations and was eager to protect its rights to the film version of *Gone With the Wind* overseas, also tipped her off when it learned of issues related to her book in foreign countries. And, as always, some of the pirating publishers were bold enough to contact her directly, presumably oblivious to the fact that she was not enamored of their endeavors. In 1947, the son of one of her Chinese translators sent Mitchell a copy of an introduction to *Gone With the Wind* that his father had written, along with a request that she send them a pair of pants, a violin, and some ginseng.[55] She had the piece translated and was touched by the effort that had gone into it. Although much of the information was incorrect or exaggerated—she was amused by references to her as "modest, pure and benevolent" and an excellent housekeeper—it reflected an honest attempt at accuracy. It gave her hope that the book might be a quality production, and she sent the young man the requested items.[56]

Her major worry remained the still-unresolved Dutch piracy litigation, which had been on hold for years now. J. A. Fruin had served as a captain in the Dutch cavalry throughout the war and only occasionally got word through. Mitchell understood from him that ZHUM had wearied of the lawsuit and was willing to move forward as an authorized publisher and pay her back royalties. Mitchell, too, was weary and willing to settle but by February 1946 had not received the promised payment or any word about where things stood. Reporters frequently asked her about the status of the case, and it embarrassed her to respond that she knew nothing. Worse, she heard rumors that ZHUM had authorized a Belgian edition of *Gone With the Wind*, as if the tentative resolution gave Adrian Stok, the publisher, the right to start selling her translation rights to third parties. Mitchell was anxious for Fruin to set matters straight. She allowed that perhaps he had been "killed in the liberation fighting" but felt some other member of his firm or perhaps a family member should have contacted her.[57] She was also frustrated with Walbridge Taft, her lawyer in New York. Despite repeated attempts to light a fire under him to get the case resolved, he seemed content to wait for Fruin to get in touch.

The Dutch lawyer reestablished contact in the spring of 1946 and promised the settlement would be resolved soon. Mitchell expected Taft to follow up, but he saw no urgency in the matter. In his estimation, Fruin had done wonders given the conditions he faced. Taft also questioned whether the negligible sum involved merited the importance Mitchell attached to it. Not willing to wait any longer, Mitchell went over Taft's head and wired Fruin directly. Three days later, word came that ZHUM had paid Fruin the settlement. For Mitchell, this good news was tempered by the fact Fruin had subtracted his fees from the Dutch publisher's payment without her approval and made no mention of when her money would be forwarded. Then, when the legal papers arrived, the settlement agreement was written poorly, and there was no record of court approval.[58] Taft again expressed no particular concern, and the author told him she no longer required his services.

She asked her accountants to review the files, and, in short order, they gave Mitchell a full report of what Fruin owed. "It is like a breath of fresh salt air in a close room to read their lucid account of what has been taking place in Holland," she wrote Stephens Mitchell in the fall of 1946. The author asked her brother to step in and wrap things up. "It has become such an unwieldy, bulky and long-drawn-out affair that I hope in some manner you can get it simplified," she told him. "The most exasperating thing about the whole situation is the bunglesomeness with which it has been handled, the many mistakes which have occurred along the way and the delay in closing up the case properly."[59]

Taking his sister's statements of what had occurred at face value, Stephens Mitchell wrote a sharp letter to J. Drost, a lawyer who had take over the case from Fruin. He received an equally sharp reply. Drost evidenced little patience for demanding Americans but expressed a willingness to address Mitchell's concerns:

> My first impression by this letter was: One more proof of the complete igno-rance of Americans about a country, occupied, ruined and plundered five long years by the Germans, slaughtered and terrorized by the Gestapo, hav-ing lost—relatively—far greater part of its population than any other allied country of Western Europe or America, having been since September 1944 without rail or car traffic, with scarce and very slow postal communications, nearly starved by cold and want of food, utterly disorganized even after its liberation in May 1945.
>
> The second impression was: I must thoroughly study its contents and then make the situation clear and put things right. This is what I will now try to do.[60]

Drost made a convincing case that his firm had not been negligent. He had not put the settlement agreement in writing earlier for fear the Germans might have found the document and punished them for dealing with Americans. Once the papers were finally drawn up, they had not been presented to the court because it was a private matter that did not need court approval under Dutch law. He assured Stephens Mitchell that the text was not poorly written in the original Dutch; he could not vouch for the translation the author had obtained.

The Belgian edition also turned out to be much ado about nothing. ZHUM had subcontracted with the Belgian publisher because Holland, which had been "far more plundered by the Germans than Belgium," did not have enough paper to print the book. Drost explained that Belgian is not a separate language from Dutch but rather a variation spoken in the Flemish section of Belgium. From that point forward, the case moved to a smooth resolution. Though the money Mitchell eventually received was nothing close to what she had spent on the litigation, the author felt she had done the right thing. She was proud of the attention she had drawn to the plight of American writers as a result of her country's failure to join the Berne Convention and regretted only that she had not accomplished a change in the law.[61] Although it had taken a decade of her life to bring ZHUM into the fold, the author held no grudge against Stok and went on to develop a productive working relationship with him. At long last, the foreign accounts appeared well in hand.

# 15

~

# A Bolt from the Blue

## Fall 1947–August 1949

By the fall of 1947, John Marsh had regained enough strength to resume working on the *GWTW* business affairs. Although he would never be well enough to return to Georgia Power—he resigned his position in early September—he wanted to take some of the heavy load off his wife's shoulders. One of his initial forays back into the role as her manager reveals the uncertain nature of his relationship with Macmillan more than a decade into their association. As meticulous as ever, Marsh went over with a fine-tooth comb the publisher's royalty statement for the previous year and spotted an irregularity in the percentages the company used to calculate the author's earnings. Instead of paying her a 15 percent royalty, the firm had used a 10 percent scale. When Marsh wrote to Macmillan about the issue that September, Brett greeted him like a long-lost friend: "Cheers and more cheers! . . . It is a delight to my heart to learn that you are up and at 'em again." The publisher explained that Macmillan had used a 10 percent figure to determine royalties because the book sold less than five thousand copies that year. According to the 1936 revised royalty agreement, the percentages dropped in any year the book sold below that threshold. "Did that clear matters up?" Brett asked optimistically.[1] It did not.

Margaret Mitchell's book had sold close to forty-five thousand copies the year in question, all formats combined; only the three-dollar edition sold fewer than five thousand. But Marsh was not content to simply point out the error and move on. Instead, he launched into a detailed explanation of why Macmillan had been unreasonable in its adjustment of her royalty

249

agreement back in the spring of 1936. He also made a passing reference to the "bad and unfair" contract Macmillan had let Mitchell sign with David O. Selznick.[2]

The publisher apologized immediately and without equivocation for the calculation error. Brett was sorry. The mistake would be corrected. As for Marsh's feeling that Macmillan had let Mitchell down on the negotiations with Selznick, Brett regretted the Marshes were unhappy with the movie contract. He stated that fifty thousand dollars was a generous amount of money back in 1936 and that Harold Latham had done as well as could have been expected at the time the sale was made.[3]

Brett's suggestion that Mitchell was grousing about the amount of money obtained for the movie rights threw Marsh into a rage. After thanking Brett for making the correction, he heaped a torrent of abuse on the startled publisher. Referring to Brett's comments as "slurring," Marsh, who apparently had been biting his tongue all these years, could restrain himself no longer:

> Our dissatisfaction with the motion picture contract did not arise from the amount of money and nobody has any right to attribute to Peggy the qualities of a welsher or a whiner. Our dissatisfaction did arise from very different factors and you are in [a] better position than anybody else to know what they are. You know, but apparently you have forgotten, how Macmillan put a blindfold over Peggy's eyes and tied her hands behind her back and delivered her over to Selznick. Macmillan was her agent and she relied on Macmillan in the contract negotiations. Then, several weeks after the movie contract was signed, we learned that Macmillan had not even tried to protect Peggy's interests, as it had pledged itself to do. Macmillan's representatives had acted solely to protect Macmillan's interests, versus Selznick and versus Peggy. . . .
>
> The numerous vague and far reaching demands upon the Author in the Selznick contract, and its almost complete lack of positive protection of the Author's interest, are why it is a bad and unfair contract and why we have been dissatisfied with it. It has forced Peggy to spend large amounts of money and it has made even greater drains on her time and strength.[4]

Marsh acknowledged he and his wife had been extraordinarily inexperienced at the time and advised Brett, "We would not have signed such a contract in 1936, excepting only for the fact that we relied upon Macmillan, as Peggy's agent, and Macmillan failed us."

Brett was thoroughly bewildered by the assault. He had had little to do with the movie negotiations, other than approving Latham's plan to bring in Annie Laurie Williams and dealing with the fallout of Mitchell's dissatis-faction with the contract. It had been Latham who kept Williams's involve-ment a secret. It had been Latham who promised to look out for Mitchell's interests and then left on vacation. It had been Richard Brett who had been at the table with Mitchell and the Selznick representatives. Unsure how to respond, George Brett forwarded the correspondence to Latham and asked for the editor's impressions of Marsh's letter. This proved to be another land mine.

Latham immediately jumped on his boss for having implied to Marsh that the editor had anything to do with the motion picture contract for *Gone With the Wind*. Latham claimed that he, too, knew little about the matter, having been on vacation that entire summer of 1936. He explained that Williams had sent him the offer while he was out of town, suggesting he had no idea why she had bothered him with it. Did Latham forget that he had volunteered to be Mitchell's agent and had assured her that he person-ally would look after matters? Apparently so. Absolving himself of any responsibility, Latham said that he knew nothing about Macmillan's position at the contract conference or why Marsh would say that the publisher blind-folded Mitchell. He even pointed out that he had never seen the contract or known any of its terms beyond the fifty-thousand-dollar payment.[5]

After establishing to his satisfaction that the problem was not his fault, Latham suggested Brett deal with Marsh in generalities. He took the liberty of drafting a response for the publisher's consideration, which Brett used verbatim for his reply to Marsh on December 8. The letter expressed regret that Marsh was disappointed but assured him of Macmillan's good inten-tions. Not grasping that Marsh's concern was a matter of principle and not of money, the letter suggested that the couple was unfairly judging matters with hindsight of what literary rights were worth in 1947 as opposed to what they had been worth in 1936.[6]

How Marsh responded to Brett's latest letter, if at all, is not known; the records do not include a reply. But for the rest of his life, Marsh main-tained the view that Macmillan was responsible for the raw deal Mitchell received in the movie contract. Mitchell, though, appears not to have shared his anger. In fact, that first week in December, she wrote friendly letters to both Brett and Latham and made no mention of the ancient history that was so vexing her husband. She told Latham that, if she ever found time to write another book, he would be the first person she told on the first day she sat down at the typewriter. She also mentioned the possibility of another book in a letter to Brett. Although she was far too well mannered to disagree publicly with her husband, these letters seem intended to let both men know where they stood in her eyes. She would hardly promise her next book, arguably the most valuable manuscript in the world, to Macmillan if she did not trust or respect the firm.

That she wrote to both Latham and Brett is also noteworthy. Over the years, it has been speculated that Mitchell had a hopeless case of hero worship for the editor but never liked her publisher. Comparing Mitchell's relationships with Latham and Brett, it does appear at first glance that she shared a more cordial one with the editor. Early in their relationship, when Latham urged her to call him by his first name, she assented, but added effusively, "I feel exactly as though I had referred to God Almighty familiarly as 'G.A.'"[7] With her editor, Mitchell always acted like something of an ingenue bewildered with all the goings-on around her. Latham brought out the Southern belle in her, and she, the paternalistic side in him.

But Mitchell was not so taken by Latham's charm that he was above reproach in her eyes. If anyone was at fault over the movie deal, ultimately it was Latham. He is the one who talked her into selling the rights. He brought Williams into the negotiations behind Mitchell's back. He then left the author hanging while he went on vacation. It must have also rankled Mitchell that Latham took all the credit for discovering her manuscript without ever publicly—and apparently not privately—giving credit to Mitchell's dear friend, Lois Cole. Cole resented Latham's handling of the matter, as she revealed in a 1956 letter to Margaret Baugh. Latham talked as if he had received a bonus for *Gone With the Wind*, Cole said. "You know how he was—anything to make other people uncomfortable." She had not received any financial recognition for her role in the manuscript's acquisition, saying the thought of acknowledging her contribution "never occurred to them."[8] Cole had not made waves though, and Mitchell followed her friend's lead in not burning bridges with Latham.

Brett, on the other hand, had gotten off on the wrong foot with the author. He had reduced her royalties and refused to apologize for the poorly handled movie deal. Yet, he quickly came around to seeing that Mitchell was a person of unique charm. Although he never explicitly admitted having done anything wrong in those early days, he appeared to spend the next several years trying to win Mitchell over, often going above and beyond the call of duty to support her interests. He volunteered to share the legal bills on the Susan Lawrence Davis case. He agreed to defer royalties for tax purposes. He reversed his brother's decision to not aid in the Billy Rose case and the Dutch piracy lawsuit. He spent countless hours helping her deal with the foreign rights. He was the one who approached Selznick about letting Mitchell off the hook on the "God Almighty clause," Mitchell and Brett did not always see eye to eye, but their relationship was all the richer for having been tested. He knew she was no pushover and certainly no fool. In 1943, British prime minister Winston Churchill famously said that "the price of greatness is responsibility." Brett borrowed that sentiment and reworked it to Mitchell's accomplishments, telling her with admiration that the price of greatness, in her case, had been labor.[9] For her willingness to pay that price with such a fine attitude, he had come to respect her greatly. He was also impressed by the level of expertise she developed in handling her publishing rights. As he wrote her in 1946, "In copyright matters I may have some knowledge, and perhaps some horse sense, but I think I bow to you. I find you too are an expert."[10] If she forgave the Dutch publisher, Adrian Stok, for all the trouble he caused, it seems unlikely she had not forgiven Brett who, despite his missteps, had been supportive of her and her brainchild.

Brett and Mitchell also seemed to enjoy each other's company in a way she and Latham never did. Whereas Mitchell's letters to her editor were warm, with Brett she seemed more comfortable showing the old Peggy, the one who enjoyed a good off-color joke. They were closer in age—only seven years apart—and shared a similar sense of humor. Indicative of her comfort with him is a response she offered to a suggestion he made in the spring of 1937 that the next commercial tie-in might be a *Gone With the Wind* corset. Even though they were not yet on a first-name basis, she had no problem taking his reference to intimate women's apparel to the next level:

> I am sure, however, that there is one ante bellum garment which will not return with the wind. That is the ante bellum pantie. Not long ago an admirer sent me a pair of her grandmother's drawers (yes, I know that sounds like a queer present, but I have received a few even queerer than this!). I tried these panties on, and I give you my word I could get both legs in one of the legs of Granny's pants. That pair of drawers was the most uncomfortable garment I ever had on, highly starched, baggy as a Turk's britches and covered with ruffles and embroidery. And chilly—my goodness! But I will not go into indelicate reasons for the chilliness of these pants, and I will only say that after trying them on I am sure ante bellum britches will not come back in style again.[11]

Only occasionally did her letters to Latham reveal the same sort of ribald spirit.

Mitchell also visited socially with Brett over the years, and it was not unusual for her to come to New York unannounced and ring him up. They would have dinner or go to the theater and usually ended the evening at the Plaza Hotel, where they talked until the wee hours of the morning.[12] He had taken her to the famous New York City nightspot, the Stork Club. Brett family lore says he was impressed with how well Mitchell could hold her liquor; he declared she could probably drink any man under the table.[13] Despite the early bumps in their relationship, he came to feel that Mitchell was closer to him than to anyone else at Macmillan. He did not think her visits with him were good diplomacy; he genuinely felt they were friends.[14] Stephens Mitchell agreed with Brett's assessment: "You are right about Margaret's liking for you. She was not much of a diplomat. If she liked people, she let them know it."[15]

With the foreign accounts back in order for the most part, Mitchell relished the sense of accomplishment. Despite all the troubles the translations had caused, the effort had been worth it. "Casting modesty to the four winds," she proclaimed to a friend, she and Baugh had "done wonders" cooking up foreign contracts and getting money out of places nobody thought possible.[16] She was impressed with her secretary's efficiency and tenaciousness, and several times expressed gratitude by presenting Baugh with copies of the foreign editions. In an Italian translation, the author paid tribute to Baugh's ability to "read a royalty report in any language" and, in a Spanish edition, offered the inscription "Senorita Margarita Baugh, From la autora Margarita Mitchell, I kees your leetel wite fooot, Senorita, for your help on this edition."[17]

Mitchell managed a veritable publishing empire from her Atlanta apartment and did a remarkable job, all things considered. Did she handle matters perfectly? Certainly not. At times, she let her pride and principles come before practicalities and business sense, especially when it came to fighting piracies. But, to her credit, she maintained her sense of humor and recognized the absurdity of what she was going through. To Baugh, she joked of writing a play about the life of a bestselling author. Whenever something ludicrous happened in the office, one of them would say, "That is something for the play."[18] Mitchell saw it as an author's duty to "scramble for themselves and fight for and defend their copyrights as best they can" and took seriously her obligation to protect *Gone With the Wind*.[19] While Brett and Walbridge Taft thought she went overboard spending so much money and time worrying about copyright problems, she had the last laugh.

Mitchell had proven that, with diligence and fortitude, foreign royalties could be profitable. Having the rights nailed down all over the world ultimately proved to her advantage when the foreign market for American books exploded after the war. Mitchell was ready to move. She had written one of the most famous novels in the world. She had a stable of reliable publishers in place. It also did not hurt that her book resonated with those rebuilding their lives amidst the ruins of World War II. A reader from Budapest, who dubbed herself "a Hungarian Scarlett O'Hara," wrote to Mitchell in 1946, telling her that in *Gone With the Wind* "every single account which describes the terrible destruction and sufferings of war is so much like our experiences that it seems as though you, too, had been living among us during those ghastly times."[20] As a result, the overseas publishing rights to *Gone With the Wind* turned out to be more profitable after the war than before. Years later, Stephens Mitchell wrote of how proud he was of his sister for her management of *Gone With the Wind*. Unlike other writers who let fortunes slip through their fingers, Margaret Mitchell's personal story was that she became a successful and diligent businessperson. Through her tireless efforts, she ensured she and Marsh were the ones to profit from her book's success.[21]

Of course, financial gain was never a driving issue for Mitchell. She had no interest in money if it were going to cause problems in her personal life. That resolve had not diminished, as Metro-Goldwyn-Mayer (MGM) learned in the fall of 1947 when the studio approached her about authorizing it to produce a sequel. Selznick had finally gotten through his head that Mitchell would never agree to such a project, but MGM, which now controlled the rights to the *GWTW* movie, wanted to revisit the idea. The studio was willing to pay Mitchell up to twenty-five thousand dollars for a two-year option to create its own continuation. Understandably wary of her reaction, Carol Brandt, an MGM executive, asked Latham to present the offer.[22] The Macmillan editor did not think there was much chance the author would accept but passed the proposal along anyway in case she might find it amusing. As Latham expected, Mitchell was not interested and did not want to discuss it with MGM. In classic Mitchell fashion, she explained:

> The weather has been too hot recently and I have been too tired for me to
> be polite and, if I am not quick and polite, before I know it people from

Hollywood will be bouncing off every plane and expecting to be entertained, and then the gossip columns will be full of the news that the great director, Mr. So-and-So, is conferring in Atlanta with the shy little author and the sequel to *Gone With the Wind* will be produced in 96 reels by day-after-tomorrow.[23]

She asked Latham to decline on her behalf. As reporter Elmer Davis once noted, Mitchell was a unique example of "self-abnegation" in the literary world. Resolving not to write again until she had something of merit to say, no matter how much money was dangled in front of her, was arguably as great an accomplishment as having written *Gone With the Wind*.[24]

With Marsh increasingly able to pitch in, Mitchell found her workload manageable for the first time in years. In the summer of 1948, Cole and her family visited Atlanta, and Mitchell relaxed in the company of old friends. Linda Taylor Barnes, Cole's daughter, fondly recalls the author taking them to lunch at the Piedmont Driving Club. Five years old at the time and decked out in a fancy dress, white socks, and patent leather shoes, Linda asked if she could get into the children's wading pool at the elegant country club. Her mother was aghast, but "Aunt Peggy" quickly took off her own shoes and stockings and happily splashed in the water with the little girl.[25]

Mitchell also found pleasure in hearing from fans. While the flood of mail had narrowed to a small stream, she was delighted that a new generation of readers was discovering her story. One eager soul took the liberty of offering a list of possible chapter titles for future editions of *Gone With the Wind*, such as "A Bolt from the Blue" for the opening chapter and "Too Late for Love" for the finale. Mitchell was especially amused by the suggestion "Perjury, Pride and Prostitutes," which she thought "would be a good title for a novel!"[26] As had been her policy since 1936, most letters received a courteous and prompt reply. That summer, a group of young women who had formed their own Literary Classics Club wrote to her with that all-too-familiar question of what happened to Scarlett and Rhett. Mitchell replied cheerfully, not letting on that she suspected a gloomy future for her lovers: "Now, girls, I can't answer that question about 'did Scarlett get him back.' Your guess is as good as mine, because I don't know. . . . I suppose some of you think one way and some the other, and either way may be right."[27]

That fall, as Mitchell approached her forty-eighth birthday, she "wanted to get all her ducks in a row," her brother recalled.[28] At her request, he stopped by the Marsh apartment on several evenings so they could talk about her investments and review the voluminous business files related to *Gone With the Wind.* The siblings also discussed what should happen to her literary legacy should she die before her husband and brother. "She wanted her writings destroyed, unless John saw fit to publish them," Stephens Mitchell said. "She wanted no sequels to *Gone With the Wind.* She wanted no comic strips, no abridgements nor condensations. She wanted everything done with dignity and, if necessary, to spend a lot of money to keep things dignified." His sister remarked that their ideas of dignity differed but that she trusted he would know what to do.[29]

In November, after a brief hospitalization for an undisclosed malady, Mitchell continued her house-in-order preparations and decided to update the will she had written in 1938 in the aftermath of the *Gone With the Wind* juggernaut. She now found the original document "too long, and perhaps a little stuffy."[30] After talking to her brother about some of the legal technicalities, Mitchell wrote a new will in longhand, its language simple and conversational—no wherefores, herebys, or pledges of sound mind and body. The opening sentence got straight to the point: "I want John, Steve Mitchell and the Trust Co. of Ga. to be the executors of my will." She made several bequests, including forgiving a loan she held on housekeeper Bessie Jordan's house and paying in full an annuity she was buying for Baugh. She left property or cash gifts to nieces and nephews on both sides of the family, to three godchildren—including Cole's son—and to several Atlanta institutions.

It has been rumored that Mitchell's will specifically forbad her executors from authorizing a sequel to *Gone With the Wind*, but it did not. Both her husband and brother were fully aware of her feelings about continuing the story of Scarlett and Rhett, and she trusted them to follow her wishes and use their best judgment. What she committed to paper was concise and specific. She referred to her novel—her most valuable asset—only twice in the five-page will. Halfway down the third page, she specified that "all rights to *Gone With the Wind*, domestic and foreign" would go to Marsh. On the fourth page, she granted her executors the power "to renew all copyrights." She did not address the issue of protecting her privacy that had been so prominent in the previous will, nor did she put specific restrictions on what should be done with her manuscript, research material, and letters other than noting that "all my papers and written matter of all kinds" would go to Marsh.[31] She wanted the remainder of her estate divided one-fourth to her brother and three-fourths to her husband.[32] When she finished the document that would govern the future of the world's bestselling novel, she asked three friends to drop by and witness her signature.

At Christmas, a group of local schoolchildren came to the couple's apartment to sing carols. When thanking their teacher, Mitchell commented that seeing "so many good looking and good mannered children makes us feel better about the future of our country."[33] The author also seemed to feel better about the direction her own life was taking. Marsh's health continued to improve, and he regained enough strength to finally venture out of the house. Some nights, they walked across the street to the Piedmont Driving Club for supper; on others, she drove them to a friend's house to visit or to a nearby theater to see a movie. That spring, they saw *Gone With the Wind* again at the Tenth Street Theatre near their former apartment on Crescent Avenue. The manager had sent free passes, and she wrote to tell him how much they enjoyed the film and how interested they were to see the theater was full. "A great many people seemed to be repeaters, for they knew beforehand what was going to happen and started laughing or crying before the cause for laughter or tears appeared on the screen."[34]

While Mitchell was glad to see people taking pleasure in her story, she remained uncomfortable with many aspects of being a celebrity. In early 1949, Associated Press correspondent Hal Boyle revisited the *GWTW* phenomenon in an article picked up by newspapers across the country. He had talked with Mitchell at a recent meeting of the Georgia Press Institute in Athens and related how the author still received inquiries from readers, such as a drunk who called late one night about the color of Scarlett's hair. When she read the caller a passage from the book that proved her heroine had black hair, he moaned, "That cost me fifty bucks. I bet Scarlett had red hair. Are you sure she doesn't?"[35]

To keep these types of disturbances to a minimum, Mitchell did her best to stay out of the public eye. In April 1949, Carl W. Ackerman, dean of the school of journalism at Columbia University, invited her to appear on a series of radio and television programs about Pulitzer Prize winners. She thanked him for his interest but declined, citing a personal "policy of not appearing on radio or making other public appearances." She worried such a program would stir up renewed interest and "hullaballoo" about the dramatic, radio, and television rights to her novel, something she desperately wanted to avoid. Mitchell noted that her Pulitzer certificate, which hung on her wall, "is one of my real treasures and I will always remember my excitement and pride when I first learned that my novel had won it," but participating in his show was something she could not do.[36] She also turned down an offer from Ward Green of King Features Syndicate who wanted to turn *Gone With the Wind* into a comic strip. Although his offer was generous, such a retelling of her story was bound to stir things up again.[1]

By the spring, Marsh was well enough to travel. In late May, the couple went to Delaware to see his mother and then to New York, where they visited with the Taylors. While in town, they had lunch with Latham in their suite at the Waldorf Astoria. Correspondence between author and editor had trailed off in recent years, but Latham received occasional letters from her usually full of cheerfulness and lively anecdotes.[38] She also tried to visit Brett while in the city but had been unable to make their schedules work.

Now that she had more free time, would Mitchell finally begin writing again? When *Gone With the Wind* was published, Mitchell swore she would never be crazy enough to write another book given the hardships the novel had imposed on her. Also, as her brother recalled, she believed that "no one (Shakespeare excepted) has more than three good stories in him. If he has three, he is a genius. If he has two, he is wonderful. Most of the great authors have only one." Mitchell had told her story, and it was a good one.[39] The only thing she had published in the past thirteen years was the war bonds article in 1942. When asked about the possibility of a second book, she said repeatedly there was no time to consider it given the incessant demands on her time from being a bestselling author.

As the years went by, Mitchell remained opposed to writing a sequel to *Gone With the Wind* but, as a born storyteller and someone who had been writing since childhood, apparently could not resist forever the urge to put words on paper. Throughout the 1940s, she frequently jotted down notes and various ideas that came to her at odd times, such as when waiting in a doctor's office or if unable to sleep at night. Sometimes it was a few sentences of conversation; other times, it was several paragraphs. She kept a notebook for jotting down her thoughts but often used whatever paper was handy, including the backs of envelopes. On occasion, she turned the notes over to Baugh to type. "They all had the same come-on as *Gone With the Wind* and left you licking your chops for more," the secretary recalled.[40]

Mitchell acknowledged authors were prone to swearing off additional books and then changing their minds: "I have heard other writers make that same remark and then observed that they were stricken suddenly with a novel while in their bath or woke up in the night with a violent attack of short story."[41] By 1949, she appeared on the verge of such an attack herself. Mitchell began to discuss with family and friends specific ideas she had for future projects. Though she was certain she would never write a sequel to the story of Scarlett and Rhett, she remained interested in the Civil War era and was even open to developing some of the minor characters from *Gone With the Wind*, such as the Tarletons.[42] Baugh recalled that Mitchell had also expressed an interest in Union general William T. Sherman's march to Atlanta. The author once asked her secretary to look through a biography of Confederate general Leonidas Polk, who was killed defending the city, to substantiate reports that he had kept a cow with him throughout the war so he would have fresh milk daily. "She was going to use that somewhere up the road," Baugh surmised.[43]

There were several other topics floating around her head as well. To friend Richard Harwell, a collector of Confederate memorabilia and fellow history enthusiast, Mitchell mentioned an interest in the eccentric Georgia poet Thomas Holley Chivers and the Confederate medical corps in North Georgia during Sherman's assault on Atlanta. She told Harwell she had also made notes on the Confederados, a band of former Confederate soldiers who established a colony in Brazil after the Civil War.[44] With her brother, Mitchell discussed the possibility of a detective novel set in the Civil War period that might include a reference to the Ladies Gunboat Association, a fundraising group of Confederate women.[45] Marsh thought she was semiseriously considering the play about an author's life that she and Baugh joked about; she certainly had the raw material.

While it seems that Mitchell may have been on the verge of embarking on a new project, something always seemed to pop up to keep her occupied with her firstborn. With the world economy rebuilding, book sales were strong in the United States and abroad, which meant the Marshes had plenty to do keeping an eye on *Gone With the Wind*. When Mitchell received Macmillan's annual royalty statement in 1949, she learned that American readers had bought another 17,400 copies of her novel over the previous year, the vast majority the $1.98 cheap edition but some of the regular three-dollar edition as well. This translated to about $1,400 in royalties—a tidy sum from a twelve-year-old title.[46] Overseas, 1948 proved a banner year as well with Mitchell pulling in more than forty thousand dollars from the foreign accounts.[47]

Although they were glad to be earning something after all the years of hard work on the foreign accounts, the influx of income equated to a tremendous amount of work. The Marshes spent hours reviewing correspondence and sales reports in a variety of languages. And problems continued to creep up that needed her attention. In England, *Gone With the Wind* was out of print because of postwar paper shortages and inflation, and she received complaints from British fans who wanted her to send them copies of the American edition. Hating to have the book unavailable for sale when demand remained strong, she agreed to accept a reduced royalty to get the British edition back on the market.[48]

In Japan, the status of her copyright had improved after the war. In light of the Allied occupation, Japanese publishers wanting to release American books now had to enter into contracts with authors and pay royalties.* Once again, Mitchell demonstrated her willingness to not hold a grudge and entered into a contract with Mikasa Shobo, one of the Japanese firms that had published her work before the war. The edition was an immediate bestseller, its sales aided by the perception that the book offered valuable insights into American history. It performed so well that the publisher struggled to keep up with demand in the face of an acute paper shortage. All seemed well until Mitchell discovered that the first volumes of the new edition did not contain the proper copyright notice. She fired off a letter to the firm canceling the contract. The publisher apologized immediately, blaming the mistake on his poor English skills. He took extraordinary steps to make things right, including adding the credit to all copies still in stock, running notices in newspapers, and printing special posters for bookstores pointing out the error.[49] Mitchell allowed the book to remain in print, but it was another reminder that she could never let her guard down. Like any good parent, she needed eyes in the back of her head.

In June, she received a letter from a Parisian named Madame Henri Pajot, who declared she had written a sequel to *Gone With the Wind* titled "Lady de Tara" and wanted Mitchell's permission to publish it. The Frenchwoman asserted she had altruistic motives for her action: she wanted to please readers who did not approve of the way Mitchell ended her story. Pajot suggested she was well within her rights given that Mitchell had not bothered to write a sequel herself after all these years. Should Mitchell decline to grant permission, Pajot threatened, her French publisher was prepared to go ahead with the project and simply change the names of the

---

* Mitchell was so pleased with this turn of events that she wrote General Douglas MacArthur, head of the Allied occupation, and thanked him for his efforts defending American interests.

characters. The name Pajot rang a bell. Mitchell reviewed her correspondence files and was irritated to discover that the Frenchwoman had proposed a sequel to the author in 1941 and had been denied permission then; it would not be granted now. Mitchell reminded the woman of their earlier correspondence, and warned: "I have successfully prevented dishonest people from using my characters in the past, and I will prevent you and your publisher from doing it too." As for the argument that Mitchell had waived her sequel rights, the author responded, "This is the same as if I had money in my pocket [for several years] and you and your publisher decided that, as I had not spent it, then you two were entitled to spend it for me."[50] Mitchell described the incident to Latham, admitting these types of battles were taking more and more out of her. "I have had to give so much time, energy, thought—and in some cases to take legal action—to such things that it would have been easier to write six sequels than to circumvent the sequels of well meaning but thick-skulled people, all the way from Korea to Kokomo."[51]

Also on the author's mind were her affairs in eastern Europe, where the Soviets were rising to power. As country after country fell behind the Iron Curtain, Mitchell found it increasingly difficult to conduct business in that part of the world. Her Yugoslavian publisher, whom Mitchell described as a "beautiful young Serbian lady," had lost her publishing business, and her Czech publisher's firm had been nationalized. Wanting to support her many associates who were struggling under Soviet rule, Mitchell packed and shipped boxes of food, vitamins, and clothing for them. She was not sure the items ever reached the recipients but was afraid to ask too many questions. To Wallace McClure, she wrote, "Sometimes when I am out in crowds I find I do not have too much conversation about what is going on in Georgia because I have been wrestling with international financial regulations and wondering about people who cannot possibly escape from the encirclement of Russia."[52] But she did not have any regrets over her foreign entanglements. Dealing with the overseas rights during the war years and the period of rebuilding in Europe had given her "a box seat at the world's biggest show." She did not know anyone in government service or otherwise who had had the privilege of learning about as many foreign countries as she. "I realize now that my book has taken me to many countries and made many friends for me."[53]

And there was the recurrent rumor mill, which Mitchell continued to monitor through her clipping service. She was distressed to receive an article from a Massachusetts newspaper that quoted Granville Hicks, a literary critic and an adviser to Macmillan, as telling an audience that the publisher had taken a chance on *Gone With the Wind* after reading only a single chapter. Mitchell wrote to him, asking that he not repeat the mistake in future presentations. While her sensitivity might seem extreme, the former reporter could never accept the carelessness of those who felt compelled to write a story about her, yet could not be bothered to check the facts. "The story of how Mr. Latham secured the manuscript of *Gone With the Wind* has been printed and reprinted until I would think everyone in the United States had heard it until they were sick of hearing it," she told Hicks. She did not care so much how the story affected her—it wouldn't really—but she worried his comments would have a "troublesome effect" on young writers who romanticized the life of an author. She thought writing "the hardest work in the world" and did not want her name associated with any story that suggested otherwise.[54] Hicks apologized for her being bothered but denied having made such a representation. He recalled having said that Latham knew he had a bestseller after having read a single chapter. He chastised Mitchell for believing everything she read in the newspapers and blamed the "garbled account" of his speech on a public relations man at the college where he had spoken.[55]

Another error-ridden story appeared that summer, but this time Mitchell could not maintain a polite facade. She was horrified to see a reader-submitted anecdote in *Reader's Digest* that, in her mind, questioned her skill as a writer. The filler piece in the July 1949 issue was headlined "Facts to the Contrary" and claimed there was a discrepancy in the timeline of *Gone With the Wind*, with Ashley Wilkes dying at Gettysburg in July 1863, fourteen months before his wife gave birth to their son in September 1864. As readers of the book (and even those who had seen only the movie) knew, Ashley did not die at Gettysburg, or at any point in the story. Therefore, the entire premise of the comment was faulty. But the rest of the piece made it worse, painting Mitchell as knowingly careless with facts and flippant when a mistake was pointed out.

> When the publisher called Margaret Mitchell's attention to the timing, the author was silent for a moment. Then she said, "Well, I know the Yankees will never change the date of the Battle of Gettysburg, and I'm certainly not going to change the date of the Battle of Atlanta." The publisher moved uncomfortably in his chair. "But—how will we explain it to the public, Miss Mitchell?" Miss Mitchell shrugged. "Let's hope they will be so interested in

the story they will overlook the discrepancy of time; if not," she added, "we'll just say that southern women do things more leisurely."[56]

Recalling the months of grueling fact-checking, copyediting, and rewriting she and Marsh had endured in 1935 and 1936, Mitchell was devastated and enraged. She had always been grateful to readers who pointed out mistakes in the text, happy to have them corrected in a future printing, but now a national publication made it appear she did not know her history and, worse, did not care.

Her frustration escalated when on June 17, 1949, she received a letter from the magazine's managing editor, Alfred S. Dashiell, admitting error and professing, not very sincerely, to be "greatly embarrassed." He explained that the reader who submitted the anecdote was a former Atlanta resident, suggesting that gave the tale an air of credibility. When the magazine sent the woman a draft of the piece and a check for fifty dollars, she proudly showed it to a friend, who pointed out the mistake. The submitter contacted *Reader's Digest* that same day and returned the fifty dollars, but it was too late; the magazine had been printed. Dashiell offered the services of his employees to help with any correspondence Mitchell might receive about the mix-up. Just wrap the letters up and send them along, he suggested cheerfully. He closed with "deep apologies" but did not mention running a correction.[57]

Mitchell fumed at the inadequate response, offended that the magazine thought she could be pacified so easily. As she explained to Latham,

> I was more incensed by their thinking that I would let people like them answer my personal mail than I was by the original error. I wonder why they thought I'd let people who told such a big lie about me have the chance to write some more lies and cover up their errors. They appeared to have no comprehension of any damage they had done me, nor did they appear to care. In fact, they have acted like a hit-and-run driver that had damaged an innocent pedestrian, and have been trying to get away from the scene as fast as possible.[58]

She vowed she would not let the magazine bully her. "I suppose they don't know that I never have been frightened by people being large or rich and have never ducked out of a fight either. . . . [I] never have any hesitancy about spending money or time when someone has damaged me, as they have done." Her ire was not only on her own behalf; she thought the anecdote reflected badly on Macmillan. "I resented how they made you look

like an ass too, and made The Macmillan Company to be the sort of publisher who would put up with such inaccuracy. (My goodness, Miss Prink
wouldn't have let me get away with that!)"

Wearily and angrily, the Mitchell-Marsh family picked up its battle gear
once more. She wanted a correction run and was determined to get one. In
a letter to Dashiell dated June 21, Stephens Mitchell demanded a retraction
and that the correction be worded in such a way "that the truth may be
aided in catching up with the lie."[59] The author also took her story to the
press to set the record straight. In an interview with the *Atlanta Journal*, she
alleged the *Reader's Digest* piece had "professionally damaged" her reputation because it portrayed her as "an author with a flippant view toward
accuracy rather than a painstaking researcher's attitude."[60] When the *Digest*
story was picked up in the *Milwaukee Sentinel*, Mitchell wrote to editor Buck
Herzog, demanding he print a retraction as well. Herzog's reply painted her
as unnecessarily alarmed. The editor felt no retraction was necessary because
he had attributed the story to the *Digest* and used "[sic]" after the mention
of Ashley's death. He also hinted that the entire thing had been a grand
publicity stunt for one of his favorite books, which, by the way, he would
not mind having the author autograph.[61] Mitchell's files do not contain a
copy of a response to Herzog.

Mitchell was not alone in her outrage. Many readers wrote to her, to
Macmillan, and to *Reader's Digest*, pointing out the error. The magazine
reportedly received more than eight thousand phone calls about the matter
in a single day and so much mail that it prepared a form letter in response.[62]
When the *Digest* realized the level of support Mitchell had and that she was
not going to go away quietly, it agreed to run a correction. At Marsh's insistence, the editors worked closely with him on the exact wording, and
Mitchell triumphantly announced her victory to Latham on July 29: "I
believe the long record of our successful legal moves against people who
had misused my name or literary material finally convinced the *Reader's
Digest* that they were going to have a great deal of trouble with me. I think
their idea was to print some sort of something in September that would
make me look like an ass and you and the Macmillan Company, too, but
we stopped all that."[63]

Victory came with a price. Between battling the magazine, the Pajot
incident, and the trouble in Japan, the couple's workload had increased so
much that in July they were forced to hire a second secretary. "We should
have done it years ago, as Margaret Baugh has had more than any one person could carry even if she worked twenty-four hours a day," Mitchell

noted to Latham. "We always hoped that things would quiet down and life become simpler, but here it is a great many years since 1936, and the work growing out of *Gone With the Wind* is so heavy we have to have additional help."[64]

They needed more than secretarial help, though. In the midst of resolving the *Reader's Digest* matter, Mitchell began to receive inquiries about developing the television rights to her novel. Being unfamiliar with how this new medium operated, the Marshes decided to bring in an outside adviser. Unwilling to deal with strangers, they asked Kay Brown, who was now an agent with Music Corporation of America, to represent them in negotiating the television rights.[65] Although it may have seemed odd to turn to somebody who played such a major role in securing the movie contract that caused the Marshes so much expense and angst, the couple never held a grudge against Brown. They admired the way she handled herself and welcomed her expert guidance.

~

After supper on Thursday, August 11, 1949, the Marshes decided to see a movie. Mitchell drove them the short distance to the Peachtree Arts Theatre, where the 1944 British film *A Canterbury Tale* was showing. Parking on the west side of Peachtree, she helped Marsh out of the car. Dusk was beginning to settle. Taking his arm, Mitchell looked both ways and said, "It looks safe now," then began crossing the thoroughfare her book had made world famous. As they reached the middle of the street, she apparently sensed something; she leaned around her husband and, looking south, spotted a car speeding toward them out of a broad curve. Suddenly, her comment a few weeks earlier to Latham about an "innocent pedestrian" seemed eerily prescient. As Marsh would recall later, they both hesitated, and then, without speaking, she turned and headed back to the curb they had just left.

By now, twenty-nine-year-old Hugh Gravitt, an off-duty taxi driver at the wheel of his own car, had spotted the couple in the middle of the street. He blew his horn and swerved to the left, slamming on his brakes. The car went into a skid and seemed to be chasing Mitchell, witnesses recalled. The vehicle struck her and threw her to the pavement. Marsh shakily rushed to his wife's side. An ambulance arrived in minutes and raced the author to Grady Hospital.

The next morning's *Atlanta Constitution* carried a large photograph of the author and the banner headline "Margaret Mitchell Struck by Car, Gravely Injured; Driver Held." Atlanta began a vigil for the woman who had brought them such pride and attention. Over the next several days, newspapers around the world updated their readers. Calls, letters, and telegrams—from President Harry Truman, Selznick, and Brett, among many others—poured in, inquiring about her condition and offering prayers Mitchell had suffered a skull fracture and internal injuries. Each day, the Atlanta newspapers carried front-page updates on the author. On Saturday, Mitchell seemed to rally slightly, but on Sunday her condition worsened. She had murmured a few words—"it hurts" and "it tastes bad" when given some orange juice to drink. On several occasions, she rose up and said a few phrases such as "I'll take care of that in the morning" before falling back into unconsciousness. On Tuesday, August 16, doctors talked about operating to relieve the pressure on her brain. But it was too late; Margaret Mitchell died just before noon.

The funeral was scheduled for Thursday. In an effort to control what was sure to be a large crowd, the family had 350 admittance cards printed and hand delivered to friends, family members, and dignitaries across the city, including Georgia governor Herman Talmadge and Atlanta mayor William B. Hartsfield. Brett offered the services of Macmillan employees in the Atlanta office to help answer the telephone and record telegrams and other messages for Mitchell's family. He also ordered two floral arrangements—one from the officers and directors of Macmillan, the other from its employees.[66] He flew to Atlanta Wednesday night.

Latham had heard a radio broadcast about the accident on the morning of August 12, the day he was leaving for a month's vacation in Maine and Canada. The news frightened him, he later wrote; he sensed Mitchell would not recover. Though unable to attend her funeral, the editor recalled with fondness his lunch with the Marshes that spring at the Waldorf. His last vivid recollection of Mitchell was her excitement over an unusual orchid corsage he had sent her that day.[67]

Cole and Allan Taylor also were on vacation. By the time they heard of Mitchell's death, they could not make the necessary flight connections from their family cabin in the remote reaches of the Adirondack Mountains.[68] Devastated, they wrote Marsh a personal and heartrending letter, fretting about not having immediately left for Atlanta upon hearing of the accident. To Cole and her husband, the timing of their friend's death was inescapably cruel given how close the Marshes seemed to be at starting a "happier, less harried life."[69] Cole later told Baugh, "Allan and I will never have a friend like her again—and I could have lost anyone but her."[70]

Condolences streamed in from around the world. In a telegram to

Marsh, President Truman lauded Mitchell as "an artist who gave the world an eternal book" and said she would be remembered "as a great soul who exemplified in her all too brief span of years the highest ideals of American womanhood."[71] Governor Talmadge noted, "The people of Georgia, the people of the nation and millions in foreign lands who have read and been inspired by her great and famous book will be saddened."[72] Marsh received many touching letters from fans, including a blind boy who wrote to him in Braille and several Catholic nuns who said they were having masses said for the author.[73] The family requested memorial donations be made to Grady Hospital, but many people also sent floral tributes, including a spray of red roses from actress Olivia de Havilland; an arrangement from Gallimard, Mitchell's French publisher; and a vase of flowers from New York with a card signed simply "M.S.," presumably Marion Saunders.[74]

On August 18, a large crowd gathered in front of the prestigious H. M. Patterson Funeral Home on Spring Street and listened to the service on loudspeakers that had been set up at Mayor Hartsfield's request. Calling Mitchell Atlanta's "greatest and most beloved citizen," the mayor urged city residents to pause for a moment of silent prayer. After a ten-minute ceremony, the funeral procession headed toward the city's historic Oakland Cemetery, where thousands of fallen Confederate soldiers lay. As the hearse crossed Peachtree Street, "a shaft of sunlight broke through the clouds, and seemed to light up that historic thoroughfare," the *Atlanta Journal* reported.[75] Thousands of Atlantans lined the sidewalks or stood on their front porches to watch the cortege, some crying quietly, men removing their hats in respect. Slowly, the cars made their way between the cemetery's narrow brick gateposts and toward the plot where Mitchell's parents were buried. At the grave, John Marsh, Stephens Mitchell, Margaret Baugh, Bessie Jordan, and other friends and family members said their goodbyes while, at a distance, photographers from the local newspapers and the national media, including the Associated Press and *Life* magazine, snapped photos.

That same week, the September *Reader's Digest* appeared on newsstands containing a lengthy correction regarding the Ashley Wilkes piece. The editors admitted the anecdote was inaccurate and regretted they had given the impression Mitchell had been careless with the historical details of her book. It was a final triumph for the author to whom history and accuracy meant so much—but one that came too late for her to savor.

# 16

~

# Inherit the Wind

## August 1949–1959

In the days after Margaret Mitchell's death, the newspapers and magazines that had so closely followed her in life now offered tributes and commemorations. Even the *Saturday Review of Literature*, which had objected to her book's Pulitzer Prize on the grounds that *Gone With the Wind* was inferior to several other novels on the same theme, conceded that she deserved credit for having written "the most popular novel in the world." *Review* editor Harrison Smith tipped his hat to Mitchell for the way she handled the circus her life had become.[1]

With the blitz of media attention, sales of *Gone With the Wind* jumped sharply in August 1949. Bookstores in Atlanta sold out quickly and placed hundreds of orders for both the full-priced and cheap editions. Similar demand for the novel was reported throughout the South. At the end of the month, when Atlanta's Piedmont Drive-In showed the movie—the booking had been made before her death—thousands of patrons jammed the roads near the theater, creating a three-mile backup.

John Marsh assumed responsibility for his wife's literary legacy. He gave the task his full attention despite his immense grief. After battling health problems for so many years, Marsh considered himself well trained in "living with a wholly obnoxious state of affairs." As he wrote to Harold Latham, "Peggy herself was preparation for the experience of losing her. She went through some awfully tough experiences, and over and over she whipped them. She would have whipped the last one if the son-of-a-bitch

Gravitt★ had been driving even a little slower and given her one additional second of time in which to escape." Mitchell had written a book about survival and how people faced the "major upheavals of life." With that before him, Marsh said, "I just could not afford to fail."[2]

One of the first actions he took was to write a will providing for disposition of the *GWTW* rights upon his death. Consistent with Mitchell's wishes, he specified that all the rights, income, and property related to the novel would pass to her brother Stephens Mitchell. Next, Marsh confronted the painful task of sorting through his wife's papers. Knowing she had not wanted a biography written or her working papers viewed by the public, he began burning her personal correspondence, as well as the bulk of the manuscript of *Gone With the Wind*. The process proved agonizing for the distraught husband, so he asked Margaret Baugh to continue the chore on his behalf. After instructing her to destroy hundreds of items, Marsh began to have second thoughts. He wanted to respect his wife's wishes but came to see that he was erasing the record of her remarkable life and that of her novel. He instructed Baugh to stop for the time being.[3]

Not surprisingly, in the wake of Mitchell's death, some opportunists sought to profit from her memory. Marsh was appalled by an advertising agency in Georgia that featured his wife's name and photograph in a series of ad templates called "Interesting Information About Georgia and Her People." The tidbits were designed to be used by banks, funeral homes, and other small businesses as part of their own newspaper promotions. He let his distaste be known to the Georgia Press Association, which, in turn, warned its members in a special bulletin. He also wrote sharply worded letters to the ad agency, the individual companies that sponsored the ads, and the newspapers in which they appeared, demanding the promotions be stopped. "Commercialization and exploitation of her name and picture were highly offensive to her in her lifetime," he said, "and I do not intend to have her commercialized and exploited now."[4]

He did not object, however, to his wife being remembered in tasteful ways. That fall, the *Atlanta Journal Sunday Magazine* announced plans to publish a Margaret Mitchell memorial edition. Mitchell's longtime friend Medora Field Perkerson spearheaded the project and asked for Marsh's cooperation. The widower knew that his wife did not want her life dis-

---

★ Hugh Gravitt, originally charged with drunk driving, speeding, and driving on the wrong side of the road, was tried for involuntary manslaughter in November 1949. The court found him guilty and sentenced him to eighteen months in prison, of which he served almost eleven.

sected in the press yet also saw that her interests would not be well served by the family refusing to discuss her. He agreed to work with Perkerson in pulling together the issue. After its release that December, Marsh expressed satisfaction with the publication and thought it would serve as a useful reference about his wife's life.[5]

Pleased with Marsh's reaction, Perkerson proposed to Macmillan that she write a biography of the author, hinting that Marsh approved of the project. When she discussed the idea with Latham, the editor let it be known that the company was emphatically against such a book.[6] He thought releasing a biography so soon after Mitchell's death would smack of commercialism, as if the publisher was cashing in on her memory. Moreover, he felt Mitchell—a "dignified, Southern lady"—would not have approved. Latham encouraged Marsh to give the idea careful consideration.

Though he knew Mitchell had been against such a project, Marsh had not ruled out authorizing a biography. As he explained to Latham, a "nagging thought" kept his mind open to the idea: "*How in the hell did she do it?* That question has never been answered. . . . When you look over the list of people who have achieved sudden fame, you mostly find suicides, scandals, catastrophes. You will have a hard time finding even one, other than Peggy, who survived the first shock and thereafter for thirteen years grew steadily in public esteem." And, if such a project were to be done, Perkerson was Marsh's first choice. He thought the articles she had written about Mitchell over the years revealed "a grasp and an understanding" of the author that enabled her to "present Peggy's personality and career understandingly."[7]

Despite Marsh's support, Perkerson's chances of being designated the official biographer evaporated the following spring. The family asked her to contribute an article about Mitchell for a special issue of the Atlanta Historical Society's monthly bulletin, and Perkerson submitted a piece she had written for the *Atlanta Journal*'s magazine. Stephens Mitchell rejected the recycled article and questioned Perkerson's loyalty to his sister if she could not be bothered to write something new. According to Baugh, he got so "hot under the collar," Perkerson told him never to speak to her again.[8] If a biography were to be written, Perkerson was out of the running.

With Latham's opposition and no qualified candidate in line to tackle the project, the biography failed to gain momentum. The question remained, though, what should become of Mitchell's papers. Although it has been reported that Marsh and Baugh burned most of them, the truth is that the vast majority was spared. The bulk of her business and personal correspondence survived as did many documents related to the writing of

*Gone With the Wind.* Among those that escaped the flames were assorted draft chapters of the novel, typewritten by Mitchell with corrections and changes in her handwriting; edited proof sheets containing corrections in both Mitchell's and Marsh's handwriting; several chronologies of events in the novel; notes Mitchell made while revising the manuscript, including lists of facts to be checked and the resulting answers; and some of the original manila envelopes in which she kept the book's chapters, with her handwritten notes on the outside.

In July 1951, Marsh decided that some of these working papers ought to be preserved in case anyone ever challenged his wife's authorship of the novel. To that end, he put a selection of drafts and notes in a large envelope, which he placed in a safe-deposit box at Citizens & Southern National Bank in Atlanta. Through a codicil to his will, he established a trust fund to cover the cost of the box rental indefinitely and left instructions that the envelope be opened only if proof were needed that Mitchell wrote *Gone With the Wind.* Should such a challenge be raised, he directed the contents were to go to the Atlanta Historical Society or the Atlanta Public Library. If need for such proof never arose, he wanted the envelope eventually to be destroyed unopened, although he specified no end date for the trust.[9]

Marsh determined that the rest of Mitchell's papers, including carbon copies of her extensive correspondence related to *Gone With the Wind,* would be preserved for the time being to help the estate manage the ongoing business of the book and in case a qualified biographer came to the forefront. However, he had no plans of making them publicly available to researchers. In fact, a few months after he signed the codicil, David C. Mearns of the Library of Congress asked Marsh to place his wife's papers in the library's Rare Books and Manuscripts Division. Marsh was flattered but declined. He explained Mitchell's views on privacy and stated he was doing his best to carry out her wishes.[10]

In addition to preserving his wife's legacy, Marsh continued to manage the *Gone With the Wind* rights. Her death did little to diminish the seemingly endless stream of details that needed to be looked after. A perennial annoyance was the people wanting to write a sequel. One hapless man from Italy wrote about a female friend who, after learning of Mitchell's death, was told in a dream, "Continue the book!" The friend began writing a sequel, with the words pouring out as though guided by the mysterious voice. After several days, the woman found it difficult to continue working on the book because of her day job. Would it be possible, the man wondered, for Mac-millan to help her financially so she could spend more time writing?[11] When an Oregon woman claimed that Margaret Mitchell had encouraged her to write a *GWTW* continuation, Marsh quickly put the would-be author in her place. Quoting his wife's earlier correspondence with the woman, Marsh blasted back that Mitchell had never urged the woman to write a sequel and that "there is nothing in Mrs. Marsh's letter that might be inter-preted as giving any such suggestion."[12]

Requests for new editions of *Gone With the Wind* came in periodically from overseas, and as usual, there were few simple answers. In 1951, Marsh received an inquiry from a Vietnamese translator but was uncertain how to proceed because Vietnam was fighting for independence from France. Marsh did not know what the country's legal status was under the Berne Convention and had to work through the assorted legalities. As for the pub-lishers with whom the estate already had contracts, Marsh had plenty to do tracking down royalties still overdue from the war years. Because of postwar currency restrictions in some countries, Mitchell's estate had money in limbo in various banks around the world. Doubting the funds would ever be released for export to the United States, Marsh put them to good use when he could. When two hundred dollars accumulated in a Tokyo bank, Marsh donated the money to the city's Union Church, a nondenomina-tional congregation whose original building was destroyed by Allied bombing.[13]

And, at long last, Marsh resolved the Marion Saunders saga. Word of her embezzlement apparently never reached a wide audience in the publish-ing industry, and she had managed to stay in business. After seven years of sending regular payments, she satisfied her debt in 1951. Marsh wrote the agent expressing pleasure that the matter was settled; he promised to "try to forget about the past."[14]

Marsh was less forgiving though of George Brett, against whom the widower still held various grudges. The two men maintained a cordial rela-tionship after Mitchell's death, but Marsh remained quick to find fault with the publisher's management of *Gone With the Wind*. Their discord bubbled to the surface when Mitchell and her novel were the subject of an episode of *The Author Meets the Critics*, a television program on the fledgling American Broadcasting Company network. The show featured critics Leo Gurko and Edith Walton, as well as a writer beginning to make a name for himself, Truman Capote. The program opened with a shot of Mitchell's novel and the announcer intoning that few books in the last half-century of American literature had had a greater impact than *Gone With the Wind*. While Gurko and Capote termed Mitchell's story a readable melodrama, neither cared for her writing or the book. Capote called the novel a "triumph of amateur women's writing" but deemed it otherwise unmemorable. Only Walton praised Mitchell. She called *Gone With the Wind* "a bang-up job" that was much better than highbrow critics would admit and predicted it would continue to be widely read in the years to come.

Walton's supportive words were not enough for Marsh, who felt "our side took a beating" in the program. Who did he blame? Brett, of course. The widower reproached the publisher for not letting him know about the program in advance, as he was confident that working together they "could have arranged to get a better break" for their side. "I am not taking the attitude that Peggy's book is deathless literature and the world's greatest novel," he said. "However, I don't think we should lose by default to this super-intellectual element."[15] Brett refused to accept any blame for Marsh's dissatisfaction and schooled him about how those types of shows operated. Publishers could not rig the content, Brett explained, because the producers wanted such shows to be controversial in order to draw an audience. In any event, it had been Macmillan who planted Walton on the show. She was a regular literary adviser for the company and a close friend of Lois Cole and Allan Taylor.[16]

Marsh had further cause for complaint when Brett presented him with a proposal from the Book-of-the-Month Club for a new edition of *Gone With the Wind*. According to Brett, the estate would receive a 10 percent royalty on an initial test run of the proposed edition. Marsh sensed something was not quite right with Brett's numbers. He responded by air-mail letter that, although they had agreed to numerous royalty adjustments over the years, he could not find any basis for a 10 percent royalty. Marsh thought the estate was entitled to 15 percent. If Brett had a document that said otherwise, Marsh requested that he be provided a copy.[17] Once again, Macmillan had to concede error: the estate was entitled to 15 percent. Latham, who responded on Brett's behalf, called it a typographical error.[18] With regular incidents like this—as innocent as they may have been— Marsh felt he had to always be on his toes to prevent the company from slipping one by him. Surely adding to Marsh's discontent, the proposed edition never came to fruition. Before signing a contract with Macmillan, the book club asked its readers to rank their interest in seven titles, including *Gone With the Wind*. To the club's surprise and embarrassment, Mitchell's novel came in last. The club's president, Meredith Wood, apologized for having been "dizzy" in his conception of how the book would fare, surmising that too many of the club's subscribers had bought the book over the years.

Brett accepted that he was on Marsh's bad side and did his best to avoid conflict. That spring, Marsh moved to a house on Walker Terrace, a few doors from the Della Manta apartment. He set up a home office and notified business associates of the new address for the entity that was now his life's work: the Margaret Mitchell Marsh Estate. Upon receipt of Marsh's change-of-address notice, Brett warned his staff to make sure that all future communications with the estate were directed to the new location so as not to give Marsh any excuse for complaint. "Marsh is one of the fussiest administrators of authors' estates that we have to deal with," he cautioned.[19]

Brett was not the only one on the receiving end of Marsh's sharp temper. When the widower moved, he hired a local woman to help pack and transfer his files and books. Although Marsh instructed her that she was not to publicly discuss her work for him, the woman apparently could not contain herself. She drafted a short article about her experience, comparing her brief time packing the *GWTW* files to "a trip around the world." From what she wrote, it was clear she had leafed through the foreign editions of *Gone With the Wind* and read letters in the business files. Hoping to have the piece published, she sent copies to Marsh and to the *Atlanta Journal*. Furious, Marsh telephoned the woman to remind her that she had been told in the beginning that he "wanted to hire somebody who could keep her mouth shut."[20] The article was not published.

Even family members felt Marsh's ire when he suspected his wife's interests were being compromised. According to notes in his files, he confronted Stephens Mitchell's sister-in-law about her sneaking some of Margaret Mitchell's childhood writings out of the family home on Peachtree Street. After the death of the author's father, Stephens Mitchell and his wife, Carrie Lou, continued to live in the house with their two sons. Carrie Lou had died in 1950, and in May of the following year, Stephens Mitchell ordered some old trunks in the basement of the house cleaned out and the contents destroyed. According to Marsh's notes, Marguerite Reynolds, the wife of Carrie Lou's brother, went into the basement and rummaged around. Later, Marsh said she gave him "the impression that she had discovered a quantity of Peggy's papers, dating back to her childhood and early girlhood, and that she had taken these papers to her home." Reynolds specifically mentioned finding what appeared to be the author's first attempt at writing her own name—a torn sheet of paper on which Eugene Mitchell had written out the word "Margaret" for his daughter to copy.[21]

Marsh did not take this invasion of privacy lightly. He explained to Reynolds that all his wife's writings belonged to him and demanded that she return them. Over the next several weeks, Reynolds promised to give the items back but dragged her feet. She eventually returned just the scrap of paper with the author's signature scrawled on it. According to Marsh's notes, Reynolds insisted "that she had nothing else belonging to Peggy, and that Steve and I had misunderstood her if we thought she said she had found and taken a quantity of Peggy's stuff."[22] Though Marsh felt he had to accept her statement at face value, he impressed upon Reynolds that he "would not hesitate to sue someone who tried to exploit [his wife] by publication or sale of her private papers."*

Also on Marsh's mind were the dramatic rights to *Gone With the Wind.* David O. Selznick remained interested in staging an extravagant theatrical production of Mitchell's story and was trying to structure a deal that appealed to Marsh. In the midst of those discussions, Annie Laurie Williams, the agent who brokered the original movie contract, reentered Marsh's life. She had gone on to a productive career since 1936 and now had a stable of respected clients, including John Steinbeck. In January 1951, on behalf of famed lyricist Alan Lerner, she offered Marsh three thousand dollars for a two-year option on the *GWTW* musical rights.[23] Without letting on that he was close to reaching a deal with Selznick, Marsh replied vaguely that unspecified circumstances compelled him to delay consideration of the offer.[24]

Still no pushover, Williams ignored the brush-off. An associate of hers, Frankie McKee Robins, a movie reviewer for *McCall's* magazine, happened to be speaking in Atlanta the following month and agreed to meet with Marsh on Williams's behalf. With no small degree of effort, Robins arranged a dinner with him at the Piedmont Driving Club. As she described

---

* In 1996, two hundred pages of Mitchell's childhood stories, essays, and journal entries were discovered in the basement of an Atlanta home owned by Wailes Thomas, a nephew of Marguerite Reynolds. Thomas had inherited the house from his mother, who had lived there at one time with Reynolds. Marsh's suspicions about Reynolds taking papers from the Mitchell home never came to light, and the estate granted permission to publish the papers as *Before Scarlett: The Girlhood Writings of Margaret Mitchell.*

their meeting, Marsh was as suspicious of her as if she had been a bank robber. "Lord! Has he ever got his guards up!" she reported to Williams. As was often the case, Marsh's reserved demeanor came across as less than collegial, and he presented a "stone wall" about his plans for the subsidiary rights. However, he gave Robins an earful about the "son of a bitch" movie contract and how Macmillan had acted in a "high-handed" manner by hiring Williams without Mitchell's consent. Robins sensed he was "sore as a bear" about how things had been handled. As for Williams's offer on the dramatic rights, Marsh said he might have something to say about it that summer but for now did not want to be bothered. Robins's overall assessment of Marsh was that he was "a very peculiar person."[25]

Summer came and went without Marsh taking action on the theatrical rights, but he remained in talks with Selznick. By the following spring, they appeared close to reaching a deal. As Selznick put out feelers to industry sources who might be interested in investing in the production, word leaked to the press that he was in talks with the estate. To Selznick's distress, the *Hollywood Reporter* ran a small notice asking, "Since when is a musical version of *GWTW* news? Billy Rose staged one at Fort Worth's Casa Manana in the '30s."[26] Worried the blurb gave the impression he was rehashing something that had already been done, Selznick asked the estate to demand a retraction.[27] Marsh wrote the paper on April 25, 1952, explaining at length the history of the Rose production and why the *Reporter*'s statement was "misleading" and "damaging to a valuable property—the *GWTW* dramatic rights."[28]

A clarification appeared in the paper's May 2 edition: "John R. Marsh, husband of the late Margaret Mitchell, *Gone With the Wind* author, clarified that the *GWTW* musical bit put on by Billy Rose in Fort Worth in 1937 was not a musical version of the book but merely a song number, also that it was unauthorized and Rose subsequently made amends for the infringement."[29] Marsh likely never saw the notice. He died at home early on the morning of May 5, 1952, after suffering another heart attack. The "papa and mamma" of *Gone With the Wind*—as dubbed by the *Atlanta Journal*—were gone.

∽

According to the will Marsh wrote after his wife's death, all the author's rights to *Gone With the Wind* devolved to Stephens Mitchell. Marsh's brother-in-law also received all the author's personal papers and the business records of *Gone With the Wind*.★ As the new owner of one of the world's most valuable literary properties, Stephens Mitchell might have been tempted to hire an agent to manage the estate's business affairs, while he and his family enjoyed the profits of his sister's labor. But Margaret and John had trusted him to watch over the book's interests, so that is what he resigned himself to do. Having been involved with *GWTW* legal matters for many years, the author's brother felt well qualified to assume the mantle of leadership.

He asked Baugh—whom Margaret Mitchell once described as "the office angel" and "the bringer of order to chaos"[30]—to stay on and assist with the estate's administrative duties. The secretary had helped manage the business of *Gone With the Wind* since January 1937 and had an in-depth knowledge of the records, issues, and people related to its history. He first set her up in the basement of his house, then eventually moved her to an office across the hall from his downtown law practice. He granted her a great deal of independence managing the daily affairs of the estate. The two communicated by telephone or memoranda and sometimes did not interact in person for weeks at a time.[31]

Baugh found the transition to her new role difficult. After having spent so much time working side by side with the Marshes in their home, she found the isolation of this arrangement unsettling. Moreover, Stephens Mitchell's way of operating was quite different from how the Marshes handled the business of *Gone With the Wind*. He changed his mind often, a practice Baugh found irritating. As she vented to Cole, "After 15 years of John and Peggy, who thought everything through to the end, knew what they thought, and stuck to it, it is very confusing."[32] Baugh also expressed concern about the lawyer's lack of attention to appearances. When he allowed himself to be photographed in his home office without having the room straightened up, Baugh told Cole, "Peggy would die. After all those years of the careful front she put up to the public! . . . If we come through this without disgracing her, it will surprise me. (By 'this' of course, I mean the next 2 or 3 decades.)"[33]

That Stephens Mitchell's approach differed from that of the Marshes is no surprise. Unlike the couple, who made *Gone With the Wind* the focus of their lives and devoted most of their waking hours to its care, he had a career

---

★ Mitchell's personal collection of souvenirs and mementos of her literary career went to the Atlanta Public Library, including the typewriter on which she wrote most of the novel, her copy of the original galleys, her Pulitzer Prize certificate, the National Book Award, and her personal collection of almost seventy foreign editions of her novel.

and a family to tend to. Furthermore, because the Marshes treated *Gone With the Wind* as if it were their child, defending its honor was their highest priority; making money off it was a secondary concern. Stephens Mitchell could not afford to take the same high-minded approach. His two sons would ultimately inherit the estate, and he felt an obligation to maximize the value of the literary rights for their benefit. In a letter to George Brett, the author's brother offered insight into how the business of *Gone With the Wind* would be different under his direction:

> During her life, Margaret set up a certain standard of values and stuck to it. She spent a great part of the money she made policing the world to maintain these standards. This redounded mainly to the profit of other people, such as Selznick, Loew's and foreign publishers, and to the prestige she desired. At the present time I do not have the money, the time nor the desire to be such a policeman.[34]

Brett appreciated what a monumental task faced Mitchell's brother in handling *Gone With the Wind*. "Believe me, Steve, . . . I sympathize with you in what I know will be your burden in complying with [Peggy] and John's wishes," the publisher responded.[35]

One of the estate's top priorities after Marsh's death was wrapping up negotiations with Selznick for the dramatic rights to *Gone With the Wind*. Having no experience with theatrical matters, Stephens Mitchell looked to Kay Brown for advice on what the rights were worth. By September 1952, Mitchell and Selznick signed a contract authorizing the producer to release what they termed a "Dramatico-Musical production" of the novel. The estate received a $2,500 advance and would earn a percentage of the box-office receipts and proceeds from a recording of the show's music. Consistent with his sister's wishes that Scarlett and Rhett's story not be expanded upon, the contract also noted that "no right of sequelization is granted . . . neither the plot nor the story nor the lives of the characters shall be carried beyond the point where they end on the last page of the Novel." Mitchell was also careful not to give Selznick the right to create a book or script version of his production; there was no need to provide competition for the novel. Mitchell admitted to Brett that he "may have been over cautious in this respect, but I wished to assure you that we were looking after every interest of The Macmillan Company."[36]

Selznick promised that a musical titled "Scarlett O'Hara" would be onstage in two years. When word of the deal reached Robins, she could not help wonder why Marsh had been so secretive about Selznick's interest when she had approached him the year before. "*That* John Marsh!" she wrote Williams. "I'll bet he's the sneaky-est angel floating around in the other side of Paradise."[37] She likened his passion for secrecy to "more than a phobia—almost a private cult."[38]

Robins's reaction was not an unusual one. Ever since Margaret Mitchell retreated from the public spotlight in 1936, the Marshes had struggled with the image question, knowing that their behavior at times seemed odd or paranoid. The perception of his sister as an eccentric had always troubled Stephens Mitchell. In a letter to Brett, he lamented that his sister had been presented to the public as "a lay figure, as flat and formal as a Byzantine portrait." Now that he was in charge, he did not intend for her to be remembered as a neurotic, hypersensitive recluse. He knew he had "no business knocking down the ikon" but did not "intend to gild it."[39] For the rest of his life, he would go to great lengths to balance his sister's desire for privacy with his sense of responsibility for protecting her reputation.

Stephens Mitchell understood his sister's reasons for wanting to shield her personal life from public scrutiny. The siblings had been raised with the mores of the Southern intellectual elite. Showiness was abhorred. Private matters were kept private. Thus, when it came to his sister's personal life, he vigorously respected her wishes. Most dramatically, after he remarried and built a new house, Mitchell made arrangements for the Mitchell family home on Peachtree Street to be razed. He told the press that he and his sister had agreed that only Mitchells should ever live there. They also did not want the house opened as a tourist attraction.[40] It probably came as no surprise to him that *Gone With the Wind* fans hauled away bricks and other pieces of the building as souvenirs.

Mitchell also accepted his sister's views about not wanting the *GWTW* manuscript and working papers made public. After Marsh's death, he and Baugh discovered in the widower's office the 1951 codicil related to the *GWTW* manuscript, along with the sealed envelope of papers. According to notes found with the material, Marsh had intended to add more items to the cache but had died before finishing the task. Mitchell returned the envelope to the bank and later added an additional envelope of materials specified by Marsh, including chapters 44 and 47 from the final manuscript showing edits by Macmillan and the Marshes. The second envelope was taped to the original, and the double package remains in a safe-deposit box to this day.[41]

As for the rest of the author's papers, of which thousands remained, Stephens Mitchell took a more measured approach. At Baugh's behest, he proceeded cautiously before destroying anything related to the business of *Gone With the Wind*. Recalling that she and Marsh had burned some letters that contained valuable information, Baugh insisted on "re-reading and considering" each document carefully. "It's a great responsibility," she told Cole.[?] They limited the destruction to personal items, such as the author's childhood report cards, handwritten verses of poetry, and letters about Clifford Henry, her World War I fiancé.[43] The bulk of Margaret Mitchell's correspondence related to *Gone With the Wind* survived—but to what end?

That question would plague Stephens Mitchell for more than a decade. While he went about the business of managing his law practice and his sister's estate, the nagging issue remained: what to do about *Gone With the Wind*'s literary legacy. After mulling over the issue for several years, Mitchell decided that the estate needed to authorize a biography to establish the record of her life and that of her literary progeny. It was only a matter of time before an unauthorized work appeared, and it did not take much imagination to predict what such a project would look like: either a hatchet job by a critic or an inadequate portrayal by a well-meaning fan.

Mitchell considered hiring an outside writer to tell the story but ultimately decided to tackle the job himself. In the mid-1950s, he began drafting a memoir about his sister's life with a focus on her experiences writing and managing *Gone With the Wind*. He relied on Baugh's assistance a great deal, and the project would be the source of considerable friction between them. When Mitchell once threatened to tear up a section they had worked on together, Baugh told Cole, "If I die young, you'll know why, and you can put up a monument accordingly."[44] They would struggle over the task well into the next decade.

~

During the years that Stephens Mitchell worked on a biography, he also managed the ongoing business of *Gone With the Wind*. There were still crackpots hoping to capitalize on the book's success, such as a man who showed up demanding money for the help he claimed to have given Mitchell in writing the manuscript. And some of the old troublemakers reared their heads, including the persistent French sequelist Madame Henri Pajot.

Stephens Mitchell heard from a Catholic priest who had been convinced by Pajot that her "Lady of Tara" was the true story of actual people named Scarlett and "Rebb," as supposedly told to Pajot by Margaret Mitchell. The author's brother had to tell the man of the cloth that the creative Parisian had "spun an elaborate yarn."[45] The rumor mill also required tending. Mitchell and Baugh routinely sent letters of correction any time the press misrepresented the record of the author's life. When publisher Bennett Cerf's syndicated column reprinted the anecdote from *Reader's Digest* about Ashley Wilkes being killed at Gettysburg and Melanie's ill-timed pregnancy, Baugh wrote Cerf at length pointing out his errors. If Ashley had died, she said, "the story would have been entirely different—and some 800 pages shorter."[46] Cerf quickly apologized, noting he heard from other readers about the mistake, and ran a correction.

But not all of the estate's work was adversarial. Fan letters still arrived on a regular basis, and the author's grave became a tourist mecca. One of her biggest admirers turned out to be Adrian Stok of ZHUM, the Dutch publisher she had fought in court for so many years. He donated one hundred dollars to a hospital memorial in her honor and sent tulip bulbs to be planted on her grave every fall. In the mid-1950s, he came to the United States to visit family and made a special trip to Atlanta to pay tribute to the author. Baugh took him on a sightseeing tour of the city; when they visited Mitchell's grave, he left a basket of gladioli and peonies "to our Margaret."[47]

The people of Atlanta also continued to cherish *Gone With the Wind* and Mitchell's memory. When the city considered renaming its utilitarian-sounding Atlanta Municipal Airport in 1954, several area residents wrote the *Atlanta Constitution* to suggest the airfield be called Margaret Mitchell Airport, Scarlett O'Hara Airport, or Gone With the Wind Airport. Noted one reader about the latter name: "It is catchy. Airplanes go like the wind, and *Gone With the Wind* is known all over the United States and in foreign countries."[48] Although longtime mayor William B. Hartsfield eventually won the honor of having the airport named for him, there was no shortage of local pride for the book that made the city famous.

The following year, Atlanta's WSB Radio and Television—the call letters of which were promoted as standing for "Welcome South, Brother"—began planning the dedication of its new headquarters. Station officials wanted to present guests with a souvenir of the event and decided on a limited edition of *Gone With the Wind*. The station made arrangements with Macmillan and the estate to produce five hundred leather-bound copies. George Brett took an active interest in the publication, even suggesting that the copies not be numbered so as to avoid causing hard feelings for those who received the higher-numbered books. Telling Stephens Mitchell that it was an honor for *Gone With the Wind* to be selected as the gift by the broadcasting firm,[49] Brett encouraged the estate to waive its royalty. Stephens Mitchell did not want to go quite that far but agreed to donate the estate's share of the proceeds to the Atlanta Historical Society.[50]

Foreign interest in *Gone With the Wind* remained steady. The novel appeared for the first time in Portugal, Lebanon, and Iran, and in new editions in Finland, France, Germany, Italy, Japan, Spain, and Sweden. Pirated editions popped up on occasion, such as in Mexico and Greece, but Stephens Mitchell did not have the drive to fight them as vigilantly as had the Marshes. He told Brett he did not "have the money or the desire or the time to sit on the steam boiler safety valve all my life." The lawyer generally tried to come to some sort of agreement with the perpetrators, even if for a modest sum. He did not want to waste time trying to "keep from the market something for which there is a market."[51] If unauthorized publishers refused to sign contracts, he was content to hope that they did not make any money.[52]

Still, Stephens Mitchell had not completely abandoned his sister's position against the injustices of literary piracy. In the fall of 1953, he paid tribute to her memory by taking a stand on an issue that had been near and dear to her heart—the failure of the U.S. government to protect the literary rights of its authors in overseas markets. After World War II, pressure built for the United States to join the Universal Copyright Convention, an international agreement developed by the United Nations as an alternative to the Berne Convention. Leading the charge on behalf of the publishing industry was the American Book Publishers Council. Its managing director, Dan Lacy, approached Brett about including testimony from the Mitchell estate regarding the difficulties the author had faced because of the failure of the United States to join Berne. Curiously, Brett initially dismissed the idea, saying it was his impression that the author had not experienced many problems managing the foreign copyrights because she had received assistance from the Department of State.[53] Margaret Mitchell would have been appalled at Brett's flippancy. Certainly, Wallace McClure and other government officials had helped, but the bulk of the foreign copyright battles had fallen on her and her husband. Brett forwarded Lacy's request to Stephens Mitchell, who seemed eager to tell the story.

The following spring, Stephens Mitchell traveled to Washington, D.C., to testify before a Senate committee. He told of twenty-three separate cases of copyright infringement that his sister had fought. He pointed out that the business of policing the book's copyright around the world involved hiring a full-time secretary in Atlanta, along with local lawyers and accountants in each country where the book was published. He estimated the Marshes had spent at least $15,000 in legal fees fighting the 1937 Dutch piracy and another $3,500 on the Chilean piracy. It was a point of pride for the author's brother when Congress approved membership in the convention.

∾

From Macmillan's perspective, the 1950s represented a new era in the life of *Gone With the Wind*. Latham retired in 1952, and the book seemed to have run its course among a large population of readers. The yearly totals in American sales had fallen in 1951 and 1952 to less than thirteen thousand copies per year. Although still an impressive number for such an old title, sales were showing a distinct downward trend. But Brett refused to put the old girl out to pasture just yet. In 1953, he solicited offers from discount publishers that might be willing to reissue the book in a cheap format aimed at a new generation of readers. He received only two bids. One was from the New American Library for what he considered a paltry twenty-five thousand dollars. The other, which far exceeded his expectations, was from Doubleday & Company; it guaranteed a minimum payment of $87,500 for the rights to produce three new inexpensive editions of the book, including the first pocket-sized paperback. In proposing the deal to Stephens Mitchell, who would receive half the payout on the contract, Brett called the offer a gold mine waiting to be tapped.[54] Mitchell accepted and congratulated the publisher on his efforts. "That is an old story—ever ancient, ever new—but I want you to know that it is appreciated by me," he wrote, apparently not sharing his brother-in-law's animosity toward Brett.[55]

The Doubleday deal received considerable attention because it was the first time Macmillan had licensed an outside firm to publish *Gone With the Wind*. At least one reporter expressed surprise that there was anyone who had not yet read the book, and a member of the American Book Publishers Council jokingly referred to the release as "Gone With the Second Wind."[56] The three new editions, released in 1954, garnered further attention when Doubleday gave Margaret Mitchell's book a dramatic facelift. The two hardcover versions—one sold to book club members, the other through bookstores—received a dynamic new dust jacket design featuring prominent images of Scarlett and Rhett, who looked a great deal like Vivien

Leigh and Clark Gable. Doubleday also reset the type so that all three unabridged versions took up far fewer pages than readers were used to seeing. The new paperback version contained a relatively svelte 862 pages. A columnist in the *New York Herald Tribune* speculated that the new format would be short enough to read in a single evening—if the reader lived in the Arctic.

In case the updated look was not enough to attract readers, publication of the new editions was timed to coincide with a rerelease of Selznick's motion picture. To celebrate the movie's fifteenth anniversary that year, Metro-Goldwyn-Mayer (MGM) launched another run through the national theater circuit. Atlanta hosted a kickoff celebration with a special showing of the film at Loew's Grand Theatre. Doubleday's bet on Mitchell proved well placed. The updated formats, along with long lines of moviegoers, breathed new life into Mitchell's book. Within a year, the three editions had sold a combined total of more than 840,000 copies.[57] Eager to tout this success, Macmillan reported to the estate that, with these additional copies in circulation, English-language sales of *Gone With the Wind* since 1936 now stood at a remarkable 5,251,931 copies.

While Stephens Mitchell shared a more pleasant relationship with Brett than had Marsh, the Mitchell family never took anything at face value. When Mitchell read Macmillan's claim about total sales, the number did not seem right to him. He reviewed nearly two decades' worth of royalty statements and determined that the figure was more than a million copies higher than the sales indicated in the estate's records. The Marshes and the estate always kept a careful eye on the royalty statements, and Stephens Mitchell felt certain Macmillan had overstated the numbers. "Margaret and John were proud of the sales, and very careful about their records," he wrote Brett, seeking clarification. "They would hardly have lost sight of a million copies. If they have been lost, we'd like to find them."[58] At first, Brett was convinced the mistake was in Atlanta, but when Mitchell insisted his records could not be reconciled to get the higher figure, Macmillan accountants went to work on a year by year analysis of sales. Brett warned his staff that they better get it right this time. He did not want Mitchell to start asking questions about where the extra royalties were.[59] Within days, the publisher conceded the "horrible" mistake had been on its part.[60]

Even with a red face, Macmillan had cause to celebrate, as did the estate. Margaret Mitchell's story had proven itself a survivor on par with Scarlett O'Hara herself. In less than two decades, the book had sold more than four million copies in the English language; overseas, it had been translated into twenty-four languages in thirty-one countries and sold almost another three million copies.[61] And, as evidenced by Doubleday's venture, *Gone With the Wind* still captured the public's imagination. Indeed, Macmillan continued to receive fan mail about the book—an average of ninety letters a month.[62] Baugh summed up the book's remarkable history to Cole: "The whole goldarned 20 years have read like a romance to me, seeing it all unfold."[63]

The Doubleday deal served as George Brett's last *Gone With the Wind* hurrah. As the 1950s came to an end, he retired, turning over the reins of Macmillan to his son, Bruce Y. Brett. Shortly thereafter, Macmillan merged with Crowell-Collier Publishing Company. Macmillan would remain its own imprint, but its reign as the preeminent American publishing house was over. Bruce Brett met with Stephens Mitchell to assure him that the transition would be a smooth one. Macmillan would have the same setup and be the same company but with additional capital. The younger Brett hoped that Macmillan and the Mitchell family could continue their dealings in the same informal manner they had enjoyed for so many years. "I did not reply to this," Mitchell wrote in his notes of their discussion, acknowledging only that they had "always gotten on fine."[64]

# 17

# Minding Scarlett's Business

## *1960–May 1983*

The new Macmillan began the decade planning for a major milestone in the history of *Gone With the Wind*—the twenty-fifth anniversary in 1961 of the novel's publication. Conveniently, that year would also mark the beginning of a nationwide commemoration of the Civil War centennial. The publisher revamped its full-priced hardback edition of Margaret Mitchell's novel with tweaks to its binding and dust jacket and developed three new editions—two paperbacks (one under the Macmillan imprint, the other through Pocket Books) and a deluxe hardcover anniversary volume featuring original illustrations. Included with the slipcased anniversary edition was a souvenir booklet titled "*Gone With the Wind* and Its Author Margaret Mitchell" that brought a new generation of readers up to date on the history of the book.

Once again, the new editions were tied to a rerelease of the movie. The film had another gala opening—its fourth—in Atlanta. Vivien Leigh and Olivia de Havilland attended, as did David O. Selznick, who had not yet managed to capture Mitchell's story in a musical stage version. The producer had recently renewed his option with the estate—one of many such renewals—and brought to Atlanta as potential collaborators poet Ogden Nash, of "candy is dandy, but liquor is quicker" fame, and musician Leroy Anderson. The producer wanted the men to "get the feel of the region and get to know the people of the *Gone With the Wind* country." Selznick declined to speculate on casting but promised the press his project would "retain the dignity and beauty of Miss Mitchell's story."[1]

Stephens Mitchell was not impressed with the producer's big talk. As the years had dragged on with no production, the lawyer had become impatient with Selznick for failing to get the show staged; other producers were interested and might have a better chance of turning the novel into a moneymaking Broadway hit. Hoping to stir Selznick into action or force him to abandon the project, Mitchell had been gradually raising the price of the option. As he explained to Kay Brown, "When I played poker as a college boy, there was a saying that 'the best way to discourage vice is to make it expensive.'"[2] The strategy had not worked so far, but Mitchell sensed Selznick would eventually have to throw in his cards. After the producer's visit to Atlanta, the author's brother told Brown that Selznick "does not look nor act like a man who is about to produce a musical."[3]

Selznick's unfulfilled promises aside, *Gone With the Wind* as book and film again proved a dynamic duo. The movie filled theaters across the nation, and the four editions sold more than five hundred thousand copies that first year.[4] A reporter aptly referred to Mitchell's magnum opus as "a geriatric literary curiosity, a veritable Methuselah."[5]

~

After almost a decade of maintaining a dual life as a lawyer and the manager of his sister's estate, as well as part-time biographer, Stephens Mitchell decided to take a step back from the literary career that had been thrust upon him at John Marsh's death. When he assumed responsibility for the estate in 1952, Mitchell must have thought that the responsibilities of looking after his sister's literary rights would diminish with time. However, Scarlett and Rhett showed no sign of slowing down. In the early 1950s, the estate earned between thirty thousand and forty thousand dollars a year from the literary rights. In 1954, the money had shot up dramatically in the wake of the three successful Doubleday editions: $67,000 in 1954, $71,000 in 1955, and $109,000 in 1956. Since then, the yearly income had not dropped below $68,000. The *GWTW* literary rights were not a sideline Mitchell could deal with in his spare time. If he was to maximize the value of those assets, it made sense to bring in professional help. In 1961, the lawyer contacted Brown, still an agent with Music Corporation of America (MCA), and asked her to take over management of the *GWTW* rights.

Margaret Baugh was not happy with the new arrangement. She considered Brown well qualified to handle the dramatic and musical rights but hated to see Stephens Mitchell bring an agency in on "all of the *GWTW* business." Specifically, she questioned MCA's ability to manage the publish-

ing and commercial side of things to Margaret Mitchell's exacting specifications. She wrote to her boss: "MCA, like any other agent, is in for making
the most money with the least time expenditure. They won't try to run
down Argentine etc. pirates they will farm out sequels build Taras they
will not know or understand [Margaret Mitchell's] policies, or care anything
about such." Baugh thought Stephens Mitchell's two adult sons, Eugene,
an economist, and Joseph, who worked for Metro-Goldwyn-Mayer
(MGM), far better suited to the task: "I see no reason why Eugene and Joe
can't operate the business—by just paying a little attention to routine and
details. They doubtless will surprise you when they really have the responsibility."[6] Baugh's entreaty did not sway Stephens Mitchell to change course.
Presumably, he did not want to weigh down his sons with managing their
aunt's affairs.

Brown's first priority in her new role was dealing with the copyright
on *Gone With the Wind*, which was set to expire in 1964, twenty-eight years
after the book's original publication. Under U.S. law at the time, authors or
their estate could renew a book's copyright for another twenty-eight years,
after which the work would enter the public domain, allowing anyone to
print and sell copies. For *Gone With the Wind*, a renewal would mean protection through 1992. Stephens Mitchell wanted the rights to remain
profitable, so he had every incentive to renew. But the renewal was equally
important to Macmillan and MGM. If the copyright on the book lapsed,
other publishers and movie studios could release their own versions of *Gone
With the Wind*. To prevent that, Macmillan and Selznick, in their original
contracts with Margaret Mitchell, had obtained the right to renew the
copyright if she or her estate failed to do so. However, a 1960 decision by
the U.S. Supreme Court established that a grant of renewal rights was void
if an author died before time for copyright renewal. In a case like Mitchell's,
only the author's heirs controlled the right to renew.[7] Thus, the Mitchell
estate had Macmillan and MGM over a barrel. If Stephens Mitchell did not
renew the copyright, the value of the publisher's and studio's investments
in *Gone With the Wind* would decline precipitously.

The lawyer seized on the situation as a way of redeeming himself for
not better protecting his sister's interests in the 1936 movie negotiations. If
MGM wanted him to renew the copyright, it would have to renegotiate its
contract with the estate. This time around, Stephens Mitchell went to the
table with Brown on his side. His faith in the agent was justified when, in
1963, the estate and MGM signed a contract that, in exchange for the estate
renewing the copyright, gave Mitchell a lump sum payment of five hundred

thousand dollars, plus 10 percent of MGM's domestic box-office gross from the film above five million dollars. Additional payments were tied to other income streams, including the film's worldwide box-office receipts and earnings from television broadcasts. At long last, Margaret Mitchell— through her estate—would receive a share of the profits Hollywood made on the story of Scarlett and Rhett. MGM also expressed interest in acquiring rights to produce a sequel, but Stephens Mitchell refused. He inserted a clause into the contract stating that "Metro shall have no right to produce any motion picture or other production with the plot or the story of the characters of the Novel, in which the lives of the characters therein shall be carried beyond the time of the ending of the Novel."[8]

Stephens Mitchell also attempted to use the copyright renewal to obtain additional compensation from Macmillan. Brown estimated the book rights were worth $280,000 and suggested the estate request a bonus from Macmillan for extending the copyright and an adjustment in royalties from 15 percent to 20 percent.[9] The estate signed a new contract with Macmillan, but the details were not made public.

⌒

While Brown managed most of the estate's business affairs, Stephens Mitchell and Baugh labored over his still-unfinished memoir. After sorting through assorted drafts, Lois Cole convinced the estate to bring in an outside writer to turn the manuscript into a publishable book. Frank Lloyd Wright biographer Finis Farr was selected and became the first outsider granted access to the *GWTW* files. He was not given a free hand, though. Mitchell, Baugh, and Cole vetted every word of Farr's manuscript, parsing details large and small, from whether Mitchell had freckles to how Adrian Stok, the Dutch publisher, should be portrayed. Stephens Mitchell also took pains to ensure Cole would receive long-overdue credit for her role in discovering the *GWTW* manuscript.[10]

Farr was close to completing his work when, on March 12, 1965, Hollywood gossip columnist Louella Parsons announced that a former journalist named Jacob Mogelever was trying to sell the movie rights to a book he was writing titled "That Mitchell Girl." Mogelever claimed his story presented a version of Margaret Mitchell's life that was more exciting than the stories she had written about in *Gone With the Wind*. He promised readers juicy details on "Atlanta's most scintillating flapper" and the inside story of her book, including his theory that Rhett Butler was based on Mitchell's first husband, "Red" Upshaw, whom Mogelever claimed she still loved after their "sensational" divorce. It was exactly the sort of project the estate had been hoping to preempt, and Stephens Mitchell moved with alacrity to make sure Mogelever did not land a production deal.

The estate contacted Parsons and asked her to get word out to the industry that Mogelever had not had access to the author's papers and, therefore, could not be relied upon to offer an accurate depiction of Margaret Mitchell's life. Cole issued a press release touting Farr's book as the only authorized and complete story. Baugh compiled a list of movie production companies and sent them notices about Mogelever's status as an unauthorized biographer. Whether the estate was responsible for killing the project is not known, but the journalist did not sell the movie rights to his story. He died a few years later, never having finished the manuscript.[11]

Farr's book, *Margaret Mitchell of Atlanta*, was released later that year. It did not offer a full exposition of the author's life but provided a timeline of the major events and insights into *Gone With the Wind* that had never before been made public. With the story told, Stephens Mitchell finally resolved what would become of his sister's papers. Researchers still sought access, but he was not prepared to throw open the files. At the same time, he did not agree with his sister that they should be destroyed. He reached a compromise and donated the bulk of the documents to his alma mater, the University of Georgia. Among eleven three-drawer file cabinets shipped to Athens were Civil War–era letters between her grandparents, three short stories the author had written as a girl, thousands of fan letters and carbon copies of Mitchell's replies, and much of the voluminous business records associated with management of the *GWTW* literary rights. In tacit acknowledgment that his decision contradicted the author's instructions, he imposed tight restrictions on the ability of researchers to copy and quote from the papers. Mitchell was not comfortable opening his sister's life for public consumption but at least had ensured the materials would be preserved for the sake of posterity.★

~

Selznick died in 1965 without having realized his dream of bringing *Gone With the Wind* to the stage. Although there had been periodic rumors of impending productions, he never managed to finance his extravaganza. When all was said and done, he ended up paying the estate more than one

---

★ Over the years, the estate has added to the collection, as have third parties. Today, the university's Hargrett Rare Book and Manuscript Library houses more than sixty thousand Mitchell-related items.

hundred thousand dollars for options on a production that never happened. But Selznick's death did not signal the end of Scarlett and Rhett's theatrical aspirations; rather, it freed the estate to pursue other opportunities.

Toho Company, Ltd., a Japanese firm, purchased the theatrical rights from the estate and produced a lavish production that divided Mitchell's story into two separate shows. On November 3, 1966, the first installment, covering events from the Twelve Oaks barbecue to Scarlett and Melanie's return to Tara after the fall of Atlanta, made its debut at Tokyo's Imperial Theater, with members of the Japanese royal family in attendance. The production ran from 3:00 p.m. to 8:00 p.m., with a one-hour dinner break. Stephens Mitchell flew to Japan for the opening. After the premiere, he was "swarmed" for his autograph, "just like a movie star!" reported his wife.[12] Although originally scheduled for a two-month run, the producers extended the show until April 1967, by which point it had been seen by more than 380,000 people.[13] Tokyo Scarlett was a hit. The following summer, the second part of the story ran a mere four hours. It played to large crowds for four months, after which the two stage versions were combined into a single six-hour production that had another successful run in the consolidated format.

Encouraged by the reception, the Japanese producers obtained permission from the estate in 1968 to mount a musical version of the story. The Japanese-language musical *Scarlett*, with a score by American composer Harold Rome, opened in Tokyo in January 1970. Two years later, an English-language version opened on London's West End, where it ran for almost a year—397 performances—featuring such numbers as "Two of a Kind," a Rhett and Scarlett duet, and "Bonnie Gone," a spiritual-like dirge mourning the young girl who was killed when thrown from her pony. While popular with tourists, the critics were not impressed. British playwright Noël Coward, who attended opening night when an onstage horse relieved itself during a key scene, found the young actress who played Bonnie especially irritating. Afterward, the famous wit supposedly commented that the producers could have taken care of two problems in one fell swoop if they had shoved the girl's head "up the horse's arse."

When the show made its way across the pond, American audiences proved hard to please. A revamped production featuring Lesley Ann Warren as Scarlett and Pernell Roberts as Rhett played short runs in Los Angeles and San Francisco. A traveling show with different leads made brief stops in Dallas, Kansas City, and Atlanta. Neither production was a success. Scarlett and Rhett returned to Japan, where the country's famous all-female Takarazuka Revue produced several versions of the story over the next several decades. Perhaps because of their experience as an occupied nation after World War II, the Japanese seemed to identify with Scarlett and her promise of a brighter tomorrow.

Regardless of how American audiences felt about a musical *Gone With the Wind,* the estate continued to prove a profitable venture. From 1960 through 1967, it earned nearly $750,000. But there was more to come. MGM again released the film in U.S. theaters in October 1967, this time touting that the movie could be viewed in the "splendor of widescreen." (Actually, technicians rescanned the original film and cut off the top and bottom of many scenes to make the picture more rectangular.) To go along with the new format, MGM issued updated movie poster artwork with an extra dash of sex appeal: Clark Gable, his white shirt open to the waist, holds Leigh, her red gown cut low, against a backdrop of garish orange flames. After another opening in Atlanta, the film traveled across the country. Moviegoers flocked to theaters; in some cities, the film played for months. By the end of 1968, Selznick's *Gone With the Wind* had grossed another thirty million dollars in the United States alone, making it one of the top box-office attractions of the year. Thanks to the 1963 agreement with MGM, the estate shared in the riches. At the same time, Pocket Books issued a new paperback edition of the novel featuring the provocative movie artwork on its cover. Margaret Mitchell would have been horrified to see her Pulitzer Prize–winning novel so adorned. Yet, with its more contemporary look, the book earned new fans—and more royalties.

Throughout the 1960s, with Brown still handling the business details, Stephens Mitchell and Baugh managed the estate's assets and served as the public face of *Gone With the Wind.* Baugh continued to work alone from the estate office, which was now located in a separate building from Mitchell's law firm. She enjoyed a public reputation as a leading authority on Margaret Mitchell's book and took pride in overseeing matters in a manner consistent with the author's wishes. *Gone With the Wind* had become her main purpose and focus in life. She and Stephens Mitchell had never developed a friendly relationship—she remained devoutly loyal to the way Margaret Mitchell had handled things, while he took a more practical approach—and it appears she viewed herself as the true keeper of the Mitchell flame. Even after suffering a serious case of throat cancer that left her dependent on a mechanical device for speech, she continued in her role as the self-dubbed "nursemaid to the prodigy."[14] In a 1966 letter to Cole, Baugh reflected on how little some aspects of her work had changed despite the passage of so many years. Although the volume of correspondence had dropped off, the same issues that existed "in Peggy's day" still popped up—everything from inquiries about new foreign editions to requests from students for help with articles and term papers. Fans still traveled from "Massachusetts or Japan or Timbuctoo" to find the real Tara or Aunt Pittypat's house and were often disappointed to find instead "40-story buildings all over the place and the roar of traffic and the sound of riveting and welding."[15]

Stephens Mitchell continued to practice law, refusing to sacrifice his career to the business of *Gone With the Wind*. The family firm where he had worked for many years had been disbanded after the deaths of his father and an uncle, and Mitchell now practiced with two younger partners: Thomas Hal Clarke, a fellow member of the Atlanta Historical Society, and Paul Anderson, a friend of Clarke's. Like Mitchell, Clarke and Anderson specialized in real estate law. Mitchell went to great lengths to keep his literary work separate from that of their firm, Mitchell, Clarke & Anderson. He never invited his partners to the estate office and did not discuss *GWTW* affairs with them.[16] But, Mitchell would not be able to maintain that divide forever.

In April 1967, the lawyer, then seventy-one, suffered serious injuries in a bizarre accident. While walking on a sidewalk in downtown Atlanta, he was struck by a large wooden crate that fell from a passing truck. The crate knocked him into the side of a bus, breaking both of his arms. He continued to work after the accident but was never quite the same. His condition placed added responsibility on Baugh, who was also in poor health. A further blow to the estate occurred when, in December, she passed away at the age of sixty-eight. Although Stephens Mitchell and Baugh had not always shared a common vision for how the literary rights should be handled, she had been an invaluable resource, and he remembered her to the press respectfully as "a right quiet and peaceful little lady."[17]

Without Baugh, Mitchell was forced to rely on Clarke and Anderson for assistance in managing the estate. Brown and her firm continued to handle much of the day-to-day issues relating to the rights, but looking ahead, Mitchell prepared his partners to oversee the estate after his passing. Although neither of the two lawyers had a personal affiliation with the author—Clarke had met Margaret Mitchell only socially—her brother trusted them to handle matters appropriately. "Steve was very diligent about

*Gone With the Wind*'s history and business, and kept good records," Clarke said. "He was very conscious of doing that and would get on us younger fellows to see that we did the same."[18]

Stephens Mitchell also relied on Cole for support. They had always been on friendly terms, and she kept an eye out for him in the New York publishing world. When Harold Latham died in March 1969, Cole sent flowers on Mitchell's behalf and forwarded him a copy of Latham's obituary from the *New York Times*. Though Cole never publicly voiced any complaints about the editor, she let her guard down with Mitchell. Included with the clipping was a letter that revealed continued resentment for Latham's having taken the credit for *Gone With the Wind*. The *Times* story claimed the publishing executive had "found" Margaret Mitchell and edited the manuscript of *Gone With the Wind*. Cole noted, "I should be old enough to laugh it off, but it still irks me when people take credit for what they didn't do. . . . No one, as you know, edited *GWTW*. . . . But, oh, well, what does it matter?"[19]

*Gone With the Wind* remained profitable as it approached its fifth decade. In the United States, Macmillan kept the original hardback edition in print and also trotted out special hardcover editions on occasion, such as for the seventy-fifth anniversary of Mitchell's birth in 1975, when it issued a slipcased volume with a foreword by author James Michener. The publisher had also periodically authorized third parties such as the Limited Editions Club to issue new versions. As for the paperback rights, Macmillan granted a license to Avon Books, which released several new editions. All of these books resulted in an impressive revenue stream for the estate, along with its share of the income earned from the movie, which MGM regularly rereleased.

The story continued to be extraordinarily popular overseas as well, especially in countries that were opening their doors to the West for the first time in decades. Selznick's film was one of the first foreign movies released in China when the Communist Party loosened cultural restrictions. A three-volume paperback was published in East Germany in the late 1970s, and about that same time, the first Burmese translation, which local critics claimed was better than Mitchell's original, won the country's National Literature Award.[20] The first Russian edition of *Gone With the Wind* appeared in the Soviet Union. Not all the editions were authorized, but they continued to introduce Scarlett's story to new audiences.

Brown generally had a free hand managing the rights, but Stephens

Mitchell did not hesitate to step in if matters took a turn he did not like. When French publisher Gallimard issued an illustrated edition for young people that contained a running commentary alongside the text, much of it unflattering to Margaret Mitchell and the South, Stephens Mitchell nearly ended the decades-old relationship with the firm. "Never have I heard of a publisher putting notes in a book . . . to show the ignorance, incompetence and prejudice of an author of a novel from which he has derived profits," the author's brother declared.[21] When Gallimard failed to apologize, Mitchell laid out his viewpoint in stark terms, comparing the situation to having a foreign edition of a French patriotic story set in World War II "commented on paragraph by paragraph by Herr Joseph Goebbels."[22] When inquiries in France indicated a lawsuit would not be successful, Mitchell reluctantly let the matter drop. However, he insisted the additional material in the book not be used in other countries and instructed Brown to tighten future contracts to ensure publication of his sister's text would be verbatim, with no commentary or notes of any kind.

For the most part though, Stephens Mitchell had mellowed over the years. He still felt loyal to his sister's preferences about how matters should be handled but gradually broadened the scope of what he deemed appropriate. He had spent two decades at the helm of the estate opposing commercial enterprises that tried to take advantage of *Gone With the Wind*. There had been proposals for *GWTW*-themed tourist attractions, property developments, and myriad other projects. He had opposed them all on the grounds that his sister would not have approved. Then, in 1969, he had given up fighting the inevitable and granted permission for Clayton County, Georgia, to designate itself the "Home of *Gone With the Wind*." So long as matters were handled tastefully, he now saw no harm in capitalizing on Scarlett and Rhett's continued appeal. Perhaps it was due to age, the changing times, or maybe, without Baugh reminding him of what the Marshes would have done, he felt more comfortable relying on his own instincts.

In 1975, Stephens Mitchell took steps down another path his sister never wanted traveled: he considered authorizing a sequel to *Gone With the Wind*. Over the years, the estate had regularly received inquiries from writers interested in continuing Scarlett and Rhett's story. Most of these correspondents went to great lengths to assure the author's brother they were uniquely qualified to take on such an important task. He thought these writers should put their talents to good use and create their own characters and story lines, and often told them so. To all offers and suggestions for a continuation, Mitchell had stood firm, repeating his sister's oft-used argument that the story ended where it ended and there was no need to go further: "Mrs. Marsh always said emphatically no. When I inherited the rights, we were offered $500,000 for sequelization rights and we said no. We shall always say no."[23]

What made him change his mind? The renewed copyright on the novel was scheduled to expire in seventeen years, at which point he suspected there would be multiple unauthorized sequels rushing to reunite Scarlett and Rhett. Concerned about the quality of such books and how they might affect the reputation of *Gone With the Wind*, he felt it prudent to authorize a continuation of the story while it was still under copyright. Not only would he ensure the story was handled respectfully, but also the estate would reap the benefits of Scarlett and Rhett's future adventures and hopefully dampen the market for unauthorized sequels. "I am 80 years old," he explained, "and do not have the ability to police the publishing world, the motion picture world, and the dramatic world to catch up with infringements. I have done this for 40 years, and am weary."[24]

Mitchell turned to Brown, now working for International Creative Management, to lead the way. She encouraged him to develop a film sequel, predicting it would generate higher revenues than a book version.[25] With Mitchell's go-ahead, she approached independent film producers David Brown and Richard Zanuck, who were riding high after their recent box-office successes *The Sting* and *Jaws*. As David Brown later said, it did not take much convincing. They thought about the offer for "a microsecond" before saying they wanted to work out a deal with the Mitchell estate.[26]

But they were not the only interested party. When MGM heard a sequel deal was in the works, it elbowed its way to the table by virtue of its earlier contractual relationships with Margaret Mitchell and the estate. Stephens Mitchell did not necessarily agree that MGM had a say in the matter but did not want to jeopardize the project by having the studio file a lawsuit. He allowed MGM to be part of the negotiations with Zanuck/Brown Productions. On June 8, 1976, Mitchell signed a contract with Universal Pictures, the studio with which Zanuck/Brown Productions was affiliated. In exchange for a three-year option on a film sequel to be produced jointly by Universal and MGM, Universal would pay five hundred thousand dollars to the Mitchell family. Universal also obtained the option to purchase a one-year extension for an additional one hundred thousand dollars. Upon commencement of principal photography, Mitchell and his sons would receive another five hundred thousand dollars and, once the film was made, 10 percent of the movie's profits. As part of the deal, Zanuck and Brown would hire an author to write a "novelization" of their sequel, to be released in paperback when the movie opened, or up to a year before.

News of a sequel to the most successful film in Hollywood history made front-page headlines. It seemed everyone wanted to know: Would the lovers reunite? Who would play Scarlett and Rhett? *New York Times* arts critic Ralph Tyler surveyed literary VIPs such as Isaac Asimov, James Dickey, and John Updike for their story line suggestions. Their clever replies ran the gamut, from Rhett founding *New South* magazine and hiring Belle Watling as a gossip columnist to Scarlett running a Colonel Sanders fried chicken franchise restaurant. Edward Albee suggested the producers ought to ask Margaret Mitchell to write the script and, if she were not available, perhaps William Makepeace Thackeray. If neither could do it, he suggested the project be scrapped because it was just a moneymaking scheme anyway.[27]

While the general public seemed eager to see what Hollywood would do with the story, a cadre of die-hard *GWTW* fans agreed with Albee that the project was ill advised. Aware of Margaret Mitchell's opposition to a sequel, some saw her brother's actions as a betrayal. A man in West Virginia who operated a *Gone With the Wind* fan club wrote to the estate, cautioning that, if the views of his club members were any indication, the project would fail. Calling the movie sequel an "obvious attempt to gain a financial windfall," he added that a continuation would probably harm the great esteem in which so many held the original book and film. Evidencing some sympathy for the estate's situation, though, the man described it as a "damned if they do, damned if they don't" scenario: the public always wanted a sequel but would likely not admire the result.[28]

Stephens Mitchell did not disagree with this assessment. He suspected the sequel might not have popular appeal, and for that reason wanted no say in the casting of the film, the selection of an author to write the sequel, or the plot—"unless," the ever-watchful guardian said, "it contains indecent or illegal matter." In his estimation, his sister's book ended at the right place: "where the woman who had a good man (and did not know it) finds out that he is the man for her, and also finds out that it is too late to do anything about it."[29] Yet, he explained to the man from West Virginia, he felt he had no choice but to go down this road. He summed up what his life had been like since his sister's death:

> After you realize the enormous number of people who have written sequels, and the trouble of fighting them off, and realize that your copyright will not

last forever, and realize that you are getting old, and that no one else is going
to devote his life to the everlasting task of preventing abridgments, varia-
tions, sequels, etc. you can come to the conclusion that (1) It is just as well
to let the public see what a sequel would be like. (2) You might as well quit
spending the continuing large sums of money, which it has taken and still
takes, to prevent such a thing.

He closed by noting, "There are perhaps a group of wealthy vestal virgins
willing to spend their lives and fortunes protecting *Gone With the Wind*. If
there are, and were, I have never met them."[30]

Just months after the sequel deal announcement, Congress extended
the copyright of works then in their renewal period—including *Gone With
the Wind*—an additional nineteen years. Under the new law, the copyright
on Mitchell's book enjoyed protection until 2011. The extension gave the
estate some breathing room from aspiring sequel writers, but Stephens
Mitchell expressed no regrets over having signed the sequel deal. When
asked how the copyright extension might have affected his decision-making
process, he refused to speculate. "I do not know what my decision would
have been had I known that the Act amending the copyright law would
pass. There is no way to tell how an 'if' would have turned out," he noted
in a letter to a fan.[31]

The movie sequel deal was not *Gone With the Wind*'s only turn in the spotlight in 1976. MGM took in another five million dollars when NBC
acquired the rights to broadcast *Gone With the Wind* for the first time on
network television in the United States. The estate's share was five hundred
thousand dollars. The movie aired over two nights that fall. The first part,
which ran on November 7, 1976, drew a record 33,890,000 viewers, the
largest audience ever to watch a single television broadcast. The final segment, shown the following night, attracted 33,750,000 viewers, the second-
largest audience in television history. As had happened when MGM rereleased the movie in theaters, interest in the novel picked up. Avon Books
went to press with its paperback edition three times in the wake of the
showing.[32]

That same year, another novel about life in the Old South took the
nation by storm. Alex Haley's *Roots*, which purported to trace the author's
family tree back to Africa, became a bestseller, and several commentators
termed Haley's book a counterpoint to *Gone With the Wind*. An intriguing

mystery arose when a handful of readers in Connecticut and Wisconsin purchased copies of *Roots* from a book club and were startled to find the text of *Gone With the Wind* bound inside the cover of Haley's book. Press reports referred to the incident as "*Roots* Traduced" or "The Revenge of the Confederacy," but the *New York Times* investigated and determined there had been no nefarious plot. According to the publisher, it had been an accident—albeit an ironic one—that occurred at a bindery where both Haley's and Mitchell's books were being produced. Only about two dozen copies of the mismatched volume made it into circulation.

During Mitchell's lifetime, the racial themes in her book had been discussed but rarely came to the forefront. Forty years later, standards of tolerance had changed, and many commentators questioned the ongoing relevance of Mitchell's version of life in the Old South. Yet, despite the increased sensitivity to racial considerations, *Gone With the Wind* remained commercially popular. The racial issue would escalate in years to come but had not yet dampened enthusiasm for Mitchell's story. It certainly did not unduly concern executives at CBS, who in April 1978, paid thirty-five million dollars for the exclusive privilege of broadcasting *Gone With the Wind* on television for the next twenty years. The deal earned the estate another $3.5 million.

In late 1976, after considering a long list of potential writers, David Brown and Zanuck chose Vivien Leigh biographer Anne Edwards to develop the story on which their movie would be based. After two years of research and writing, Edwards produced a manuscript titled "Tara: The Continuation of *Gone With the Wind*." In the 650-page story, which opens after Melanie's death, Scarlett convinces Rhett to reconcile. However, when he becomes suspicious of her continuing interest in Ashley, he finds comfort in the arms of Belle Watling, who later dies of yellow fever. Rhett returns to Scarlett but is killed in a Ku Klux Klan raid while fighting to protect Tara. Screenwriter James Goldman was hired to turn Edwards's story into a screenplay, and his treatment follows some of her plot line, but adds a new husband for Scarlett and spares Rhett's life in the end. After reviewing the draft treatment, Universal and MGM came to loggerheads over how the script should be finalized. They could not settle their differences during the three-year option period, and so, in 1979, Zanuck and Brown paid the estate one hundred thousand dollars to extend the option for another year. Even with the extra time, Universal and MGM could not agree on a story line, and the project foundered. In 1980, the movie deal was off.

Although the copyright extension alleviated any sense of urgency on issuing a sequel, Stephens Mitchell maintained an interest in authorizing a continuation of *Gone With the Wind* as a way of protecting the content and, of course, sharing in the profits. However, an incident occurred that caused him to reconsider MGM's involvement. In 1980, MGM attorney Herbert S. Nusbaum alerted the estate to an unauthorized sequel that was being shopped around to Hollywood studios. Anderson, who now handled much of the *GWTW* work, contacted the sequel's author and warned him that the project violated the estate's rights. Nusbaum also wrote to the man, advising him that MGM owned the *Gone With the Wind* motion picture rights, including sequels.[33] Anderson, who had been copied on the letter, quickly responded to Nusbaum, taking exception to his claim about MGM's rights. "Metro-Goldwyn-Mayer owns only such motion picture rights in connection with *Gone With the Wind* as it has acquired by contract, and it owns no sequel rights whatsoever," he said.[34] Those few words would serve as the launching pad for a multiyear court battle.

The estate hired an attorney specializing in copyright issues to review the series of contracts between Margaret Mitchell, Selznick, the estate, and MGM to determine what, if any, rights the studio had in a *GWTW* sequel. The lawyer concurred with the estate's view that MGM had no sequel rights in the United States. If the estate wanted to establish that point definitively, he recommended, it would have to file for a declaratory judgment in court nullifying MGM's claims. Although the case would be an expensive undertaking, Kay Brown urged the estate to push ahead, noting that MGM's claim reduced the value of the sequel rights. Zanuck and David Brown, who remained interested in tackling a movie sequel, were supportive as well. They offered one hundred thousand dollars for a new option on a movie sequel if the estate negated MGM's claim.[35] In June 1981, the estate filed suit against MGM in federal court, asserting that Margaret Mitchell, and later her estate, controlled the right to continue her story and that such rights had never been granted to Selznick, or his successor in interest, MGM. In response, MGM maintained there was ambiguity over who controlled the sequel rights and that, by allowing MGM into the 1976 agreement with Universal, Stephens Mitchell implicitly recognized MGM's rights.

While that case wended its way through the judicial system, the estate prepared for trial on another copyright matter—this one related to the

*GWTW* dramatic rights. In 1979, an Atlanta theater group called Plump Bess Productions had attempted to stage a dinner theater production called *Scarlett Fever: The Comic Retelling of a Southern Legend*. When the estate claimed copyright infringement, the theater group maintained its show was a parody and, therefore, permissible under fair use laws, which authorize limited public use of copyrighted material for purposes such as critique or commentary. The distinction between what constitutes infringement versus fair use is not clearly defined, but the estate felt confident that the theater company was making excessive use of Margaret Mitchell's copyrighted material and filed a lawsuit. The estate obtained a temporary restraining order, preventing Plump Bess Productions from staging the play, and the case finally went to trial in the summer of 1981. On September 3, the court ruled in favor of the estate, permanently barring the production and awarding five hundred dollars in damages.[36]

Stephens Mitchell won that round but would not live to see the results of his struggle with MGM over the sequel rights. That case remained unresolved when he died on May 12, 1983, at the age of eighty-seven.* Of all the people integrally involved in the life of *Gone With the Wind*, he had dedicated the most time and energy to its care. And he, more so even than his sister, had ensured its lasting value. According to his will, the rights to *Gone With the Wind* now passed to two new trusts, which he referred to jointly as the Stephens Mitchell Trusts, that he had set up for the benefit of his sons. Responsibility for managing those rights transferred to a committee consisting of Anderson, Clarke, and Atlanta tax lawyer Herbert R. Elsas, in conjunction with the Trust Company of Georgia as executor of the estate. Some of the most highly publicized events related to the business of *Gone With the Wind* lay ahead, including, at long last, an answer to the question readers had been asking for half a century: what happened to Scarlett and Rhett?

---

* Stephens Mitchell was not, however, the last survivor of the core group involved with the book's original publication. That distinction goes to George Brett, who died the following year at the age of ninety-one. Cole had died in 1979 at age seventy-six.

# 18

# Tomorrow Is Another Book

## June 1983–2011

For the first time in almost half a century, the Mitchell family was not managing the business of *Gone With the Wind*. Though the author's two nephews inherited the income earned from the book and other deals and served as the final arbiters of how the rights would be handled, they were not involved with the day-to-day decisions related to the protection and exploitation of the *GWTW* copyright. Their father had entrusted that responsibility to the trio of attorneys in Atlanta who served as committee members of the Stephens Mitchell Trusts.

Like Stephens Mitchell before them, none of the three lawyers was trained in copyright or publishing law, and none had aspirations for careers in the literary rights world. But they shared a loyalty to their friend Stephens Mitchell and a willingness to carry out his wishes regarding the estate. While the author's brother did not leave specific instructions as to how he expected the trustees to handle matters, the lawyers were well aware of his intentions. "We knew pretty much what he would have wanted," Paul Anderson said. He and Thomas Hal Clarke had helped with the Universal sequel deal, the Metro-Goldwyn-Mayer (MGM) litigation, and the lawsuit over the stage version of *Scarlett Fever*, so they were familiar with how Mitchell thought and operated. Most decisions came down to "what made sense and what was the right answer to the problem."[1]

The committeemen asked Kay Brown and her firm, International Creative Management (ICM), to continue as the estate's agent, and she remained responsible for coordinating publishing contracts and the dra-

matic, motion picture, and television rights. Despite her advanced years—
she turned eighty-one the year Stephens Mitchell died—she remained an
integral part of the *GWTW* team, as Mitchell would have wanted. Indeed,
he had credited the agent with much of his success in preserving the value
of his sister's literary assets. As he once admitted to Brown, "One of the
smart things I have done in developing and making a paying proposition
out of these rights to *Gone With the Wind* was to hold on to your hand
while you led me through the morasses and caverns of the theatrical
world."[2]

In June 1984, a little more than a year after Stephens Mitchell's death,
a federal trial court issued a decision in the lawsuit against MGM: the rights
to authorize a sequel to *Gone With the Wind* belonged to Margaret Mitchell's estate. MGM appealed, but in September 1985, the Eleventh U.S. Circuit Court of Appeals upheld the ruling, establishing that the estate alone
controlled the future of Mitchell's characters.[3] Resolving the matter had cost
the estate more than three hundred thousand dollars in attorney's fees. It
was an expensive but worthwhile investment given the value of the rights
at stake.[4]

With the sequel train back on track, the trustees moved to make up
for lost time in developing *Gone With the Wind*'s continuation. Brown recommended the estate change course and authorize a book sequel that could
later be sold to a movie studio. The committee members were in favor of
this approach, and she began vetting writers. As word spread throughout
the entertainment industry that the estate was again developing the sequel
rights, industry players sensed something big in the works. The William
Morris Agency, a rival of Brown's firm, approached the trustees and made a
pitch to take over representation of the *GWTW* rights. Although the committee members were confident of Brown's abilities, they had a fiduciary
duty to protect the estate's interests and were willing to hear what William
Morris had to say. The Morris agency agreed with Brown that a book sequel
was the best route but impressed the trustees with grand plans for exploiting
other subsidiary rights through subsequent sequels or perhaps an episodic
*Gone With the Wind* television program.[5] In the summer of 1986, the trustees advised Brown they were bringing William Morris into the fold. Reluctant to sever ties with her, the committee asked Brown if she would
continue working with the estate on a freelance basis. Her boss at ICM
refused to allow the arrangement and, so, after a quarter of a century, Brown
was out. It would fall to the William Morris Agency—a firm that had no

personal relationship with Margaret Mitchell—to find the heir to her literary legacy.[6]

*   ➤   *

In addition to signaling the end of Brown's involvement with *Gone With the Wind*, 1986 represented a landmark year in the book's life: the novel turned fifty. To mark the golden anniversary, Macmillan printed sixty thousand facsimiles of the book's May 1936 printing. The special edition, which featured a reproduction of the original dust jacket and binding, sold out quickly, bringing Margaret Mitchell back to the *New York Times* bestseller list for five weeks that summer.[7] (According to the *New York Times Book Review*, the only other book in recent memory to make a reappearance on the list so many years after its original publication was George Orwell's *1984*, which had experienced a resurgence of interest two years earlier.)[8] The Book-of-the-Month Club offered its own commemorative edition of Mitchell's novel, and in Atlanta, an informal weeklong celebration of bus tours, exhibits, and lectures took place. Even the U.S. Postal Service acknowledged the occasion by issuing a one-cent stamp honoring Margaret Mitchell in its "Great Americans" series.★

The year also brought Scarlett and Rhett together with media mogul Ted Turner, whose devotion to their story—he named one of his sons Rhett—would do much to ensure their enduring legacy in pop culture. That summer, Turner purchased the film studio MGM/UA Entertainment Company for $1.5 billion. Three months later, he sold many of the studio's assets but held on to what he most coveted, its film and TV library, which included *Gone With the Wind*. Taking advantage of the attention surrounding the book's anniversary, Turner Entertainment Company jump-started a craze of *Gone With the Wind* collectibles by licensing independent manufacturers to create a tidal wave of plates, beach towels, calendars, music boxes, dolls, figurines, and T-shirts bearing the likenesses of characters and scenes from the movie.

When the trustees saw the money Turner was making off of Mitchell's characters, they questioned whether the estate had a stake in those proceeds. Margaret Mitchell had granted the commercial tie-in rights to Loew's, MGM's parent company, but had Turner acquired those rights in his deal with MGM/UA? The trustees concluded not and advised Turner that he

---

★ Since then, the U.S. Postal Service has issued five additional *GWTW*-related stamps, including one in 1998 that pictured the novel on a thirty-two-cent stamp as part of a "Celebrate the Century" series.

had exceeded the bounds of his authority. The estate and Turner Entertainment worked out a deal: Turner would manage the commercial products and pay the estate a share of the royalties on all licensed products, which, going forward, would be released under both the Turner Entertainment and Stephens Mitchell Trusts names. Within a few years, the pact generated more than three million dollars for the estate.[9]

Not all of the trustees' efforts to protect the estate's interests were as successful. In 1986, French author Regine Deforges released a book in the United States titled *The Blue Bicycle*; it was an English-language version of a novel she had published in France several years earlier to great success. Deforges admitted the opening section of her story was an updated version of *Gone With the Wind*. Set in World War II France, the narrative opens at a garden party at which Lea is rebuffed by Laurant, who marries his cousin Camille. Laurant leaves for war, and Lea falls for the dashing François, who helps her escape Paris after the Germans invade. Believing Stephens Mitchell would not have tolerated Deforges's blatant use of Margaret Mitchell's plot, the trustees, acting through the Trust Company of Georgia, filed a plagiarism lawsuit against the author in Los Angeles and then in France. Not the least bit intimidated, Deforges defended her right of free expression, claiming the bank could not claim exclusive rights to the classic literary theme of a love triangle in which a woman loves a man who loves another woman. The legal proceedings dragged out for several years, with the estate winning twice at the trial court level and Deforges prevailing both times on appeal. Not eager to incur the cost of a third trial, the trustees let the matter drop.[10] Anderson and Clarke were serious about protecting the copyright but would not fall on their sword to prove a point.

While Margaret Mitchell had fought every usurper as a matter of principle, the committee lawyers endeavored to take a measured approach to managing the *GWTW* rights. Anderson has said the committee tries "not to make a federal case" out of every situation where someone is violating the book's copyright. "There's a point where you have to exercise judgment about it, and we try to do that."[11] For instance, when an unauthorized translation of *Gone With the Wind* appeared in Ethiopia in 1986, the trustees took no action, presumably given the unusual circumstances of the book's production. In the late 1970s, an inmate at an Ethiopian prison smuggled in an English-language copy of Mitchell's novel. The prisoners took turns reading it an hour each day. Fascinated with Scarlett and Rhett, a political prisoner named Nebiy Mekonnen began translating *Gone With the Wind* into his native language, Amharic. He wrote with a smuggled pen on the sole source of paper available—the back side of foil linings from cigarette packets. His fellow prisoners were so pleased with his efforts that they relinquished their allotted hours with the book so he could have more time to work. They also donated their cigarette wrappers to McKennon, a non smoker. Over the years of his imprisonment, the translator filled an estimated three thousand scraps of paper, which he smuggled out for safekeeping with fellow inmates as they were released. After he gained his own freedom, the translator tracked down the papers and borrowed money to publish twenty thousand copies of *Negem Lela Ken New*, which translates to "Tomorrow Is Another Day."[12]

The April 1988 issue of *Life* magazine announced that, at long last, the Mitchell estate had chosen an author to write a sequel to *Gone With the Wind*. The successor to Margaret Mitchell's literary legacy would be Alexandra Ripley, a novelist from Charleston, South Carolina. Acknowledging Mitchell was a tough act to follow, the South Carolinian prepared herself for the task by reading *Gone With the Wind* six times and making a detailed outline of its plot. She also copied by hand hundreds of pages of Mitchell's novel to get a physical feel for her predecessor's writing style. Yet, the pressure of living up to the expectations of Mitchell's fans did not frighten her. "Yes, Margaret Mitchell writes better than I do," she said, "but she's dead."[13]

Ten days after the announcement, the estate held an auction for publishers to bid on the rights to release the new book. Several firms tossed their wallets into the ring, though noticeably absent was Macmillan. Warner Books won the auction with a bid of $4.94 million as an advance on royalties, narrowly beating out the underbidder, Delacorte/Dell, which offered $4.8 million. For Warner, it was money well spent. Within six months, the publisher recouped most of its investment by securing more than four million dollars in advances from publishers in Brazil, England, France, Japan, Sweden, and West Germany eager to issue translations of Ripley's continuation.

Although Warner Books announced the sequel would be released in the spring of 1990, the work took Scarlett's "foster mother"—as Ripley considered herself—longer than anticipated. Ripley did not submit a draft of her one thousand–page manuscript to the publisher until March of that year. Warner was not happy with what it saw, asked for extensive rewrites, and delayed the book's release until fall. Then, just before the June American Booksellers Association convention, where publishers unveil their upcoming titles, Warner yanked the book from the company's autumn lineup. Ripley and her editor at Warner were at an impasse, and industry insiders speculated that the effort to produce a sequel might again fall apart.[14]

The publisher and the Mitchell estate agreed to hire and split the cost of an independent editor to work on Ripley's manuscript. They retained the services of Jeanne Bernkopf, known in the industry as a "book doctor," to assess the draft and facilitate rewrites. After several frantic months of work, Warner Books approved a revised manuscript in early 1991. Downplaying rumors swirling around the project, the publisher blamed the delay on the length of the manuscript and the care Ripley was taking to ensure fans of the original book would be pleased.[15] To the relief of everyone involved, Scarlett and friends would see another day. Especially grateful, the estate paid Bernkopf a fifteen-thousand-dollar bonus on top of its share of her thirty-thousand-dollar fee.[16]

The sequel was scheduled for a fall 1991 release, and the publicity department at Warner Books began trumpeting that "Tomorrow Is Here, at Last. . . ." The publisher had high expectations for Ripley's novel, titled *Scarlett: The Sequel to Margaret Mitchell's* Gone With the Wind, and announced a first printing of a half million copies.[17] Warner's marketing strategy differed dramatically from the approach Macmillan had taken with Mitchell's original. Whereas Macmillan had been anxious to build buzz by getting the book into the hands of as many reviewers as possible, Warner embargoed *Scarlett*, meaning it did not release review copies until immediately before publication. This is a modern technique publishers use to prevent reviewers from stealing the thunder of a hotly anticipated book. If all goes well, an embargo helps the publisher create a buying frenzy on release day. The only hint Warner gave of what Ripley had to offer was an excerpt it released in *Life* magazine six weeks before publication day. Keeping the book under wraps worked. In the days leading up to the release, advance orders streamed in, and numerous additional overseas publishers signed contracts for translations. Warner increased the first run to 750,000 copies and ordered an additional 350,000 copies as of publication day.[18] Like *Gone With the Wind*, the sequel was a guaranteed bestseller before its release.

Macmillan president Barry Lippman took the opportunity to get in a dig at Warner Books, saying that the quality of Ripley's book did not matter; it was destined to succeed simply for being what it was.[19] He predicted people would be buying *Gone With the Wind* long after *Scarlett* ran its course.

His disdain did not stop Macmillan from capitalizing on Ripley's work though. The firm produced more than fifty thousand copies of Mitchell's novel to coincide with the sequel's release. (Warner did not dispute Lippman's assessment of *Gone With the Wind*'s lasting appeal; it later acquired the paperback rights to Mitchell's original from Macmillan.)

Fifty-five years after Rhett said he didn't give a damn, Warner Books unveiled Ripley's book on September 25, 1991. The story opens at Melanie's burial, after which Scarlett returns to Tara, where her beloved Mammy dies. A tryst with Rhett in Charleston leaves Scarlett pregnant, but when he becomes involved with another woman, Scarlett flees to her father's family in Savannah. She later accompanies a cousin to Ireland, where she gives birth to Rhett's daughter. After numerous adventures in the O'Hara homeland, Scarlett and Rhett reunite and head off to face new challenges. It was not the ending Mitchell had in mind for her famous lovers, but Ripley felt obligated to offer a happy resolution for the fans. Her daughter Merrill Geier says that Ripley "did not want to pander to the lowest common denominator" yet understood the business side of what it meant to write a *Gone With the Wind* sequel. "Nobody was trying to break literary ground here."[20]

Eager fans lined up outside a B. Dalton Booksellers near Atlanta to be among the first to buy a copy when the store opened at midnight. By the end of the first day, readers in the United States had snapped up 250,000 copies. Booksellers were harried but thrilled to report that customers were grabbing the books as quickly as the boxes were opened. Some fans even claimed the cartons as souvenirs. The nation's two leading bookstore chains at the time—B. Dalton and Waldenbooks—both set one-day sales records. Warner Books was ecstatic and amazed by the public's reaction; its president, Laurence J. Kirshbaum, deemed *Scarlett* a phenomenon.[21]

Book reviewers were not so impressed. The notices were scathing. A newspaper in Richmond, Virginia, judged that Ripley didn't "know nothin' 'bout writin' no sequels," while columnist Molly Ivins quipped that more probable plot lines could be found in episodes of *Gilligan's Island*. Once they read the book, many readers also expressed disappointment. The story had a fantastical element to it that some found not in keeping with Mitchell's original, while others were disconcerted that the bulk of the action took place outside Georgia. Ripley shrugged off the criticism, saying she doubted fans would have been happy with a sequel written by Margaret Mitchell herself.

The harsh critical reaction did not appear to have any negative impact on *Scarlett*'s sales. By the end of the first week, more than five hundred thousand copies had been sold. Ripley energetically promoted the sequel, appearing at signings across the country. Thousands turned out to see her, and she was a good sport along the way. At a book signing at a Rich's department store in Atlanta, the author found herself waiting in a long line at the women's restroom. She bartered a place up front for a signed copy of her book, which she inscribed in the stall: "From the ladies room at Rich's." After developing tendinitis in her wrist from signing more than ten thousand copies of *Scarlett*, she felt a special kinship with Margaret Mitchell. She joked to the press about putting her arm in a sling and going into seclusion.[22]

When 1.5 million copies had moved after one month, *Scarlett* was proclaimed by some sources to be the fastest-selling novel in U.S. history.[23] The book spent thirty-four weeks on the *New York Times* bestseller list, its first sixteen weeks in the top spot. By the end of the year, Warner Books had printed 2,100,000 hardback copies of *Scarlett*.[24] *Gone With the Wind* tagged along for the ride, landing on the bestseller list yet again, this time for ten weeks. And despite Lippman's distaste for *Scarlett*, he must have been pleased by its success. Macmillan went back to press three times that fall, printing approximately forty-five thousand more copies of Mitchell's original.

Book buyers outside the United States were equally enthusiastic about Scarlett's new adventures. Publishers in more than thirty countries released translations. Within months, foreign sales topped four million, including 670,000 copies in Germany and 500,000 in France.[25] Ripley made appearances in both countries, where she received the full celebrity treatment. In Biarritz, France, she stayed at a luxury hotel and, according to her daughter, "learned what it was like to be a rock star."[26] As in America, the sequel revived interest in Mitchell's original, leading to numerous new editions of *Gone With the Wind* overseas, some packaged with copies of *Scarlett*.

As the trustees and William Morris had hoped, the sequel's overwhelming success caught the attention of producers interested in translating the story to the screen—although this time it would be the more compact medium of television. In November 1991, with *Scarlett* riding high on bestseller lists, Hungarian producer Robert Halmi bid nine million dollars for the rights to turn the book into a miniseries. While working on the teleplay, Halmi let it slip that he intended to jettison Scarlett's move to Ireland and take the characters to the Wild West instead. Not so fast, the trustees responded. They had authorized one sequel in Ripley's novel; they had no intention of allowing Halmi to rewrite the book into a second one. They forced the producer to carry on with Ripley's basic plot.[27]

Like David O. Selznick, Halmi conducted an extensive talent search for an actress to play Scarlett. He claimed to have received more than twenty thousand applications. After holding auditions in the United States, England, Germany, Ireland, and Spain, he brought nine of the most promising candidates to Atlanta in October 1992 for a contest broadcast live from the Georgia State Capitol. At the end of the program, in which viewers watched hopefuls perform screen tests, Halmi announced the winner was none of the above. The search continued. A year later, the producer again followed in Selznick's footsteps by settling on a little-known British actress to play the most famous Southern belle in history. He selected thirty-one-year-old Joanne Whaley-Kilmer to portray Scarlett O'Hara Hamilton Kennedy Butler. Former James Bond, Timothy Dalton, was to be her Rhett. The six-hour miniseries aired on CBS in November 1994 to respectable ratings but was a critical failure.★

Hoping financial lightning would strike twice, the trustees and the William Morris Agency began planning for a second sequel. Ripley had no interest in participating. She was eager to return to her own writing and had earned enough to allow her that luxury—she anticipated taking in more than six hundred thousand dollars from the sequel.[28] For *Scarlett* redux, the estate settled on British novelist Emma Tennant, who had written a sequel to Jane Austen's *Pride and Prejudice*.[29] The trustees auctioned the rights on January 24, 1995, and the prize went to St. Martin's Press with a $4.5 million bid.[30] Tennant produced a manuscript that October, but St. Martin's identified problems with the story line, character development, setting, and writing style. Tennant refused to make substantive changes, and St. Martin's fired her.[31] Though neither the estate nor the publisher publicly disclosed the problematic plot, the disappointed author revealed salient details in an interview with *The Mail* in London. Her story, titled "Tara," takes Scarlett to New York and later Washington, D.C., where she becomes the mistress of President Rutherford B. Hayes. Rhett finds himself entangled with a criminal gang, forcing Scarlett to infiltrate the mob as a moll to save his life. He flees to South America, and Scarlett marries Ashley, but eventually Rhett staggers home, and the couple reunites.[32]

---

★ The week before, a made-for-television movie titled *A Burning Passion: The Margaret Mitchell Story* aired. Starring Shannen Doherty as Mitchell, the story focused on the author's relationship with her first husband, "Red" Upshaw; John Marsh and *Gone With the Wind* were relegated to the periphery.

With Tennant out of the picture, St. Martin's embarked on a hunt for a new writer. Interest in Scarlett's further adventures remained high, and the pressure was on for the publisher to fill that demand before someone else did. In Russia, a group of writers took advantage of the delay and churned out a series of unauthorized sequels with titles such as *We Call Her Scarlett* and *The Secret of Rhett Butler.*[33] The Mitchell estate apparently chose not to waste resources fighting the rogue publishers, and many of these books became bestsellers in the former Soviet Union. At home, the estate took a firmer hand. In 1996, a mother-daughter team in North Carolina self-published a book called *My Beloved Tara* that takes Mitchell's characters into the early years of the twentieth century. The duo earned the distinction of producing the first unauthorized sequel published in book form in the United States. The Mitchell trustees insisted the book be withdrawn. The authors complied, but St. Martin's and the estate knew time was of the essence in hiring a new writer if they hoped to avoid an onslaught of other unauthorized continuations. Their next candidate would come indirectly through Macmillan.

The sixtieth anniversary of *Gone With the Wind*'s publication in 1996 marked the end of Macmillan's role as its publisher. In the late 1980s, the firm had been acquired by Robert Maxwell, a controversial British media tycoon. A few years later, Maxwell's body was discovered floating in the ocean near his yacht, and it came to light that the financier was nearly broke. His assets were divvied up among creditors in a complicated series of transactions that resulted in the Scribner publishing firm acquiring the rights to Mitchell's novel. Beginning with the 106th printing of *Gone With the Wind* in 1996, Scribner replaced Macmillan's name on the spine of the *GWTW* dust jacket. One of the publisher's inaugural acts as custodian of the novel was to issue a sixtieth anniversary edition. The book featured a foreword by novelist and Atlanta native Pat Conroy, who sang the book's praises and recalled his mother's admiration for Margaret Mitchell.

Intrigued by Conroy's commentary, St. Martin's approached him about writing the second sequel, although not necessarily a continuation of *Scarlett*. Conroy, who had been baptized in the same Atlanta church as Margaret Mitchell and fondly remembered her book as his first foray into the world of literature, eagerly accepted the invitation. In 1998, St. Martin's announced that Conroy would offer readers Rhett's point of view of the events in *Gone With the Wind* in a book to be titled "Rules of Pride: The Autobiography of Captain Rhett Butler, CSA." Many of Conroy's friends expressed surprise that he would agree to be associated with what they considered a racist book. Conroy stood his ground, declaring in a letter to the Mitchell trustees that he had nothing to be ashamed of. Mitchell admired the blacks in her story, he said, and had depicted them as finely as characters created by African American writers Toni Morrison and Alice Walker. Conroy considered it an honor to step into Mitchell's shoes and wanted to do her proud.[34]

The honeymoon was not to last, though. As the project progressed, Conroy chafed at restrictions the estate imposed on his creative process. He claimed the committee members forbade him from touching on such topics as homosexuality and miscegenation and nixed plans he had to kill off Scarlett in what he promised would be one of the great death scenes in literature. In early 1999, Conroy withdrew from the project. As a jab at the trustees, Conroy joked that he had planned on beginning his book with Rhett and Ashley in bed together—and Rhett asking Ashley, "Did I ever tell you my grandmother was black?" It was back to the drawing board for St. Martin's.

In 1998, Congress extended the U.S. copyright term on creative works for another twenty years. Under the new law, *Gone With the Wind*'s copyright is protected until 2031, ninety-five years after the book's original publication. The extension caused a firestorm of controversy. Free speech advocates claimed that locking down the rights to books for such a lengthy period of time beyond an author's death was unfair to living artists and unnecessary because the vast majority of old artistic works no longer had commercial value. They dubbed the extension the "Mickey Mouse Protection Act," arguing that it benefited only a small group of highly profitable entertainment and literary estates, such as Walt Disney's and Margaret Mitchell's. Opponents filed a lawsuit in federal court, arguing that Congress had exceeded its authority.

The federal government, with the support of Walt Disney Company and other media interests, defended the copyright extension on the grounds that liberal copyright laws encourage progress in the arts by ensuring that artists, and later their heirs, receive the income derived from the artists' labors. Advocates of copyright extension equated artistic rights to traditional property rights. If someone builds an apartment building and leaves it to their grandchildren, those heirs are entitled to collect rents in perpetuity. Why should creative works be held to a different standard? Both sides dug in their heels, and the case would spend years moving through the federal court system.

Mitchell trustees Clarke and Anderson—Herbert R. Elsas had died in 1995—chose not to join the battle. "What happens, happens," Anderson said of the estate's stance.[35] So, as the century came to an end, the future of *Gone With the Wind* was up in the air. Would the estate have only another decade to profit from the copyright?

While the litigation dragged on, the search continued for a new sequel writer. In early 2001, the estate and St. Martin's chose Virginia's Donald McCaig, author of the critically acclaimed Civil War novel *Jacob's Ladder*. McCaig was no *Gone With the Wind* enthusiast—he had never read the novel before being approached about the sequel. After studying Mitchell's work, though, he came to view it as "astonishing" and deemed Scarlett O'Hara the "finest woman character in American literature."[36] As had been Conroy's proposed approach, McCaig would focus on the enigmatic Rhett Butler. Thinking a conventional sequel or prequel would pale by comparison to the original, he agreed to write what perhaps can best be termed a "requel"—a retelling of the story before and during the events in Mitchell's book, combined with his version of what happened afterward.

As St. Martin's prepared to announce McCaig's selection, publisher Houghton Mifflin Company issued advance reading copies of a novel titled *The Wind Done Gone*, which it characterized as a "rejoinder" to *Gone With the Wind*. Written by African American songwriter Alice Randall of Nashville, Tennessee, *The Wind Done Gone* presented the fictional diary of a former slave named Cynara, a mulatto, green-eyed daughter of a plantation owner called Planter and a slave woman named Mammy. The story retells *Gone With the Wind* from Cynara's perspective, and includes Cynara's half-sister, Other, and her longtime lover, R.; Beauty, the owner of an Atlanta brothel; Mealy Mouth and her husband, Dreamy Gentleman; and plantations called Tata and Twelve Slaves Strong as Trees. Randall said that she had enjoyed reading *Gone With the Wind* as a girl but had come to object to the book on the grounds that it turned slavery into a form of entertainment. She wrote her rejoinder to address the damage she felt Mitchell's work had caused blacks, pointing specifically to the stereotypes of the overweight Mammy and scatterbrained Prissy. Randall noted difficulties she faced traveling overseas where, for many people, *Gone With the Wind* is the sole reference point for what African Americans are like.[37]

On March 16, 2001, the Mitchell estate moved to halt publication of *The Wind Done Gone*, calling it a "blatant and wholesale theft" of Mitchell's "characters, settings, plot lines and other copyrighted elements." The suit also claimed that allowing Randall to use the thinly disguised characters in *Gone With the Wind* would diminish or preclude the estate's ability to control future derivative works. The complaint sought ten million dollars in damages and asked for a preliminary injunction to prevent Randall's book from being sold while the lawsuit made its way through the legal system.

Randall expressed shock at the estate's reaction, saying she had "sought to dismantle *Gone With the Wind*, not freeload off it."[38] Houghton Mifflin maintained *The Wind Done Gone* was a classic parody of Mitchell's work and thus fell within the fair use exception to the estate's copyright. According to the publisher, Mitchell's book had become such a seminal source of information about American plantation life that the public interest necessitated another perspective being brought forth.[39] Houghton Mifflin lined up a team of influential authors, editors, and scholars to support its position. Nobel and Pulitzer prize-winning author Toni Morrison submitted a declaration to the court praising Randall's efforts to offer a more accurate version of slave life and referring to her prose as "evocative, wry, plangent."[40] Pat Conroy joined the fray by e-mail from the deck of a ship en route from Egypt to Turkey. He commended Randall for her clever play on *Gone With the Wind* and declared her "uncommonly talented." He excoriated Anderson and Clarke for their tenaciousness in protecting *Gone With the Wind*, referring to them as "rapacious" and lacking any sense of humor. Conroy also played the race card, expressing indignation that the estate was trying to prevent an African American woman from publishing her first novel.[41]

At a hearing that April before a U.S. District Court in Atlanta, the estate took issue with the accusations of Mitchell and her book being racist. It introduced into evidence Conroy's 1998 letter about Mitchell's fine characterization of African American characters. Moreover, it argued, through outside counsel hired to handle the litigation, race was not germane to the case: "It's not about whether Margaret Mitchell wrote a racist book that may or may not need correcting, and it's not that Ms. Randall cannot write a book, fiction or non-fiction, that expresses the view that slavery was horrible." The salient issue, the estate argued, was a legal one: had Randall gone too far in using Mitchell's copyrighted work in making her point?[42]

The court declared *The Wind Done Gone* "unabated piracy" of Mitchell's novel and ordered Houghton Mifflin to stop "further production, display, distribution, advertising, sale, or offer for sale" of the book pending disposition of the case. The opinion stated that Randall's use of Mitchell's copyrighted material went "well beyond" what was necessary to critique *Gone With the Wind*, thus removing Randall's book "from the safe harbor of parody."[43] Houghton Mifflin immediately appealed, and on May 25, a three-judge panel of the Eleventh U.S. Circuit Court of Appeals lifted the injunction, ruling that the publisher was entitled to a hearing on the merits of the case before the book could be barred from distribution. The Mitchell estate sought a rehearing before the full appeals court, but it would take months to obtain a ruling on that request.

Meanwhile, the legal battle had garnered extensive press coverage, which Houghton Mifflin put to good use. Within days of the appellate court's decision, the publisher had *The Wind Done Gone* in the nation's bookstores, with a dust jacket declaring it "The Unauthorized Parody" of *Gone With the Wind*. Randall became an overnight sensation by giving impassioned press interviews declaring the appeals court decision a victory for free speech. Booksellers treated *The Wind Done Gone* as an imminent blockbuster. They placed large orders, displayed it prominently, and offered promotional discounts—perks generally reserved for books with glowing reviews or a proven sales record.[44] In the short run, the bets paid off as the book quickly landed on bestseller lists.

But the fascination did not last long. Critical reviews of Randall's work were mixed. While *Booklist* called it "brilliant" and *Publishers Weekly* credited Randall with "sharp" insights, *The Wind Done Gone* left many critics unsatisfied. In the *New York Times*, Megan Harlan said the lawsuit over the book was more interesting than the book itself.[45] Lisa Schwarzbaum of *Entertainment Weekly* called *The Wind Done Gone* "a shack" compared to the "impregnable fortress" of *Gone With the Wind*.[46] Other critics questioned Randall's motives, suggesting that she had written the book as a publicity stunt rather than as a thoughtful political commentary. A nationally syndicated editorial cartoon depicted Randall in front of her computer working on her "next book"—"The Mockingbird Done Died."[47]

Randall's celebrity appeal suffered further when she made an impolitic appearance that summer at the Margaret Mitchell House, an Atlanta museum located in the Crescent Avenue apartment building where Mitchell wrote most of *Gone With the Wind*. During a question-and-answer period, a young African American woman on the staff of the facility expressed her view that Margaret Mitchell was not a racist. According to press reports, Randall shrieked at the woman, claiming that the staffer had been duped into admiring *Gone With the Wind*. When the young woman tried to apologize for causing offense, Randall asked her to sit down, announcing that she was not going to debate an employee of the Mitchell House. In an effort to smooth over the awkward moment, the facility's director, Mary Rose Taylor, began to speak about "dignity" and "building bridges." As she did, another African American woman approached the microphone to ask a question. Randall interrupted Taylor, reports said, and declared indignantly, "Here we are, silencing another black woman!"[48] Troy Patterson, a critic for *Entertainment Weekly,* was in the audience that day and summed it up as "grotesquely weird."[49] Angela Webster of the *Times-Herald* in Newnan, Georgia, wrote an editorial piece, equating Randall's outburst to "an especially petulant child embarrassing his mother" in a grocery store. "You just want to crawl under a rock and pretend you haven't seen what you've just seen," she wrote, struggling to "convey the awfulness of watching a grown woman lose it so publicly." Webster wrote a parody of her own titled "The Mind Done Gone," with Randall's and Taylor's parts played by characters named Bitter and Nervous.[50]

By the time the Eleventh Circuit denied the estate's request for a rehearing that October, *The Wind Done Gone* had fallen off the *New York Times* bestseller list. Anderson and Clarke decided that a costly legal battle fighting Randall's book was not worth the effort. Over the next several months, the parties reached an out-of-court settlement under which the estate agreed to drop the suit in exchange for Houghton Mifflin making a donation to Atlanta's Morehouse College, a historically black school where Margaret Mitchell anonymously provided financial aid to black medical students in the 1940s. Neither side publicly disclosed the amount of the donation.[51] Houghton Mifflin continued to distribute Randall's book under the parody label.

The media treated the Mitchell trustees as if they had admitted defeat and widely criticized them for having picked on Randall. The copyright extension litigation remained pending, and *The Wind Done Gone* case was cited as a textbook example of a greedy literary estate seeking to block the creative process of a living artist. The backlash of being perceived as overly hawkish did not bother Clarke, then eighty-six, or Anderson, eighty-two, who felt they had nothing for which to apologize. When asked about their image as bad guys, Clarke assured a reporter that he and Anderson did not have horns.[52] They owed a fiduciary duty to the Mitchell estate and, equally important, had made a promise to Stephens Mitchell that they would look after his sister's literary rights. While it might seem overzealous to go after well-intentioned or minor infringements, Anderson pointed out that they do not have the luxury of sitting back and letting people chip away at *Gone With the Wind* a little bit here, a little bit there. At some point, they'd be left with nothing. That said, if he had it to do over again, Anderson later admitted he would not necessarily bother going after Randall. "If we had done absolutely nothing, that book would have faded into the shadows pretty quickly," he stated.[53]

In an interview almost a decade after her book's release, Randall took issue with any suggestion that her book benefited from the publicity surrounding the litigation. While the hype undoubtedly sold books, she suggested the media circus did more harm than good. Many reviewers rushed through *The Wind Done Gone* in an effort to meet publication deadlines, she said, and failed to give it the attention it required. "It was meant to be a difficult book. It's a coded parody grounded in other texts. Many of the critics didn't take the time to read it for what it was." As a result, she said, they missed the point, and her book was dismissed too quickly by a broad segment of readers.[54] But Randall appeared to hold no grudges against the Mitchell estate. "In all honesty, if I had to guess, I think the lawyers actually believed I was trying to steal fans of *Gone With the Wind* for my own financial gain. I suspect it never occurred to them that there are people who actually hate *Gone With the Wind* and what it stands for." The author saw her conflict with the estate as a clash of purposes. "Their focus was on the business of the literary rights. Mine was on the art, heart, and reality of life in the South. They tried to take me to the other side of the street, and that just isn't where my work goes." She maintained that her aim in writing the book was to provoke discussion, a goal she unquestionably achieved. Long past the controversy, Randall said her book "is still doing good work."[55] In the decade since its publication, *The Wind Done Gone* has sold approximately two hundred thousand copies in the United States.[56]

In January 2003, the U.S. Supreme Court upheld the 1998 copyright extension act.[57] This meant *Gone With the Wind* would remain the exclusive property of the Mitchell estate in the United States until 2031, giving the estate another twenty-eight years to control Scarlett and Rhett in the United States. But where did the copyright stand in the rest of the world?

The European Union had granted copyright extensions similar to those in the United States, but not all nations were as generous. In countries where the copyright has expired, *Gone With the Wind* is no longer the exclusive property of the Mitchell estate. The Australian copyright, for instance, expired in 1999, fifty years after Mitchell's death. At least one American writer took advantage of the situation and published through an Australian firm a *Gone With the Wind* sequel that the estate had blocked in the United States several years earlier. The book cannot legally be sold in the United States, but is available for purchase online, making its distribution difficult to police. Also of concern to the estate, in 2004, the Australian version of Project Gutenberg—an online association of volunteers who upload noncopyrighted works onto the Internet—posted an electronic version of *Gone With the Wind* on its server. The estate contacted the organizers and asked them to remove the book or take measures to prevent access in countries where *Gone With the Wind* remained under copyright. Presumably unwilling to battle the estate, Project Gutenberg took the book down.[58] Although the estate denied having forced the site's hand, cyberspace pundits criticized Mitchell's representatives for picking on the innocent and law-abiding Australian book lovers and expecting them to keep up with and enforce American copyright law. The following year, the website reposted Mitchell's book online.

∼

Nearly thirteen years after St. Martin's won the right to publish an authorized sequel to *Gone With the Wind*, the firm released McCaig's *Rhett Butler's People*. McCaig dedicated the 2007 book to Anderson, "Faithful Fiduciary," and offered readers a look at Rhett's life before he met Scarlett and during the long stretches in *Gone With the Wind* in which he was offstage. Ultimately, the couple reunites, albeit in entirely different circumstances than Ripley had imagined.

As had been done for *Scarlett*, St. Martin's embargoed the release. Taking full advantage of the intervening years' worth of technological advancements, an interactive website and e-newsletter offered fans teasers, tidbits, and trivia quizzes. Although many *GWTW* enthusiasts enjoyed the approach, the efforts were seen by some as overly contrived. Valley Haggard, a book reviewer in McCaig's home state of Virginia, said of the process, "It got old. It got boring. I wanted to talk with this so-called-amazing author that the Mitchell Estate handpicked to write the second authorized sequel and I wanted to read his book, not take some stupid quiz."[59]

Once they finally read the book, many critics—including Haggard—were impressed. Few reviews were out-and-out raves, but the overall sense was that McCaig had done greater justice to Mitchell's story than had Ripley. His book debuted at number 5 on the *New York Times* bestseller list and remained on the list for eight weeks. Though *Rhett Butler's People* failed to take America by storm, it stoked interest overseas in Mitchell's original novel, and numerous new editions of *Gone With the Wind* appeared when McCaig's novel was released in at least fifteen countries, including Brazil, Finland, Japan, Korea, Poland, and Russia.

When asked about the possibility of a third sequel, Anderson said he did not think so but would not make any promises. "Something could come along that we couldn't turn down. Never say never."[60] With the second authorized sequel behind them, Anderson and Clarke prepared to turn over the estate's affairs to a new generation of lawyers, their sons Paul Anderson, Jr., and Thomas Hal Clarke, Jr. As the senior Clarke officially retired and the senior Anderson began to step back from his day-to-day duties, their sons were designated trustees. Responsibility for the future of *Gone With the Wind* now rests largely in the younger generation's hands.[61]

In 2008, Scarlett O'Hara had another chance to prove herself onstage. After the Harold Rome musical production failed to set the British or American theatrical worlds on fire in the 1970s, other stage versions of her story— some musical—played in France, Greece, and South Korea, but all met with mixed success. Only in Japan did she seem fully comfortable before the footlights. Undaunted by this track record—or perhaps unaware of it— Margaret Martin, a Los Angeles–based public health expert who dabbled in songwriting as a hobby, decided to try her hand at creating a *Gone With the Wind* musical. Unlike many of the previous adaptors, she focused on Mitchell's book for source material rather than on Selznick's film.

Martin asked the Stephens Mitchell Trusts for the rights to produce her vision of Mitchell's novel, knowing the chances of the estate entrusting such a valuable property to a novice were remote. Indeed, Anderson, Jr., later recalled having thought Martin's proposal a "dead duck."[62] Yet, the committeemen heard her out and came away impressed. After months of discussions, they granted her the rights. Martin scored her next coup when she convinced Sir Trevor Nunn of *Les Miserables* and *Cats* fame to direct the production.

With Nunn's involvement, Martin succeeded in pulling together the necessary financing for her *Gone With the Wind*. She had high expectations for the $9.5 million show when it opened on April 22, 2008, in London's West End. Among the invitation-only guests at the 1,100-seat New London Theatre were the trustees, actress Joan Collins, fashion model Twiggy, and television host Sir David Frost. The production, which starred American actress Jill Paice as Scarlett and Scottish singer Darius Danesh as Rhett, opened with a rousing song titled "Born to Be Free," sung by the slaves at Tara, while narrators set the scene with words from Mitchell's first chapter. The three-and-a-half-hour show closed to a lengthy standing ovation.

Afterward, audience members made their way to the first night party at the nearby Waldorf Hilton hotel. All along the five-block walk down London's famed Drury Lane, theater employees were stationed with candle-lit lanterns and large signs reading: "Road to Tara This Way." The street entrance to the hotel's Palm Court ballroom was flanked with two large torches. Inside, Confederate flags and red, white, and blue bunting decorated the rooms, and a small orchestra played. Guests could sample various Southern dishes, including "Mammy's Jambalaya," "Prissy's Alabama Barbecue," "Big Sam's Three-Bean Chili," and "Cookie's Cajun Sausages," while waiters wearing aprons proclaiming "I'll Never Be Hungry Again" circled the rooms with trays of hors d'oeuvres and glasses of champagne.

Any sense of elation Martin or the estate may have enjoyed came crashing down when the British critics weighed in. Their reviews were brutal. The *Sunday Times* blasted the "interminable tiffs and tantrums" between Rhett and Scarlett "expressed in limp, forgettable songs,"[63] while the *Telegraph* called it a "soullessly efficient" production that "merely feels like one damn thing after another."[64] Scarlett and Rhett closed up their tent after only seventy-nine performances.

Theatrical failings aside, *Gone With the Wind* rolls on. As of 2010, more than thirty million copies of Mitchell's novel have been printed in the United States and abroad, and its publisher expects a profitable future for the remainder of the copyright term. A sure sign of Scribner's faith in the title is that, when Warner Books' paperback license rights expired in 2005, Scribner declined to renew. It wanted the rights for itself. After decades of farming the paperbacks out to independent publishers, Scribner began issuing its own softcover editions of Mitchell's novel. Seventy-five years after its original publication, new editions also continue to appear across Europe and Asia. In China, more than two dozen editions have been issued in the past few years. New countries continue to enter the *Gone With the Wind* family as well; in 2009, the book appeared for the first time in Albania. The motion picture still attracts viewers and regularly lands on "all-time favorites" lists. Clark Gable's famous exit line—"Frankly, my dear, I don't give a damn"—nabbed the number 1 ranking on the American Film Institute's list of one hundred all-time favorite movie quotes. The 1939 film classic remains the most-watched movie in history and, when figures are adjusted for inflation, also still leads the list of top grossers. The movie has gone on to live a new life on videotape, DVD, and Blu-ray as well. When Margaret Mitchell ended her novel with Scarlett's vow that tomorrow would be another day, she never imagined the unending tomorrows her book would experience.

As a new generation of readers reaches maturity with a fresh set of perspectives and tolerances, can Scarlett and Rhett maintain this remarkable pace? The two surviving original trustees believe so. Clarke suggests *Gone With the Wind* is a cultural heirloom for many people: the book was a "big, big thing in those days, and the people who became so intimate with it have passed it down through the years. It's a part of the history of the South."[65] Anderson points to the seemingly unstoppable synergy between Mitchell's novel and Selznick's movie: "It's the unusual combination of a first-class book with a first-class picture."[66] The two men expect the book's literary rights will require careful tending until 2031, when its current copyright term expires, and far beyond. Regardless of whether Congress extends the copyright again, the *Gone With the Wind* trademark remains protected indefinitely, and the estate holds the copyright on the two authorized sequels, both of which will enjoy legal protection for decades beyond Mitchell's original.

No matter what tomorrow holds for the legalities or business affairs of *Gone With the Wind*, one thing is sure: Scarlett O'Hara, the "flighty, fast bit of baggage"[67] Margaret Mitchell created, will live on in the imagination of millions of readers. In 1937, a fan complimented the author on how vividly the book's characters were drawn: "I have heard Scarlett discussed exactly as if she were real; that she is still alive no one seems to doubt. I pointed out to one group that she must be an old, old lady now—ninety years old. But they insisted that one so vitally alive couldn't possibly die."[68] Mitchell agreed, noting that Scarlett had plenty of life left to live, with or without Rhett Butler: "As you say, she would be quite an old lady now, but I cannot help feeling that she is still the same Scarlett, and probably scandalizing her great-grandchildren by refusing to be a lady of the old school."[69]

# Epilogue

The unprecedented success of *Gone With the Wind* earned Margaret Mitchell several hundred thousand dollars amidst the Great Depression. Though only a fraction of that money found its way into her wallet given the skyscraping income tax rates of the era, the author zealously guarded her financial stake in the novel. World War II slowed the income to a trickle but ultimately served to establish Scarlett's story as an international symbol of inspiration. Due to her meticulous protection of *Gone With the Wind*'s copyright, Mitchell was well poised to take advantage of a post-war resurgence of interest. The author's death did not diminish the good fortune of her novel. Stephens Mitchell's careful management and exploitation of his sister's book and its subsidiary rights—including his savvy movie percentage deal in 1963—turned a rising stream of income into a veritable flood. Since his death, the trusts he established to manage the *GWTW* literary rights have generated tens of millions of dollars through two popular sequels, a television miniseries, a menagerie of marketing tie-ins, and, of course, numerous editions of the original novel that continue to be published in the United States and abroad.

Where has all the money gone? The author's two nephews have enjoyed the benefits of their aunt's success but not in an ostentatious way. Stephens Mitchell's older son, Eugene, made several large charitable donations, including $1.5 million to fund a Margaret Mitchell Chair in Humanities and Social Sciences at Atlanta's historically black Morehouse College, another $1.5 million for scholarships at Morehouse's medical school, and $667,000 to preservation efforts at Atlanta's historic Oakland Cemetery, where most of his family is buried. He died in 2007, at the age of seventy-six, survived by his wife. This left the younger son, Joseph—who, like his brother, had no children—the last member of Margaret Mitchell's immediate family. Joe Mitchell still lives in the one-story house in Atlanta where his father moved after tearing down the family home on Peachtree Street in the early 1950s. The estate has not revealed who will inherit the rights going forward.

# Acknowledgments

Don't let our names on the title page fool you. It takes more than two individuals to write a book. Throughout this project we have received assistance and guidance from many people. It would be impossible to list everyone who contributed, but we would like to acknowledge those who made it possible for us to tell this story.

One of the most meaningful aspects of this endeavor has been working with the family members and representatives of the people who played a role in the life of *Gone With the Wind*. In this regard, we owe a special debt of gratitude to the committee members of the Stephens Mitchell Trusts: Paul Anderson, Paul Anderson, Jr., Thomas Hal Clarke, and Thomas Hal Clarke, Jr. In addition to granting us access to and permission to quote from Margaret Mitchell's papers, these gentlemen served as an invaluable source of information about the inner workings of the *GWTW* literary rights. As noted earlier, Lois Cole's children, Linda Taylor Barnes and Turney Allan Taylor, Jr., were also an essential resource; we are honored they allowed us access to their mother's correspondence. Other contributors who shared memories of their relatives include the following: Anne Poland Berg and Karen Berg Kushner (Norman Berg); Brad Brett, Betsy Carpenter, Barrie and Ralph Gonzalez, and Ann Zagari (George Brett, Jr.); Clare Brett Smith and Betsy Carpenter (Richard Brett); Kate Barrett (Kay Brown); Bill Leigh

(W. Colston Leigh); Jane Dieckmann and Craig Zane (John Marsh); Wallace B. McClure and Wallace McClure, Jr. (Wallace McClure); Bonnie Louise Mogelever Pollack (Jacob Mogelever); Merrill and Osmund Geier (Alexandra Ripley); Augusta Saunders (Marion Saunders); Lucie Baird (Walbridge Taft); and Joy Bailey (Annie Laurie Williams). We appreciate the time each of them spent being interviewed and responding to our requests for photographs and documents.

Numerous institutions gave invaluable help as well, either through research assistance, the granting of permissions, or, in several cases, both. We especially wish to thank the staff at the Hargrett Rare Book and Manuscript Library at the University of Georgia for their many courtesies. Mary Ellen Brooks, Melissa Bush, and Mary Linnemann, in particular, responded with grace and thoroughness to our requests. Others who helped along the way include the following: Christine Lee at Simon & Schuster; Thomas Lannon at the New York Public Library; Steve Wilson and Katherine Feo at the Harry Ransom Center at the University of Texas at Austin; Peggy Allan-O'Brien, Joan Hart, and Julie McCarthy at the Kearny Library in Kearny, New Jersey; Daniel Snydacker at the Pequot Public Library in Southport, Connecticut; Tara Craig with the Rare Book and Manuscript Library of Columbia University; Kelly Cornwell and Richard Cruse in the Special Collections department of the Atlanta-Fulton Public Library; Julie Bookman, Diane Lewis, and Mary Rose Taylor, formerly of the Margaret Mitchell House; Beth Bailey and Megan Spears at the Road to Tara Museum; Susan Boone with the Special Collections Division of the Smith College Libraries; Marianne Bradley in Special Collections at McCain Library at Agnes Scott College; E. Kathleen Shoemaker at the Manuscript, Archives, and Rare Book Library of Emory University; Tom Camden and David Grabarek at the Library of Virginia; Sue VerHoef, reference manager at the Atlanta History Center; Shaunna Hunter at Bortz Library of Hampden-Sydney College; and the kind reference librarians at the Richmond Public Library. In addition, permissions were generously granted by the *Atlanta Journal-Constitution*, the *Hollywood Reporter*, Houghton Mifflin Harcourt, the Junior League, *Life*, the *Los Angeles Times*, Mondadori Editore, the *Nation*, Newnan *Times-Herald*, the *New Republic*, *Publishers Weekly*, Random House, *Reader's Digest*, R. R. Bowker, and *Svenska Dagbladet*.

Many individuals kindly provided assistance or consented to be interviewed, including Mel Berger, John Dawes, Evan J. Goldfried, Valley Haggard, Shawn McIntosh, Angela Webster McRae, Joseph Mitchell, Troy

Patterson, Alice Randall, Tom Sabulis, Thomas Selz, Mart Stewart, George Wead, and Daniel Yezbick.

On a personal level, our family and friends have offered endless inspiration and support. For their interest and a large variety of thoughtful suggestions, we thank the following who read the manuscript as it progressed: Eleanor Bridges, Orran Brown, Alan Carter, Linda Collins, Roya Ewing, Ellen P. Firsching, Georgia Kukoski, and Harriett Wiley. We are also fortunate that two Margaret Mitchell and *Gone With the Wind* experts agreed to vet the manuscript: Marianne Walker, author of *Margaret Mitchell and John Marsh: The Love Story behind Gone With the Wind,* whose excitement about this project almost equaled her love for "John and Peggy"; and Herb Bridges, dean of *Gone With the Wind* collectors and a veritable encyclopedia about the book and the film. Herb's enthusiasm, advice, and ready ear have been essential to this project, while his generosity in sharing his collection and his immense knowledge with John Wiley over the past thirty years has made John's experience with *Gone With the Wind* all the richer.

Others whose advice and enthusiasm have helped along the way include Em Bowles Locker Alsop, Susan Atkinson, Anne and Ryland Brown, Chris and Orran Brown, Jr., Lucas Brown, Beverly Buxton, Carly Buxton, Doug Buerlein, Martha Davenport, Boo Echols, Kevin Finto, Raymond Firsching, Marsha Hawkins, Tom Heyes, Joslin Hultzapple, Sarah Innes, Kelly Kyle, Mary Beth McIntire, Joseph Papa, Roma Petkauskas, Coleen Butler Rodriguez, Landon Simpson, Letty Tate, Tasha Tolliver, Mary Wittleder, and the wonderful folks of the James River Writers. Thanks as well to two exceptional high school English teachers—Kathryn Russell for Ellen and Elizabeth Koudelka for John—who inspired and encouraged us in our literary endeavors.

We also are pleased to acknowledge the role of our agent, Jeanne Fredericks, who went far beyond the call of duty on many occasions. And at Taylor Trade Publishing, we are especially grateful to Rick Rinehart, Flannery Scott, Kalen Landow, Alden Perkins, and copyeditor extraordinaire Naomi Burns.

Every effort has been made to obtain necessary permissions for use of copyrighted material. If there have been any omissions, we apologize and will be pleased to make appropriate acknowledgments in any future edition. Of course, shortcomings or mistakes in this book are entirely our own.

~'

# Notes

## KEY TO ENDNOTES

### *Abbreviations*

| | |
|---|---|
| ALW | Annie Laurie Williams |
| GB | George Brett, Jr. |
| HL | Harold Latham |
| JM | John Marsh |
| LC | Lois Dwight Cole Taylor |
| MB | Margaret Baugh |
| MM | Margaret Mitchell Marsh |
| MS | Marion Saunders |
| RB | Richard Brett |
| SM | Stephens Mitchell |

### *Document Repositories*

| | |
|---|---|
| AHC | Margaret Mitchell Collection, James G. Kenan Research Center, Atlanta History Center, Atlanta |
| Barnes | Private collection of Linda Taylor Barnes and Turney Allan Taylor, Jr. |
| Columbia | Annie Laurie Williams Collection, Rare Book and Manuscript Library, Columbia University, New York |
| Emory | Margaret Mitchell Collection, Manuscript, Archives, and Rare Book Library, Emory University, Atlanta |
| HRC | Harry Ransom Humanities Research Center, University of Texas at Austin |
| NYPL | Macmillan Company Records, Manuscripts and Archives Division, New York Public Library, Astor, Lenox, and Tilden Foundations, New York |
| Smith College | Authors Collection, Sophia Smith Collection, Smith College, Northampton, Mass. |
| UGA | Hargrett Rare Book and Manuscript Library, University of Georgia Libraries, Athens, Ga. |

## CHAPTER 1: THIS WOMAN HAS SOMETHING

1. MM to Julia Collier Harris, April 28, 1936, Smith College.
2. Finis Farr, *Margaret Mitchell of Atlanta* (New York: Morrow, 1965), 15; "How *Gone With the Wind* Was Written: An Interview by Medora Perkerson," *Atlanta Journal Magazine*, May 23, 1937.
3. MM to Julia Collier Harris, April 28, 1936, Smith College.
4. MM to Henry Steele Commager, July 10, 1936, UGA.
5. *Facts and Fancies* (Atlanta: Washington Seminary, 1918).
6. Turney Allan Taylor, Jr., interview by Ellen F. Brown, October 2009.
7. Farr, *Margaret Mitchell of Atlanta*, 54.
8. MM to Allen Edee, July 31, 1920, AHC.
9. MM to Julia Collier Harris, April 28, 1936, Smith College.
10. Frances Marsh Zane, "Peggy," 1981, UGA.
11. SM, "Memoir of Margaret Mitchell," 1975, 205, UGA.
12. Frances Marsh Zane, "To J.R.M.," n.d., UGA.
13. MM to Julian Harris, April 21, 1936, Smith College.
14. MM to Florence Billikopf, August 29, 1936, UGA.
15. MM to Mrs. E. L. Sullivan, August 18, 1936, UGA.
16. Julia B. Willet, "Margaret Mitchell," *Junior League Magazine*, November 1936.
17. MM to Julian Harris, April 21, 1936, Smith College.
18. MM to J. Bean, July 25, 1936, UGA.
19. Lamar Q. Ball, "Writing of *Gone With the Wind* Beset by Difficulties, Says Author," *Atlanta Constitution*, November 9, 1936.
20. Willet, "Margaret Mitchell."
21. "How *Gone With the Wind* Was Written."
22. Willet, "Margaret Mitchell."
23. Ball, "Writing of *Gone With the Wind*."
24. Ball, "Writing of *Gone With the Wind*."
25. MM to Stephen Vincent Benét, July 9, 1936, UGA.
26. MM to Harvey Smith, n.d., circa 1928–1929, Emory.
27. Quoted in Farr, *Margaret Mitchell of Atlanta*, 86.
28. Medora Field Perkerson, "Was Margaret Mitchell Writing Another Book?" *Atlanta Journal Magazine*, December 18, 1949.
29. MM to HL, April 16, 1935, NYPL.
30. Linda Taylor Barnes, interview by Ellen F. Brown, November 2009.
31. Barnes, interview.
32. Lois Dwight Cole, "The Story Begins at a Luncheon Bridge in Atlanta," *New York Times*, June 25, 1961.
33. Cole, "The Story Begins."
34. Taylor, interview.
35. LC to MM, December 1, 1933, Barnes.
36. Notes by MM to Norman Berg, October 22, 1936, UGA.
37. MM to HL, April 16, 1935, NYPL.
38. "Harold Latham Searching South for Good Manuscripts," *Atlanta Journal*, April 12, 1935.
39. MM to Thomas W. Palmer, November 25, 1938, NYPL.
40. "Harold Latham Searching South for Good Manuscripts."
41. Memorandum by HL, July 17, 1935, NYPL.
42. HL to LC, April 13, 1935, Barnes.

43. MM to LC, December 14, 1935, Barnes.
44. MM to Mary Marsh, April 17, 1936, UGA; Notes by MM to Norman Berg, October 22, 1936, UGA
45. MM to Mary Marsh, April 17, 1936, UGA
46. HL to MM, April 13, 1935, Barnes
47. MM to Mary Marsh, April 17, 1936, UGA.
48. HL to LC, April 13, 1935, Barnes.
49. MM to J. Donald Adams, July 9, 1936, UGA.
50. MM to HL, April 16, 1935, NYPL.
51. HL to LC, April 18, 1935, Barnes.
52. HL to MM, April 18, 1935, quoted in Farr, *Margaret Mitchell of Atlanta*, 95.
53. Memorandum by LC, n.d., Barnes.
54. HL to MM, July 15, 1935, NYPL.
55. MM to HL, July 9, 1935, NYPL.
56. Memorandum by HL, July 17, 1935, NYPL.
57. HL to MM, July 15, 1936, NYPL.
58. Report by Charles W. Everett, quoted in Farr, *Margaret Mitchell of Atlanta*, 101. Farr reprints large parts of Everett's assessment and thus presumably had access to the report. However, the document's whereabouts today are unknown. It does not appear to be in either the Macmillan files at the New York Public Library or the Margaret Mitchell Marsh papers at the University of Georgia's Hargrett Rare Book and Manuscript Library.
59. Farr, *Margaret Mitchell of Atlanta*, 97.
60. Farr, *Margaret Mitchell of Atlanta*, 101.
61. Wolfgang Saxon, "George P. Brett Is Dead at 91; Headed Macmillan Company," *New York Times*, February 15, 1984.
62. James A. Michener, "Introduction," in *Gone With the Wind*, by Margaret Mitchell, anniversary ed., iii–xii (New York: Macmillan, 1975).
63. Memorandum by HL, July 17, 1935, NYPL.
64. HL to MM, July 17, 1935, NYPL.
65. MM to LC, July 13–17, 1935, Barnes.
66. MM to HL, July 17, 1935, NYPL.
67. HL to MM, July 22, 1935, NYPL.
68. MM to LC, July 25, 1935, Barnes.
69. MM to HL, July 27, 1935, NYPL.
70. MM to HL, August 1, 1935, NYPL.
71. HL to MM, August 5, 1935, NYPL.
72. LC to MM, August 5, 1935, NYPL.
73. MM to HL, August 6, 1935, NYPL.
74. HL to MM, August 9, 1935, NYPL.

## CHAPTER 2: A MANUSCRIPT OF THE OLD SOUTH

1. HL to MM, August 13, 1935, NYPL.
2. MM to HL, July 27, 1935, NYPL.
3. Farr, *Margaret Mitchell of Atlanta*, 107.
4. SM, "Memoir," 88; MM to Gilbert Govan, October 15, 1937, UGA; Margaret Mitchell, *Gone With the Wind* (New York: Macmillan, 1936), 397.

5. Cole, "The Story Begins."

6. MM to HL, July 27, 1935, NYPL.

7. MM to LC, November 11, 1935, Barnes.

8. Ball, "Writing of *Gone With the Wind.*"

9. MM to HL, September 3, 1935, NYPL.

10. JM to LC, February 9, 1936, NYPL.

11. Statement by MM, August 1, 1939, *GWTW* Literary Rights office, Atlanta.

12. MM to HL, September 3, 1935, NYPL.

13. HL to MM, September 10, 1935, NYPL.

14. Statement by MM, August 1, 1939, *GWTW* Literary Rights office, Atlanta.

15. "How *Gone With the Wind* Was Written"; *Margaret Mitchell and Her Novel* (New York: Macmillan, 1936), 20–21.

16. MM to HL, June 1, 1936, UGA.

17. MM to Harry Slattery, October 3, 1936, UGA; MM to Harry E. Ransford, January 4, 1937, UGA; MM to Franklin Garrett, February 23, 1939, UGA.

18. MM to Mr. and Mrs. Francis M. Swords, May 8, 1944, UGA.

19. MM to LC, October 3, 1935, NYPL.

20. MM to Frances Beach, October 19, 1936, UGA.

21. Everett Hale to Mr. Lund, October 28, 1935, NYPL.

22. LC to MM, October 30, 1935, NYPL.

23. MM to HL, October 30, 1935, NYPL.

24. MM to HL, October 30, 1935, NYPL.

25. MM to HL, October 30, 1935, NYPL.

26. HL to MM, November 4, 1935, NYPL.

27. LC to MM, November 7, 1935, NYPL.

28. JM to LC, January 30, 1936, NYPL.

29. MM to LC, November 11, 1935, Barnes.

30. LC to MM, November 14, 1935, Barnes.

31. LC to Mr. Lund, November 4, 1935, NYPL.

32. LC to Mr. Lund, November 4, 1935, NYPL.

33. Daniel Yezbick, interview by Ellen F. Brown, January 2009.

34. MM to Wilbur G. Kurtz, November 19, 1935, UGA.

35. MM to Henry Stuckey, December 3, 1935, UGA.

36. LC to MM, December 6, 1935, Barnes.

37. LC to MM, December 6, 1935, Barnes.

38. LC to MM, December 18, 1935, NYPL.

39. LC to MM, December 19, 1935, NYPL.

40. MM to LC, December 19, 1935, NYPL.

41. LC to MM, December 20, 1935, NYPL.

42. JM to LC, January 20, 1936, NYPL.

43. Notes by JM, circa April 1952, UGA.

44. JM to Mary Marsh, March 22, 1936, UGA.

45. MM to Mary Marsh, January 13, 1936, UGA.

46. JM to LC, January 31, 1936, UGA.

47. Michener, "Introduction."

48. Hugh Eayrs to GB, April 4, 1938, NYPL.

49. Hugh Eayrs to GB, April 4, 1938, NYPL.

50. Everett Hale to J. P. Smith, January 3, 1936, NYPL.

51. MM to Mary Marsh, January 13, 1936, UGA.

52. MB to LC, January 7, 1936, NYPL.

53. LC to MM, January 11, 1936, NYPL.
54. MB to LC, January 16, 1936, NYPL.
55. MB to LC, March 4, 1936, UGA.
56. GB to MM, April 24, 1936, NYPL.
57. "Publisher Notes Changed Habits of Reading," *Atlanta Journal*, January 19, 1936.
58. Cole, "The Story Begins."
59. Marianne Walker, *Margaret Mitchell and John Marsh: The Love Story behind* Gone With the Wind (Atlanta: Peachtree Publishers, 1993), 233.
60. JM to LC, January 28, 1936, NYPL.

## CHAPTER 3: IN COLD TYPE

1. Barnes, interview.
2. LC to Everett Hale, February 3, 1936, NYPL.
3. LC to JM, February 3, 1936, NYPL.
4. JM to LC, January 31, 1936, NYPL.
5. JM to LC, January 31, 1936, NPYL.
6. LC to Everett Hale, February 3, 1936, NYPL.
7. LC to JM, February 3, 1936, NYPL.
8. LC to MM, February 6, 1936, NYPL.
9. Memorandum by HL, July 17, 1935, NYPL.
10. LC to MM, February 6, 1936, NYPL.
11. Michener, "Introduction."
12. Anne Zagari, interview by Ellen F. Brown, December 2009.
13. LC to MM, February 6, 1936, NYPL.
14. JM to family, March 22, 1936, UGA.
15. JM to GB, October 29, 1947, UGA.
16. LC to MM, February 5, 1936, NYPL.
17. Westbrook Pegler, "Fair Enough," *Atlanta Constitution*, November 28, 1936.
18. MM to Mary Marsh, April 17, 1936, UGA.
19. William W. Hawkins, Jr., to Everett Hale, February 12, 1936, NYPL.
20. MM to Henry Stuckey, February 3, 1936, UGA.
21. JM to LC, February 13, 1936, NYPL.
22. LC to MM, February 20, 1936, NYPL.
23. JM to LC, February 13, 1936, NYPL.
24. LC to JM, February 15, 1936, NYPL.
25. LC to JM, February 15, 1936, NYPL.
26. LC to MM, February 20, 1936, NYPL.
27. MM to Mary Marsh, February 25, 1936, UGA.
28. Howard McLellan, "The Making of a Best Seller," *American Business*, April 1937.
29. Clare Brett Smith, interview by Ellen F. Brown, December 2009; Betsy Carpenter, interview by Ellen F. Brown, December 2009.
30. Helen C. Smith, "Auction Gets Rare *GWTW*," *Atlanta Constitution*, May 27, 1976.
31. Yolande Gwin, "Margaret Mitchell's Novel Depicts Three Major Periods," *Atlanta Constitution*, February 6, 1936.
32. MM to Yolande Gwin, February 10, 1936, quoted in Yolande Gwin, ed., *I Remember Margaret Mitchell* (Lakemont, Ga.: Copple House Books, 1987).

33. Farr, *Margaret Mitchell of Atlanta*, 112.

34. JM to LC, February 9, 1936, NYPL.

35. LC to JM, February 13, 1936, NYPL.

36. MM to Julia Collier Harris, April 28, 1936, Smith College.

37. MM to Paul Jordan-Smith, May 27, 1936, UGA.

38. MM to LC, March 18, 1936, NYPL.

39. George Stevens, *Lincoln Doctor's Dog, and Other Famous Best Sellers* (Philadelphia: J. B. Lippincott, 1939), 68.

40. Charles Lee, *The Hidden Public: The Story of the Book-of-the-Month Club* (New York: Doubleday, 1958), 70.

41. LC to MM, March 9, 1936, NYPL.

42. LC to James Putnam, February 19, 1936, NYPL.

43. James Putnam to Basil Davenport, February 26, 1936, NYPL.

44. LC to MM, March 7, 1936, NYPL.

45. LC to MM, March 9, 1936, NYPL.

46. MM to LC, March 14, 1936, NYPL.

47. MM to Frances Marsh Zane, April 10, 1936, UGA.

48. LC to MM, March 19, 1936, NYPL.

49. HL to Everett Hale, December 31, 1935; Everett Hale to J. P. Smith, January 3, 1936, NYPL.

50. JM to family, March 22, 1936, UGA.

51. MM to LC, March 18, 1936, NYPL.

52. JM to family, March 22, 1936, UGA.

53. MM to LC, March 22, 1936, NYPL.

54. LC to MM, March 24, 1936, NYPL.

55. Deposition by GB, December 15, 1937, UGA.

56. HL to William Allen White, March 23, 1936, NYPL.

57. HL to William Allen White, March 23, 1936, NYPL.

58. William Allen White to HL, March 24, 1936, NYPL.

59. W. Colston Leigh to MM, March 27, 1936, NYPL.

60. LC to MM, March 31, 1936, NYPL.

61. MM to LC, April 14, 1936, Barnes.

62. MM to W. Colston Leigh, April 9, 1936, NYPL.

63. W. Colston Leigh to HL, April 15, 1936, NYPL.

64. W. Colston Leigh to MM, May 20, 1936, NYPL.

65. MM to HL, May 25, 1936, NYPL.

## CHAPTER 4: A BOOK WITH DEFINITE POSSIBILITIES

1. MM to LC, March 14, 1936, NYPL.

2. LC to MM, March 9, 1936, NYPL.

3. Howard Fast, *Being Red* (Boston: Houghton Mifflin, 1990), 161.

4. ALW to LC, March 5, 1936, Columbia.

5. LC to MM, April 29, 1936, NYPL; Taylor, interview.

6. LC to MM, March 9, 1936, NYPL.

7. MM to ALW, March 10, 1936, Columbia.

8. MM to LC, March 14, 1936, NYPL.

9. LC to MM, March 16, 1936, NYPL.

10. LC to MM, April 9, 1936, NYPL.

11. MM to LC, April 14, 1936, Barnes.

12. LC to JM, February 3, 1936, NYPL.; HL to J. P. Smith, May 8, 1936, NYPL.

13. McLellan, "The Making of a Best Seller."

14. Daniel Yezbick, "Riddles of Engagement: Narrative Play in the Children's Media and Comic Art of George Carlson," *ImageTexT: Interdisciplinary Comics Studies*, 2007, at www.english.ufl.edu/imagetext/archives/v3_3/yezbick (accessed August 12, 2010).

15. Frank Daniel, "Simplicity, Loyalty and Love Produced *Gone With the Wind*," *Atlanta Journal*, August 17, 1949.

16. JM to LC, January 31, 1936, NYPL.

17. LC to Mr. Lund, February 3, 1936, NYPL.

18. Summary of remarks by [GB], April 25, 1938, NYPL.

19. Meredith Wood to GB, April 15, 1936, NYPL.

20. Deposition by GB, December 15, 1937, UGA.

21. HL to J. P. Smith, May 5, 1936, NYPL.

22. HL to MM, May 5, 1936, NYPL.

23. LC to MM, April 21, 1936, NYPL.

24. MM to LC, April 27, 1936, NYPL.

25. MM to LC, April 27, 1936, NYPL.

26. Frances Marsh Zane, "My Dearly Beloved Young Lady," n.d., 11, UGA.

27. Robert R. Nathan, "National Income in 1937 Largest since 1929," *Survey of Current Business*, June 1938.

28. Deposition by GB, December 15, 1937, UGA.

29. LC to MM, May 18, 1936, NYPL.

30. "The New N.G.B.R. Displays," *Publishers Weekly*, June 20, 1936.

31. McLellan, "The Making of a Best Seller."

32. LC to MM, April 29, 1936, NYPL.

33. Ida Wilkinson to Norman Berg, May 28, 1936, NYPL.

34. Quoted in LC to ALW, June 16, 1936, NYPL.

35. LC to MM, April 29, 1936, NYPL.

36. First edition of *Gone With the Wind*, inscribed to MB, Special Collections, McCain Library, Agnes Scott College, Decatur, GA.

37. MM to LC, May 5, 1936, NYPL.

38. LC to MM, May 29, 1936, NYPL.

39. Ruth Rae to LC, April 15, 1936, NYPL.

40. LC to MM, April 21, 1936, NYPL.

41. MM to LC, April 27, 1936, NYPL.

42. MM to LC, May 5, 1936, NYPL.

43. LC to MM, April 29, 1936, NYPL.

44. MM to LC, April 27, 1936, NYPL.

45. MM to HL, January 8, 1937, NYPL.

46. MM to LC, May 5, 1936, NYPL.

47. MM to LC, May 5, 1936, NYPL.

48. MM to Julia Collier Harris, June 29, 1936, UGA.

49. MM to Julia Collier Harris, June 29, 1936, UGA.

50. MM to HL, May 25, 1936, NYPL.

51. SM to GB, September 21, 1936, NYPL.

52. LC to ALW, May 6, 1936, NYPL.

53. ALW to LC, May 11, 1936, NYPL.

54. Everett Hale to HL, May 18, 1936, NYPL.

55. Kay Brown to David O. Selznick, July 7, 1936, HRC.
56. Everett Hale to HL, May 18, 1936, NYPL.
57. ALW to HL, May 19, 1936, NYPL.
58. HL to GB, May 20, 1936, NYPL.
59. ALW to HL, May 19, 1936, NYPL.
60. HL to ALW, May 26, 1936, Columbia.
61. Macmillan London to Macmillan New York, telegram, April 2, 1936, NYPL.
62. HL to Macmillan London, April 3, 1936, NYPL.
63. Macmillan London to Macmillan New York, April 6, 1936, NYPL.
64. Macmillan London to Macmillan New York, April 7, 1936, NYPL.
65. HL to William A. Collins, April 6, 1936, NYPL.
66. GB to Harold Macmillan, April 4, 1936, NYPL.
67. GB to Macmillan London, April 16, 1936, NYPL.
68. Macmillan London to Macmillan New York, April 17, 1936, NYPL.
69. James Putnam to William A. Collins, April 22, 1936, NYPL.
70. William A. Collins to James Putnam, April 23, 1936, NYPL.
71. William A. Collins to HL, April 23, 1936, NYPL.
72. GB to Harold Macmillan, April 23, 1936, NYPL.
73. Harold Macmillan to GB, April 24, 1936, NYPL.
74. GB to HL, April 24, 1936, NYPL.
75. GB to MM, April 24, 1936, NYPL.
76. William A. Collins to Macmillan New York, April 20, 1936, NYPL.
77. William A. Collins to Macmillan New York, May 4, 1936, NYPL.
78. HL to Harold Macmillan, May 5, 1936, NYPL.
79. HL to William A. Collins, May 5, 1936, NYPL.
80. William A. Collins to HL, May 6, 1936, NYPL; William A. Collins to HL, May 15, 1936, NYPL.
81. William A. Collins to HL, May 7, 1936, NYPL.
82. HL to William A. Collins, May 6, 1936, NYPL.
83. HL to William A. Collins, May 18, 1936, NYPL.
84. MM to HL, May 13, 1936, NYPL.
85. HL to MM, May 18, 1936, NYPL.
86. MM to HL, May 21, 1936, NYPL.
87. HL to GB, May 25, 1936, NYPL.
88. Harold Macmillan to HL, May 26, 1936, NYPL.
89. HL to GB, June 1, 1936, NYPL.

## CHAPTER 5: FANNING THE FLAME

1. Book-of-the-Month Club to Thomas Seltzer, May 16, 1936, NYPL; Everett Hale to J. P. Smith, May 18, 1936, NYPL.
2. Macmillan, advertisement for *Gone With the Wind*, *Publishers Weekly*, May 23, 1936.
3. HL to MM, May 21, 1936, NPYL.
4. MM to HL, May 25, 1936, NYPL.
5. HL to MM, May 27, 1936, NYPL.
6. LC to MM, May 28, 1936, NYPL.
7. LC to MM, May 28, 1936, NYPL.

8. JM to GB, October 29, 1947, NYPL.

9. MM to LC, May 29, 1936, NYPL.

10. MM to HL, June 1, 1936, NYPL.

11. MM to HL, May 25, 1936, NYPL; MM to HL, June 1, 1936, NYPL.

12. HL to Sonia Chapter, May 11, 1936, NYPL.

13. LC to MM, May 18, 1936, NYPL.

14. Simone de Beauvoir, *Letters to Sartre* (New York: Arcade, 1991), 414.

15. MS to MM, May 1, 1936, NYPL.

16. MM to MS, May 8, 1936, UGA.

17. MS to MM, May 11, 1936, NYPL.

18. MM to MS, May 13, 1936, NYPL.

19. MM to LC, May 14, 1936, NYPL.

20. LC to MM, May 18, 1936, NYPL.

21. HL to Sonia Chapter, May 11, 1936, NYPL.

22. MS to MM, May 22, 1936, NYPL.

23. HL to Sonia Chapter, May 26, 1936, NYPL.

24. MM to MS, May 27, 1936, UGA.

25. MM to W. F. Caldwell, June 16, 1936, NYPL.

26. MM to HL, May 21, 1936, NYPL.

27. JM to LC, July 13, 1936, NYPL.

28. Deposition by GB, December 15, 1937, UGA.

29. GB to J. A. Fruin, April 25, 1938, NYPL.

30. John S. Kidd & Son to Patron, June 18, 1936, NYPL.

31. Deposition by GB, December 15, 1937, UGA.

32. Everett Hale to HL, September 13, 1949, NYPL.

33. Deposition by Hugh Eayrs, Exhibit G, July 8, 1938, UGA.

34. ALW to Maurice Hanlon, June 15, 1936, Columbia.

35. ALW to HL, June 10, 1936, Columbia.

36. Rosalie Stewart to ALW, July 3, 1936, Columbia.

37. ALW to HL, May 27, 1936, NYPL.

38. Kay Brown to David O. Selznick, May 26, 1936, HRC.

39. ALW to HL, May 27, 1936, NYPL.

40. HL to MM, June 17, 1936, as quoted in SM to GB, September 21, 1936, NYPL.

41. HL to LC, June 14, 1936, as quoted in SM to GB, September 21, 1936, NYPL.

42. SM to GB, September 21, 1936, NYPL.

43. MM to LC, June 15, 1936, NYPL.

44. ALW to LC, June 24, 1936, NYPL.

45. David Thomson, *Showman: The Life of David O. Selznick* (New York: Knopf, 1992), 130.

46. Kay Brown to David O. Selznick, May 21, 1936, HRC.

47. David O. Selznick to Kay Brown, May 25, 1936, HRC.

48. Kay Brown to David O. Selznick, May 26, 1936, HRC.

49. JM to Mary Marsh, June 26, 1936, UGA.

50. "The Night before Publication," n.d., AHC; "Mrs. Luise Sims Gives Dinner in Honor of Margaret Mitchell," *Atlanta Journal*, June 23, 1936.

51. MM to Julia Collier Harris, July 8, 1936, NYPL.

52. MM to Marian Sims, June 20, 1936, AHC.

53. JM to Mary Marsh, June 26, 1936, UGA.

54. MM to Julia Collier Harris, June 29, 1936, Smith College.

55. Lamar Q. Ball, "Margaret Mitchell Seeks in Vain for Time to Get Her Hair Washed," *Atlanta Constitution*, November 10, 1936.

56. MM to LC, April 27, 1936, NYPL.

57. SM, "Memoir," 198.

58. MM to Julia Collier Harris, June 29, 1936, Smith College.

59. MM to Ruth Hinman Carter, June 22, 1936, UGA.

60. LC to MM, June 5, 1936, NPYL.

61. LC to Charles J. Trenkle, June 10, 1936, NYPL.

62. Ruth Hinman Carter to MM, June 20, 1936, UGA.

63. MM to GB, June 6, 1936, NYPL.

64. JM to Ernest Camp, Jr., June 25, 1936, UGA.

65. MM to Clark Howell, June 28, 1936, UGA; "Atlanta Historical Society Will Honor Mrs. John R. Marsh," *Atlanta Constitution*, June 26, 1936.

## CHAPTER 6: THE MAKING OF A COLOSSAL UPPER-CASE SUCCESS

1. LC to MM, June 30, 1936, NYPL.

2. Ralph Thompson, "Books of the Times," *New York Times*, June 30, 1936.

3. ALW to Bosley Crowther, June 15, 1956, Columbia.

4. LC to Louis Freedman, July 1, 1936, NYPL.

5. Richard Harwell, *An Enduring Legacy: Margaret Mitchell's* Gone With the Wind (Dublin, Ga.: Gone With the Wind Forum '91, 1991), 12; Anne Edwards, *Road to Tara: The Life of Margaret Mitchell* (New Haven, Conn.: Ticknor & Fields, 1983), 208.

6. "The Night before Publication," n.d., AHC.

7. "Davison-Paxon Remodels Book Department," *Publishers Weekly*, November 20, 1937.

8. J. P. Smith to Everett Hale, July 1, 1936, NYPL.

9. George Brett, Sr. to MM, July 1, 1936, NYPL; notes on Finis Farr draft by MB, October 1964, UGA.

10. MM to LC, July 4, 1936, NYPL.

11. Reviews quoted in Mertice James, ed., *The Book Review Digest* (New York: H. W. Wilson, 1937).

12. Quoted in *Literary Digest*, July 25, 1936.

13. "Three Historical Novels," *New Yorker*, July 4, 1936.

14. J. Donald Adams, "A Fine Novel of the Civil War," *New York Times Book Review*, July 5, 1936.

15. Henry Steele Commager, "The Civil War in Georgia's Red Clay Hills," *New York Herald Tribune Books*, July 5, 1936.

16. Julian Meade to HL, July 16, 1936, NYPL.

17. Sara Field to Macmillan, July 4, 1936, NYPL.

18. "The Difficulties of Success," *Publishers Weekly*, September 19, 1936.

19. Robert Garland to Macmillan, [June] 1936, NYPL.

20. William W. Hawkins, Jr., to Everett Hale, July 1, 1936, NYPL.

21. Macmillan, advertisement, *Publishers Weekly*, July 4, 1936.

22. MM to Herschel Brickell, July 7, 1936, UGA.

23. MM to LC, July 3, 1936, NYPL.

24. LC to Alec Blanton, July 6, 1936, NYPL.

25. MM to LC, July 2, 1936, NYPL.

26. MM to LC, July 3, 1936, NYPL.

27. MM to J. Donald Adams, July 9, 1936, UGA.
28. MM to GB, March 15, 1937, UGA.
29. JM to LC, July 13, 1936, NYPL.
30. LC to Alec Blanton, July 6 1936, NYPL; JM to Alec Blanton, July 22, 1936, NYPL.
31. James Putnam to JM, July 2, 1936, NYPL.
32. JM to Mary Marsh, July 19, 1936, UGA.
33. MS to Everett Hale, July 16, 1936, NYPL.
34. James Putnam to Hugh Eayrs, July 13, 1936, NYPL.
35. Ellen Elliott to James Putnam, July 14, 1936, NYPL.
36. James Putnam to Ellen Elliott, July 27, 1936, NYPL.
37. Kay Brown to David O. Selznick, July 7, 1936, HRC.
38. LC to JM, July 8, 1936, NYPL.
39. LC to MM, July 8, 1936, NYPL.
40. JM to LC, July 13, 1936, NYPL.
41. SM, "Memoir," 111.
42. JM to LC, July 13, 1936, NYPL.
43. JM to LC, July 13, 1936, NYPL.
44. ALW to Bosley Crowther, June 5, 1956, Columbia.
45. LC to JM, July 14, 1936, NYPL.
46. LC to JM, July 15, 1936, NYPL.
47. JM to LC, July 27, 1936, NYPL.
48. JM to LC, July 27, 1936, NYPL.
49. MM to HL, August 13, 1936, UGA.
50. MM to Herschel Brickell, July 26, 1936, quoted in SM, "Memoir," 111.
51. ALW to Para Lee Brock, March 16, 1956, Columbia.
52. MM to GB, May 20, 1938, NYPL.
53. SM, "Memoir," 111–12.
54. Martin Shartar, "The Winds of Time and Chance: Stephens Mitchell Surveys Seven Decades in Atlanta," *Atlanta*, July 1974.
55. MM to Kay Brown, September 3, 1936.
56. SM to Kay Brown, December 19, 1967, UGA.
57. SM to GB, September 21, 1936, NYPL.
58. Extract of draft letter from JM, June 1937, UGA.
59. Barnes, interview.
60. SM, "Memoir," 112.
61. SM, "Memoir," 113-A.
62. SM, "Memoir," 112.
63. SM, "Memoir," 113-A.
64. JM to Edwin Granberry and Herschel Brickell, July 30, 1936, Tom Heyes Collection, Los Angeles.


## CHAPTER 7: THAT BOOK ABOUT THE WIND

1. Frank Luther Mott, *Golden Multitudes* (New York: Macmillan, 1947), 256–57.
2. "*Gone With the Wind* Book of Many Names," *Richmond Times Dispatch*, August 9, 1936.
3. Mott, *Golden Multitudes*, 257.

4. Memorandum by Macmillan, July 15, 1936, NYPL.

5. Hugh Eayrs to GB, April 4, 1938, NYPL.

6. "Books: North v. South," *Time*, March 7, 1938.

7. J. P. Smith to Everett Hale, July 1, 1936, NYPL; "Margaret Mitchell's Novel Literally *Gone With Wind*," *Atlanta Journal*, August 9, 1936.

8. LC to Silas Peavy, August 8, 1936, NYPL.

9. McLellan, "The Making of a Best Seller."

10. Macmillan, advertisement, *Publishers Weekly*, August 15, 1936.

11. Jack Phillips to Alec Blanton, September 25, 1936, NYPL.

12. Silas Peavy to LC, August 24, 1936, NYPL.

13. LC to Silas Peavy, August 28, 1936, NYPL.

14. JM to James Putnam, August 11, 1936, NYPL.

15. Hellmut Lehmann-Haupt, *The Book in America: A History of the Making and Selling of Books in the United States* (New York: R. R. Bowker, 1952), 378.

16. "The Difficulties of Success."

17. Ginny Morris to MM, n.d., UGA.

18. Memorandum by Macmillan, n.d., NYPL.

19. "Currents in the Trade," *Publishers Weekly*, April 10, 1937.

20. E. Smalley to Mrs. G. C. Barnum, December 12, 1936, NPYL.

21. Howard Otten to Macmillan, March 22, 1937, NYPL.

22. Howard Otten to Macmillan, March 26, 1937, NYPL; Harvey E. Runner, "Macy's Resells 35,940 Copies of Best Seller to Macmillan Co.," *New York Herald Tribune*, March 24, 1937.

23. JM to James Putnam, July 23, 1936, NYPL; James Putnam to JM, July 27, 1936, NYPL.

24. London to James Putnam, August 24, 1936, NYPL; Charles Morgan, *The House of Macmillan (1843–1943)* (New York: Macmillan, 1944), 230.

25. James Putnam to JM, August 25, 1936, NYPL.

26. GB to MM, November 25, 1936, NYPL.

27. David O. Selznick to Kay Brown, July 15, 1936, HRC.

28. Dorothy Modisett to LC, December 9, 1936, NYPL.

29. Russell Birdwell to Louis N. Freedman, October 6, 1936, Columbia.

30. JM to K. T. Lowe, August 3, 1936, UGA.

31. James Putnam to H. O. Owen, August 31, 1936, NYPL.

32. James Putnam to JM, August 11, 1936, NYPL.

33. ALW to HL, October 16, 1936, NYPL.

34. SM, "Memoir," 113-B.

35. SM, "Memoir," 113-C.

36. SM, "Memoir," 114-A.

37. JM to GB, October 6, 1936, UGA.

38. James Putnam to JM, August 11, 1936, NYPL.

39. GB to JM, September 3, 1936, as quoted in SM to GB, September 21, 1936, NYPL.

40. SM to GB, September 21, 1936, NYPL.

41. MM to Allan Taylor, October 5, 1936, UGA.

42. Paul Anderson, interview by John Wiley, Jr., January 2010.

43. MM to Allan Taylor, October 5, 1936, UGA.

44. Allan Taylor to MM, October 3, 1936, UGA.

45. MM to HL, September 23, 1936, NYPL.

46. MM to HL, September 23, 1936, NYPL.

47. MM to HL, September 25, 1936, NYPL.

48. HL to MM, October 6, 1936, NYPL.

49. HL to MM, October 6, 1936, NYPL.

50. Henry W. Taft to GB, October 6, 1936, NYPL.

51. James Putnam to JM, October 6, 1936, NYPL.

52. SM, "Memoir," 114-A.

53. JM to LC, October 20, 1936, NYPL.

54. HL to JM, October 26, 1936, NYPL.

## CHAPTER 8: THE RELUCTANT CELEBRITY

1. Sidney Howard to MM, November 18, 1936, UGA.

2. JM to GB, November 28, 1947, NYPL.

3. Oscar R. Strauss, Jr., to MM, August 17, 1936, UGA.

4. HL to Accounting, November 6, 1936, NYPL.

5. HL to Mr. Myers, October 15, 1936, NYPL.

6. "*Gone With Wind* Pages Are Recovered by Ruse," *Atlanta Constitution*, November 14, 1936.

7. "Random Notes on the N.Y. Times Book Fair," *Publishers Weekly*, November 21, 1936.

8. MM to Herschel Brickell, December 8, 1936, UGA; MM to Kay Brown, September 12, 1938, UGA.

9. George W. Stimpson to Macmillan, November 9, 1936, NYPL; LC to George W. Stimpson, November 18, 1936, NYPL.

10. MM to Julia Willett, September 9, 1936, UGA.

11. MM to LC, April 8, 1937, NYPL.

12. Ralph McGill, "*Gone With the Wind*," *Red Barrel*, September 15, 1936.

13. MM to Raymond G. Carpenter, July 25, 1936, UGA.

14. MM to Vivian Coates, November 4, 1936, UGA.

15. Kathryn Clack to MM, November 30, 1936, UGA.

16. Mrs. Will Carter to MM, February 1937, UGA.

17. MM to HL, December 3, 1938, NYPL.

18. Walker, *Margaret Mitchell and John Marsh*, 340.

19. MM to HL, May 31, 1937, NYPL.

20. Mitchell, *Gone With the Wind*, 668.

21. R. E. Hutchinson to James Putnam, September 2, 1936, NYPL.

22. Norman Berg, "The Real Story of *Gone With the Wind*," *Atlanta Constitution*, November 29, 1936.

23. JM to Mary Marsh, September 26, 1936, UGA.

24. MM to James Putnam, April 22, 1937, NYPL.

25. MM to Herschel Brickell, October 9, 1936, UGA.

26. Albert C. Leitch, "*Gone With Wind* Presses Going Strong, Pass 656,000," *Atlanta Constitution*, October 21, 1936.

27. MM to GB, November 17, 1937, NYPL.

28. Katharine Bleckley to MM, September 2, 1936, UGA.

29. MM to LC, March 5, 1937, UGA.

30. Edwin Granberry, "The Private Life of Margaret Mitchell," *Collier's*, March 13, 1937.

31. Zane, "My Dearly Beloved Young Lady," 21.

32. Zane, "Peggy," 11.

33. MM to LC, March 5, 1937, UGA.

34. MM to Robert L. Bullard, March 15, 1937, UGA.

35. MM to Harris Dunn, December 12, 1936, Smith College.

36. MM to K. T. Lowe, August 29, 1936, UGA.

37. JM to James Putnam, August 11, 1936, NYPL.

38. MM to Mr. Osbourne, November 30, 1936, UGA.

39. MM to Mrs. Williams, March 11, 1937, AHC.

40. MM to Mary Davenport Combes, August 19, 1948, UGA.

41. Medora Field Perkerson, "Double Life of Margaret Mitchell," *Atlanta Journal Sunday Magazine*, May 16, 1937; MM to Lucy Caldwell, November 17, 1936, UGA.

42. MM to Herschel Brickell, November 17, 1937, UGA.

43. MM to Paul Jordan-Smith, September 23, 1936, UGA.

44. Paul Jordan-Smith to MM, October 11, 1936, UGA.

45. L. Markowitz to MM, October 27, 1936, UGA.

46. MM to L. Markowitz, October 28, 1936, UGA.

47. MM to Alec Blanton, September 23, 1936, NYPL.

48. Alec Blanton to MM, September 29, 1936, NYPL.

49. Ball, "Margaret Mitchell Seeks."

50. SM, "Memoir," 118.

51. Ball, "Margaret Mitchell Seeks."

52. Lamar Q. Ball, "Fame's Tempo Has Been Quickened, According to Margaret Mitchell," *Atlanta Constitution*, November 11, 1936.

53. Lamar Q. Ball, "All Modern Publishing Records Smashed by *Gone With the Wind*," *Atlanta Constitution*, November 13, 1936.

54. Ball, "All Modern Publishing Records."

55. SM, "Memoir," 118.

56. MM to Ginny Morris, April 21, 1937, UGA.

57. Ginny Morris to MM, April 29, 1937, UGA.

58. LC to MB, December 12, 1954, UGA.

59. Barnes, interview.

60. "*Gone With Wind* Nearing Million," *Atlanta Constitution*, December 3, 1936.

61. Macmillan sales statement for *Gone With the Wind*, August 1, 1937, NYPL.

62. Michener, "Introduction."

63. Notes on Farr manuscript by MB, May 21, 1965, Emory.

64. "News from Publishers," *Publishers Weekly*, December 5, 1936.

65. MM to LC, December 4, 1936, NYPL.

66. HL to GB, December 8, 1936, NYPL.

67. MM to HL, January 8, 1937, NYPL.

68. MM to Gladys Platner, April 18, 1940, Smith College.

69. JM to Mary Louise Nute, December 14, 1936, as quoted in Walker, *Margaret Mitchell and John Marsh*, 343.

70. MM to LC, April 23, 1937, NYPL.

71. Zane, "My Dearly Beloved Young Lady," 15.

72. Statement by MM, August 1, 1936, *GWTW* Literary Rights office, Atlanta.

## CHAPTER 9: GONE WITH THE WIND, INC.

1. Statement by MM, August 1, 1939, *GWTW* Literary Rights office, Atlanta.

2. Statement by MM, August 1, 1939, *GWTW* Literary Rights office, Atlanta.

3. Zane, "Peggy," 12.

4. MM to LC, March 5, 1937, UGA.

5. Ruth Hinman Carter to MM, November 21, 1936, UGA.

6. MM to LC, March 5, 1937, UGA

7. MM to LC, March 5, 1937, UGA

8. MM to LC, March 5, 1937, UGA.

9. MM to Herschel Brickell, February 8, 1937, UGA.

10. Perkerson, "Double Life of Margaret Mitchell."

11. Faith Baldwin, "The Woman Who Wrote *Gone With the Wind*, An Exclusive and Authentic Interview," *Pictorial Review*, March 1937.

12. JM to Edwin Granberry, notes, n.d., UGA.

13. Granberry, "The Private Life of Margaret Mitchell."

14. MM to LC, January 19, 1937, Barnes.

15. Andrew Sparks, "Margaret Mitchell Wanted No Memorials," *Atlanta Journal*, April 9, 1961.

16. MM to LC, January 19, 1937, Barnes.

17. "Record of Sales Mitchell: *Gone With the Wind*," August 1, 1937, NYPL.

18. McLellan, "The Making of a Best Seller."

19. SM, "Memoir," 114-A.

20. SM, "Memoir," 127.

21. SM, "Memoir," 129.

22. Extract of draft letter from JM, June 1937, UGA.

23. Photo caption, *Publishers Weekly*, February 27, 1937.

24. MM to HL, June 7, 1937, NYPL.

25. MM to Miss Thompson, October 5, 1936, NYPL.

26. Ginny Morris to MM, June 2, 1937, UGA.

27. MM to Mrs. Wilbur Kurtz, February 5, 1937, UGA.

28. MM to Norman Berg, notes, October 22, 1936, UGA.

29. "Romance Unending," *The Times*, October 3, 1936.

30. Ball, "Fame's Tempo Has Been Quickened."

31. MM to Herschel Brickell, April 8, 1937, UGA.

32. "Give and Take of Bestsellers," *Publishers Weekly*, December 26, 1936.

33. MM to Herschel Brickell, February 22, 1937, UGA.

34. LC to JM, January 14, 1938, UGA.

35. Statement by MM, August 1, 1939, *GWTW* Literary Rights office, Atlanta.

36. MS to MM, January 14, 1938, UGA.

37. MS to SM, October 20, 1936, UGA; MS to SM, January 25, 1937, UGA.

38. MS to SM, January 25, 1937, UGA.

39. JM to MS, January 28, 1937, UGA.

40. MM to Mary Marsh, April 17, 1936, UGA.

41. "National Book Awards for 1936," *Publishers Weekly*, February 27, 1937.

42. MM to Julian Harris, May 5, 1937, Smith College.

43. MM to GB, May 3, 1937, NYPL.

44. MM to GB, May 10, 1937, NYPL.

45. MM to HL, May 11, 1937, NYPL.

46. [Harrison Smith], "*Gone With the Wind*," *Saturday Review of Literature*, September 3, 1949.

47. RB to Mr. McGill, May 7, 1937, NYPL; "Pulitzer Prizes Awarded," *Publishers Weekly*, May 8, 1937.

48. MM to Marsh family, June 21, 1937, UGA.

49. J. G. Robertson, Jr., to MM, May 11, 1937, UGA.

50. Nobel Prize, "Nomination and Selection of Literature Laureates," at http://nobelprize.org/nobel_prizes/literature/nomination (accessed August 19, 2010).

## CHAPTER 10: DEFENDING SCARLETT'S HONOR

1. GB to MM, February 26, 1937, UGA.

2. SM to Macmillan, February 23, 1937, NYPL.

3. GB to MM, February 16, 1937, UGA.

4. Reed Harris to Editor-In-Chief, May 2, 1937, NYPL.

5. Edwin Smith to GB, June 18, 1937, NYPL.

6. GB to Walbridge Taft, June 21, 1937, NYPL.

7. Walbridge Taft to GB, June 24, 1937, NYPL.

8. HL to GB, May 17, 1937, NYPL.

9. HL to MM, May 20, 1937, NYPL.

10. GB to SM, July 25, 1937, NYPL.

11. GB to SM, July 27, 1937, NYPL.

12. GB to Miss Hutchinson, September 21, 1937, NYPL.

13. GB to MM, March 14, 1938, NYPL.

14. GB to SM, March 4, 1938, NYPL.

15. MM to GB, March 8, 1938, NYPL.

16. MS to HL, April 7, 1937, NYPL.

17. SM to GB, April 12, 1937, NYPL.

18. GB to SM, April 14, 1937, NYPL.

19. SM to GB, April 23, 1947, NYPL.

20. Lucius Beebe, "This New York," *New York Herald Tribune*, June 5, 1937.

21. Sidney L. Samuels to SM, July 1, 1937, NYPL.

22. Thompson & Barwise to Mitchell & Mitchell, July 24, 1937, UGA.

23. W. L. Brusse to MS, April 10, 1937, NYPL.

24. Everett Hale to W. L. Brusse, April 22, 1937, NYPL.

25. Macmillan Canada to Everett Hale, May 21, 1937, NYPL.

26. Hugh Eayrs to Everett Hale, May 21, 1937, NYPL.

27. Frederic Melcher to MS, May 25, 1937, NYPL.

28. MS to HL, June 29, 1937, NYPL.

29. MM to Julian Harris, July 28, 1937, Emory.

30. MM to Mrs. Louis Davent Bolton, July 22, 1937, AHC.

31. Transcript of telephone conversation between Richard Brett and William Bratter, August 3, 1937, NYPL.

32. SM to GB, August 4, 1937, NYPL.

33. RB to Walbridge Taft, August 5, 1937, NYPL.

34. RB to SM, August 12, 1937, NYPL.

35. RB to Hugh Eayrs, August 5, 1937, NYPL.

36. RB to Alec Blanton, August 17, 1937, NYPL.

37. H. C. Beaty to RB, August 24, 1937, NYPL.

38. RB to SM, August 25, 1937, NYPL.

39. GB to SM, September 15, 1937, NYPL.

40. GB to JM, September 2, 1937, UGA.

41. MM to GB, September 24, 1937, UGA.

42. JM to MS, August 23, 1937, NYPL.

43. GB to JM, September 3, 1937, NYPL.

44. MM to GB, September 24, 1937, UGA.

45. JM to GB, September 8, 1937, NYPL.

46. MS to GB, September 11, 1937, NYPL.

47. MM to GB, September 24, 1937, UGA

48. MM to GB, September 24, 1937, UGA

49. William M. Doerflinger to Herschel Brickell, June 28, 1937, NYPL.

50. Macmillan, press release, July 2, 1937, NYPL.

51. "From the Macmillan Company," [1937], NYPL.

52. Macmillan, notice for *Gone With the Wind*, *Publishers Weekly*, September 25, 1937.

53. Memorandum by W. M. Doerflinger, June 22, 1937, NYPL.

54. MM to GB, September 24, 1937, UGA.

55. HL to MM, October 5, 1937, NYPL.

56. MS to GB, June 1, 1938, NYPL.

57. Czechoslovakian edition of *Gone With the Wind*, inscribed to HL, Kearney Public Library, Kearney, New Jersey.

58. MM to GB, October 19, 1937, NYPL.

59. MM to GB, November 1, 1937, NYPL.

60. GB to MM, October 25, 1937, NYPL.

61. Kakon Stangerup, review of *Gone With the Wind*, *Nationaltidende*, September 1937.

62. Ven Nyberg, review of *Gone With the Wind*, *Svenska Dagbladet*, October 1937.

63. Review of *Gone With the Wind*, *Kaleva*, December 1937.

64. GB to MM, November 15, 1937, NYPL.

65. Madeleine Baxter to MM, August 13, 1938, UGA.

66. Lukacs Gyula to MM, [1937], UGA.

67. "Amazing Demand for American Novel," *Cape Argus*, August 28, 1937.

68. MM to HL, July 15, 1940, NYPL.

69. MS to MM, March 14, 1938, UGA.

70. MM to HL, May 30, 1938, NYPL.

71. MS, "GWTW: Report on Foreign Publishers," December 3, 1943, UGA.

72. Howard S. Cady to John M. Born, April 21, 1938, NYPL.

73. MM to MS, October 27, 1937, UGA.

74. MM to HL, November 18, 1937, NYPL.

75. Walbridge Taft to SM, December 2, 1937, NYPL.

76. MM to GB, November 9, 1937, NYPL.

77. MM to GB, November 15, 1937, NYPL.

78. Wallace McClure to SM, November 16, 1937, UGA.

79. MM to GB, December 17, 1937, NYPL.

80. GB to MM, November 12, 1937, NYPL.

81. Walbridge Taft to SM, December 13, 1937, NYPL.

82. MS to MM, January 8, 1938, NYPL.

83. Dutch edition of *Gone With the Wind*, inscribed to HL, Kearney Public Library, Kearney, New Jersey.

## CHAPTER 11: FROM GREENLAND'S ICY MOUNTAINS TO INDIA'S CORAL STRAND

1. LC to MM, January 17, 1938, Barnes.

2. JM to GB, January 3, 1938, NYPL.

3. MM to MS, March 11, 1938, UGA.

4. MM to HL, July 11, 1938, NYPL.

5. MM to GB, March 8, 1938, NYPL.

6. MS to MM, March 14, 1938, UGA.

7. Walbridge Taft to SM, January 24, 1938, NYPL; Joaquin Abogado to Cadwalader, Wickersham & Taft, January 19, 1938, NYPL.

8. MS to Mr. Sanchez, January 7, 1938, NYPL.

9. JM to GB, January 13, 1938, NYPL.

10. JM to GB, January 13, 1938, NYPL.

11. MS to MM, January 8, 1938, UGA.

12. JM to GB, January 7, 1936, NYPL.

13. Joaquin Abogado to Cadwalader, Wickersham & Taft, January 19, 1938, NYPL.

14. Walbridge Taft to SM, January 24, 1938, NYPL.

15. MM to GB, November 29, 1938, NYPL.

16. MM to William Lyon Phelps, January 21, 1938, UGA.

17. MM to MS, January 6, 1938, UGA.

18. HL to GB, January 28, 1938, NYPL.

19. MM to GB, January 20, 1938, NYPL; HL to GB, January 28, 1938, NYPL.

20. GB to MM, May 18, 1938, NYPL.

21. Walbridge Taft to SM, January 28, 1938, NYPL.

22. GB to MM, May 18, 1938, NYPL.

23. MM to GB, May 20, 1938, NYPL.

24. Alec Blanton to Wycliffe A. Hill, September 10, 1938, NYPL.

25. LC to Kay Brown, February 6, 1937, NYPL.

26. LC to Mr. Browne, February 6, 1937, NYPL.

27. MM to LC, July 8, 1938, Barnes.

28. GB to MM, June 20, 1938, NYPL.

29. Michener, "Introduction."

30. Howard S. Cady to Ingeborg Barth, July 7, 1938, NYPL.

31. MM to GB, July 7, 1938, NYPL.

32. GB to MM, August 16, 1938, NYPL.

33. JM to GB, August 19, 1938, NYPL.

34. Alec Blanton to GB, September 8, 1938, NYPL.

35. "Low-Priced Edition of *Gone With the Wind*," *Publishers Weekly*, September 24, 1938.

36. GB to JM, October 21, 1938, NYPL.

37. JM to GB, October 24, 1938, NYPL.

38. "*Gone With the Wind* in Cheap Edition Gets Great Sales," *Publishers Weekly*, November 12, 1938.

39. "Macmillan to Issue *Gone With the Wind* at 69 Cents," *Publishers Weekly*, August 12, 1939.

40. SM, "Memoir," 113-C.

41. MM to Kay Brown, July 7, 1938, UGA.

42. *Trust Co. Bank v. MGM/UA*, 772 F.2d 6424, 6425 (11th Cir. 1985).

43. MM to LC, September 12, 1938, NYPL.

44. C. L. Bouvé to LC, September 7, 1938, NPYL.

45. JM to LC, November 21, 1938, NYPL.

46. JM to MS, August 31, 1938, UGA.

47. MS to JM, September 2, 1938; MS to JM, September 5, 1938, UGA.

48. JM to MS, September 6, 1938, UGA.

49. JM to MS, November 8, 1939, UGA.
50. JM to family, May 29, 1938, NYPL.
51. MM to Mr. Mermin, draft, September 30, 1938, NYPL.
52. SM, "Memoir," 173.
53. MM to Mr. Shipp, July 11, 1938, Emory.
54. George Gallup, "56,500,000 Hope to See *Gone With Wind* and Public Approves Vivien, Gallup Finds," *Atlanta Constitution*, February 20, 1939.
55. MM to HL, December 27, 1938, NYPL.
56. MM to Clifford Dowdey, January 2, 1939, UGA.

## CHAPTER 12. ME AND MY POOR SCARLETT

1. MM to Kay Brown, January 31, 1939, UGA.
2. GB to MM, February 23, 1939, NYPL.
3. MM to HL, March 15, 1939, NYPL.
4. "Letter from Paris," *New Yorker*, March 25, 1939.
5. MM to HL, May 6, 1939, NYPL.
6. MM to MS, November 2, 1939, UGA.
7. MM to Wallace McClure, October 9, 1939, UGA.
8. MM to Wallace McClure, August 16, 1940, UGA.
9. MM to Wallace McClure, August 8, 1940, UGA.
10. JM to MS, March 10, 1939, UGA.
11. MS to MM, September 29, 1939, UGA.
12. Ginny Morris to MM, March 13, 1939, UGA.
13. MM to Ginny Morris, March 16, 1939, UGA.
14. MM to Ernest V. Heyn, April 15, 1939, UGA.
15. MM to MS, March 17, 1939, UGA.
16. Agreement between Margaret Mitchell Marsh, Selznick International Pictures, and Loew's, July 17, 1939, UGA.
17. JM to GB, July 24, 1939, NYPL.
18. GB to Kay Brown, August 1, 1939, NYPL.
19. Miscellaneous correspondence, August 1939, NYPL.
20. GB to MM, August 11, 1939, UGA.
21. MM to GB, August 8, 1939, UGA.
22. Charles Trenkle to Alec Blanton, July 31, 1939, NYPL.
23. "Macmillan to Issue *Gone With the Wind* at 69 Cents."
24. H. Cady to HL, August 16, 1939, NYPL.
25. David O. Selznick to Howard Dietz, August 24, 1939, NYPL; unsigned memorandum, August 25, 1939, NYPL.
26. James Putnam to Lovat Dickson, August 31, 1939, NYPL.
27. GB to MM, September 14, 1939, NYPL.
28. MM to GB, September 15, 1939, NYPL.
29. GB to MM, September 18, 1939, NYPL.
30. Memorandum of conversation with JM by [GB], September 22, 1939, NYPL.
31. GB to MM, September 26, 1939, NYPL.
32. GB to MM, October 6, 1939, UGA.
33. GB to MM, October 23, 1939, UGA.
34. GB to MM, October 23, 1939, UGA.

35. MM to GB, October 28, 1939, UGA.

36. MM to GB, October 28, 1939, UGA.

37. GB to MM, October 30, 1939, UGA.

38. MM to GB, November 7, 1939, UGA.

39. GB to MM, November 8, 1939, NYPL.

40. GB to MM, December 7, 1939, NYPL.

41. Russell Birdwell to GB, October 4, 1939, NYPL; GB to Russell Birdwell, October 9, 1939, NYPL.

42. GB to MM, December 13, 1939, NYPL.

43. JM to Mrs. Lamar Rutherford Lipscomb, January 17, 1940, UGA.

44. Kay Brown to MM, August 3, 1939, UGA.

45. Kay Brown to MM, August 10, 1939, UGA.

46. MM to Kay Brown, August 26, 1939, UGA.

47. Mildred Seydell to H. F. Juergens, October 23, 1939, John Wiley, Jr., Collection, Midlothian, Va.

48. Mildred Seydell to MM, October 12, 1939, John Wiley, Jr., Collection, Midlothian, Va.

49. Mildred Seydell to H. F. Juergens, October 23, 1939, John Wiley, Jr., Collection, Midlothian, Va.

50. H. F. Juergens to Mildred Seydell, October 30, 1939, John Wiley, Jr., Collection, Midlothian, Va.

51. MM to Edwin Granberry, April 11, 1940, in *Letters from Margaret*, ed. Julian Granberry, 79 (Bloomington, Ind.: 1st Books Library, 2001).

52. HL to GB, December 1, 1939, NYPL.

53. First edition of *Gone With the Wind*, Margaret Mitchell Marsh Collection, Special Collections, Atlanta-Fulton Public Library, Atlanta.

54. GB to MM, December 7, 1939, NYPL.

55. "Cashing In on *Gone With the Wind*," *Business Week*, December 30, 1939.

56. Hattie McDaniel to MM, December 11, 1939, UGA.

57. MM to Hattie McDaniel, December 13, 1939, UGA.

58. David O. Selznick to MM, December 6, 1939, UGA.

59. Inez Robb, "Retiring Author and Stars in Three-Hour Chat," *Atlanta Georgian*, December 14, 1939.

60. Vivien Leigh to MM, December 14, 1939, UGA.

61. LC, interview by Linda Barnes, transcript, 1977, Barnes.

62. "Publisher of *GWTW* Here for Premiere," *Atlanta Journal*, undated clipping, UGA.

63. LC, interview.

64. Brett Smith, interview; Carpenter, interview.

65. "Petite Atlantan Meets Film Stars for the First Time," *Atlanta Constitution*, December 16, 1939.

66. Barnes, interview.

67. MM to Mr. and Mrs. Clark Gable, January 10, 1940, UGA.

68. Signed copy of *Gone With the Wind*, Medora Field Perkerson Papers, UGA.

69. LC, interview.

70. LC, interview.

71. MM to Susan Myrick, February 28, 1939, UGA.

72. David O. Selznick to Sidney Howard, January 6, 1937, in *Memo from David O. Selznick*, ed. Rudy Behlmer, 144 (New York: Viking, 1972).

73. JM to family, January 1940, UGA.

74. WSM Radio recording, December 15–16, 1939, John Wiley, Jr., Collection, Midlothian, Va.

75. HL to MM, December 19, 1939, NYPL.

76. Barnes, interview,

77. MM to Hattie McDaniel, December 16, 1939, UGA.

## CHAPTER 13: TOTING THE WEARY LOAD

1. JM to Mary Marsh, December 20, 1939, as quoted in Walker, *Margaret Mitchell and John Marsh*, 432.

2. "Cashing In on *Gone With the Wind*."

3. Memorandum by GB of telephone conversation with Howard Dietz, December 27, 1939, NYPL.

4. GB to JM, January 18, 1940, UGA.

5. GB to Kay Brown, January 18, 1939, NYPL.

6. "January Reprint Best Sellers," *Publishers Weekly*, February 14, 1940.

7. GB to MM, March 27, 1940, NYPL.

8. LC to HL, January 25, 1940, NYPL.

9. JM to Richard Anderson, January 15, 1940, UGA.

10. Zane, "Peggy," 6.

11. Mary Butler correspondence file, November 6, 1939–April 17, 1940, UGA.

12. Kay Brown to MM, May 3, 1940, UGA.

13. Vivien Leigh to MM, February 8, 1940, UGA.

14. MM to David O. Selznick, March 2, 1940, UGA.

15. JM to David O. Selznick, March 21, 1940, UGA.

16. "Notice to the Trade," *Publishers Weekly*, February 24, 1940.

17. "Unauthorized *Gone With the Wind* Withdrawn," *Publishers Weekly*, March 16, 1940.

18. MM to HL, October 6, 1940, UGA.

19. HL to MM, October 8, 1940, UGA.

20. GB to MM, July 2, 1940, NYPL.

21. "Strip-Dancer May Face Suit for *Gone With the Wind* Act," *Atlanta Constitution*, December 12, 1940.

22. MM to Edwin Granberry, April 11, 1940, in *Letters From Margaret*, ed. Julian Granberry, 80 (Bloomington, Ind.: 1st Books Library, 2001).

23. MM to Carol Clemens and Joan Wylie, April 9, 1940, UGA.

24. SM to the Celilia Company, August 8, 1940, NYPL.

25. *Trust Co. Bank v. MGM/UA*, 772 F.2d 740 (11th Cir. 1985); Kay Brown to MM, June 6, 1940, UGA.

26. MM to David O. Selznick, August 31, 1940, UGA [letter not sent]

27. Kay Brown to JM, September 24, 1940, UGA.

28. MM to David O. Selznick, December 11, 1940, UGA.

29. SM to R. E. Samuels, March 8, 1941, UGA.

30. Harold Martin, "Gone Are the Wind-sors for *Gone With Wind* Revival," *Atlanta Constitution*, November 9, 1940.

31. "Triplets Named Gone, With, Wind," *Atlanta Constitution*, December 13, 1940.

32. J. A. Fruin to Cadwalader, Wickersham & Taft, June 4, 1940, NYPL.

33. MS to JM, January 30, 1940, UGA.

34. MS to SM, December 27, 1940, UGA.

35. JM to GB, April 25, 1940, UGA.

36. MM to LC, September 22, 1941, Barnes.

37. JM to MS, November 14, 1940, UGA.

38. GB to MM, May 15, 1942, NYPL.

39. MM to GB, May 18, 1942, NYPL.

40. MM to Wallace McClure, August 8, 1940, UGA.

41. JM to GB, June 24, 1940, NYPL.

42. JM, "Foreign Book Contracts—Gone With the Wind," memorandum, March 1945, UGA.

43. JM to MS, November 27, 1943, UGA.

44. MM to MS, November 2, 1939, UGA.

45. Handwritten notes by JM, September 30, 1943, UGA.

46. Dorothy Black to MM, June 1, 1941, UGA.

47. Betty Mears to GB, August 18, 1955, NYPL.

48. Zane, "My Dearly Beloved Young Lady," 17.

49. MM to HL, December 26, 1941, NYPL.

50. David O. Selznick to Kay Brown, September 29, 1941, UGA.

51. Kay Brown to David O. Selznick, October 1, 1941, UGA.

52. Actor Cordell, "Margaret Mitchell Pallbearer May Hold Clue to Scarlett, Rhett Mystery," *Atlanta Journal-Constitution*, November 28, 1985.

53. David O. Selznick to Kay Brown, October 7, 1941, UGA.

54. RB to HL, August 11, 1941, NYPL.

55. HL to RB, August 26, 1941, NYPL.

56. JM to Kay Brown, December 13, 1941, UGA.

57. Alec Blanton to HL, April 29, 1942, NYPL.

58. MM to HL, May 14, 1942, NYPL.

59. MM to HL, August 17, 1942, NYPL.

60. David O. Selznick and John Hay Whitney to MM, August 22, 1942, UGA.

61. MM to David O. Selznick and John Hay Whitney, August 31, 1942, UGA.

62. Kay Brown, interview by George Wead, n.d., John Wiley Collection, Midlothian, Va.

63. M. Thomas Inge, "Tara vs. Dogpatch: Cartoonist Al Capp Recounts His Legal Run-in with *GWTW* Author," *The Scarlett Letter*, Summer 2004.

64. David O. Selznick to MM, December 3, 1942, UGA.

## CHAPTER 14: RECONSTRUCTION

1. MM to LC, December 12, 1942, Barnes.

2. JM to MS, August 10, 1943, UGA.

3. MS to JM, August 12, 1943, UGA.

4. MS to JM, September 20, 1943, UGA.

5. MS to JM, October 1, 1943, UGA.

6. MS to JM, October 6, 1943, UGA.

7. "Owing to MMM by MS," October 7, 1943, UGA.

8. Memorandum to JM and SM, October 7, 1943, UGA.

9. Agreement dated October 8, 1943, UGA.

10. Notes by MB, February 1965, UGA.

11. JM to GB, March 4, 1944, NYPL.
12. Handwritten notes by JM, October 14, 1943, UGA.
13. MS to JM, October 12, 1943, UGA.
14. MS correspondence files, Fall 1943, UGA.
15. MS to JM, October 18, 1943, UGA.
16. JM to MS, November 27, 1943, UGA.
17. JM to MS, October 25, 1943, UGA.
18. JM to MS, November 27, 1943, UGA.
19. JM to MS, November 29, 1943, UGA.
20. JM to MS, November 27, 1943, UGA.
21. Handwritten notes by JM, December 1, 1943, UGA.
22. MS to JM, December 2, 1943, UGA.
23. JM to MS, December 6, 1943, UGA.
24. MS to HL, December 8, 1943, UGA.
25. GB to MM, February 18, 1944, NYPL.
26. JM to GB, March 4, 1944, NYPL.
27. HL to GB, March 10, 1944, NYPL.
28. GB to JM, March 15, 1944, NYPL.
29. JM to GB, April 4, 1944, NYPL.
30. JM to MS, July 22, 1944, UGA.
31. MM to Hervey Allen, July 6, 1944, UGA.
32. Draft contract with Leland Hayward, c. 1944–1945, UGA.
33. MM to Jenny Bradley, January 13, 1944, HRC.
34. MM to GB, November 22, 1944, UGA.
35. Supplementary Memorandum on Publishers and Agents by MS, November 1944, UGA.
36. MM to W. S. Traer, November 7, 1945, UGA.
37. Macmillan, press release, December 11, 1945, NYPL.
38. SM, "Memoir," 187.
39. GB to MM, July 29, 1946, NYPL.
40. MM to Jesse Draper, June 29, 1942, Smith College.
41. MM to Eddy Gilmore, August 6, 1946, UGA.
42. SM, "Memoir," 180.
43. MM to Wallace McClure, March 31, 1947, UGA.
44. MM to Jenny Bradley, February 18, 1947, HRC.
45. MM to Gaston Gallimard, May 21, 1945, HRC.
46. MM to W. S. Traer, November 7, 1945, UGA.
47. Price, Waterhouse & Co. re: Mrs. Margaret Mitchell Marsh, May 16, 1946, UGA.
48. MM to GB, August 5, 1946, NYPL.
49. GB to MM, July 8, 1946, NYPL.
50. MM to GB, August 5, 1946, NYPL.
51. Friedrich Geisler to MM, November 23, 1946, NYPL.
52. MM to GB, January 10, 1947, NYPL.
53. MM to Wallace McClure, July 1, 1947, UGA.
54. GB to MM, February 20, 1947, NYPL.
55. MM to Katherine P. Carnes, September 2, 1947, UGA.
56. MM to Dr. W. B. Burke, May 14, 1947, UGA.
57. MM to GB, February 25, 1946, NYPL.
58. MM to GB, June 3, 1946, UGA.

59. MM to SM, September 30, 1946, UGA.
60. J. Drost to SM, November 26, 1946, UGA.
61. MM to GB, December 8, 1948, UGA.


## CHAPTER 15: A BOLT FROM THE BLUE

1. GB to JM, September 23, 1947, NYPL.
2. JM to GB, October 29, 1947, NYPL.
3. GB to JM, October 31, 1947, NYPL.
4. JM to GB, November 28, 1947, NYPL.
5. HL to GB, December 4, 1947, NYPL.
6. GB to JM, December 8, 1947, NYPL.
7. MM to HL, August 13, 1936, UGA.
8. LC to MB, April 19, 1956, UGA.
9. GB to MM, May 27, 1947, NYPL.
10. GB to MM, July 12, 1946, NYPL.
11. MM to GB, March 15, 1937, NYPL.
12. GB to SM, December [12], 1955, NYPL.
13. Zagari, interview.
14. GB to SM, December [12], 1955, NYPL.
15. SM to GB, December 13, 1955, NYPL.
16. MM to Helen Dowdey, September 4, 1947, quoted in SM, "Memoir," 187.
17. Italian and Spanish editions of *Gone With the Wind*, inscribed to MB, Special Collections, McCain Library, Agnes Scott College, Decatur, Ga.
18. MB to LC, April 16, 1964, UGA.
19. MM to A. E. Zucker, September 24, 1946, NYPL.
20. "Hungarian Scarlett O'Hara Writes Again, 'We're Alive,'" *Atlanta Constitution*, December 23, 1956.
21. SM, "Memoir," 114-A.
22. Carol Brandt to HL, September 3, 1947, NYPL.
23. MM to HL, September 1947, NYPL.
24. Elmer Davis, "The Economics of Authorship," *Saturday Review of Literature*, November 23, 1940.
25. Barnes, interview.
26. Van Ness H. Bates to MM, January 1949, UGA; MM to Julia Willett, January 14, 1949, UGA.
27. MM to Delores Baptista, June 3, 1948, UGA.
28. SM, "Memoir," 188.
29. SM, "Memoir," 188–89.
30. SM, "Memoir," 174-B.
31. Will of Margaret Mitchell Marsh, November 21, 1948, Fulton County Courthouse, Atlanta.
32. Will of Margaret Mitchell Marsh.
33. MM to Julia Clifton, January 24, 1949, UGA.
34. MM to Harold E. George, May 6, 1949, UGA.
35. "Drunks Still Call 'Peggy' About Scarlett's Hair," *Atlanta Journal*, February 21, 1949.
36. MM to Carl Ackerman, May 3, 1949, UGA.

37. Notes by MB, Ward Green file, n.d., UGA.

38. Statement by HL, n.d., NPYL.

39. SM, "Memoir," 198.

40. MB to LC, April 16, 1964, UGA

41. MM to J. Donald Adams, July 9, 1936, UGA.

42. MB to LC, April 8, 1964, UGA

43. MB to LC, April 16, 1964, UGA.

44. Richard Harwell, "Introduction," in Gone With the Wind *as Book and Film*, ed. Richard Harwell, xxi (Columbia: University of South Carolina Press, 1992).

45. Sparks, "Margaret Mitchell Wanted No Memorials."

46. "English Language Sales GWTW," n.d., UGA.

47. Affidavit by GB, July 5, 1950, UGA.

48. MM to GB, February 2, 1949, NYPL.

49. MM to GB, June 15, 1949, UGA.

50. MM to Madame Henri Pajot, June 24, 1949, NYPL.

51. MM to HL, July 12, 1949, NYPL.

52. MM to Wallace McClure, July 26, 1949, UGA.

53. MM to Wallace McClure, July 26, 1949, UGA.

54. MM to Granville Hicks, February 7, 1949, UGA.

55. Granville Hicks to MM, February 11, 1949, UGA.

56. "Facts to the Contrary," *Reader's Digest*, July 1949.

57. Alfred S. Dashiell to MM, June 17, 1949, NYPL.

58. MM to HL, July 12, 1949, NYPL.

59. SM to Alfred S. Dashiell, June 21, 1949, UGA.

60. Dozier Cade, "Peggy Mitchell Hits Magazine 'Falsity,'" *Atlanta Journal*, June 19, 1949.

61. Buck Herzog to MM, July 8, 1949, UGA.

62. HL to Mr. Norris, August 1, 1949, NYPL.

63. MM to HL, July 29, 1949, NYPL.

64. MM to HL, July 12, 1949, NYPL.

65. Brown, interview.

66. GB to JM, August 16, 1949, NYPL; GB to Marcia Carroll, August 17, 1949, NYPL.

67. Statement by HL, n.d., NPYL.

68. Barnes, interview.

69. Allan Taylor to JM, August 30, 1949, UGA.

70. LC to MB, August 18, 1949, UGA.

71. Harry S. Truman to JM, August 17, 1949, UGA.

72. Herman Talmadge to JM, August 16, 1949, UGA.

73. Zane, "Peggy."

74. "General Correspondence—Condolences" file, UGA.

75. William Key, "Margaret Mitchell Laid to Rest as Sun Breaks Leaden Clouds," *Atlanta Journal*, August 18, 1949.

## CHAPTER 16: INHERIT THE WIND

1. [Smith], "*Gone With the Wind*."

2. JM to HL, April 4, 1950, NYPL.

3. MB to LC, December 22, 1953, UGA.
4. JM to B. L. Tante, August 14, 1950, UGA.
5. JM to HL, April 4, 1950, NYPL.
6. HL to JM, March 2, 1950, NYPL.
7. JM to HL, March 9, 1950, NYPL.
8. MB to LC, December 9, 1955, UGA.
9. Codicil to JM will, July 26, 1951, Fulton County Courthouse, Atlanta.
10. Walker, *Margaret Mitchell and John Marsh*, 512.
11. A. Limongelli to Macmillan, September 1, 1951, UGA.
12. JM to Martha Purdy, January 5, 1950, NYPL.
13. "*GWTW* Royalties Help Rebuild Japan Church," *Atlanta Journal*, July 19, 1951.
14. JM to MS, December 7, 1951, UGA.
15. JM to GB, February 7, 1950, NYPL.
16. GB to JM, February 20, 1950, NYPL.
17. JM to GB, February 2, 1951, NYPL.
18. HL to JM, February 6, 1951, NYPL.
19. GB to HL, et al., May 28, 1951, NYPL.
20. Memorandum by JM of telephone conversation between JM and Mrs. Nell W. Simmons, November 21, 1951, UGA.
21. Memorandum by JM, "Personal Effects and Their Disposal" file, n.d., UGA.
22. Memorandum by JM, "Personal Effects and Their Disposal" file.
23. ALW to JM, January 26, 1951, Columbia.
24. JM to ALW, February 7, 1951, Columbia.
25. Frankie McKee Robins to ALW, February 17, 1951, Columbia.
26. Mike Connolly, "Rambling Reporter," *Hollywood Reporter*, April 16, 1952.
27. David O. Selznick to JM, April 18, 1952, UGA.
28. JM to Mike Connolly, April 25, 1952, UGA.
29. Mike Connolly, "Rambling Reporter," *Hollywood Reporter*, May 2, 1952.
30. French edition of *Gone With the Wind* inscribed to MB, Special Collections, McCain Library, Agnes Scott College, Decatur, Ga.
31. MB to LC, June 9, 1954, UGA.
32. MB to LC, December 22, 1953, UGA.
33. MB to LC, June 9, 1954, UGA.
34. SM to GB, January 21, 1953, NYPL.
35. GB to SM, February 20, 1953, NYPL.
36. SM message for GB, n.d., NYPL.
37. Frankie McKee Robins to ALW, September 22, 1952, Columbia.
38. Frankie McKee Robins to ALW, October 9, 1952, Columbia.
39. Quoted in MB to LC, June 9, 1954, UGA.
40. Andrew Sparks, "Why Were Margaret Mitchell's Letters Burned?" *Atlanta Journal Magazine*, October 5, 1952.
41. SM memo, July 20, 1953; SM to Harvey Hill, July 24, 1953.
42. MB to LC, December 22, 1953, UGA.
43. MB notes, "Correspondence and Papers Destroyed" file, UGA.
44. MB to LC, December 9, 1955, UGA.
45. SM to Reverend N. Henry Brazier, March 5, 1963, UGA.
46. MB to Bennett Cerf, July 3, 1952, UGA.
47. "Hollander Pays Honor to Margaret Mitchell," *Atlanta Journal*, May 8, 1956.
48. "Many Show Interest in Selecting an Appropriate Name for Airport," *Atlanta Journal*, March 30, 1954.

49. GB to SM, September 15, 1955, NYPL.

50. GB to Mr. Lewis, January 26, 1956, NYPL.

51. SM to GB, January 21, 1953, NYPL.

52. SM, "Memoir," 115.

53. GB to Dan Lacy, November 17, 1953, NYPL.

54. CB to SM, December 11, 1953, NYPL.

55. SM to GB, December 18, 1953, NYPL.

56. "Trade Winds," *Saturday Review,* April 10, 1954.

57. SM to GB, February 11, 1955, NYPL.

58. SM to GB, January 12, 1955, NYPL.

59. GB to Mr. Swanson, January 27, 1955, NYPL.

60. GB to SM, February 7, 1955, NYPL.

61. GB to George de Kay, April 26, 1954, NYPL.

62. Secretary to the president to J. M. Hedrick, December 8, 1960, NYPL.

63. MB to LC, April 11, 1956, UGA.

64. Memorandum by SM, on trip to New York, n.d., UGA.

## CHAPTER 17: MINDING SCARLETT'S BUSINESS

1. Sam Lucchese, "Selznick Envisions Musical *GWTW,*" *Atlanta Journal,* March 9, 1961.

2. SM to Kay Brown, November 7, 1955, UGA.

3. SM to Kay Brown, March 21, 1961, UGA.

4. "English Language Sales GWTW."

5. Ralph McGill, "Little Woman, Big Book: The Mysterious Margaret Mitchell," *Show,* October 1962.

6. MB to SM, January 16, 1961, UGA.

7. *Miller Music Corp. v. Charles N. Daniels, Inc.,* 362 U.S. 373 (1960).

8. Agreement between Stephens Mitchell and Metro-Goldwyn-Mayer, Inc., December 4, 1961, UGA.

9. Notes by SM, telephone conversation with Kay Brown, February 7, 1961, UGA.

10. Notes by MB, February 1965, NYPL.

11. Bonnie Mogelever, interview by Ellen F. Brown, December 2009.

12. Notes by MB, c. 1966, UGA.

13. Kevin J. Wetmore, Jr., "From *Scaretto* to *Kaze to Tomo Ni Sarinu*: Musical Adaptations of *Gone With the Wind* in Japan," in *Modern Japanese Theatre and Performance,* ed. David Jortner, Keiko McDonald, and Kevin J. Wetmore, Jr., 237–50 (Lanham, Md.: Lexington Books, 2006), 239.

14. MB to Mrs. Leland R. Colbeck, October 25, 1939, UGA; Herb Bridges, interview by John Wiley, Jr., March 2010.

15. MB to LC, June 29, 1966, UGA.

16. Anderson, January 2010 interview.

17. "Margaret Baugh Is Dead: Margaret Mitchell's Secretary," *Atlanta Constitution,* December 28, 1967.

18. Thomas Hal Clarke, interview by John Wiley, Jr., April 2010.

19. LC to SM, March 10, 1969, UGA.

20. Moe Hein, "Lost and Found in Translation," October 1, 2006, at www.uiowa.edu/~iwp/EVEN/documents/MoeHein.lostandfoundintranslation.final.9.21.pdf (accessed August 12, 2010).

21. SM to Jenny Bradley, January 13, 1977, UGA.

22. SM to Claude Gallimard, May 17, 1977, UGA.

23. SM to Susan Lanier, June 27, 1969, UGA.

24. Draft responses by SM to questions about sequel project, July 13, 1976, UGA.

25. Paul H. Anderson, "The *Gone With the Wind* Copyright," n.d., *GWTW* Literary Rights office, Atlanta.

26. Dennis Brown, "*Gone With the Wind* II: Whatever Happened to the Sequel?" *Los Angeles Times*, December 10, 1989.

27. Ralph Tyler, "Literary Figures Offer Plots and Quips," *New York Times*, August 1, 1976.

28. Don McCulty to SM, November 30, 1977, UGA.

29. Draft responses by SM to questions about sequel project, July 13, 1976, UGA.

30. SM to Don McCulty, January 3, 1978, UGA.

31. SM to John Wiley, Jr., January 7, 1977, UGA.

32. William Pratt, *Scarlett Fever: The Ultimate Pictorial Treasury of* Gone With the Wind (New York: Collier, 1977), 306.

33. Herbert S. Nusbaum to Harry Clay Pendleton, Jr., June 4, 1980, UGA.

34. Paul Anderson to Herbert S. Nusbaum, June 16, 1980, UGA.

35. "Analysis of *GWTW* Motion Picture Sequel," April 10, 1981, UGA.

36. U.S. District Court judgment, September 3, 1981.

## CHAPTER 18: TOMORROW IS ANOTHER BOOK

1. Anderson, January 2010 interview.

2. SM to Kay Brown, December 19, 1967, UGA.

3. *Trust Co. Bank v. MGM/UA*, 772 F.2d 740 (11th Cir. 1985).

4. Anderson, "The *Gone With the Wind* Copyright."

5. Steve Oney, "A 2nd *Wind* in the Cards for Scarlett," *Orlando Sentinel*, January 8, 1987.

6. Anderson, January 2010 interview.

7. Edwin McDowell, "*Gone With the Wind* Best Seller Again at 50," *New York Times*, June 24, 1986.

8. Esther B. Fein, "Another Day, Lots of Dollars as Scarlett Returns to Tara," *New York Times*, October 3, 1991.

9. Anderson, "The *Gone With the Wind* Copyright."

10. Anderson, "The *Gone With the Wind* Copyright."

11. Paul Anderson, interview by John Wiley, Jr., March 2010.

12. Carol Huang, "Tomorrow Is Another Day: An Ethiopian Student Survives a Brutal Imprisonment by Translating *Gone With the Wind* into His Native Tongue," *American Scholar* 75, no. 4 (Autumn 2006): 79–88; Paul Theroux, *Dark Star Safari: Overland from Cairo to Cape Town* (Boston: Houghton Mifflin, 2003), 124–47.

13. Claudia Glenn Dowling, "The Further Adventures of Scarlett O'Hara," *Life*, May 1988.

14. Edwin McDowell, "Book Notes," *New York Times*, February 20, 1991.

15. McDowell, "Book Notes."

16. Anderson, "The *Gone With the Wind* Copyright."

17. McDowell, "Book Notes."

18. "Scarlett Takes World's Readers by Storm," *The Scarlett Letter*, November 1991.

19. "Scarlett Takes World's Readers by Storm."

20. Merrill Geier, interview by Ellen F. Brown, April 2010.

21. Fein, "Another Day, Lots of Dollars as Scarlett Returns to Tara."

22. Geier, interview.

23. "Scarlett Takes World's Readers by Storm."

24. Daisy Maryles, "Winning Strategies," *Publishers Weekly*, January 1, 1992.

25. "Scarlett Takes World's Readers by Storm."

26. Geier, interview.

27. Phil Kloer, "Battle Brews on Changes in *Scarlett*," *Atlanta Journal-Constitution*, March 26, 1992.

28. Joy Winstead, "A 3rd *Gone With the Wind*? Not by This Author," *Publishers Weekly*, September 25, 1991.

29. Nadine Brozan, "Chronicle," *New York Times*, November 8, 1994.

30. "*Gone With the Wind* to Have Second Sequel," *New York Times*, January 25, 1995.

31. Sarah Lyall, "Book Sequel Creates a New Civil War," *New York Times*, June 3, 1996.

32. Michael Burke, "The Story of Scarlett They Did Not Want You to Read," *The Mail* [London], June 9, 1996.

33. Alessandra Stanley, "Frankly My Dear, Russians Do Give a Damn," *New York Times*, August 29, 1994.

34. Pat Conroy to Hal Clarke et al., November 10, 1998, "Information about Suntrust Bank v. Houghton Mifflin Company-Court Papers," at www.hmhbooks.com/features/randall_url/courtpapers.shtml (accessed September 23, 2010).

35. Anderson, March 2010 interview.

36. "MMH Party Launches *Rhett Butler's People*," *The Scarlett Letter*, Winter 2007.

37. Alice Randall, interview by Ellen F. Brown, April 2010.

38. Randall, interview.

39. Ben H. Bagdikian et al., "Letter of Support," April 10, 2001, "Information about Suntrust Bank v. Houghton Mifflin Company-Court Papers," at www.hmhbooks.com/features/randall_url/courtpapers.shtml (accessed September 23, 2010).

40. Declaration by Toni Morrison, April 15, 2001,"Information about Suntrust Bank v. Houghton Mifflin Company-Court Papers," at www.hmhbooks.com/features/randall_url/courtpapers.shtml (accessed September 23, 2010).

41. Statement by Pat Conroy, April 11, 2001, "Information about Suntrust Bank v. Houghton Mifflin Company-Court Papers," at www.hmhbooks.com/features/randall_url/courtpapers.shtml (accessed September 23, 2010).

42. "*Wind Done* Blows Back: Appeals Court Lifts Injunction Against Book Judged *GWTW* 'Piracy,' " *The Scarlett Letter*, Summer 2001.

43. Order, U.S. District judge Charles A. Pannell, Jr., *SunTrust Bank vs. Houghton Mifflin Co.*, April 20, 2001.

44. David Kirkpatrick, "MediaTalk: Legal Battle Increases Interest in Book Sequel," *New York Times*, June 11, 2001.

45. Megan Harlan, "Books in Brief: Fiction," *New York Times*, July 1, 2001.

46. Lisa Schwarzbaum, "*Wind* Storm," *Entertainment Weekly*, May 15, 2001.

47. Walt Handelsman, cartoon, Tribune Media Services, Inc., 2001.

48. Jill Vejnoska, "Author Stirs Harsh *Wind* in Tara Land," *Atlanta Journal-Constitution*, July 13, 2001.

49. Troy Patterson, "The *Wind* Mill: Author/Parodist Alice Randall Hosts a Showdown in Margaret Mitchell's Backyard," *Entertainment Weekly*, July 27, 2001.

50. Angela Webster, "The Mind Done Gone: A Parody," *Times-Herald* [Newnan], July 18, 2001.

51. Don O'Briant, "*Wind* Finale: Morehouse to Benefit from Suit Settlement," *Atlanta Journal-Constitution*, May 10, 2002.

52. Associated Press, "Pair Protects *Gone With the Wind* Copyright," *New York Times*, May 23, 2001.

53. Anderson, March 2010 interview.

54. Randall, interview.

55. Randall, interview.

56. Lori Glazer, Houghton Mifflin publicist, e-mail to Ellen F. Brown, March 19, 2010.

57. *Eldred v. Ashcroft*, 537 U.S. 186 (2003).

58. Victoria Shannon, "One Internet, Many Copyright Laws," *New York Times*, November 8, 2004.

59. Valley Haggard, interview by Ellen F. Brown, March 2010.

60. Anderson, March 2010 interview.

61. Anderson, March 2010 interview.

62. Donna Kornhaber and David Kornhaber, "A First-Timer Makes Rhett and Scarlett Sing," *New York Times*, April 13, 2008.

63. Christopher Hart, "*Gone With the Wind*," *Sunday Times*, April 27, 2008.

64. Charles Spencer, "*Gone With the Wind*: Frankly, My Dear, It's a Damn Long Night," *Telegraph*, April 23, 2008.

65. Clarke, interview.

66. Anderson, January 2010 interview.

67. Mitchell, *Gone With the Wind*, 864.

68. Lillian Craig to MM, January 23, 1937, UGA.

69. MM to Lillian Craig, January 28, 1937, UGA.

# Bibliography

## BOOKS

Badaway, Janice A. *A Feeling for Books: The Book-of-the-Month Club, Literary Taste, and Middle-Class Desire*. Chapel Hill: University of North Carolina Press, 1977.

Beauvoir, Simone de. *Letters to Sartre*. New York: Arcade, 1991.

Behlmer, Rudy, ed. *Memo from David O. Selznick*. New York: Viking, 1972.

Brooks, Paul. *Two Park Street*. Boston: Houghton Mifflin, 1986.

Burlingame, Roger. *Of Making Many Books: A Hundred Years of Reading, Writing and Publishing*. New York: Charles Scribner's Sons, 1946.

Canfield, Cass. *The Publishing Experience*. Philadelphia: University of Pennsylvania Press, 1969.

Clement, Richard W. *The Book in America*. Golden, Colo.: Fulcrum, 1996.

Compaine, Benjamin M. *The Book Industry in Transition: An Economic Study of Book Distribution and Marketing*. White Plains, N.Y.: Knowledge Industry Publications, 1978.

Coser, Lewis A. *Books: The Culture and Commerce of Publishing*. New York: Basic Books, 1982.

Edwards, Anne. *Road to Tara: The Life of Margaret Mitchell*. New Haven, Conn.: Ticknor & Fields, 1983.

Exman, Eugene. *The House of Harper: One Hundred and Fifty Years of Publishing*. New York: Harper & Row, 1967.

*Facts and Fancies*. Atlanta: Washington Seminary, 1918.

Farr, Finis. *Margaret Mitchell of Atlanta*. New York: Morrow, 1965.

Fast, Howard. *Being Red*. Boston: Houghton Mifflin, 1990.

Granberry, Julian, ed. *Letters from Margaret*. Bloomington, Ind.: 1st Books Library, 2001.

Grannis, Chandler B., ed. *What Happens in Book Publishing*. New York: Columbia University Press, 1967.

Gwin, Yolande, ed. *I Remember Margaret Mitchell*. Lakemont, Ga.: Copple House Books, 1987.

Hale, Robert D., ed. *A Manual on Bookselling.* New York: American Booksellers Association, 1987.

Harwell, Richard. *An Enduring Legacy: Margaret Mitchell's* Gone With the Wind. Dublin, Ga.: Gone With the Wind Forum '91, 1991.

———, ed. Gone With the Wind *as Book and Film.* Columbia: University of South Carolina Press, 1992.

———. *Margaret Mitchell's* Gone With the Wind *Letters, 1936–1946.* New York: Macmillan, 1976.

Hayward, Charles E. *The Publishing Process: A Manual on Bookselling.* New York: American Booksellers Association, 1987.

James, Mertice, ed. *The Book Review Digest.* New York: H. W. Wilson, 1937.

Jenkins, Herbert T. *Atlanta and the Automobile.* Decatur, Ga.: Emory University, 1977.

Jortner, David, Keiko McDonald, and Kevin J. Wetmore, Jr., eds. *Modern Japanese Theatre and Performance.* Lanham, Md.: Lexington Books, 2006.

Lee, Charles. *The Hidden Public: The Story of the Book-of-the-Month Club.* New York: Doubleday, 1958.

Lehmann-Haupt, Hellmut. *The Book in America: A History of the Making and Selling of Books in the United States.* New York: R. R. Bowker, 1952.

*Margaret Mitchell and Her Novel,* New York: Macmillan, 1936.

Mitchell, Margaret. *Gone With the Wind.* New York: Macmillan, 1936.

Morgan, Charles. *The House of Macmillan 1843–1943.* New York: Macmillan, 1944.

Mott, Frank Luther. *Golden Multitudes.* New York: Macmillan, 1947.

Peacock, Jane Bonner, ed. *Margaret Mitchell: A Dynamo Going to Waste: Letters to Allen Edee 1919–1921.* Atlanta: Peachtree Publishers, 1985.

Pratt, William. *Scarlett Fever: The Ultimate Pictorial Treasury of* Gone With the Wind. New York: Collier, 1977.

Pyron, Darden Asbury. *Southern Daughter: The Life of Margaret Mitchell.* New York: Oxford University Press, 1991.

Saint-Amour, Paul K. *The Copywrights: Intellectual Property and Literary Imagination.* Ithaca, N.Y.: Cornell University Press, 2003.

Salamon, Julie. *The Net of Dreams.* New York: Random House, 1996.

Schick, Frank L. *The Paperbound Book in America: The History of Paperbacks and Their European Background.* New York: R. R. Bowker, 1958.

Stevens, George. *Lincoln's Doctor's Dog, and Other Famous Best Sellers.* Philadelphia: J. B. Lippincott, 1939.

Tebbel, John. *A History of Book Publishing in the United States.* New York: R. R. Bowker, 1972–1981.

Theroux, Paul. *Dark Star Safari: Overland from Cairo to Cape Town.* Boston: Houghton Mifflin, 2003.

Thomson, David. *Showman: The Life of David O. Selznick.* New York: Knopf, 1992.

Unwin, Stanley. *The Truth About Publishing.* New York: Macmillan, 1960.

Walker, Marianne. *Margaret Mitchell and John Marsh: The Love Story behind* Gone With the Wind. Atlanta: Peachtree Publishers, 1993.

West, James L. *American Authors and the Literary Marketplace since 1900*. Philadelphia: University of Pennsylvania Press, 1988.

## ARTICLES

Adams, J. Donald. "A Fine Novel of the Civil War." *New York Times Book Review*, July 5, 1936.

Anderson, Paul H. "The *Gone With the Wind* Copyright." n.d., GWTW Literary Rights office, Atlanta.

Associated Press. "Pair Protects *Gone With the Wind* Copyright." *New York Times*, May 23, 2001.

*Atlanta Constitution*, "Atlanta Historical Society Will Honor Mrs. John R. Marsh," June 26, 1936.

———, "*Gone With Wind* Nearing Million," December 3, 1936.

———, "*Gone With Wind* Pages Are Recovered by Ruse," November 14, 1936.

———, "Hungarian Scarlett O'Hara Writes Again, 'We're Alive,'" December 23, 1956.

———, "Margaret Baugh Is Dead: Margaret Mitchell's Secretary," December 28, 1967.

———, "Petite Atlantan Meets Film Stars for the First Time," December 16, 1939.

———, "Strip-Dancer May Face Suit for *Gone With the Wind* Act," December 12, 1940.

———, "Triplets Named Gone, With, Wind," December 13, 1940.

*Atlanta Journal*, "Drunks Still Call 'Peggy' About Scarlett's Hair," February 21, 1949.

———, "*GWTW* Royalties Help Rebuild Japan Church," July 19, 1951.

———, "Harold Latham Searching South for Good Manuscripts," April 12, 1935.

———, "Hollander Pays Honor to Margaret Mitchell," May 8, 1956.

———, "Many Show Interest in Selecting an Appropriate Name for Airport," March 30, 1954.

———, "Margaret Mitchell's Novel Literally *Gone With Wind*," August 9, 1936.

———, "Mrs. Luise Sims Gives Dinner in Honor of Margaret Mitchell," June 23, 1936.

———, "Publisher Notes Changed Habits of Reading," January 19, 1936.

———, "Publisher of *GWTW* Here for Premiere," undated clipping, Hargrett Rare Book and Manuscript Library, University of Georgia Libraries, Athens, Ga.

*Atlanta Journal Magazine*, "How *Gone With the Wind* Was Written: An Interview by Medora Perkerson," May 23, 1937.

Baldwin, Faith. "The Woman Who Wrote *Gone With the Wind*, An Exclusive and Authentic Interview." *Pictorial Review*, March 1937.

Ball, Lamar Q. "All Modern Publishing Records Smashed by *Gone With the Wind*." *Atlanta Constitution*, November 13, 1936.

————. "Fame's Tempo Has Been Quickened, according to Margaret Mitchell." *Atlanta Constitution*, November 11, 1936.

————. "Margaret Mitchell Seeks in Vain for Time to Get Her Hair Washed." *Atlanta Constitution*, November 10, 1936.

————. "Writing of *Gone With the Wind* Beset by Difficulties, Says Author." *Atlanta Constitution*, November 9, 1936.

Beebe, Lucius. "This New York." *New York Herald Tribune*, June 5, 1937.

Berg, Norman. "The Real Story of *Gone With the Wind*." *Atlanta Constitution*, November 29, 1936.

Brown, Dennis. "*Gone With the Wind* II: Whatever Happened to the Sequel?" *Los Angeles Times*, December 10, 1989.

Brozan, Nadine. "Chronicle." *New York Times*, November 8, 1994.

Burke, Michael. "The Story of Scarlett They Did Not Want You to Read." *The Mail* [London], June 9, 1996.

*Business Week*, "Cashing In on *Gone With the Wind*," December 30, 1939.

Cade, Dozier. "Peggy Mitchell Hits Magazine 'Falsity.'" *Atlanta Journal*, June 19, 1949.

*Cape Argus*, "Amazing Demand for American Novel," August 28, 1937.

Cole, Lois Dwight. "The Story Begins at a Luncheon Bridge in Atlanta." *New York Times*, June 25, 1961.

Commager, Henry Steele. "The Civil War in Georgia's Red Clay Hills." *New York Herald Tribune*, July 5, 1936.

Connolly, Mike. "Rambling Reporter." *Hollywood Reporter*, April 16, 1952.

————. "Rambling Reporter." *Hollywood Reporter*, May 2, 1952.

Conroy, Pat. "Preface." In *Gone With the Wind*, by Margaret Mitchell, 60th anniversary ed., 12. New York: Scribner, 1996.

Cordell, Actor. "Margaret Mitchell Pallbearer May Hold Clue to Scarlett, Rhett Mystery." *Atlanta Journal-Constitution*, November 28, 1985.

Daniel, Frank. "Simplicity, Loyalty and Love Produced *Gone With the Wind*." *Atlanta Journal*, August 17, 1949.

Davis, Elmer. "The Economics of Authorship." *Saturday Review of Literature*, November 23, 1940.

DeLorme, Rita H. "Margaret Mitchell's People: Recalling Catholic Relatives of Georgia Icon." *Southern Cross*, November 29, 2007.

Dowling, Claudia Glenn. "The Further Adventures of Scarlett O'Hara." *Life*, May 1988.

Fein, Esther B. "Another Day, Lots of Dollars as Scarlett Returns to Tara." *New York Times*, October 3, 1991.

Gallup, George. "56,500,000 Hope to See *Gone With Wind* and Public Approves Vivien, Gallup Finds." *Atlanta Constitution*, February 20, 1939.

Granberry, Edwin. "The Private Life of Margaret Mitchell." *Collier's*, March 13, 1937.

Gwin, Yolande. "Margaret Mitchell's Novel Depicts Three Major Periods." *Atlanta Constitution*, February 6, 1936.

Harlan, Megan. "Books in Brief: Fiction." *New York Times*, July 1, 2001.

Hart, Christopher. "*Gone With the Wind*." *Sunday Times*, April 27, 2008.

Huang, Carol. "Tomorrow Is Another Day: An Ethiopian Student Survives a Brutal Imprisonment by Translating *Gone With the Wind* into His Native Tongue." *American Scholar* 75, no. 1 (Autumn 2006). 79–80.

Inge, M. Thomas. "Tara vs. Dogpatch: Cartoonist Al Capp Recounts His Legal Run-in with *GWTW* Author." *The Scarlett Letter*, Summer 2004.

Jones, Marian Elder. "Me and My Book: Margaret Mitchell's *Gone With the Wind*." *Georgia Review* 16, no. 2 (Summer 1962): 180–87.

*Kaleva*. Review of *Gone With the Wind*, December 1937.

Key, William. "Margaret Mitchell Laid to Rest as Sun Breaks Leaden Clouds." *Atlanta Journal*, August 18, 1949.

Kirkpatrick, David. "MediaTalk: Legal Battle Increases Interest in Book Sequel." *New York Times*, June 11, 2001.

Kloer, Phil. "Battle Brews on Changes in *Scarlett*." *Atlanta Journal-Constitution*, March 26, 1992.

Knebel, Fletcher. "Scarlett O'Hara's Millions." *Look*, December 3, 1963.

Kornhaber, Donna, and David Kornhaber, "A First-Timer Makes Rhett and Scarlett Sing." *New York Times*, April 13, 2008.

Leitch, Albert C. "*Gone With Wind* Presses Going Strong, Pass 656,000." *Atlanta Constitution*, October 21, 1936.

Lucchese, Sam. "Selznick Envisions Musical *GWTW*." *Atlanta Journal*, March 9, 1961.

Lyall, Sarah. "Book Sequel Creates a New Civil War." *New York Times*, June 3, 1996.

Martin, Harold. "Gone Are the Wind-sors for *Gone With Wind* Revival." *Atlanta Constitution*, November 9, 1940.

Maryles, Daisy. "Winning Strategies." *Publishers Weekly*, January 1, 1992.

McDowell, Edwin. "Book Notes." *New York Times*, February 20, 1991.

———. "*Gone With the Wind* Best Seller Again at 50." *New York Times*, June 24, 1986.

McGill, Ralph. "*Gone With the Wind*." *Red Barrel*, September 15, 1936.

———. "Little Woman, Big Book: The Mysterious Margaret Mitchell." *Show*, October 1962.

McLellan, Howard. "The Making of a Best Seller." *American Business*, April 1937.

Michener, James A. "Introduction." In *Gone With the Wind*, by Margaret Mitchell, anniversary ed., iii–xii. New York: Macmillan, 1975.

Mitchell, Anita C. Benteen. "Emory's Editions of *Gone With the Wind*." *Emory Alumnus*, July 1961.

Nathan, Robert R. "National Income in 1937 Largest since 1929." *Survey of Current Business*, June 1938.

*New Yorker*, "Letter from Paris," March 25, 1939.

———, "Three Historical Novels," July 4, 1936.

*New York Times*, "*Gone With the Wind* to Have Second Sequel," January 25, 1995.

Nyberg, Ven. Review of *Gone With the Wind*. *Svenska Dagbladet*, October 1937.

O'Briant, Don. "*Wind* Finale: Morehouse to Benefit from Suit Settlement." *Atlanta Journal-Constitution*, May 10, 2002.

Oney, Steve. "A 2nd *Wind* in the Cards for Scarlett." *Orlando Sentinel*, January 8, 1987.

Patterson, Troy. "The *Wind* Mill: Author/Parodist Alice Randall Hosts a Showdown in Margaret Mitchell's Backyard." *Entertainment Weekly*, July 27, 2001.

Pegler, Westbrook. "Fair Enough." *Atlanta Constitution*, November 28, 1936.

Perkerson, Medora Field. "Double Life of Margaret Mitchell." *Atlanta Journal Sunday Magazine*, May 16, 1937.

———. "The Mystery of Margaret Mitchell." *Look*, November 15, 1955.

———. "Was Margaret Mitchell Writing Another Book?" *Atlanta Journal Magazine*, December 18, 1949.

*Publishers Weekly*, "Currents in the Trade," April 10, 1937.

———, "Davison-Paxon Remodels Book Department," November 20, 1937.

———, "The Difficulties of Success," September 19, 1936.

———, "Give and Take of Bestsellers," December 26, 1936.

———, "*Gone With the Wind* in Cheap Edition Gets Great Sales," November 12, 1938.

———, "January Reprint Best Sellers," February 14, 1940.

———, "Low-Priced Edition of *Gone With the Wind*," September 24, 1938.

———, "Macmillan to Issue *Gone With the Wind* at 69 Cents," August 12, 1939.

———, "National Book Awards for 1936," February 27, 1937.

———, "The New N.G.B.R. Displays," June 20, 1936.

———, "News from Publishers," December 5, 1936.

———, "Notice to the Trade," February 24, 1940.

———, "Promotion Plans for Spring 1937," January 21, 1937.

———, "Pulitzer Prizes Awarded," May 8, 1937.

———, "Random Notes on the N.Y. Times Book Fair," November 21, 1936.

———, "Unauthorized *Gone With the Wind* Withdrawn," March 16, 1940.

*Richmond Times Dispatch*, "*Gone With the Wind* Book of Many Names," August 9, 1936.

Robb, Inez. "Retiring Author and Stars in Three-Hour Chat." *Atlanta Georgian*, December 14, 1939.

Runner, Harvey E. "Macy's Resells 35,940 Copies of Best Seller to Macmillan Co." *New York Herald Tribune*, March 24, 1937.

*Saturday Review*, "Trade Winds," April 10, 1954.

Saxon, Wolfgang. "George P. Brett Is Dead at 91; Headed Macmillan Company." *New York Times*, February 15, 1984.

*The Scarlett Letter*, "MMH Party Launches *Rhett Butler's People*," Winter 2007.

———, "Scarlett Takes World's Readers by Storm," November 1991.

Schwarzbaum, Lisa. "*Wind* Storm." *Entertainment Weekly*, May 15, 2001.

Shannon, Victoria. "One Internet, Many Copyright Laws." *New York Times*, November 8, 2004.

Shartar, Martin. "The Winds of Time and Chance: Stephens Mitchell Surveys Seven Decades in Atlanta." *Atlanta*, July 1974.

[Smith, Harrison]. "*Gone With the Wind*." *Saturday Review of Literature*, September 3, 1949.

Smith, Helen C. "Auction Gets Rare *GWTW*." *Atlanta Constitution*, May 27, 1976.

~~Smith, Helen C. "Telegram Tells In II an arrised rare monounial. *Atlanta Journal*, April 9,~~ 1961.

———. "Why Were Margaret Mitchell's Letters Burned?" *Atlanta Journal Magazine*, October 5, 1952.

Spencer, Charles. "*Gone With the Wind*: Frankly, My Dear, It's a Damn Long Night." *Telegraph*, April 23, 2008.

Stangerup, Kakon. Review of *Gone With the Wind*. *Nationaltidende*, September 1937.

Stanley, Alessandra. "Frankly My Dear, Russians Do Give a Damn." *New York Times*, August 29, 1994.

Thompson, Ralph. "Books of the Times." *New York Times*, June 30, 1936.

*Time*, "Books: North v. South," March 7, 1938.

———, "The Press: Apology for Margaret," January 11, 1943.

*The Times*, "Romance Unending," October 3, 1936.

Tyler, Ralph. "Literary Figures Offer Plots and Quips." *New York Times*, August 1, 1976.

Vejnoska, Jill. "Author Stirs Harsh *Wind* in Tara Land." *Atlanta Journal-Constitution*, July 13, 2001.

Webster, Angela. "The Mind Done Gone: A Parody." *Times-Herald* [Newnan], July 18, 2001.

Wetmore, Kevin J., Jr. "From *Scaretto* to *Kaze to Tomo Ni Sarinu*: Musical Adaptations of *Gone with the Wind* in Japan." In *Modern Japanese Theatre and Performance*, ed. David Jortner, Keiko McDonald, and Kevin J. Wetmore, Jr., 237–50. Lanham, Md.: Lexington Books, 2006.

Willett, Julia B. "Margaret Mitchell." *Junior League Magazine*, November 1936.

Winstead, Joy. "A 3rd *Gone With the Wind*? Not by This Author." *Publishers Weekly*, September 25, 1991.

Yezbick, Daniel. "Riddles of Engagement: Narrative Play in the Children's Media and Comic Art of George Carlson." *ImageTexT: Interdisciplinary Comics Studies*, 2007. www.english.ufl.edu/imagetext/archives/v3_3/yezbick (accessed August 12, 2010).

## INTERVIEWS

Anderson, Paul. Interview by John Wiley, Jr., January and March 2010.

Barnes, Linda Taylor. Interview by Ellen F. Brown, November 2009.

Bridges, Herb. Interview by John Wiley, Jr., March 2010.

Carpenter, Betsy. Interview by Ellen F. Brown, December 2009.

Clarke, Thomas Hal. Interview by John Wiley, Jr., April 2010.

Geier, Merrill. Interview by Ellen F. Brown, April 2010.

Haggard, Valley. Interview by Ellen F. Brown, March 2010.

Mogelever, Bonnie. Interview by Ellen F. Brown, December 2009.

Randall, Alice. Interview by Ellen F. Brown, April 2010.

Smith, Clare Brett. Interview by Ellen F. Brown, December 2009.

Taylor, Turney Allan, Jr. Interview by Ellen F. Brown, October 2009.

Yezbick, Daniel. Interview by Ellen F. Brown, January 2009.

Zagari, Anne. Interview by Ellen F. Brown, December 2009.

## MISCELLANEOUS

Dickey, Jennifer Word. "'A Tough Little Patch of History': Atlanta's Marketplace for *Gone With the Wind* Memory." PhD diss., Georgia State University, 2007.

"*Gone With the Wind* Translated into Russian." CNN Sunday Morning News, March 25, 2001. http://transcripts.cnn.com/TRANSCRIPTS/0103/25/sm.08.html (accessed August 12, 2010).

Hein, Moe. "Lost and Found in Translation." October 1, 2006. www.uiowa.edu/~iwp/EVEN/documents/MoeHein.lostandfoundintranslation.final.9.21.pdf (accessed August 12, 2010).

# Index

*Italic numbers preceded by "p" refer to images in the photo section.*